Kashmir Śaivism

The Central Philosophy of Tantrism

Kamalakar Mishra

Department of Philosophy
Banaras Hindu University

Rudra Press

Cambridge, Massachusetts

Published by
Rudra Press
P.O. Box 13390
Portland, OR 97213

Cover design by Susan Cobb
Cover photo of Ardhanarishvara, 12th century. Courtesy of The Saint Louis Art Museum, Purchase: Friends Fund. Used by permission.
Printed in the United States of America

Library of Congress Cataloging-in-Publication Data

Mishra, Kamalakar
Kashmir Śaivism : the central philosophy of tantrism / Kamalakar Mishra.
p. cm.
Includes bibliographical references and index.
ISBN 0-915801-32-9 : $18.95
1. Kashmir Śaivism--Doctrines. 2. Tantrism. I. Title.
BL1281.1545.M57 1993111
294.5'513--dc20 93-13103
CIP

Dedicated to the memory
of my revered and beloved teacher,
Professor T.R.V. Murti,
at whose feet I learned the secrets of
Indian philosophy and religion.

Contents

Preface

The present work is an exposition of the philosophy and religion of the Trika system, popularly known as Kashmir Śaivism. Kashmir Śaivism is the most prominent system of the Tantric tradition. I consider Kashmir Śaivism the true or central philosophy of Tantrism.

My earlier book, *Significance of the Tantric Tradition* (1981, Varanasi, India), has much in common with the present work, but was written with a different objective in mind. The objective of *Significance of the Tantric Tradition*, as the title suggests, was not to present a full exposition of Tantric philosophy but to point out the significance of this philosophy from various angles — historical, epistemological, ontological, and axiological. The book's primary aim was to bring out the consistency and authenticity of Tantric thought and to make explicit the running thread of logic implicit in the system. The present work, *Kashmir Śaivism: The Central Philosophy of Tantrism*, however, is meant to be a full exposition of the Tantric system, covering all areas of Tantric philosophy. As such, it contains many topics not previously discussed and can be viewed as an elaboration of the earlier work.

Although the contribution of Tantra to Indian philosophy and culture is of immense significance, little work has been done in this field. Moreover, the Tantras, or Āgamas, have something significant and relevant to say to modern humanity. With its positive attitude towards the world and its variety of yogic *sādhanās* for self-improvement in all respects, Tantra carries a promise of help to people in their present predicament. This makes exposition and elucidation of Tantric insight worthwhile.

The mystic language of the Tantras and the rich symbolism found therein present difficulties in the exposition of Tantric thought. Abhinavagupta, the principal philosopher of Kashmir Śaivism, overcame these difficulties to make a systematic and rational presentation of Tantric wisdom in his famous work, the *Tantrāloka*. This present book is an attempt to understand the Tantric position mainly in light of the *Tantrāloka*.

Although Abhinavagupta seems to have unravelled the knots of Tantric philosophy and religion, much is left, even in his works, to be further clarified and elaborated. This is why differences of opinion and confusion exist among Tantric scholars with regard to the correct position of Tantric thought. My goal in the present work is to spell out implicit ideas, to make explicit the inner thread of logic of the Tantric system, and to fill in the gaps when possible.

In this attempt, some views might emerge that will appear new and original to the reader. But I submit that nothing is really new; everything is present, perhaps merely implicitly, in the Tantric position. For example, I have tried to present the rationale or the underlying logic of the left-handed (*vāma* or Kaula) doctrine, specifically with regard to sex. I have also interpreted and presented Tantric religion, or the Tantric way of life, in such a way as to make it quite relevant to the modern age of science and technology. All of this might seem to be my own invention, but actually it can be clearly read between the lines in the Tantras; I have simply tried to make it more explicit. What may at most be considered my own contribution is my attempt to supply the apparently missing links. But that, too, is purely on the basis of Tantric thought.

In this book, I attempt to present a logical analysis of the Tantric position of Abhinavagupta. I have also shown, according to my understanding, what remains unresolved and unanswered in his philosophy, but I admit that in the present work I am mainly playing the role of advocate of Abhinavagupta rather than critic. I am trying (a) to justify the Tantric position from the rational point of view, (b) to work out a consistent philosophy of Kashmir Śaivism, (c) to present the rationale of the abstruse Tantric *sādhanās*, (d) to trace out and clarify the inner thread of logic running through the entire system of thought, and (e) to demonstrate the soundness and significance of Kashmir Śaivism.

At places in my discussion the Advaita Vedāntin appears as the chief opponent (*pūrvapakṣin*) of Tantra for the simple reason that some of the basic principles of the Tantric system are questioned and contradicted by Advaita Vedānta. In defense, the Tantrist would not only justify him or herself but would in turn counter-question the Advaitin. My aim at those places is not to enter into polemics and refute the Advaitin but simply to clarify my own position. I hope the Advaita Vedantins will take my criticisms in that spirit.

The present work is the result of long years of study, research, thinking, teaching, and discussion on the subject. In expounding the topic, I have attempted to apply the utmost clarity of thought and explain the abstruse ideas in a simple way. The style of presentation is more like that of a teacher explaining and discussing things in an informal way than that of a pedant heavy with the weight of scholarship.

Moreover, Kashmir Śaivism is, to borrow a term from existentialism, a *praxis* — an authentic philosophy, not a mere ideology. Therefore, I have tried to present it in such a way as to impress upon the reader that this philosophy is related to life and is something of real concern. I have taken care not to be abstract in my treatment of this philosophy so that it does not lose touch with life.

In order to avoid misunderstanding and misinterpretation and to make the issues clear, I have also at times made certain repetitions. I submit that the repetitions cannot be helped, or can be avoided only at the cost of clarity and completeness of understanding. Moreover, the repetitions are of a few words or a few sentences only, and will, I hope, be excused by the reader.

Acknowledgments

I first would like to express my eternal indebtedness to my most revered and beloved teacher, the late Mahāmahopādhyāya Paṇḍita Rāmeśvara Jhā, at whose holy feet I studied the texts of Kashmir Śaivism for about twenty years. Not only was Paṇḍita Rāmeśvara Jhā a deep and insightful scholar with a spark of genius, he was also a man of spiritual experience; he lived and practiced the philosophy of Kashmir Śaivism. His spiritual insights helped me understand the secrets of Tantric philosophy more clearly. I bow in obeisance to him who was known among his students and disciples as the "modern Abhinavagupta."

I am deeply indebted to another revered and beloved teacher, the late Professor T. R. V. Murti, renowned scholar of Buddhism and Vedānta, who had penetrating insight into the problems of philosophy and religion.* He taught me Indian philosophy in general and Advaita Vedānta in particular. He used to allow me to discuss philosophical issues with him for hours at a stretch, enlightening me with his sparkling insight. I owe my training in philosophy to him.

I express my gratitude to still another revered and beloved teacher, the late Professor R. K. Tripathi. From him I learned how to develop clarity of ideas and present issues in a coherent and pointed

---

* I have had many teachers. Abhinavagupta has said, "The disciple desirous of acquiring knowledge should go from teacher to teacher, just as a bee desirous of floral flavor moves from flower to flower." (T.A. 13.335.)

way. Professor Tripathi was also a *sādhaka* for whom philosophy was a matter of practical concern. His attitude helped me appreciate philosophy as a way of life. Both Professor Murti and Professor Tripathi were Advaita Vedāntins; their criticisms of Kashmir Śaivism helped me develop my understanding of Kashmir Śaivism, and Tantrism in general, in a logically consistent way.

My respected and beloved teacher, Professor K. S. Sivaraman, an authority on Śaivism who now holds the chair of Hindu Studies at Concordia University, Montreal, Canada, enlightened me on many problems and issues in Śaivism and helped me understand the true spirit of Śaivism. He has urged me for a long time to write on Kashmir Śaivism. I express my gratitude to him.

I have benefitted from discussions on Kashmir Śaivism with many eminent scholars. Prominent among them are Dr. B. N. Pandit, Professor L. N. Sharma, Dr. Navjivan Rastogi, Dr. Sunthar Visuvalingam, and Professor K. D. Tripathi. My thanks are due to them.

I am also thankful to my students who have indirectly helped me in the preparation of this work. Their searching questions in discussion with me have helped me come out with a fuller understanding and presentation of Kashmir Śaivism.

I do not know how to thank Dr. K. P. Mishra, my former student and now a colleague of mine, who has helped me in a number of ways. He has taken great pains in correcting the typescript and checking the references.

The present work is the revised version of my Ph.D. thesis entitled "Philosophy of Abhinavagupta with Special Reference to Tantrāloka," submitted to Banaras Hindu University (B.H.U.). I am thankful to B.H.U. for giving me permission to use the thesis material in this book for publication.

I most reverently acknowledge my indebtedness to Swami Chetanandaji, director of the Nityananda Institute, for making the publication of this book possible. I would also like to give thanks to

Sharon Ward and all the people at the Institute and Rudra Press who have been so kind and helpful to me. I am grateful to my editor, Jennifer Cross. Her improvements to the language of the book are greatly appreciated.

Abbreviations

Bhagavadgītā	*Bh.G.*
Īśvara-pratyabhijñā-kārikā	*I.P.K.*
Īśvara-pratyabhijñā-vimarśinī	*I.P.V.*
Kulārṇava Tantra	*K.T.*
Mālinīvijaya Tantra	*M.V.T.*
Mālinīvijaya -vārtika	*M.V.V.*
Paramārthasāra	*P.S.*
Parātriṁśikā-vivaraṇa	*P.T.V.*
Pratyabhijñā-hṛdayam	*P.H.*
Śiva-dṛṣṭi	*Ś.D.*
Śiva-sūtra	*Ś.S.*
Śiva-stotrāvali	*Ś.St.*
Tantrāloka	*T.A.*
Tantrāloka-viveka	*T.A.V.*
Tantrasāra	*T.S.*

References that contain page numbers are from the volumes published by the Kashmir Series of Texts and Studies, Srinagar.

nirāśaṁsātpūrṇādahamiti purā bhāsayati yad
dviśākhāmāśāste tadanu ca vibhaṅktuṁ nijakalām/
svarūpādunmeṣaprasaraṇanimeṣasthitijuṣas
adadvaitaṁ vande paramaśivaśaktyātma nikhilam//

"I bow to the all-pervading, non-dual Absolute that is the ultimate Śiva-Śakti that, from its desireless and perfect state, first of all illumines itself as the pure 'I am' [the pure subject] and then in order to divide its active power, branches off into two [the subject and the object] and that, from its nature, keeps on emanating and extending itself [as creation] and again dissolving it in itself."

I.P.V. 1.1.1 (*maṅgalācaraṇa*).

Kashmir Śaivism

The Central Philosophy of Tantrism

1

Introduction

GENERAL SIGNIFICANCE OF THE TANTRIC TRADITION

Abhinavagupta is the principal philosopher of the Trika or Pratyabhijñā school, popularly known as Kashmir Śaivism. Kashmir Śaivism itself is the most prominent system in the Tantric tradition and Abhinavagupta is the chief exponent of Tantric philosophy.[1] Since Abhinavagupta is a Tantric philosopher it is quite relevant, even necessary, to give an introduction to the Tantric tradition. To demonstrate the significance of Abhinavagupta means first to show the significance of Tantric philosophy itself.

Among the general public there is a common misconception about Tantra. It is believed that in performing Tantric practices one uses mystic formulas or mantras, invokes spirits and mystic deities, and as a result acquires weird powers and uncanny experiences. But this understanding of Tantra is obviously naive, for Tantra has a much wider connotation. It stands for a particular conception of Reality and subsequently a particular way of life. It presents a set of values that are on the one hand ethically good, and on the other hand, pleasant and satisfying to the individual; it is thus quite practical.

The Tantric value system is so thorough and comprehensive that no aspect of life remains untouched. Based on the "inductive" (*āgama* or *āgamana*) experience of the seers and yogins, which was largely verified by a longstanding tradition of experimentation, Tantric wisdom forms the basis of a happy and healthy life both for the individual and society. Tantra shows how to accept and use the world and worldly values so that they become a means of Self-realization. It presents an integral view of life that synthesizes enjoyment (*bhoga*) and liberation (*mokṣa*) as well as worldly involvement (*pravṛtti*) and renunciation (*nivṛtti*). It advocates a positive yoga that embraces all and makes everything holy and good. The message of Tantra is both timely and timeless.

Another misconception, prevalent even among scholars, is that the Vedic tradition alone forms the basic trend of Indian culture, the Tantric tradition being a side current or even a perversion. This is a colossal misunderstanding. The Āgamas or Tantras have had an importance equal to the Vedas in shaping Indian culture. The Tantric tradition has something very significant to say and this must be taken into account if we wish to form a complete view of Indian philosophy and religion.

Both the Veda (*nigama*) and Tantra (*āgama*) are taken to be revelatory in character, pertaining to the extra-empirical or esoteric, knowledge of reality. If this is so, then what need is there of the Tantra if we already have the Veda? Is the Tantra redundant or does it have some special significance? Side by side with the Veda, the Tantra does have special significance; in fact it is complementary to the Veda. According to both Veda and Tantra, Ultimate Reality is Consciousness (*citi* or *saṁvit*), which is called Brahman or Śiva. The nature of this Consciousness is both knowledge (*jñāna*) and activity or dynamism (*kriyā*), and it is the dynamic aspect of Reality that is responsible for the manifestation of the world. This concept of dynamism though not explicitly explained is implicitly present in the Vedas and Upaniṣads, and the implicit is made explicit in the

Tantras. The Upaniṣadic utterances regarding Creation clearly suggest the existence of a dynamic principle in Brahman. It is said in the Upaniṣads that the world comes out of or emanates from Brahman,[2] and that "He willed: 'Let me become many and reproduce.'"[3] These statements tend to suggest *kriyā* or *spanda*. The statement that "all these things come out of Bliss itself"[4] refers in unequivocal terms to *spanda*. These statements cannot be explained away by calling them fables (*ākhyāyikās*) as the Advaitins do.[5]

Thus the Upaniṣads do accept the dynamic aspect of Reality, but they do not fully explain that dynamism. This task is fulfilled by the Tantras. In the Tantras, the dynamism of Reality is completely spelled out; the immanent aspect of Brahman is brought to the fore. As a result, in the Tantra there is an extremely positive attitude towards Creation.

There is another important sense in which Tantra is complementary to the Veda. The Veda is called *nigama* or *nigamana*, which means "deduction," while the Tantra is called *āgama* or *āgamana*, which means "induction." The Veda is believed to have been revealed from a higher source — the seers did not author the statements of the Veda; they simply received, or "perceived," them. Therefore, the Vedic statements have to be taken as accepted premises from which conclusions are then deduced. Hence Vedic knowledge is deduction (*nigamana*) from revealed premises. *Āgama*, or Tantra, on the other hand, is based on the evidence of the experience of the seers and yogins. It is really a yogic tradition. Abhinavagupta calls it the "tradition of experience" (*anubhavasampradāya*).[6]

It is not that the Veda does not believe in the verification of revealed knowledge or that the Tantra does not believe in revelation. Both believe in both, but the Vedic knowledge comes mainly through the process of revelation, whereas the Tantric knowledge comes mainly through experience. In the Indian tradition, revelation and experience are considered complementary to each other — what is revealed can also be confirmed in actual experience. The

Vedic knowledge is confirmed in experience and this experiential confirmation is the function of the Tantra. In this sense the Tantra (*āgama*) is complementary to the Veda (*nigama*).

The external form of the Tantra suggests that it is revealed by Lord Śiva, as it is presented in the form of a dialogue between Śiva and Pārvatī, the consort of Śiva. It is quite possible to conceive of the Tantra as revelation, but the special nature of the Tantra is that it is based on experience. The yogins and seers have experienced the truth; the Tantra may be understood as a record of their experience, the dialogue of Śiva and Pārvatī being a literary device meant to make that record attractive.

Abhinavagupta interprets the dialogue between Śiva and Pārvatī as a dialogue within our own consciousness, between the two levels of consciousness. He says, "The Self, which is present in every form and is self-luminous, does both the questioning and answering itself as if by dividing itself into the questioner and the answerer, both being itself at the same time."[7] It is also said that it is the Lord Śiva Himself who, taking the form of the teacher and the pupil, revealed the Tantra by way of question and answer.[8] This means that the dialogue is between the seeking self and the answering self, the answer being provided from within the Self. The questioning self is the lower self (*aṇu*) and the answering self is the higher Self (Śiva). The same interpretation may be given in the case of the dialogue between Arjuna and Kṛṣṇa in the *Bhagavadgītā*.

Even if the dialogue is understood literally and the Tantra is taken to be revelation, there is no discrepancy. The twin notions that the Tantra is revealed by God, on the one hand, and is experienced by the yogins and seers, on the other, are quite compatible, for what is revealed can also be confirmed in our own experience. The Tantric tradition accepts both points of view.

Thus we see that the Āgamic or Tantric tradition, apart from being highly significant in its own right, is also complementary to the Vedic or Upaniṣadic tradition. The Tantric ideas that are implicitly present and sometimes explicitly expressed in the Vedas and Upaniṣads are explicitly and fully spelled out by the Tantras. Thus, Veda and Tantra form one and the same line of thought. Those who compiled the Tantras in the post-Vedic period[9] were conscious of this continuity and oneness in the Vedic-Tantric tradition; they have explicitly mentioned this continuity. In the *Kulārṇava Tantra* Lord Śiva affirms to his consort, Pārvatī, "The six systems of the Vedic philosophy are the limbs of my body like feet, stomach, hands, and head; those who differentiate them actually dismember my body. And these are also the six limbs of the Kula; therefore, O dear one, know the Vedic discipline to be Kaulic (Tantric)."[10]

The Tantra does not merely enjoy the status of being complementary to the Veda. Its complementarity to the Veda is incidental. In fact, the Tantra has an autonomous and independent status. It would be quite reasonable to see the start of the Tantric tradition in the time when the seers, without any allegiance to the Veda, independently raised questions pertaining to life, made practical investigations in the direction of finding answers, and finally got the solutions. That the findings of the Tantric seers complement the Vedic store of knowledge, or complement any other tradition for that matter, is just incidental. The significance of the Tantric tradition lies not in its being complementary to the Veda or to any other tradition but in its potential to give autonomously a complete and perfect philosophy of life.

In a way the Tantra is even fuller and more important than the Veda. The reason for this claim is simple. The Tantra is Veda plus Tantra, whereas the Veda is Veda plus *implicit* Tantra. That is, the Tantra, besides its own wisdom, fully incorporates the wisdom of the Veda, but the Veda contains the wisdom of Tantra only implicitly and requires the Tantra to make it explicit.

Moreover, the *āgama* or Tantra is epistemologically more sound than the *nigama* or Veda. What is obtained through experience is scientific knowledge and is confirmed by itself; it does not require revelation to confirm it. On the contrary, revelation requires experience for its confirmation; revelation without experience remains an object of faith and does not become knowledge. Confirmation comes from experience, not from revelation.

Tantra can be called a science. In calling Tantra a science, I am neither changing the essential meaning of the term "science" nor am I misusing the term. Reason is the general principle underlying the scientific method; science is the *rational* study of anything. Reason makes it clear that a study based on speculation or faith cannot be dependable; we can depend only on what we observe or cognize. Therefore, science is based not on speculation or faith, but on actual experience or cognition.[11] Reason makes it further clear that normally we have only one mode of experience, which is the empirical or sensory mode. Experience in the context of science means empirical experience. Therefore, science can also be defined as an empirical study.

But by using the same faculty of reason it also becomes clear that science is based on *empirical* experience not by definition but simply because present-day science knows of no mode of experience other than the empirical one. If some other mode of experience were discovered, there would be no hesitation on anyone's part in calling it scientific. The only burden would be to prove that it is a genuine experience and not something such as a reverie, hallucination, or illusion. It would become scientific by virtue of being experience.

Tantra is based on the actual experience of the seers, yogins, and spiritual experimenters. They sought to investigate the inner nature and potentialities of humanity and made wide experiments at the individual and societal level. Their laboratory was the human being and, to some extent, society. They did not have modern methods and facilities for recording, processing and preserving the data; they did, of course, have their own methods of doing so. Moreover, in order that the record of their discovery be palatable and entertaining, they did not adopt prosaic scientific language, but expressed their findings in poetic terms using metaphors, symbols, and allegories.

The findings of the Tantric seers are verified and confirmed by a longstanding tradition of yogins reaching up to the present. Anyone can verify the truth of the findings for him- or herself. There is also no risk involved. Thus, Tantra is a science — a spiritual science. Just as there is material science, there is spiritual science with its methodology of spiritual investigation. Material science has an applied form, a technology. In the same way spiritual science has a technology. The technology of spiritual science is called *yoga.* Tantra presents yoga in a variety of forms. Just as the technology of material science is used in a variety of fields, Tantric yoga, the technology of spiritual science, is applied in a variety of sub-areas.

We should not labor under the illusion that everything written in the extensive corpus of the Tantra is based on experience. Just as what appears in the Veda is not all revelation, what appears in the Tantra is not all experience. The Tantric texts also contain a lot of hyperbolic and speculative material, as well as some material that can be set aside as irrelevant. If we are to take a realistic view of the Tantra without any undue sentimental attachment to the Tantric texts, we must carefully weed out the unnecessary elements in order to understand the true Tantric position.

There can be no doubt that reason is the only available tool for accomplishing this task and the only criterion for making any judgment. Even the suprarational does not oppose reason. To be beyond reason means to be unknowable by reason, not to be irrational or antirational. Therefore, reason is the best tool and the best criterion for determining the real purport of the Tantra, just as it is the best tool for judging anything else. Even when we accept revelation (*śruti*), we do so because reason tells us that we cannot know or experience Reality through reason or sense perception, and therefore we have to resort to revelation. It is only by using reason that we become aware of the limitations of reason itself and recognize the need to accept revelation. That Reality is beyond reason is made clear by reason alone. Reason is required not only to make a revelation intelligible but to make us aware of the desirability of revelation in the first place.

The position of Tantra is sound not only logically and epistemologically, but also ontologically and axiologically. Tantra gives a complete world view, satisfactorily explaining all aspects of reality. Its metaphysical concept of dynamic consciousness (*cit-śakti*) with freedom (*svātantrya*) as its nature, consistently explains all the existential problems of reality, including life and the world. The Tantric discovery points out that the phenomenon of consciousness, which we call the "Self" or the "I", that appears at the surface level is just the tip of a bigger reality lying deeper in us. Consciousness is like an iceberg, only a tiny portion of which is visible above the surface, or like an artesian spring that is invisibly connected to a deeper and vaster underground water reserve. If we accept this premise, it follows that we can reach the deeper levels of our reality step by step. Self-realization can be achieved in degrees. Even in our normal state we have some degree of Self-realization, as the power of consciousness (*citi-śakti* or *kuṇḍalinī* in the symbolic language of Tantric yoga) is already working in us in the form of our mental faculty. Obviously it is possible that in different people this consciousness will manifest in varying degrees, either naturally or by the deliberate process of uncovering or unfolding the qualities of Consciousness. We can logically stretch this process to the extent of achieving the fullest manifestation of Consciousness — Self-realization, or spiritual attainment in the highest degree.

The most significant contribution of Tantra is in the axiological field — the field of values. The Tantric seers, like Indian seers in general, were aware from the beginning that there are two basic sets of values in life. One is the ethical value of goodness or morality and the other is the material value of pleasure or happiness. The former is technically called *śreya*, meaning "*the good,* " and the latter is *preya*, or "*the pleasant.*" In the Indian system there are four values: *dharma* (morality), *artha* (money), *kāma* (satisfaction of desires), and *mokṣa* (self-realization). Morality comes under "*the good* "; money and satisfaction of desires fit under "*the pleasant.*" The seers were also aware that in actual life there is a dichotomy between "*the good*" and "*the pleasant*"; people have to undermine or sometimes even totally suppress "*the pleasant*" in favor of "*the good.*" The seers were therefore quite clear that a value system that is merely "*good*" with no element of "*the pleasant*" is not practical.

Therefore, they sought to discover a system that synthesized within itself both "*the good*" and "*the pleasant,*" or truth and beauty, or the good of oneself and the good of others. They found the answer in what is called Self-realization, or *mokṣa. Mokṣa* is not an otherworldly value, but the ground of overall success in life. All talent and all power to work efficiently and gracefully in every walk of life come from the Self, just as all the electric power that moves fans and lights lightbulbs comes from the powerhouse. All creativity, artistic or otherwise, springs forth from the Self. It is from the Self that the illumined understanding of anything comes to the mind as a spontaneous flash in a phenomenon technically called *pratibhā.* Therefore, the more a person is in line with the Self, the more the power flows. Thus, a person of Self-realization will be a better teacher, a better philosopher, a better scientist, a better leader, a better businessperson, a better manager, and so on.

Self-realization incorporates within itself both morality and the satisfaction of desires. Morality is naturally present in *mokṣa* for two reasons. First, the Self that is attained in *mokṣa* is naturally good. That is why it is called *Śiva* (literally "the benign"). It would be illogical to think that bad actions could spring forth from a naturally benign self. Ramakrishna Paramahansa used to say that just as only honey can drop from a honeycomb, only good actions can spring forth from the Śiva-state.

Second, in the state of *mokṣa*, or Self-realization, one feels one's unity with all. "He becomes one with all."[12] It is quite natural for such a person to do good to all.[13] What obstructs the Self is called ignorance (*ajñāna*). Ignorance is defined as the sense of duality (*dvaitha-prathā* or *bheda bhuddha*). It is the sense one has that something or someone is "other."[15] When this sense of duality is dispelled and one's unity with all is realized — that is, universal love is attained — then one of the most essential characteristics of Self-realization is achieved.

It is obvious that selfishness, or the sense of duality, is the root of all immorality. One can exploit a person only when one considers him or her as other than oneself. But if one considers that person a part of oneself, how can one exploit him or her? A Self-realized person will not exploit or harm anyone, as Self-realization is a state of perfect universal love. On the contrary, he or she will help all. Thus Self-realization is a state of natural, spontaneous morality.

Self-realization synthesizes within itself both the satisfaction of desires and morality, both "*the pleasant*" and "*the good.*" In Self-realization one's own best interest and the good of others become one; it is a state that is at once both good and pleasant. In our empirical experience, too, we can find at least one phenomenon that is an example of this synthesis: the phenomenon of love. In love, the good of the lover and the good of the beloved person become one. A mother, for example, feels her oneness with her child and feels happy in the happiness of the child. Love naturally prompts good action by the lover toward the beloved. Moreover, besides prompting beneficial activity towards the beloved person, love gives immense satisfaction and joy to the lover him- or herself. The rapture of love is so deep that only a true lover can fully understand it. To use a phrase from Shakespeare, "It blesseth him that gives and him that takes." Love is the very nature of the Self, and a person of Self-realization will be a true lover. Love is the chief characteristic of the saints and sages who have achieved some amount of Self-realization. The more we realize the Self, the greater is the natural flow of love in us.

The uniqueness of the Tantric conception of *mokṣa*, or Self-realization, is twofold. First, according to Tantra, *mokṣa* is not an otherworldly value, it is the ground of overall success in every walk of life. This corrects the misconception that *mokṣa* is somehow separate from the present life. Second, *mokṣa*, according to Tantra, does not consist merely of "*the good,*" but is a synthesis of both 'hat is good and what is pleasant. This notion of *mokṣa* modifies the popular Indian classification of the four values of life. According to the popular classification, money (*artha*) and the satisfaction of desires (*kāma*) come under "*the pleasant*" and morality (*dharma*) and Self-realization (*mokṣa*) both come under "*the good.*" But according to the Tantric classification, morality alone comes under "*the good*," as *mokṣa* is really a synthesis of both "*the good*" and "*the pleasant,*" and is thus a value higher than even "*the good.*" The scheme of values according to the Tantric classification would be presented in the following way:

> money (*artha*) — material value — the pleasant (*preya*)
> satisfaction of desire (*kāma*) — material value — the pleasant (*preya*)
> morality (*dharma*) — moral value — the good (*śreya*)
> Self-realization (*mokṣa*) — spiritual value — synthesis of "*the good*" and "*the pleasant.*"

HISTORY OF THE TANTRIC TRADITION

It is extremely difficult, if not impossible, to present a historical picture of the Tantric tradition. What are set out by historians as the so-called facts of Tantric history are broad conjectures based on highly inadequate data. The popular theory of the Dravidian origin of Tantra, coupled with the popular theory that Aryans came to India from outside and that the Vedic tradition of the Aryans stood in antagonism to the Tantric tradition, is nothing more than the broad guesswork of historical anthropologists. Some scholars have now begun to voice their doubts about this theory. The history of Tantra lies in deep obscurity, and we have no means at hand to delineate it with surety and sketch its contours conclusively.

But, even if we do not have a chronological account of the Tantric tradition, it does not put us at a loss, for the Tantric philosophy itself exists and can be judged on its own merits. India has never bothered itself with recording the chronological history of authors, for the simple reason that what is more important is the idea that is expressed and preserved, not the people who were the tools for the expression of the idea.

In outlining the history of Tantra, I am thus not giving the history of the people associated with it. I am instead presenting the history of *ideas*. There too, I am giving not a *chronological* history of ideas but a *logical* one. The ideas are presented in an order that weaves them into a coherent system. This is not to imply that a historical approach is not worthwhile. But in this instance, where the chronological events cannot be fixed with any certainty, it behooves us to concentrate on the ideas, which are our chief interest here.

Just as the Vedas are understood to be not just the physical corpus of writings but a body of knowledge (*jñāna*), Tantra too is understood not so much as a collection of texts or scriptures, but as a philosophy of life handed down to the present age by a longstanding tradition. Tantra is a particular philosophy or idea and in this sense Tantra may have existed from the time of the Vedas. It may be even older than the Vedas. Of course, the language of the Tantric texts presently available is the post-Vedic Sanskrit systematized by Pāṇini. This might suggest that Tantra is post-Vedic. But this is not a serious problem. Almost all the traditions in ancient India, and some of them even now, existed first in oral form and were handed down from guru to disciple, or from generation to generation.[15] It is therefore reasonable to believe, as the orthodox scholars do, that the Tantric philosophy existed in oral form from the time of the Vedas, if not earlier, and was only *written down* after the time of the Vedas.

The Tantric tradition is sometimes identified with the Śaiva tradition and ascribed to the Dravidians, who are considered the original natives of India,[16] whereas the Vedic tradition is considered Aryan. The Aryans are said to have emigrated to India from middle Asia. The theory that the Aryans were a race separate from the Dravidians and that the Aryans came to India from outside is not proven; it may at the most be regarded as a historical or anthropological hypothesis subject to correction.[17] No one knows for certain the historical truth about the Dravidians and the Aryans, and it is not necessary to consider it here. If the Dravidians existed as a separate race, and if the Tantric culture originally belonged to them, they were certainly one of the wisest races on earth, for they knew the truth that the inner nature cannot be eliminated simply by suppressing or rejecting it, and that one's basic nature can be sublimated or directed into higher channels. They discovered the way to win over nature with the help of nature's own law.

It seems the Aryans, if at all different from the Dravidians, were no less wise, for they quickly and successfully accepted and assimilated within their own culture the essence of the Dravidian culture. The blending of the two cultures, if indeed they were originally separate, was a happy event, for the two cultural traditions were complementary to each other. However, in the beginning it seems the Aryans had a contemptuous attitude towards the Tantric or Śaiva culture; that is suggested by the condemnation of the Tāntrikas or Śaivas as "phallic worshippers" (*śiśna-devāḥ*).[18] But perhaps later on the Aryans realized that the Tantric culture had significant elements; then they quickly grasped and digested the essentials of that culture — a fact suggested by the Vedic literature considered as a whole.

The above observation is based on the presumption that the Aryans were different from the Dravidians, and that the Tantric culture is originally Dravidian. But this presumption itself, by virtue of being a presumption, cannot be accepted as truth. We might just as well presume that the Tantric culture belongs to the Aryans and is not anti-Vedic. In that case we will interpret the Vedic verses mentioned and quoted above as referring not to the Tāntrikas or Śaivas but to those materialistic demons who indulge only in "eating and engaging in sex" (*śiśnodara-parāyaṇāḥ*). In my present exposition of the Tantric philosophy I am taking the view that the distinction between the Aryan and the Dravidian is dubious and that Tantric thought thoroughly belongs to Aryans, although there might have been several stages in the development of the Tantric ideas from the implicit, embryonic stage to the explicit, fully grown stage.

AMALGAMATION OF THE CULTURES OF RENUNCIATION (NIVṚTTI) AND WORLDLY INVOLVEMENT (PRAVṚTTI)

In India we can find two divergent and apparently contradictory traditional ways of life from the beginning of known history. One is the way of renunciation (*nivṛtti*) and the other is the way of worldly involvement (*pravṛtti*). The former is the path of the renunciate (*sannyāsin*) and the latter is the path of the householder (*gṛhastha*). Both these cultural traditions have their strong advocates and their followers. The significance of the Tantric way of life is that it amalgamates or synthesizes the two ways of involvement and renunciation, assimilating the merits of both and at the same time discarding the defects. The assimilation or amalgamation of the two great, but mutually divergent, currents of life into one is an event of prime significance in the cultural history of India.

In the Indian mind there has always been a fascination with the life of a self-denying renunciate. Such a person has always been looked upon with reverence by the Indian people; even now such a person is held in high esteem in Indian society. The Buddhist monk, the Jaina ascetic, or the Advaita-vedāntic sannyāsin who is the embodiment of renunciation or self-abnegation is considered the ideal person. But a deeper analysis of this phenomenon reveals that the negational ideal (*nivṛtti*) is not so healthy for the individual or for society. This life-denying ideal creates psychological problems and obstructs the process of the integration of personality in the individual, on the one hand, and has a negative effect on endeavors to reform society on the other hand.

But this ideal has its merits, too. It helps one ascend to the higher levels of spiritual life. Unless one negates the lower, one cannot ascend to the higher. In order to assimilate and synthesize the lower within oneself one is required to rise to a higher level. Taken in this sense, negation is as much a law of healthy life as affirmation is.

Unlike the ideal of renunciation, the ideal of involvement in worldly activities is life-affirming, and is therefore free from the above-mentioned defects of the life of renunciation. It has every possibility of bringing fulfillment in the life of the individual and in society. But, like renunciation, involvement has its drawbacks, although they are of a different sort. Involvement, if it is a purely materialistic way of life without the spiritual element, may limit people to the animal level and can cause chaos and unrest in the individual and in society.

Renunciation may be termed the life of spirit and involvement the life of matter. The former may also be called "*the good*" and the latter "*the pleasant.*" What is needed for a healthy life, whether individual or societal, is a synthesis or an amalgamation of the two. One without the other is not only incomplete but also conducive to serious problems. The Tantric way of life is an answer to this. The Tantric life is basically spiritual, with the material life carried out as the free expression of the spirit. Tantric spirituality is inclusive of materiality. Tantra presents a way of life in which the profane becomes sacred and material life itself becomes spiritual. The distinction between the sacred and the profane is abolished. In the Tantric way of life, enjoyment (*bhoga*) becomes yoga, so-called vice becomes virtue, and the otherwise bondage-creating world becomes the means to liberation.[19]

Thus, the Tantric way of life is a happy and perfectly successful synthesis of the aforesaid two opposite trends of Indian culture, which are both very strong but one-sided. Neither of the two traditions alone can solve all the problems of life. The amalgamation of the two, however, is a development of profound historical and cultural significance. India presents, in the form of Tantra, a philosophy of life that is complete and perfect in all respects and that has the potential to answer *all* the problems of life.

It is necessary here to clear up the misconception that Tantra is itself merely the way of involvement or indulgence because it accepts sensual and material enjoyment. Tantra is not the way of indulgence, for it does not advocate a hedonistic or materialistic way of life. Tantra is a synthesis of involvement and renunciation; the Tantric way is basically a spiritual way of life that turns the material into the spiritual. The main characteristic of Tantric yoga is that it spiritualizes material life.

It should also be made clear that if one understands the Veda as the path of renunciation relative to Tantra as the path of indulgence, one is gravely mistaken. The Veda does not advocate renunciation. It is full of prayers for material fulfillment; the Vedic sacrificial rituals are aimed at acquiring material prosperity. Even the Upaniṣads, which are interpreted by the Advaitic scholiasts as yielding the doctrine of renunciation, do not preach renunciation of material life at all. In fact, the *Īśa Upaniṣad* warns against the life of pure renunciation and advocates the synthesis of renunciation and worldliness. The Upaniṣad says, "Those who worship indulgence (*avidyā*) enter into darkness, but those who are engrossed in renunciation (*vidyā*) enter into still more darkness."[20] The best way, therefore, is a reconciliation of both, and in the same vein the Upaniṣad further says, "One who comprehends both renunciation and involvement crosses mortality with the help of involvement and attains immortality with the help of renunciation."[21] The point is that both renunciation and worldliness become the means of spiritual realization; there is actually no dichotomy between the two. This supports my contention that the Tantric philosophy is implicitly, and sometimes explicitly, present in the Upaniṣads. The Vedas and the Upaniṣads neither present a life-denying metaphysics nor conceive of Reality, or Brahman, as inactive.

THE TANTRIC DENOMINATIONS

In India there are several traditions and sub-traditions of Tantra. Some have become extinct; some are still living. We can classify them all under three major denominations: (a) Śaiva-Śākta Tantrism, (b) Buddhist Tantrism, and (c) Vaiṣṇava Tantrism. All the sub-trends of Tantrism can be placed under one or the other denomination. For example, the Nātha tradition of Gorakha Nātha and the Aghora tradition of Kīnārāma can be regarded as branches of Śaiva-Śākta Tantrism. Similarly, the Sahajiyā cult of Bengal, which might have originated from the Buddhist Sahajayāna and later on taken Vaiṣṇava form, can be safely classified as Vaiṣṇava Tantrism.

The Bāul tradition of eastern India seems to be a combination of Buddhist Tantrism, Vaiṣṇava Tantrism, and Islamic Sufism. The Bengali term *bāul,* or *bātul,* or *bāvalā,* in the dialects of Hindi, means "crazy" or "mad." The esoteric Tantric yogin is "God-intoxicated" or "mad" with spiritual ecstasy. The Bāul yogins also sing and roam as mendicants.

The Kāpālika tradition, which flourished in the medieval period and is now virtually extinct, is an offshoot of Buddhist Tantrism with a mixture of Śaiva-Śākta Tantrism. Tibetan Tantrism owes its allegiance to the Buddhist Yogācāra Vijñānavāda. It is said that Padmasambhava, an Indian Brahmin-turned-Buddhist from Nalanda, went to Tibet and Nepal and spread Buddhist Tantrism in the Himalayan regions. Tibetan Tantrism is mainly Buddhist.

The cults of Śaiva-Śākta Tantrism are divided into two lineages: the Girnārī and the Newārī. Girnār, which is a mountain in the Gujarat province, is the seat of the Lord Dattātreya. Lord Dattātreya is regarded as the original teacher of Śaiva-Śākta Tantrism. Paraśurāma and Durvāsā, who are the legendary teachers of Śaivism, are in the same lineage. The followers of the Aghora tradition owe their allegiance to Dattātreya, the Lord of Girnār; they are thus called Girnārīs. The followers of the Nātha tradition are mainly Newārī. Newār is the sub-Himalayan region, chiefly Nepal. The gurus of the Nātha tradition lived in this area. Even now Guru Gorakha Nātha is held in high esteem in Nepal. Therefore the followers are called Newārīs.

Some believe that all forms of Tantrism originated from the Buddhist Vajrayāna in the medieval period. It is true that Vajrayāna has exercised great influence on other traditions, but it is not correct to say that Vajrayāna is the source of Tantrism. In fact, Tantrism is much older; it existed even before the Buddha. Tantrism is so flexible and liberal that it can adopt any form and any terminology or symbols for its expression. It can assume Buddhist form as well as other forms. When Buddhist Tantrism came under Vaiṣṇava influence in Bengal, it had no difficulty changing into the Vaiṣṇava version. Tantrism is really one; it has only adopted different forms and terminologies like those of Buddhism, Śaiva-Śāktism, and Vaiṣṇavism.

As far as the Śaiva and Śākta denominations are concerned, I do not consider them two separate traditions. Since two words — Śaivism and Śāktism — are used in the Tantric literature, we have been led to think that they denote two different traditions that are philosophically separate from each other. Metaphysically, Śaivism and Śāktism come from the same root. The ontological position of both schools is one and the same. Śiva is both Śiva and Śakti in one. In fact, Ultimate Reality, which is called Śiva or Śakti, is Consciousness (*citi* or *samvit*). This Consciousness is conceived of as a dynamic force, and that dynamism of Consciousness is called Śakti. So, Reality is one, whether it is called Śiva or Śakti. To use an analogy, a current of water can be seen as water; it can also be seen as current, that is, a flow of water. Similarly, Consciousness can be seen as Śiva (*jñāna*) and it can also be seen as a dynamic force or Śakti (*kriyā*). Śiva and Śakti are two aspects of one and the same Reality.

The only difference between Śaivism and Śāktism is that of emphasis. Just as the current of water may be seen by one person as water and by another person as just the current or flow, the Śaiva envisages Reality as Śiva, whereas the Śākta sees it as Śakti. Added to this is a slight difference in the form of worship. The Śākta worships God as the Mother in the personified form of Durgā or Kālī. The Śaiva may worship God in the personified form of Śaṁkara of the Kailāsa Mountain together with his consort Pārvatī. But these are all symbols. The symbols may differ, but they do not signal a philosophical difference, because they denote the same Reality. The difference in emphasis cannot bring about any real philosophical difference, for the overall position remains unaltered. The Śaiva does not say that Reality is not Śakti; similarly, the Śākta cannot say that Reality is not Śiva.

The historical position of Buddhist Tantrism is a little baffling, because it does not seem to fit in with the main trend of Buddhism. The essence of the teaching of the Buddha is renunciation (*tyāga*) in the literal sense of the renunciation of worldly things. One may wonder how a Buddhist *bhikkhu*, who should be an avowed renunciate, could follow a path that uses indulgence, even in sex, which is a practice that goes against the ocher robe donned as a symbol of renunciation. The Śaiva and the Vaiṣṇava may have no difficulty accepting indulgence, for they may see the world as the sport (*līlā*) of the Lord, and therefore they need not become renunciates, but the same cannot be true of the Buddhist.

A possible explanation of the emergence of Tantrism in the Buddhist tradition of complete renunciation is that Tantrism arose as a reaction to the philosophy of extreme self-abnegation, and it served to counterbalance the extreme negativism. However, there is also another explanation. The origin of Buddhist Tantrism can be traced to the original teachings of the Buddha, and the explanation may be that the Buddha taught the Tantric ideas for a special class of elites. For the general public or for people at the lower stages of spiritual evolution, the teaching of renunciation is relevant, for such people cannot understand the higher teaching of Tantra, which envisages renunciation in the midst of enjoyment. The philosophy of ordinary renunciation is only the first half of the total spiritual *sādhanā*.

The second half is that of Tantra, which synthesizes renunciation and enjoyment. Tantrism thus might be not an incongruent aberration in the Buddhist tradition but the culmination of the inner dynamism of Buddhist thought.

THE COMMON FEATURES

Since all the Tantric denominations (Śaiva-Śākta, Buddhist, and Vaiṣṇava) are forms of Tantrism, they must have some features in common. There are two principal characteristics of Tantrism common to all these Tantric denominations. The first is the concept of spontaneous activity, or dynamism, in Consciousness, Consciousness being accepted as Ultimate Reality. This dynamism is called *ṣakti* or *kriyā*. Sentience, illumination, or knowledge (*jñāna*), is generally accepted as the essential characteristic of Consciousness; it is this that differentiates Consciousness from insentient matter. But Consciousness is not an inert principle; it has an active element in the form of thinking or creative imagination. Tantra conceives of Consciousness not merely as a knowing principle, but also as an energy, in fact, *the* energy, which not only knows but also acts. In Tantra, Consciousness is thus called Consciousness-Force (*citi-śakti*).

The knowing or illuminating aspect of Consciousness is called *jñāna*, *prakāśa*, or Śiva, and the dynamic or active aspect is called *kriyā*, *spanda*, *vimarśa*, or Śakti. It is also called *svātantrya* (freedom), as the activity is perfectly free. The dynamic (*kriyā*) aspect of Consciousness is symbolized by a woman, and the knowledge (*jñāna*) aspect by a man.[22] That is why the Śakti (energy) aspect is referred to by feminine names like Vāmā, Tripurā, Bhairavī, Sundarī, Ṣoḍaśī, Durgā, Kālī, Śivā, Umā, Pārvatī, Rādhā, Sītā, and so on. Rādhā and Sītā are the Vaiṣṇava symbols of Śakti. Similarly, masculine names like Śiva, Bhairava, Rudra, Kṛṣṇa, and Rāma are the symbols of the knowing aspect. Kṛṣṇa and Rāma are the Vaiṣṇava symbols.[23]

Tantra conceives of Reality as knowledge and activity in one. That is why Reality is called Śiva-Śakti, Prakāśa-Vimarśa, or Jñāna-Kriyā. Symbolically, Reality is depicted as a person having both the feminine and masculine aspects in one. This is called *Ardhanār-īśvara* in Śaiva Tantrism, *Yuganaddha* in Buddhist Tantrism, and *Rādhā-Kṛṣṇa* or *Sītā-Rāma* in Vaiṣṇava Tantrism.

There is a fashion among some scholars to interpret the two aspects of Consciousness in terms of polarity. The polarity, of course, is evident in the symbols of man and woman. But if we understand and analyze the nature of that which is symbolized, namely Consciousness with knowledge and activity, we find that polarity becomes meaningless. Polarity exists in a pair of opposites like the north and south poles of the earth. Man and woman, of course, form a pair of opposites. But knowledge and action, which are called Śiva and Śakti, are not opposites. They are simply two aspects of one and the same Reality.[24] They are not in opposition but in union. To understand them in terms of polarity is to impose the characteristics of the symbol on the symbolized.

The second common feature of Tantrism is a positive attitude toward life and the world, and the philosophy of using the world and worldly enjoyment in such a way that they become the means of attaining the ultimate spiritual goal, Self-realization. This feature of Tantrism is in logical conformity with the first feature — the acceptance of creative dynamism, or Śakti, in Reality, or Consciousness. This Śakti is responsible for the creation of the world. Creation is the free manifestation of Śakti, or of Śiva in its Śakti aspect. The implication is that Creation, or the world, should be taken as something holy or good, as it is the manifestation of the Divine. The world is not to be rejected as an illusion (*māyā*), obstruction, or super-imposition on Reality, but is to be accepted and embraced as the manifest form of the divine Consciousness that is our own Self. This metaphysics becomes the basis of the positive way of life that Tantra advocates. This positive attitude towards life and the world is present in every denomination of the Tantric tradition.

The common features of the different denominations of Tantrism are quite obvious; tracing out the points of difference, or the uniqueness of each denomination, is not as easy. It is not possible to catch hold of real differences. The difference in names and terms is insignificant. For example, in the case of Śaivism and Vaiṣṇavism, it would not be an over-simplification to say that in many areas the terms Śiva and Viṣṇu are interchangeable. This is true of some other terms as well. Buddhist Tantrism, of course, is philosophically somewhat different, for *nirvāṇa* is not the same as Self-realization, or God-realization. But like the Śaiva and Vaiṣṇava state of realization, *nirvāṇa* is taken not as a negative state but as a state of fullness and bliss. Although it uses the term *śūnyatā* frequently, Buddhist Tantrism falls more in line with the Yogācāra Vijñānavāda than with the Mādhyamika Śūnyavāda. Vijñānavāda is nearer to Śaivism. And as far as the practical Tantric *sādhanā* is concerned, there is no basic difference from the other schools of Tantrism. Most of the differences between the Tantric denominations are just differences in name and in the language, or mode of expression, conditioned by the philosophical tradition of each school.

As far as the Śaiva and Śākta denominations are concerned, they are one and the same tradition philosophically and religiously. One may call the tradition Śaiva or Śākta, as one likes. In order to avoid confusion, I have used the term *Śaiva-Śākta*, because according to the tradition Reality is both Śiva and Śakti in one.

SIGNIFICANCE OF THE LEFT-HANDED DOCTRINE (KAULA-MĀRGA)

As a logical corollary to the second feature common to all forms of Tantrism, that is, the positive attitude towards life and the world, and the philosophy of transforming worldly enjoyment into the means of Self-realization, what follows is a description of the left-handed doctrine (Kaula- or *vāma-sādhanā*) in which the spiritual aspirant makes use of the five M's (*pañca-makāra*) — wine (*madya*), meat (*māṁsa*), fish (*mīna*), parched grain (*mudrā*), and sexual intercourse (*maithuna*) — in order to change his or her attitude towards them. What is falsely and egotistically taken to be profane and ignoble by orthodox Hindus is used in the left-handed practice as an object of worship. Tantra introduced this practice for the special purpose of freeing the mind of the aspirant (*sādhaka*) from the false distinctions of good and bad artifically created by society.

Tantra emphasizes not the physical use of the five M's, but the change of attitude toward them. One may change one's attitude towards these so-called profane things even without physically using them. So, in the Tantric *sādhanā* the physical use of the five M's is not obligatory; one can become a Tantric *sādhaka* even without using them. In fact, the physical use of the five M's is prohibited in the case of ignorant people who do not aim at changing their attitude. The *Kulārṇava Tantra* says, "The ignorant person (*paśu*) should not smell, see, touch, or drink wine and meat; the use of these is efficacious (only) in the case of the *Kaula-sādhakas*."[25]

Among the five M's of the left-handed path, the *sādhanā* of sexual union is the most significant, for the transformation, or sublimation, of sex energy plays the most important role in the healthy development and shaping of personality. This much-misunderstood and much-misused *sādhanā* requires considerable space for a full explanation of its significance. I will discuss it in detail in Chapter 10. Here a brief reference to the *sādhanā* must suffice. According to Tantra, desire (*kāma*) is the principal form of energy (*śakti*) in human beings. It is neither possible nor desirable to destroy this energy. The libidinal energy (*kāma-śakti*), sublimated or made to flow into higher channels, can be a powerful catalyst for change. The crude sexual energy can be directed to flow upward into the higher expressions of love, aesthetic creativity, and Self-realization. Tantra presents a method or yoga for the deliberate sublimation of sexual energy.

The Tantric yoga of sex sublimation, briefly, consists of two practices. First, one has to cultivate the attitude that sex is something holy and divine. The same attitude is to be cultivated towards the sex partern and the sex organ. For example, the male should regard the female as the divine Śakti, and the female should regard the male as Śiva. The phallic worship of Śaivism — worship of the sex organ as the divine symbol — is also aimed at cultivating this attitude. This change of attitude towards sex and the sex object serves as an antidote to neutralize the poisonous feeling that sex is something unholy and dangerous. This is a necessary step in the process of sex sublimation. Second, one should feel intense love for the sex partner and perform the sex act as an expression of love, not as sensual enjoyment (*bhoga*). Through practice it is possible to completely rid the sex act of its sensual element and do it purely as an expression of love. This, on the one hand, enhances the joy of sex and on the other hand, transforms sex into love. The practice of love towards the sexual partner is a means of mastering sex by sublimation.

The Vaiṣṇava Tantrists, however, use only the fifth M, *maithuna* or sexual intercourse and avoid the other *makāras*, especially meat and wine, in their practice. This is perhaps because Vaiṣṇavism is a tradition of non-violence (*ahiṁsā*) and puritanical conduct. Their puritanical conduct includes eating pure (*sāttvika*) food and abstaining from impure (*tāmasika*) food and drink like meat and wine. Although the general Vaiṣṇava *sādhaka* still cherishes the ideal of celibacy and sexual purity, he or she extricates sex from the puritanic list. However, the Vaiṣṇava Tāntrika is not able to adopt the use of meat and wine, probably because he or she is still conditioned by the Vaiṣṇava prohibitions. This discriminative attitude of the Vaiṣṇava Tantric *sādhaka* may obstruct the process of rising fully above the artificial and egotistic barriers of good and bad. The *sādhaka* of the Śaiva-Śākta tradition of Tantrism does not have this disadvantage, as he or she uses all five M's.

In the use of the four M's, wine (*madya*), meat (*māṁsa*), fish (*mīna*), and parched grain (*mudrā*), no question of the sublimation of desire is involved; these four M's are employed to eliminate the artificial and egotistical distinction between religious and profane, or between false good and bad. But the *sādhanā* concerning the sexual M, besides being beneficial in the above way, has the added benefit of sex sublimation. The Tantric seers realized that the sexual energy, if sublimated, could work wonders. That is why Tantrism places special emphasis on the sexual *sādhanā*. Thus, the fifth M related to sex has greater significance than the other four M's.

BREAKING FALSE BARRIERS

From what we have seen about Tantra thus far, it should be clear that the Tantric way is an attempt to break the false barriers of the individual and of society. One's real self is covered with the cloaks of artificial taboos and inhibitions created out of one's individual and social ego. When one throws off these cloaks, one realizes the natural beauty of one's real self. Beauty lies in the egoless nakedness of the Self, just as in the innocent nudity of a little child. Tantrism is the way of becoming existentially nude by stripping oneself of all the artificial coatings of the individual and social personality.

Indian society and the individuals within it have been suffering from many undesirable artifically created barriers. Caste is one such barrier; it is like a cancerous growth eating into the vitals of Indian society. The social order based on the arrangement of the four functional classes of *brāhmaṇa*, *kṣatriya*, and so on, might have been a good thing in some hoary past, but it degenerated into castism. This created the false social vanity of high and low, respectable and untouchable. The Tantric seers noticed this dangerous growth and rebelled against it. Whether or not they succeeded in bringing the society back to its natural beauty is a different matter; but the fact is that Tantrism has fought against castism. This is one of the many reasons why rigid orthodox people, who were caste supporters, looked down on Tantrism.

The orthodox people did not allow all castes to have equal opportunity, even in spiritual practices. But Tantrism, being liberal and totally unorthodox, considers caste meaningless in deciding who is qualified for *sādhanā*.[26] This is in sharp contrast with the orthodox attitude that the *śūdra*, or lowest caste, does not have the right to study the Veda. The Tantric rituals of collective worship tend to abolish castism and untouchability. For example, in the collective *cakra* worship practitioners of all castes are required to eat and drink from the same pot. The rich and the poor, the princely class and the ordinary laborer, the lady of noble birth and the prostitute — all are deliberately given equal treatment. The symbolic *cakra* worship is, among other things, aimed at creating the sense of equality by freeing people from the false sense of distinction. It is also aimed at freeing people from artificially created taboos and inhibitions.

For the smooth functioning of a healthy society it is essential that its members behave in a disciplined way; this implies acceptance of social rules and taboos; yet Tantrists seem to violate all social norms. This is not to imply that Tantrists are undisciplined. The Tantrist aims at becoming free, not undisciplined. In the state of freedom there is a natural discipline that comes from within. Discipline does not mean obeying a law even if it is wrong. We all know that many social laws, like caste, untouchability, inequality based on the consideration of status, exploitation of one class by the other, and so on, are based on false premises. The Tantrist seeks to break these false laws, and in that sense he or she is a nonconformist. But this cannot be called a lack of discipline.

It is possible to have a society free from all artificial taboos. In fact, freedom from such taboos is essential for the formation of a healthy society. There are some social laws that are, in the ultimate analysis, immoral and also injurious to social health. Fundamentalist laws, for example, are made in the name of religion, but some are highly immoral and have a crippling effect on the personality development of the members of society. The Tantrist would deliberately break such laws in order to establish natural justice.

This does not mean that there should be no social or political laws. It means that these laws should not be based on the selfishness and egocentrism of some people who consciously or unconsciously try to exploit others. Moreover, people might indulge in self-deception when making decisions based on considerations of caste, social status, and so on. Some social laws might be based on sheer ignorance. Other laws, created out of egocentrism, might lead people to indulge in self-deception. Thus, there can be (a) laws created out of ignorance, (b) laws created out of selfishness, and (c) laws created out of egoism. If the Tantrist seeks to break such laws, what is wrong with that?

Of course, Tantrism does not condone the violation of laws and taboos that are not unjust and are, in fact, necessary for the happy functioning and development of society. But under special circumstances the need to allow exceptions to even these rules might arise. The exception may be perfectly in line with the spirit of the rule, and not allowing the exception may go against the spirit of the rule. If a society does not apply human considerations in executing the rules, and instead exercises them rigidly and blindly, that society does not have healthy growth. Geniuses and talented people sometimes need to be granted exceptions, and a society that deals with them strictly might hamper the growth of talent. Moreover, a rigid society with stringent laws can give rise to hypocrisy and to psychologically disintegrated personalities. People indulging in self-deception abound in such a society. The point is that a society possessing rational and flexible rules capable of adjustment to any new situation is a healthy society that can never decay. Tantrism aims at creating such a society.

ABERRATIONS

In the world of actual Tantric practices, the sacrifice of animals is widespread. Even human sacrifice was common in the medieval period; nowadays it is not common and is also declared a crime by law. Still, stray cases of human sacrifice are often reported in the newspapers. Animal or human sacrifice is believed by some so-called

Tantric practitioners to be an offering pleasing to the Goddess (Śakti). An in-depth analysis of this practice reveals that animal or human sacrifice is an undesirable aberration in the Tantric tradition. To think that the Divine Being will be appeased by the killing of an animal in an offering is to impose human fancy on the Deity. The Divine Mother wants the *sādhaka* to sacrifice and offer his or her ego, not the animal and not even his or her own physical self.

Thus, animal or human sacrifice is one of the many non-Tantric practices that have crept into the Tantric tradition. It does not have the sanction of the principal Tantras. The same is true of the practice of black magic. While practicing the Tantric yoga meant for Self-realization, the *sādhaka* automatically acquires some psychic powers, but Tantra does not permit them to be used for evil purposes. There are certain Tantric *sādhanās* that are specifically aimed at achieving psychic powers meant to be used for good purposes. Lest such *sādhanās* fall into the hands of impostors and miscreants and be abused by them, the Tantric gurus have tried their best to keep them concealed. They revealed the secrets of the psychic *sādhanā* only to deserving disciples, and they chose and accepted the disciples themselves after due scrutiny.[27] Although utmost care was taken in safeguarding the psychic *sādhanā* from undeserving persons, the *sādhanā* might have slipped into the wrong hands, as the safeguarding measures could not be one-hundred percent foolproof. Hence, in the course of Tantric history we find the misuse of such practices. This is to some extent analogous to the misuse of technological power by the wrong people. However, the general Tantric *sādhanā*, or the Tantric way of life, is safe and harmless and is also completely open and public.

We should not think, therefore, that every phenomenon that occurs in the name of Tantric practice is actually Tantrism. Practices like animal sacrifice and black magic are not proper Tantrism. The same is true of the abuse of the left-handed path, especially the *sādhanā* of sexual union, carried out by some pseudo-Tantrists.[28] We have to be very careful in discriminating between the Tantric and the non-Tantric or pseudo-Tantric.

What are the criteria for discriminating between true Tantrism and false Tantrism? I would say there are two criteria. First, we have to use reason in order to see whether a particular practice is consistent with the Tantric philosophy. Second, we have to make an in-depth analysis of the Tantras and produce evidence from the Tantric texts for or against that particular practice. If the alleged Tantric practice satisfies the two criteria, it should be accepted as Tantric, otherwise it should be rejected.

KASHMIR ŚAIVISM AS THE CULMINATION OF TANTRIC PHILOSOPHY

Although the three denominations of Śaiva-Śākta, Buddhist, and Vaiṣṇava all have forms of Tantrism, the Śaiva-Śākta tradition surpasses the others and forms the most complete model of Tantrism. The following are the reasons for placing the Śaiva, or Śaiva-Śākta, school above the other schools. First, the Śaiva school is more thorough, as it deals with almost *all* the topics and sub-topics of Tantrism. The other schools are not so thorough; they overlook many issues. Second, the concept of the dynamism (*śakti*), or activity (*kriyā*), of Consciousness, which is the key concept of Tantric philosophy, is discussed in full detail in the Śaiva tradition, and the nature of this dynamism or activity is fully brought out. Other schools do not present the concept with the same completeness. Third, the Śaiva tradition, in its use of the left-handed doctrine, more clearly demonstrates the spirit of Tantrism. The acceptance of the world and the assimilation of material values into the spiritual is brought out more logically and fully. For example, the use of the five M's is carried out to its full length, logically culminating in the *Aghora-sādhanā*, which entails using even more impure substances, such as urine and excrement.

The philosophy of Tantrism, or Śiva-Tantrism, is fully elucidated and expounded on in a systematic, logical, and rational way in the philosophical system called Trika or Pratyabhijñā, popularly known as Kashmir Śaivism. The philosophers of Kashmir Śaivism, especially Abhinavagupta, have explained all the issues of Tantrism, both in its philosophical or theoretical and religious or practical aspects. They have also drawn out the Tantric philosophy to its logical perfection. On this basis, I venture to propose that Kashmir Śaivism is the culmination of the Tantric tradition, or is the central philosophy of Tantrism.

Incidentally, we find more than one metaphysical position in the Śaiva Tantras. In this connection a question may be asked: If Tantra is taken to be revelation or as experienced truth, then why are there differing ideas within it? This question is considered in the *Tantrāloka.*[29] It is true that the Tantra advocates three metaphysical positions — difference (*bheda*), unity-in-difference (*bhedābheda*), and unity (*abheda*). Technically, the *bheda* corpus is called *Śiva* Āgama, the *bhedābheda* works are known as *Rudra* Āgama, and the *abheda* texts fall under the rubric of the *Bhairava* Āgama.[30] Different philosophical positions may ensue from these three differently-oriented Āgamas.[31] Why the difference? The difference in suitability of people for particular practices (*adhikārī-bheda*) is the answer. In the Indian tradition in general, and the Tantric tradition in particular, it is maintained that the same *sādhanā*, or path, may not be suited to all persons, because all people are not at the same spiritual level; there is a hierarchy of stages of spiritual evolution. Therefore, different paths may be prescribed for different levels of competence. The difference among the Āgamas is due to the "difference among the audience. The difference in meaning is a mere formality."[32] As far as the result is concerned, there is no difference; all of them lead to the attainment of Śiva-consciousness.[33]

In the Tantric tradition, philosophy translates into a path, or *sādhanā*; therefore, the separate philosophies of *difference*, *unity-in-difference*, and *unity* are prescribed for different types of practitioners. Some people, perhaps the majority, cannot understand unity; they can only understand difference. Therefore, only a philosophy of difference can help them. Others cannot be satisfied by the philosophy of difference; for these there is the philosophy of unity, and so on. Therefore, the contradictions in philosophy do not stem from the Āgama itself, but from the differences in the followers for whom the teaching is meant.[34] The Tantric seer is like an expert physician who does not prescribe one and the same medicine for all patients; the medicine varies according to the needs of the patients. This is why, in the course of Indian spirituality, it has often been the case that the same guru teaches different ideologies to different disciples. The guru knows the full truth, but the truth is only grasped by the disciple according to his or her own understanding.

A further question arises here: if the three types of philosophies — difference, unity, and unity-in-difference — are meant for three different types of people, with no judgment as to which is higher or lower, why is the philosophy of unity regarded as the highest, or the correct, philosophy? To this question Jayaratha, the commentator on the *Tantrāloka*, gives an interesting answer.[35] He says that the philosophy of unity includes, or synthesizes within itself, the other two, and not vice versa; therefore, it is the highest. He quotes a verse from the *Tantrāloka*: "Like fragrance in the flower, oil in the til-seed, self in the body and sweet taste in the water, Kaulism (the non-dualistic philosophy) is immanently present in every discipline (*śāstra*)."[36] He maintains that the other disciplines are able to become the means for the highest attainment, or Self-realization, because they are "saturated" with the "nectar" of absolute non-dualism.[37] Unity includes difference; difference, or manifoldness (*bheda*) is accepted, but it is given its proper place — the *many* is accepted as the free expression of the one. Abhinavagupta says that it is Śiva who "first manifests the world of difference (*bheda*) as the opponent's statement (*pūrvapakṣa*) and then again brings it to the conclusion (*uttarapakṣa*) of unity (*abheda*)."[38] It is the sport (*līlā*) of the non-dual Lord to freely manifest in duality, denying at the same time the independent status of duality by incorporating it within Himself. Therefore, unity (*abheda*) is the highest truth. The logic here is that what is more comprehensive is more true.[39]

The Advaita Vedāntin presents the same logic in a slightly different way. He maintains that unity is higher or deeper than difference, for difference presupposes unity. Two different battleships, even when they fight with each other, float upon a common sea. Moreover, the world of difference, according to the Advaitin as well as the Kashmir Śaivite, is the manifestation of unity (Brahman or Śiva); unity is not the manifestation of difference. This means that unity (Śiva or Brahman) stands independent, by itself, and is therefore higher, or truer, than difference (the world), which depends upon unity. To use an analogy, the waves are included in the ocean; the ocean is not included in the waves.[40] We can say that difference is grounded in unity like the waves in the ocean, for difference is the manifestation of unity. We cannot say that unity belongs to difference or is grounded in difference.[41] The philosophy of unity can include the philosophy of duality within itself, but the reverse is not true. That is why the dualist quarrels with the non-dualist, but the non-dualist does not quarrel with the dualist. The father of Advaita, Gauḍapāda, says, "The dualists being absolutely certain of their own positions oppose one another, but this [the philosophy of non-dualism] is not opposed to them."[42]

To conclude, non-dualism (*abheda*), being a synthetic and more comprehensive philosophy, accepts all positions — giving them their proper place, of course — and therefore is the truer philosophy. Following this logic, Abhinavagupta maintains that the Trika philosophy, or *bhairava-śāstra*, which is non-dual, is "the essence of the Śaiva discipline, divided among ten, eighteen and sixty-four Tantras."[43]

Before the rise of Śaiva Absolutism, or Śivādvaita, in the valley of Kashmir, the valley was influenced by Buddhist ideas, as the entire area including the Punjab and Kashmir had been the seat of Buddhist learning. The Buddhists denied the existence of a permanent soul; they were Anātmavādins. The idea of no-soul (Anātmavāda) did not fit in with the long-cherished Brahmanical tradition of the eternal Self (Ātmavāda). When the Buddhist no-soul doctrine became prevalent, it was natural that the beleaguered eternal Self tenet (Ātmavāda) should raise its head in reaction. First, the theistic form of the doctrine of the Self came to the fore. Later, this naturally gave way to Absolutism. The Kashmiri philosophers took advantage of the already existent Mahāyāna Absolutism and the Śabda Absolutism of Bhartṛhari, shaping Śaiva Absolutism according to the methodology of those systems.

The rise of Śaiva Absolutism is described in a legend prevalent in Kashmir and is referred to by Somānanda in his *Śiva-dṛṣṭi* and by Abhinavagupta in his *Tantrāloka.*[44] Somānanda affirms that the secrets of the Śaiva tradition in earlier times existed in the "mouths of the rishis," and with the advent of the Kali age they were concealed and were difficult to obtain.[45] The legend goes that Lord Śiva, out of grace, incarnated in the form of Śrīkaṇṭha and instructed the sage Durvāsā to salvage the Śaiva teachings. Durvāsā produced a mental son, Tryambaka, and transmitted the Śaiva wisdom to him. Then Tryambaka began to propagate the system. That is why the tradition is called the Tryambaka tradition, or *Teramba* in Kashmiri colloquial language.[46]

THE ETYMOLOGY OF TANTRA AND ĀGAMA

It will not be out of place to investigate the meaning of the words *tantra* and *āgama. Tantra* means a discipline or a system. The meaning includes the sense of a logically worked out, self-consistent discipline. The discipline is both in the field of philosophy, or metaphysics, and in the field of religion, or practical life. In other words, *tantra* means a philosophical discipline, as well as a religious and cultural one.

Tantra, or *tantraṇa*, is also used in the sense of the extension, stretching, or spelling out of ideas. In *tantra* any idea, proposition, or philosophy is "stretched" out to its logical extent. This final meaning is in line with the first meaning. *Tantra* means a system logically stretched to its fullest extent.

The word *āgama* is the same as *āgamana*, which means induction or inductive experience, as opposed to *nigama*, or *nigamana*, which means deduction. Here the word *āgamana* is used for all experience, not merely sense experience. Since the Tantra is based on actual experience acquired by yogins and seers, it is called Āgama.

There is also another meaning of the word *āgama*. It means "that which comes," or "that which comes automatically" (*āgacchati iti āgamaḥ*). When the spiritual impurity (*mala*) is removed from the Self, knowledge dawns, or the intuitive experience automatically arises from within the Self. This phenomenon is technically called *pratibhā*. The person who attains knowledge in this way, by himself and without the teaching of a guru, is called "spontaneously perfected" (*saṁsiddha*).[47] Since the Tantra is a record of the intuitive experience of the *saṁsiddhas*, inductively acquired, it is called *āgama*. This knowledge is called *āgama* in a third sense also: *āgama* also means "that which comes by tradition." What comes by tradition has its origin or basis in the inductive experience (*āgamana*) of the seers.

The two words *tantra* and *āgama* taken together mean a fully and logically worked out discipline or body (*tantra*) of knowledge that has come down by tradition, and that is originally based on the inductive experience (*āgama*) of the seers.

THE TEXTUAL HISTORY

Since my object is to present an exposition of the philosophy of Abhinavagupta — Kashmir Śaivism — in giving the textual history I will restrict myself to the texts of Kashmir Śaivism instead of tracing the history of the entire Tantric corpus, which is neither possible nor relevant here.[48] I will divide the texts into two categories: (a) the scriptures or Tantras that provide the source and the basis for Kashmir Śaiva philosophy, and (b) the philosophical treatises written by the philosophers of Kashmir Śaivism.

As Kashmir Śaivism is a non-dualistic system, its philosophers, especially Abhinavagupta, accept mainly those Tantras, or Āgamas, in which the non-dualistic, or monistic, position is reflected. Traditionally the number of Āgamas projecting the philosophy of unity is believed to be sixty-four. Ten Āgamas reflect the philosophy of difference, and eighteen propound unity-in-difference.[49] Out of the sixty-four texts setting forth the doctrine of unity, only a few are available. Abhinavagupta, in his *Tantrāloka*, quotes from a number of Āgamas which are now lost. Important available Tantras are the *Mālinīvijaya*, or *Mālinīvijayottara* — also called the *Śrīpūrva-śāstra*; the *Svacchanda*; the *Rudrayāmala*; the *Vijñānabhairava*; the *Parātriṁśika* or *Parātrīśikā* or simply *Trīśikā*, which forms part of the *RudrayāmalaTantra* and enjoys an independent position like the *Gītā* in the *Mahābhārata*; the *Kulārṇava*; the *Vāmakeś-varī*; the *Netra*; and the *Mṛgendra*, which forms part of a bigger *Āgama* called the *Kāmika*.

The *Mālinīvijayottara* is said to be a summary of a remarkable Tantra of gigantic size, called the *Siddhayogīśvarī Tantra*, referred to by Abhinavagupta as *Siddhayogīśvarī-mataṁ.*[50] The *Vijñānabhairava* is believed to be the essence of the *Rudrayāmala*, and the *Parātriṁśikā* is an actual part of the *Rudrayāmala*. The *Netra* and *Mṛgendra* Tantras are believed to carry a primarily dualistic purport, but they are interpreted by the Kashmir Śaiva philosophers in a non-dualistic way, hence they are listed among the source texts of Kashmir Śaivism.

Abhinavagupta places the *Mālinīvijayottara* above all the Tantras and regards it as the essence of the Trika system. Whenever he refers to it, he does so with great respect. He says, "There is nothing here (in the *Tantrāloka*) which is not in the *Mālinīvijayottara*," and "Trika is the essence of the Śaiva tradition, and the *Mālinī* is the essence of Trika."[51]

As far as the antiquity of the Tantras is concerned, I have already pointed out that the Tantric tradition existed in oral form, transmitted from guru to disciple, from the time of the Vedas. It was rendered into written form only later. Scholars differ over the time of the written Tantras, with dates ranging from the second or third century B.C. to the seventh or eighth century A.D. Since the language of the Tantras is post-Pāṇini Sanskrit, we can conclude that the Tantras were compiled and put into writing during the period ranging from the second or third century B.C. to the third or fourth century A.D.

Some of the Tantras mentioned above have commentaries written by various authors. Abhinavagupta, who lived from the end of the tenth century to the beginning of the eleventh century A.D., wrote a *Vārtika*[52] on the *Mālinīvijayottara* Tantra, known as the *Mālinīvijaya-vārtika.* Kṣemarāja, in the eleventh century A.D., wrote commentaries (called *udyota*) on the *Netra*, *Svacchanda*, and *Vijñānabhairava* Tantras, although the commentary on the *Vijñānabhairava* is written partly by Kṣemarāja and partly by Śivopādhyāya. Ānandabhatta also wrote a commentary, called *Kaumudī*, on the *Vijñānabhairava.* Abhinavagupta has written an illustrious commentary on the *Parātriṁśikā.* Abhinavagupta also mentions three commentaries on the *Parātriṁśikā*, by Somānanda, Kalyāṇa, and Bhavabhūti.[53] Professor K. C. Pandey has discovered two more commentaries by Lakṣmīrāma and Lāsaka, found in Kashmir.[54]

After the scriptural literature — the Tantras, or Āgamas — we come to the works of the philosophers of Kashmir Śaivism, who flourished from the ninth to the twelfth centuries A.D. Almost all of them lived in Kashmir. Maheśvarānanda, author of the *Mahārthamañjarī*, and Varadarāja, author of the *Śivasūtra-vārtika*, were probably the only important writers of this system who hailed from outside Kashmir, but they are reported to have visited Kashmir and to have accepted the Kashmiri gurus.

The first name in the history of Kashmir Śaivism is Vasugupta, who flourished in Kashmir during the end of the eighth century and the beginning of the ninth century A.D. His *Śiva-sūtra* is the first presentation of the non-dualistic Śaiva philosophy in the form of *sūtras.* The orthodox view is that Vasugupta did not author or compose the *sūtras* himself; instead the *sūtras* were revealed to him by Lord Śiva. Therefore, orthodox pandits regard the *Śiva-sūtra* as an Āgama or Tantra, and like to classify it among the scriptures.

The legend associated with Vasugupta and his *Śiva-sūtra* is that Lord Śiva instructed Vasugupta in a dream to go to Mahādeva Mountain in Kashmir, find the *sūtras* inscribed on a stone slab there, and then propagate them among the people. The legend goes that Vasugupta, as instructed by Śiva, went to the mountain and found the *sūtras* accordingly. The purport of the legend, if interpreted rationally, would be that Vasugupta received the non-dual Śaiva philosophy in a state of spiritual inspiration and then presented it in the form of *sūtras.*

Vasugupta's disciple, Bhatta Kallaṭa, who lived in the mid-ninth century, wrote the famous *Spanda-kārikā.* But there is a controversy regarding the authorship of this work. Some, including Kṣemarāja, uphold the view that it was authored by Vasugupta himself. Others, including Utpala Bhaṭṭa, the author of *Spanda-pradīpikā,* believe that it was composed by Kallaṭa, who received the doctrine from his guru, Vasugupta. The following are the commentaries on the *Spanda-kārikā:* (a) Kallaṭa's own short commentary, the *Spanda-vṛtti,* (b) Rāmakaṇṭha's *Spanda-vivṛti,* (c) Kṣemarāja's *Spanda-nirṇaya* and *Spanda-sandoha,* which is an exhaustive commentary on the first sutra of the *Spanda-kārikā,* and (iv) the *Spanda-pradīpikā* of Utpala Bhaṭṭa, who is not to be confused with Utpaladeva.

The *Śiva-sūtra* and *Spanda-kārikā* are more or less written in an inspired way without using the philosophical method of reasoning. The *Śiva-dṛṣṭi* (literal meaning: "Śaiva philosophy") of Somānanda, of the late ninth century, is the first Kashmir Śaiva philosophical treatise to use the method of refuting the opponent's view and supporting one's own view (*khaṇḍana* and *maṇḍana*). An incomplete commentary by Utpaladeva on the *Śiva-dṛṣṭi* is available. It only goes up to the 74th verse of the 4th chapter. Abhinavagupta probably wrote a commentary called *Śivadṛṣṭyālocana,* but it is not available.

Somānanda is the father of the Pratyabhijñā school. His *Śiva-dṛṣṭi* is a tough work, however. His disciple, Utpaladeva, also known as Utpalācārya, who lived from the end of the ninth century to the beginning of the tenth century, improved upon his teacher's work and presented the Pratyabhijñā philosophy in the *Īśvara-pratyabhijñā-kārikā* with more precision and in a less difficult style. Abhinavagupta characterizes the work as reflecting the wisdom of Somānanda.[55] Abhinavagupta has written two commentaries on the *Īśvara-pratyabhijñā-kārikā.* One is the *Vimarśinī,* also called the *laghvī* ("smaller") commentary, and the other is the *Vivṛti-vimarśinī,* also called the *bṛhatī* ("larger") commentary. Utpala himself had written a commentary (*vivṛti)* on his *Pratyabhijñā-kārikās*; Abhinava's *Vivṛti-vimarṣinī,* or *bṛhatī* commentary, is based upon that, but unfortunately Utpala's commentary is not available. Utpala also wrote *Ājaḍapramātṛ-siddhi, Īśvara-siddhi,* and *Sambandha-siddhi,* together known as *Siddhi-trayī.* Another very important work of Utpala is *Śiva-stotrāvalī,* a collection of philosophically profound verses composed as a prayer to Lord Śiva.

After Utpala comes the greatest philosopher of Kashmir Śaivism, Abhinavagupta, the grand-disciple of Utpaladeva. Abhinava was the direct disciple of Lakṣmaṇagupta, who in turn was a disciple of Utpala. Professor K. C. Pandey has done extensive research on the history and works of Abhinavagupta.[56] We can divide the works of Abhinava into two parts, namely, (a) the commentaries, and (b) independent works. His commentaries are as follows:

1. *Īśvara-pratyabhijñā-vimarśinī* (*laghvī vṛtti).* A commentary on the *Īśvara-pratyabhijñā-kārikā* of Utpaladeva.
2. *Īśvara-pratyabhijñā-vivṛti-vimarśinī* (*bṛhatī vṛtti*). A larger commentary on the *Īśvara-pratyabhijñā-kārikā* of Utpala-deva, based on the lost commentary of Utpala.
3. *Parātriṁśikā-vivaraṇa.* A commentary on *Parātriṁśikā.*
4. *Bhagavadgītārtha-saṅgraha.* A short commentary on the *Gītā.*
5. *Śivadṛṣṭyālocana.* A commentary on the *Śiva-dṛṣṭi* of Somānanda (not available).

Following are the independent works of Abhinavagupta:

1. *Tantrāloka.* This is the *magnum opus* of Abhinavagupta. It is a huge work presenting the philosophy, religion, and yogic *sādhanā* of the non-dual Śiva-Tantric tradition, Kashmir Śaivism. Rājānaka Jayaratha, of the twelfth century A.D., has written an equally extensive commentary, the *Viveka*, on the whole of the *Tantrāloka.* The *Tantrāloka* was first published along with the *Viveka* by the Kashmir Series of Texts and Studies, Srinagar, in 12 Volumes. It is composed in verse.
2. *Tantrasāra.* This is a prose summary of the main topics of the *Tantrāloka.*
3. *Tantra-vaṭa-dhānikā.* This is a further summarization, in verse, of the *Tantrāloka.* It is like the seed (*dhānikā*) of the banyan tree (*vaṭa*) of Tantra.[57]
4. *Mālinīvijaya-vārtika.* This is an extensive exposition of the *Mālinīvijayottara* Tantra.
5. *Paramārthasāra.* This is a non-dualistic rendering of Śeṣa Muni's semi-dualistic work, the *Ādhāra-kārikās.* Yogarāja, of the second half of the eleventh century A.D., has written a commentary on the *Paramārthasāra.*

Besides the above-mentioned works, Abhinavagupta has authored a number of short works, including his *stotras*; some of them, like the *Anuttarāṣṭikā*, contain profound philosophical wisdom.[58] They are as follows:

1. *Anuttarāṣṭikā.*
2. *Paramārtha-dvādaśikā.*
3. *Paramārtha-carcā.*
4. *Mahopadeśa-viṁśatikam.*
5. *Kramastotram.*
6. *Bhairava-stavaḥ* (*Bhairava-stotram*).
7. *Dehastha-devatā-cakra-stotram.*
8. *Anubhava-nivedanam.*

In addition to these works in philosophy, religion and yogic practice, Abhinavagupta has to his credit two illustrious works on poetics in commentary form:

1. *Dhvanyāloka-locana.* A commentary on the *Dhvanyāloka* of Ānandavardhana, a work expounding on the *vyañjanā*, or suggestion theory of Indian poetics.
2. *Abhinava-bhāratī.* A commentary on the famous *Nāṭya Śāstra* of Bharata, expounding on the Indian theory of *rasa*, or aesthetic enjoyment.

Although these two works are on aesthetics, they have a philosophical background, as Abhinavagupta attempts to present, especially in his commentary on the *Nāṭya Śāstra*, Indian aesthetic theory from the point of view of Śaiva spiritual philosophy.

Abhinavagupta is virtually the last philosopher contributing to the advancement and improvement of Kashmir Śaivism. The post-Abhinavagupta writers either repeat, clarify, or simplify the position of Abhinavagupta. Among the post-Abhinava philosophers, Kṣemarāja, a disciple of Abhinava, who lived in the eleventh century A.D., is the most important. His works are as follows:

1. *Pratyabhijñā-hṛdayam.* A simplified introduction to the essence of the Pratyabhijñā philosophy, written in the form of sūtras and commentary.
2. *Parā-praveśikā.* A booklet written with a view to helping the layman understand the Śaiva philosophy.
3. *Śiva-sūtra-vimarśinī.* A commentary on the *Śiva-sūtra.*
4. *Spanda-nirṇaya.* A commentary on the *Spanda-kārikās.*
5. *Spanda-sandoha.* An exhaustive commentary on the first *sūtra* of the *Spanda-kārikās.*
6. *Stavacintāmaṇi-vivṛti.* A commentary on the *Stava-cintāmaṇi* of Bhaṭṭanārayaṇa.
7. *Svacchanda-udyota.* A commentary on the *Svacchanda Tantra.*

8. *Netrodyota.* (*Netra-udyota*) A commentary on the *Netra Tantra.*
9. *Vijñānabhairava-udyota.* A commentary on the *Vijñāna-bhairava Tantra* (incomplete).
10. Commentary (*ṭīkā*) on the *Śivastotrāvalī.*
11. Commentary (*ṭīkā*) on the *Sāmbapañcāśikā.*

Other post-Abhinava works and philosophers include the following:

1. *Śiva-sūtra-vārtika* of Varadarāja, an eleventh century disciple of Kṣemarāja, from Kerala.
2. Commentary (*vivṛti*) on the *Paramārthasāra* of Abhinavagupta by Yogarāja, another eleventh century disciple of Kṣemarāja.
3. *Vṛtti* on *Mṛgendra Tantra* by Nārāyaṇa Kaṇṭha of the eleventh century.
4. *Viveka,* the famous commentary on the *Tantrāloka* of Abhinavagupta by Jayaratha, of the twelfth century. Also a commentary on the *Vāmakeśvarī-matam* by the same author.
5. *Mahārthamañjarī* of Maheśvarānanda, a twelfth century non-Kashmiri, written in the Maharastrian *Apabhraṁśa* language, a corrupt colloquial form of Sanskrit. It is a text of the Kula tradition, written in line with Abhinavagupta.
6. *Mahānaya Prakāśa* of Rājānaka Śitikaṇṭha, who lived in the second half of the twelfth century, a text in line with the Kula tradition, written in the Kashmiri *Apabhraṁśa.*
7. *Devīnāmavilāsa* of Sahib Kaula in which he synthesizes Śaiva non-dualism and Vedānta.
8. *Lallā-Vāk* of Lalleśvarī, or Lallā, a female mystic saint of Kashmir who wrote in Kashmiri in the 14th century.
9. Śivopādhyāya wrote part of the commentary (*udyota*) on the *Vijñānabhairava Tantra.* He also wrote an independent work, the *Śrividyā.*

10. Bhāskarakaṇṭha has written a commentary called *Bhāskarī* on the *Vimarśinī* of Abhinavagupta. He has also translated the work of Lalleśvarī into Sanskrit (*Lalleśvarī vākyaṁ*).

The textual history of Kashmir Śaivism would not be complete without the mention of two recent authors who are from outside Kashmir but who lived in Kashmir for some time. One is Amṛtavāgbhava, a saint and yogi, who wrote *Ātmavilāsa* in Sanskrit verse along with his own commentary, *Sundarī*, in Hindi, first published in 1936 and re-edited by his disciple, B. N. Paṇḍit, with notes, in 1983. Amṛtavāgbhava's work is notable in that he presents a synthesis of Advaita Vedānta and Kashmir Śaivism.

The other philosopher is Mahāmahopādhyāya Paṇḍita Rāmeśvara Jhā, or Rāmeśvarācārya, popularly known among his disciples as the modern Abhinavagupta, a person who lived his philosophy. He wrote, among other things, the famous *Pūrṇatā Pratyabhijñā*, a treatise on the Pratyabhijñā philosophy in Sanskrit verse, first published in 1960. It was later published by Joshi Brothers, Varanasi, in 1984, with the Hindi translation by Pandit Kamalesh Jha. *Pūrṇatā Pratyabhijñā* is a simpler and logically more precise rendering of Abhinavagupta's philosophy. Abhinavagupta is a difficult writer; Paṇḍita Rāmeśvara Jhā presents a clearer and simpler, but logically more compact version of Abhinavagupta. In places, he unravels some of the knots in Abhinava's philosophy. His claim that the Pratyabhijñā philosophy that came down through Utpala and Abhinava attained its perfection in him is not mere vanity.[59]

THE SPECIAL SIGNIFICANCE OF ABHINAVAGUPTA

I hinted in the very beginning of this work that the general significance of Abhinavagupta would be the same as the significance of the Tantric tradition itself. Besides being important in this general way, Abhinavagupta is highly significant in a special way, also.

His own contribution to the understanding of Tantric philosophy is of the utmost value; he is indispensable for the student of Tantra. Certain ideas are uniquely his own and help the student understand the Tantric position as a logical and rationally self-consistent whole. As is natural, those ideas fill in the gaps in Tantric philosophy to a great extent.

The esoteric knowledge of the Tantra is expressed in a symbolic language that sometimes becomes quite unintelligible. The Tantric symbols cannot be understood in the absence of clues from within the tradition itself. Abhinavagupta has given ample clues for understanding Tantric symbolism. The clues that he gives are not merely the outcome of his rational understanding; he derives them from the tradition itself. Abhinavagupta belongs to the tradition, and he studied with several illustrious gurus. He acknowledges them for enlightening him on certain difficult problems.[60] Thus, the explanation of the intricate symbolism of the Tantra presented by Abhinavagupta is rooted in the tradition, on the one hand, and is shaped by his brilliant insight, on the other. Without Abhinavagupta, it would be difficult to cut clear pathways through the thorny jungle of Tantric symbolism.

Abhinavagupta presents the otherwise difficult philosophy of Tantra in a cogent and coherent way that makes the Tantric position logically and rationally acceptable. What is complex in Tantra becomes simple in his treatment; what is esoteric and mystical becomes rationally understandable.

The clarity and precision with which Abhinavagupta has advocated the Tantric philosophy, and the ingenuity and insight with which he has interpreted the Tantric position, have had a tremendous impact on the Tantric thinkers who followed him. The powerful impact is really due to the unusual clarity and insight with which he tackles the problems. The beauty of Abhinavagupta is that he is relevant even now. His name, *Abhinava*, which means "novel" or "new," becomes literally meaningful: *Abhinavagupta* is "ever-new."

Abhinavagupta also provides the thread of unity among the different sub-trends of the Kashmir Śaiva tradition, weaving them into one whole of the Trika, or Pratyabhijñā, philosophy of Kashmir Śaivism. At the time of Abhinava, Kashmir Śaivism had four main sub-traditions — the Spanda, Krama, Kula, and Pratyabhijñā schools. The Spanda school emphasized the dynamic aspect of Consciousness, technically called *spanda* or *kriyā*. It advocated catching the thread of spontaneous activity as the means of realizing the Self. The Krama school, which emphasized the successive steps of manifestation of the Self, or Śiva, in the form of the world of creational forms (*vikalpas*), tended to make use of the creational forms to reach the Self in a successive way. The Kula school, which emphasized the unity of Śiva and Śakti symbolically expressed in the union of man and woman, aimed at Self-realization through the left-hand path (*vāma-mārga*), using the five M's (*pañcamakāra*), especially the fifth M of sexual union.

The Krama tradition could be called the "way of the ant" (*pipīlikā-mārga*): the spiritual aspirant (*sādhaka*) slowly and gradually crosses each successive stage like an ant slowly crawling along. The Kaula school is more like the "way of the bird" (*vihaṅgama-mārga). The sādhaka*, having already shaken off much of his or her ignorance in the present or a previous life, reaches the goal directly like a bird that takes off from the ground and flies to the treetop. The bird does not have to advance by successive steps. The ant, however, has to go all the way along the tree trunk in order to reach the top.

The Pratyabhijñā school, which emphasized the knowledge (*jñāna)* aspect of Reality, promoted the attainment of Self-realization by recognizing one's unity with all beings through universal love. *Pratyabhijñā* means both the removal of ignorance, which means the sense of duality, and the attainment of the awareness of the absolute unity of oneself with all things.[61]

Abhinavagupta picks up the concept of *pratyabhijñā* and uses it as a thread to string the different flowers of the sub-trends of Kashmir Śaivism into a single garland. For him Pratyabhijñā becomes *the* philosophy, and all the other forms are incorporated within it. He may point out that Spanda, or Śakti, is another name for the natural dynamism of Śiva, or Consciousness, which is at once both Śiva and Śakti. Thus, Pratyabhijñā, which is the knowledge of the Self, or Śiva, cannot be separated from Spanda. Krama is also included in Pratyabhijñā, for the creational forms are the manifestation of the Self, or Śiva, and Śiva can be reached through these successive steps too. It is just a question of different means (*upāya*). Krama would mainly come under what is technically called *Śāktopāya.*[62] As far as the Kula school is concerned, it is not at all different from Pratyabhijñā. Kula just advocates using a special means for attaining Self-realization (*pratyabhijñā*). This special means is the use of the five M's in a highly technical way, which aims at helping the *sādhaka* above the artificial duality of the so-called religious and profane. It is also meant to sublimate the aspirant's sexual energy into pure conjugal love, which in turn releases the imprisoned flow of universal love. The main aspect of the Kula *sādhanā* is the transformation of sex into pure forms of love, until it finally reaches the stage of universal love, which is the correlate of Self-realization, or Pratyabhijñā.

Thus Abhinavagupta succeeds in making a happy synthesis of the Spanda, Krama, and Kula in the body of Pratyabhijñā. Hence it is quite appropriate to identify the Pratyabhijñā philosophy with Kashmir Śaivism, particularly in the context of Abhinavagupta. Abhinavagupta can be called the "Complete Śaiva." The Pratyabhijñā school, which started with Somānanda and was further developed by Utpaladeva, reached its perfect culmination in Abhinavagupta, who left nothing unexplained and wove all the separate strands into a coherent system.

Within the Pratyabhijñā school itself, which began with Somānanda, Abhinava's contribution is two-fold. First, he corrects and modifies the position of Somānanda to make Pratyabhijñā a fully self-consistent system that is also compatible with other systems. Second, he takes the ideas of his predecessors to their fullest extension, making actual the potentials of the system and distinguishing and clarifying the subtle nuances of the issues involved.

The first point becomes evident when we investigate Somānanda's treatment of the Grammarian school of Bhartṛhari. Somānanda seems to think that the language philosophers do not accept Consciousness as Reality, and so their theory of the Word as Supreme (*śabda-brahmavāda*) is untenable, for the things of the world cannot be reasonably conceived of as manifestations of "the Word," or language (*śabda*), unless "the Word" is identified with Consciousness. Moreover, Somānanda also thinks that the Grammarians do not accept transcendental speech (*parā vāk)*, which is the matrix of the creational states of *paśyantī*, *madhyamā*, and *vaikharī.* He sarcastically remarks that "for the 'simpleton' grammarians, *paśyantī* is the highest state."[63]

Although Abhinavagupta does not openly criticize Somānanda, he seems to reject Somānanda's criticism of Bhartṛhari. He explains Reality, or Consciousness, in terms of Speech (*śabda*, or *vāk*), in his *Parātriṁśikā-Vivaraṇa* and elsewhere, and makes it clear that the position of the Trika philosophy is not different from that of the Grammarians. The Grammarians identify Speech with Consciousness and *do* accept the transcendental state (*parā* or *parapaśyantī)*, which is the matrix of everything. Of course, the process of creation, just as in Kashmir Śaivism, starts with *paśyantī.* Since the Grammarians are more interested in the process of Creation, they start with *paśyantī.* But this does not mean that they omit the transcendent (*parā*). Abhinavagupta corrects and modifies the unjustified attitude of Somānanda towards Bhartṛhari so that the non-duality of Consciousness (*cidadvaita*) of Kashmir Śaivism becomes coherent with the non-duality of Sound (*śabdādvaita*) of Bhartṛhari.

The second point — namely that Abhinavagupta is the culmination of the Pratyabhijñā philosophy — becomes evident in a study of the works of Somānanda, Utpaladeva, and Abhinavagupta. We receive the first glimpse of the Pratyabhijñā philosophy in

Somānanda's *Śiva-dṛṣṭi*, but it is stated in almost a summary form. Moreover, the *Śiva-dṛṣṭi* is very difficult in style. Therefore, Utpaladeva developed the philosophy of Somānanda with greater detail and in a simpler style. But even in Utpala all the issues were not fully spelled out. The aspect relating to spiritual practice (*sādhanā*), for example, was touched on only briefly.

Abhinavagupta fulfilled the task of developing the Pratyabhijñā philosophy to completion. The seed of the philosophy of Self-recognition (*ātma-pratyabhijñā*), or Self-realization, sprouts in Vasugupta, becomes a sapling in Somānanda, and grows into the form of a small tree in Utpaladeva. With Abhinavagupta it develops into a fully grown tree with all its branches and boughs laden with fruits and flowers.

An additional point regarding the significance of Abhinavagupta is that he expounded the Indian theory of aesthetics, and he did that in the light of Śaiva philosophy. As I already mentioned, Abhinavagupta wrote well-known commentaries on the *Nāṭya-śāstra* of Bharata and on the *Dhvanyāloka* of Ānandavardhana. In his Commentary on Bharata, called *Bhāratī* or *Abhinavabhāratī*, he expounded on the theory of *rasa* ("aesthetic enjoyment"), from the Śaiva standpoint, to perfection.

2

Epistemology[1]

THE PROBLEM OF CONSCIOUSNESS

Can there be a "science" of spiritual experience? Is the term *science* not a misnomer in the context of the spiritual? What does the word *spiritual* mean, exactly? Does the alleged entity called *Spirit, Consciousness*, or *Self* really exist, and is the so-called spiritual experience a true objective phenomenon? Can we successfully use scientific methodology in the realm beyond empirical experience? Can we make rational inquiry into the extra-empirical realm, assuming it even exists? I propose to discuss these and other questions in the present chapter.

It is obvious that along with the body there is a knowing or thinking principle in us. I call this the "I," "The self," or "consciousness." The existence of this consciousness is asserted by Descartes's "I think, therefore I am," Advaita Vedānta's "One who denies the self, that denier itself is the self,"[2] and Kashmir Śaivism's "The self is present as the doer and the knower at the very beginning of all behavior."[3] But it is also clear that the arguments of Descartes, Advaita Vedānta, and Kashmir Śaivism do not succeed in proving the ontological self. All they prove is that there is an epistemological principle of knowing or thinking. It is beyond our reach to know whether this epistemological principle is just the "synthetic unity of pure apperception," as Kant would have it, which is just a formal unity, or is also a metaphysical reality, or entity. It is from this point that metaphysical speculations and scientific hypotheses about the self, or consciousness, start.

Logically, we cannot rule out the possibility that consciousness, or the self, is not merely an epistemological principle but also an ontological entity. Besides accepting the existence of the ontological self as a possibility, we can also accept it as a hypothesis as legitimate as the biological theory that consciousness is a cerebral activity. We cannot say that the spiritual hypothesis has less weight than the biological one; the spiritual hypothesis of consciousness explains mental phenomena better, perhaps, than the biological hypothesis does.

The biologist might think that he or she has proved for certain that consciousness is a product or a function of the body. In order to press this point he or she may put forth the two following arguments: (a) consciousness is never found independent of the body — it is always found in and through the body; (b) a change in the state of the body brings about a change in the state of consciousness. For example, when the body meets with an accident, the person becomes unconscious, and when the body is brought back to its normal condition by medical treatment, consciousness returns. The accident brings about a change in the bodily processes, which in turn effects a change in the state of consciousness. The medical treatment produces an opposite change in the bodily processes, resulting in the restoration of consciousness.

The above arguments, the biologist might think, prove conclusively that consciousness is a bodily product or function and that consciousness is not an entity over and above the body. The spiritually-minded thinker might retort that the above two arguments prove only that consciousness, in order to express itself, requires a body in a condition of fitness. They do not prove that consciousness is not an independent entity. The following analogy illustrates the point. For the expression or flow of electric current there are two conditions that must be met: (a) there must be wire or some other medium — the flow of electricity is not possible without a medium, and (b) the negative-positive circuit must be unbroken — that is, the wire must be in a condition of fitness. When the circuit is cut, the electricity ceases to flow, and when the circuit is re-connected, the flow of electricity resumes. However, just because the flow of electricity depends upon the wire, and a change in the condition of the wire brings a change in the ability of the electricity to flow, this does not mean that the electricity is a product of the wire. Electricity is an independent substance that operates through wire, or through any other medium, when that medium is in a condition of fitness. Similarly, consciousness might be an independent entity that expresses itself through the body when the body is in a fit condition.

Consciousness thus might be more than just a cerebral activity. That consciousness could be an independent entity expressing itself through the nervous system is a perfectly legitimate hypothesis. Tantric epistemology starts with the logically valid presupposition that consciousness is not merely a knowing function but is also a non-material entity (*tattva*) present within the body.

It is obvious that the axiology of a system is based on its ontology, or metaphysics, and the ontology is, in turn, based on the epistemology the system holds. Epistemology, therefore, is the basis of philosophy. Though in the history of philosophy it is difficult to find an epistemology free of ontological presuppositions, an effort can be made, as Kant did, to present the epistemology independently. The same can be done in the case of Tantric epistemology. It is true that the Tantric theory of knowledge as given in the texts is intermingled with ontology, and sometimes it becomes difficult, even impossible, to understand the epistemological position without having the ontological presupposition in mind. However, it is not altogether impossible to extricate the epistemology of Tantra from its ontology and present it in an independent way.

KNOWLEDGE AS THE NATURE OF CONSCIOUSNESS

In order to understand the nature of knowledge it is necessary to understand its relation to consciousness, or the self. The Nyāya-Vaiśeṣika system takes knowledge to be an incidental attribute of the self. The basis of this contention is perhaps Nyāya's view of sleep: in sleep the self is present, yet there is no process of knowing.

Sāṁkhya, Vedānta, and many other systems hold that knowledge is not a quality of the self, much less an incidental one. To them, knowledge is the very nature of the self, or consciousness. Tantra joins them in maintaining that knowledge is the nature of the self. The popular analogy given in this context is that of light and illumination. Light and illumination are not two different things, because light is nothing but illumination. Illumination is not a quality (*guṇa*) of light, it is the very nature (*svarupa*) of light.

The substance-quality relationship entails an ontological difference between the two. A quality merely *resides* in a substance; it is not one with the substance. The sweetness of sugar, for example, is different from the sugar itself; sugar is merely the substratum of sweetness. It would be wrong to say that sugar *is* sweetness; the correct expression would be that sugar *has* sweetness. In the case of light and illumination, however, it is wrong to say that light *has* illumination; the right expression is that light *is* illumination, because illumination is the *nature* of light, not a *quality* of light.

The adherent of Nyāya would object that if knowledge is the nature of the self, it should be present in deep sleep also. The Tantrist would answer that in deep sleep the self, or consciousness, is covered; therefore it does not illumine itself or others. When the sun is covered by clouds, it is not that the sun is devoid of illumination; the rays of the sun are just obstructed by the clouds.[4] The moment the clouds disperse, the sun is again visible. Similarly, during sleep, consciousness is clouded. When we wake up — that is, when the obstruction is removed from consciousness — it shines again. During deep sleep the self, or consciousness, itself, is covered; therefore illumination, or knowing, which is the very nature of the self, is also obscured.

Consciousness and knowledge are substantially one. They are *two* only connotatively; denotatively they are one and the same. Knowledge may be understood as the natural and essential function of consciousness just as illumination is the natural function of light.

KNOWLEDGE AS ACTIVITY

On the issue of the nature of knowledge, the most significant contribution of Tantra is the concept that knowledge (*jñāna*) is also an activity (*kriyā*), though an effortless one. Advaita Vedānta, which stands in sharp contrast to this position, holds that knowledge is a state of passivity. According to Advaita, there may well be states of activity which lead to knowledge, but in the moment of knowledge itself we are passive. The awareness, or knowledge, of an object comes of its own accord, we do not make it happen. Take the knowledge of sweetness of a fruit, for example. We pick up the fruit, chew it, and devour the morsel — all of this is activity. But as far as the actual awareness of sweetness is concerned, we do not *do* it, we simply *receive* it. The point the Advaita Vedāntins are emphasizing here is that we do not actively bring the awareness of sweetness in the way that we actively put the fruit in our mouths; we are passive in that moment. Knowledge is dependent on the object (*vastutantra*) in a way that activity is not. We cannot *choose* to perceive or not perceive an object, or decide the way in which it will be known. But in activity we are free to choose—whether to do the activity or not, and how we will do it. Activity depends upon the subject (*puruṣatantra*).

The Tantrist would point out that although knowledge seems to be a state of passivity or inactivity, it really is not so. It is a state of passivity only in the sense that there is no voluntary doing or choosing on the part of the knower. But, insofar as knowing the object means *grasping* it, it implies a positive and active involvement on the part of the knower. Knowledge, or knowing, is a kind of activity, though effortless and automatic. The famous analogy of reflection used by the Advaitin to press this point does not completely fit in the case of knowledge. The phenomenon of knowledge is generally said to be analogous to reflection — as in the reflection of the moon in a pond. The pond is said to be like the mind and the reflection of the moon like the image of the object reflected in the mind. It is further believed that just as the pond remains passive and unresponsive when the moon is reflected in it, so does the mind when the object is reflected in it. But the question arises, Is the knowing of an object just like the reflection of the moon in a pond? Of course, this analogy has some points in common with knowledge, and sometimes the Tantrist even uses this analogy, but there is a fundamental difference. The pond does not actively grasp the moon. The pond does not have to understand, or become aware of, the moon — it is simply a case of physical reflection. But in the case of knowledge, the mind has to understand, or become aware of, the object; in knowledge, there is a grasping, or an active "catching" on the part of the knower. The pond is not actively involved in the process of reflection, but the knower is.[5]

The main point here is that unless there is grasping, that is, understanding, or being aware of, the object on the part of the knower, it cannot be a case of knowledge. It will be mere sensation, or it will be like the literal reflection of the moon. This means that the mind *is* active in knowing an object. Sensation becomes perception only when consciousness, or the knower, turns itself to the sensation and understands it. If the mind or the attention of the knower is diverted elsewhere, the sensation cannot be understood, even if it has entered into the mind. Grasping or being aware of the sensation is a positive involvement or activity of the knowing consciousness. But why, as the Advaita Vedāntin points out, does the phenomenon of knowledge appear to be a state of passivity? To this the Tantrist replies that this is because the activity in the knowledge or knowing is not voluntary, but automatic and effortless. We involuntarily grasp or understand the object. Since this activity is involuntary, it may be misconstrued as not being there at all. The pond does not become aware of the reflection, but the mind does. Therefore knowledge is actually *knowing*, which suggests activity; the term *knowing* is not a linguistic misnomer.

KNOWLEDGE IS SELF-ILLUMINED

Knowledge reveals objects, but how is knowledge itself known? The Nyāya theory is that knowledge is known just as the table or the chair is known: knowledge is made the object of knowing, but that knowledge is known by an after-knowledge (*anu-vyavasāya*). "I know the table" is knowledge in the first moment. "I know that I know the table" is after-knowledge in the second moment, which is the knowledge of knowledge.[6] In the first place the *table* is the object of knowledge, and in the second moment the *knowledge* of the table is the object of knowledge.

There are two difficulties in the Nyāya theory of after-knowledge. First, knowledge cannot be known as an object, because knowledge is a part of the knower and not of the known. Knowing the knowledge is the same as knowing the knower. The knower cannot be made into an object, because the knower, including the knowing or knowledge always stands as the subject prior to the object. To know the knowing subject as an object in the subject-object mode of knowledge is a contradiction in terms. Since knowing, or knowledge, always stands outside the object known, it cannot itself be made an object.[7] If we make an object of knowledge, it ceases to be knowledge — the object itself is not knowledge; the *knowing* of that object is knowledge.

Second, if knowledge is not revealed or known by itself and if it requires an after-knowledge in order to be revealed, it will cause an infinite regress. Knowledge is revealed by after-knowledge, but this after-knowledge itself, being knowledge, requires a second after-knowledge, and the second one will require a third one, and so on *ad infinitum.* If knowledge is not illumined, or known, *by itself* in the very first moment of knowing, it cannot be known by after-knowledge. The Nyāya theory of after-knowledge is obviously naive; it is not tenable.

Knowledge cannot be known as an *object.* Yet it is a fact that when we know something we also know that we know it — we know our knowledge. This simply means that the mode of knowing the knowledge differs from the subject-object mode of knowing. This mode is what is called self-illumination (*svayamprakāśa*).[8] Knowledge is revealed or illumined by itself in the very first moment of revealing the object.[9] I know the table and at the same time I automatically know that I know the table. Knowledge is like light. Light reveals or illumines the object, and it also reveals itself in the process. But the remarkable thing is that light does not reveal itself in the same way that it reveals the table and the chair. It reveals the table by falling on the table — that is, by making the table its object, but in order to reveal itself it does not turn around and fall on itself. Light does not make itself its object, yet it does illumine itself. It illumines itself *subjectively.* Light is self-illumined (*svayamprakāśa*). Similarly, knowledge becomes aware of itself not by making itself its object; it does so through self-illumination.

CONSCIOUSNESS AS *THE* MEANS OF KNOWLEDGE

The systems of Indian philosophy accept several means of valid knowledge (*pramāṇas*), the number ranging from one to ten. Perception (*pratyakṣa*), inference (*anumāna*), and verbal testimony (*śabda*) are the most prominent ones. Tantrism is not particular about the number of these means. It may accept all of them, but it has a deeper insight into the problem of the means of knowledge. The Tantric insight is that it is the consciousness that is the foundation, or underlying principle, of all means of knowledge.[10] Consciousness, therefore, is the real means of knowledge, or *the pramāṇa.*[11] All the other means are its extension, or the means which the consciousness uses for its own ends.

What makes a means of knowledge valid? What reveals the truth of a particular means? The answer is consciousness. Call it reason or understanding or the self — it is this that is the basis of every means of knowledge. After all how do we know that perception, for example, is a means of valid knowledge? It is our reason that ascertains the truth of perception. Moreover it is consciousness that perceives through the tools of perception (*pratyakṣa*). The mere contact of the sense organ with its object does not result in knowledge through perception. It is the inner consciousness operating through the sense-object contact that makes perception a means of knowledge. This is the case with the other means of knowledge also. Scriptural authority (*āgama-pramāna*), which is said to be the real means of knowledge, is actually understood in the sense of consciousness (as in the super-consciousness of the yogins and seers, or even of God). It is said, "Āgama is another name given to the linguistic expression of the inner ideation or knowing of Śiva whose nature is consciousness and this (*āgama*) is the life of perception (*pratyakṣa*), etc."[12]

From what is said above it follows that consciousness, which is *the* means of knowledge, uses the other means (perception, etc.) as its means. In other words, the other means are really an extension of consciousness. In perception, for example, consciousness, or the self, is the knower. Here it knows through the sensing organs making contact with the object. Similarly in the case of inference (*anumāna*) it is consciousness that knows through the inferential mechanisms (*vyāpti*, etc.). Tantrism differs from Sāṁkhya, which maintains that it is the intellect (*buddhi*) and not the self or consciousness (*puruṣa*) directly that knows. The Tantrist would clarify that the intellect or the sense organ (*indriya*) is merely a means or a mechanism of knowing. The apparatus itself does not see or know. For example, when I know or see a table, it is not the eye, the visual apparatus, or the intellect, the mental apparatus, that sees; it is really I, the self, or consciousness, who am seeing. I am seeing *through* the eyes or with the help of the eyes. I am hearing *through* the ears and so on.

Tantrism emphatically denies the independent status of the intellect and the sense organs, which are seen simply as the means of knowing. Consciousness, or the self, uses them in order to know. Thus, the different means of knowledge are the varieties or extensions of one and the same means (*pramāṇa*), which is consciousness.

An objection may be raised here. If consciousness or the self is the real knower, why is it that things that lack consciousness sometimes seem to "know"? Plants, for example, sometimes seem to act intelligently. The answer is that this is possible because the consciousness latent in the plant or in other inanimate objects, becomes expressed. Tantrism holds that consciousness is present everywhere in latent form. When it for some reason becomes manifest, then the so-called unconscious matter also begins to perform conscious activity. But this is strictly because the consciousness latent in matter is now to some extent awakened. It is the consciousness, not the matter itself, that knows. Sāṅkhya mistakes the intellect (*buddhi*), an evolute of matter (*prakṛti*), for the knower. The *buddhi* does not know; it is the self or consciousness (*cit*) that knows *in and through the buddhi.*[13]

The question may be asked, If the sense organs are only the means of knowing, and consciousness is the real knower, can consciousness function independent of those means, or must it always depend on them? The answer is that consciousness can function independently. When it is tainted with impurity (*mala*) and is confined to and bound by the body, consciousness has to depend upon the sense organs for knowledge. When one is confined within the walls of a house, one needs windows to peep out of in order to see the outside world. The moment one is free from the confinement of the house, one can see directly without windows or any apparatus. Similarly, when the self or consciousness is free from the confinement of the body, it can perceive without the sense organs. The yogin who attains extra-sensory perception by being freed from impurity to some extent can also function without any sensory apparatus. The level of independence of consciousness is proportionate to the freedom from impurity. Complete freedom from impurity results in perfect independence, as in the case of the *jīvanmukta.* In that state one can still use the physical means freely. This is like a king who, although entitled to ride in the state chariot, adopts foot locomotion of his free will.

CONSCIOUSNESS IS SELF-ILLUMINED

It is the consciousness that knows or proves the existence of the object through various means, but how is consciousness itself known or proved? Consciousness is self-illumined and, therefore, self-proved. I have already demonstrated that knowledge is self-illumined (*svayamprakāśa*); the same is true for consciousness also. Knowledge and consciousness, or the self, are both self-illumined. In fact, consciousness and knowledge are substantially one. It is consciousness that illumines or proves the other means of proving; it cannot itself be illumined by the other means.[14] That which is the ground of all cannot itself be grounded upon something else; it must be self-grounded. Logic demands that unless consciousness is self-illumined, it cannot illumine other things. Experience also reveals that consciousness is self-illumined.

In the second verse of the *Īśvarapratyabhijñā-kārikā*, Utpaladeva summarizes the argument that the self, or consciousness, is self-proved. The self is the doer and the knower. The activities of doing and knowing are obvious; they do not require any proof. Doing presupposes a doer and knowing presupposes a knower. There can be no doing without the doer, no knowing without the knower. Therefore, the self is logically presupposed in all doings and knowings (*ādi-siddha*).[15]

The self is already present in all assertions and denials. When I assert or deny anything, I am present as the asserter or the denier.

Even if I deny the self and say, "I am not," this statement itself proves that I am. *I am* before anything is. *I am* the logical presupposition, or the epistemological ground, of everything.

Abhinavagupta argues that acceptance of a knowing consciousness is a logical necessity. Without consciousness the world would remain unknown.[16] It is an obvious fact that the world is illumined, or known. This fact of the world's being known entails the existence of a knowing consciousness. The world is insentient matter; therefore it cannot be known by itself. In order to become known, it requires a knowing consciousness. And it is a fact that the world *is* known. This means that a knowing consciousness does exist.

The same argument, in almost the same words, is used by Vācaspati Miśra, an Advaita Vedantin, in his famous commentary called *Bhāmatī.* He argues that in the absence of the knowing consciousness the world will become "dark," that is, the world will become unknown. Therefore, consciousness, or the self, must be accepted on this account.[17]

In Western philosophy, Kant has taken virtually the same position in establishing the *a priori* existence of "reason" or "understanding," over and above empirical objects. "Percepts," or empirical sensations are blind; they cannot be aware of themselves. In order to be known they require a knowing "reason," or "understanding." This transcendental epistemological principle of knowing exists *a priori*; in its absence there would be no knowledge at all.

This should not lead us to think that the self is not directly experienced and is only known by logical implication, however. The self is also known directly. We directly experience ourselves, as the self is self-illumined (*svayamprakāśa*). The existence of the self is proved by logic and confirmed by experience.

That the self or consciousness is self-illumined and therefore self-proved is the basic understanding of all the systems of Indian philosophy that accept the concept of the self. All of them advance more or less the same argument. Sāṁkhya, for example, proves the existence of the self (*puruṣa*) by the argument that the self is the ground (*adhiṣṭhāna*) of all mental activities.[18] Jainism and Śaiva Siddhānta, while criticizing the no-soul theorist (Nairātmyavādin), retort that the very statement of the Nairātmyavādin that "the self is not" proves that the self *is*, as the existence of the self is implied in this very denial of it. The Advaitins present the argument perhaps in the clearest and the most sustained way. I have already mentioned the "dark" argument of Vācaspati. Śaṅkarācārya says that even when one denies the self, one really proves its existence, for the denier is actually the self.[19]

In Western philosophy, Descartes is the champion of this argument. He starts with *doubting*, then it becomes clear to him that what is doubted may be true or false, but the fact of doubting is quite obvious. Therefore, the *doubting* itself cannot be doubted. He further observes that doubting presupposes a *doubter*. What is true in the case of doubting is true in the case of thinking in general; Descartes thus shifts the argument from doubting to thinking and concludes "I think, therefore, I am" (*cogito ergo sum*). It should also be clear from the Cartesian treatment of the knowledge of the self that Descartes accepts the existence of the self not merely on the basis of this logical demand, but also because he is directly aware of himself. The doubting or thinking is an aid in turning his attention to the self.

It is only the epistemological self and not the ontological self that is proved by self-illumination and by the above argument. In Tantrism the ontological nature of the self is accepted on the basis of the *āgama-pramāṇa*, which is direct knowledge. These points will be discussed at the end of this chapter.

ĀGAMIC KNOWLEDGE

As far as the knowing capacity is concerned, we may broadly divide consciousness into two levels, or stages — the ordinary and the extraordinary. The ordinary level is that of the bound self (*paśu*). At the bound level, consciousness is tainted, or covered with impurity (*mala*); therefore, knowledge at this stage is limited. This is the level of ordinary knowledge where we use the empirical means of knowledge — perception, inference, and so on. The extraordinary level is that of the freed consciousness. Here one need not use the empirical means of knowledge because at this level consciousness, freed from impurity, is independent of the physical means of knowledge. This is the stage of direct, intuitive (*āgama*) knowledge. *Āgama* is another name for the deep, inner, intuitive experience of the seer who has risen to the level of Śiva-consciousness.[20]

Tantra does not have much to say about the empirical means of knowledge like perception and inference, as it is not interested in ordinary knowledge as much as intuitive (*āgama*) knowledge. It is intuitive knowledge that reveals Reality. The Tantrist therefore attempts to deal with intuitive rather than empirical means of knowledge. Therefore, we will direct our attention to the Āgamas. It should be made clear from the beginning that an Āgama is not merely a scripture or text; it is the record of higher experience. *Āgama* primarily means the knowledge or experience of consciousness at the intuitive level. As mentioned above, Abhinavagupta interprets the dialogue between Śaṅkara and Pārvatī that forms the structure of the Āgamas as the inner dialogue within our own consciousness. *Āgama* is really a particular level of knowledge, or consciousness.

Even if the Āgamas are taken to be revelation, it makes no difference, because in the Indian tradition revelation and higher experience are one and the same. The Indian concept of revelation is different from the Semitic one. In the Semitic religions such as Christianity and Islam revelation is understood as knowledge given by God to humanity through the agency of the prophets. One cannot obtain it through one's own effort, or *sādhanā*; it is wholly a prerogative of God. In the Indian tradition, however, revelation is taken to be the knowledge of one's own Higher Self, which can be acquired through *sādhanā*. Since God is the Higher Self of humanity, revelation is the voice of one's own Self. This is why it is natural for Abhinavagupta to interpret the Āgamic dialogue of Śaṅkara and

Pārvatī as the interaction between the higher and lower selves within our own consciousness.[21] Revelation in the Semitic tradition is, more or less, a one-way affair. God reveals the truth to humankind. We cannot verify it; we have to accept it on faith. But in the Indian conception of revelation there is the premise that it can be verified in actual experience by anyone who follows the required path. The aspirant, by perfecting his or her *sādhanā*, can come to know the truth of revelation; it will not remain an object of faith.

The consciousness of the yogin rises to the level of Śiva or Brahman and becomes one with it. It is at *this* stage that the seer acquires the knowledge that is called revelation. He or she knows Brahman by *being* Brahman.[22] Anyone rising to this level can receive the revelatory knowledge, as this knowledge is the nature of one's *real* Self. Therefore, it is perfectly all right to use *revelation* and *higher experience* as synonyms. Indian tradition in general and Tantrism in particular use the two synonymously. The truth is that it is at once both revelation and experience. It is revelation because it is spontaneously revealed in the higher state of consciousness; it is a communication from the Higher Self to the lower one. And it is experience, obviously, because it is actually experienced by a person within his or her own Self, not transmitted from an external transcendent God.

In the Indian tradition it is experience, not revelation in the Semitic sense that is accepted as the source of knowledge. The Indian seer after having achieved higher spiritual experience attains the knowledge of Reality, and shows others the way to have the same attainment. Buddha, for example, vouched that he had seen the Truth, and he called upon others to see the truth for themselves. He told his disciples, "O Bhikkhus, accept my words not because of my greatness, but accept them only after duly verifying them."[23] He used to say, "come" and "see." Buddhism is thus called the "come-and-see" religion (*ehi-passako-maggo*) or (*ehi-paśyaka-mārga*). The point is that nothing need be accepted on mere faith or authority; everything should be examined and verified in experience.

The *Bhagavadgītā* also points out that the truth is actually experienced by the seers. Arjuna is thus required to accept the word of Kṛṣṇa not simply because it is uttered by Kṛṣṇa, but because it is experienced by the seers. The *Gītā* says, "What is false cannot become true, and what is true cannot become false; the seers have seen both truth and falsity up to the end."[24]

Western epistemologists, particularly Hume and Kant, have tried to show that our knowledge is confined to the realm of sense experience. Any existence beyond the reach of the senses is doubtful, according to Hume; the *reality* of an object or the *thing-in-itself* is unknowable for Kant. Any attempt to go beyond the realm of the senses is seen as either speculation or faith; it is not considered knowledge.

The obvious extension of the tenets of Hume and Kant is that philosophy should not entertain any speculation about *reality*. However, the speculative idealism of Fichte and Schelling arose immediately after Kant, and culminated in Hegel. Soon, however, there was a sharp reaction against Hegelian speculation, and a return to the ideas of Hume and Kant. The basic Humian-Kantian insight that we cannot go beyond sense experience and know metaphysical reality was appreciated. This gave rise to several systems of philosophical thinking, each one starting from the same Humian-Kantian premise but moving in different directions and drawing different conclusions. Logical positivism, for example, rejected metaphysics as "meaningless" because metaphysical statements cannot be verified, and embraced science, which alone is accessible to our senses. Phenomenology restricted philosophical inquiry to the actual phenomenon available, namely, the knowing consciousness and what is met in experience. Existentialism also rejected ontological speculation about the essence of humankind and the world as "inauthentic" and concentrated upon the actual living existence of humanity. The starting point of all these movements is the aforesaid Humian-Kantian position. Humian-Kantian theory is thus the basis of Western epistemology in the contemporary period.

This basic insight of Western epistemology is accepted and appreciated in Indian philosophy in general and Tantrism in particular. Since the Upaniṣadic-Tantric era it has been clear to the Indian mind that our ordinary knowledge does not have access to the realm of Reality; it is confined to the phenomenal world of sense experience, technically called *saṁvṛti* in Buddhism, *vyavahāra* in Advaita-Vedānta, *ābhāsa* in Kashmir Śaivism, and *saṁsāra* or *jagat* in some other systems of Indian philosophy. The Tantrist fully appreciates the Humian-Kantian idea and wholly agrees with it, but Tantrism, like a typical Oriental system, does not end with sense experience. It moves a step forward, claiming that there is a way of knowing higher than sense experience—a higher way that reveals *reality*. Behind this claim there is the very strong Indian tradition of higher knowledge, which bears the promise of verification.

In the Indian tradition, the concept of metaphysics is different from the Western concept. In the West, metaphysics is mainly speculative and therefore subject to the contemporary criticism that it is "meaningless," "inauthentic," or "unscientific." In the Indian tradition, especially in Tantrism, however, metaphysics is not speculation; it is experience (*anubhava*) acquired by induction (*āgamana*). In this sense it is worthy to be called *science* (*vijñāna*). Therefore, it is neither "meaningless" nor "inauthentic."

While the empiricist is perfectly right in accepting the validity of sense experience, there are no grounds for rejecting the possibility of a way of knowing other than the sensory one. It is epistemological dogmatism to claim that sense experience is the *only* valid means of knowledge and that, therefore, empirical science is the *only* meaningful study. It is rigid dogmatism to reject without careful investigation the claims of yogins to higher experience.

The Āgama thus provides an experiential basis for philosophy. If a philosophy originates purely from the imagination of the philosopher, it is nothing but speculation; it can never become a praxis. Logical positivism and some of the other contemporary philosophies are correct in their assertion that purely speculative philosophy has no meaning. The Tantrist would fully agree with the positivist assessment, but would move a step further and add that the empirical is not the only realm of experience — there is also an extra-empirical experience. This higher yogic experience, the Tantrist would say, is not a mere theoretical possibility, nor is it the privilege of the Āgamic seer only. It can be had by all. In fact, in all ages the yogins, saints, and sages have succeeded in having it. The existence of this state can be verified if the means of verification is not confined to empirical evidence.

AGAMIC KNOWLEDGE IS SCIENTIFIC

I propose that the Agamic knowledge is a science because it is based on the scientific method, and has the possibility of being verified. Let us first see what is meant by science and whether we can legitimately use the word in that sense. Generally speaking, there are two essential features of science that must be present in any inquiry that claims to be scientific. First, science is based not on imagination or faith, but on experience. Since ordinarily sense experience is the only mode of experience, scientific inquiry is confined to the realm of sense experience. But the question here is whether the emphasis of scientific inquiry is on experience in general or sense experience in particular. I think the emphasis must be on experience in general. Science is confined to sense experience not because it is bound to be so by definition — it is not — but because it knows no other mode of experience. If some other mode of experience is found to exist, there should be no objection from science to including it within its realm. The burden, then, is not to show that a non-sensory experience is scientific, but to show that such an experience really exists.

The second feature of science, which is related to the first, is the objectivity of experience. We call the knowledge of a table scientific, because the table can be cognized objectively. Here, again, it must be made clear that objectivity does not mean externality of experience; externality is a product of the sense organs, it is not the nature of objectivity itself. The psychological experience of emotions and ideas is essentially internal, but the objectivity of these cannot be denied since we can experience them within ourselves. Objectivity only means that experience should be *true*, that is, there should be no illusory content in one's experience. It is immaterial whether one has the *true* experience from within or from without.

If we accept the meaning of science given above, we are led to revise the meaning of *verification.* What is called verification in science need not be confined to sense experience. The testing of truth in any kind of objective experience is worthy of being called *verification.*

In this context it is significant to note that the Tantra is called *Āgama*, or *Āgamana. Āgamana* literally means "induction." Since the Tantra is based on inductive experience, it is rightly called *Āgama*; that is why Abhinavagupta calls it the "School of Experience" (*anubhava-sampradāya*).[25] In the Indian tradition *induction* is not used merely in the sense of sensory experience, it connotes all experience in general. The meaning of *induction*, like that of *science*, should not be confined to sense experience. Induction has a wider connotation including the yogic experience of the seers within its realm.

What is written in the Upaniṣads and in the Āgamas is the word of those seers who experienced the Truth. The truth of these texts is ultimately based on yogic experience. When a geography teacher says that there are Rocky Mountains in North America, describing the topography of the region, we know that the teacher's words are ultimately based on the experience of the surveyors who have actually visited the region of the Rocky Mountains. So, also, is the truth of the Āgamic statements ultimately based on the findings of the seers and yogins. While the Āgama may be the word of God, it is also the word of those who attained realization describing their actual experience.

The Āgamic experience can be called *scientific* for the simple reason that it is true experience and we can have it even now. This true objective experience was had by saints and seers of the past and it has continued to be experienced down through the ages. Indians long ago acquired this experience and applied it to the problems of life. They widely experimented with its application to the different areas of life. Thus they developed a science of such experiences. The means of acquiring this experience was called yoga. There are various forms of yoga, both theistic and non-theistic, but in essence yoga is independent of theistic beliefs because it is based on practical experience not faith. In this sense the yogic approach is perfectly rational. We can call it yogic science. The knowledge of this science was handed down from guru to disciple through personal contact.[26] It was also recorded in texts on yoga and allied subjects, but unfortunately most of the records are lost. Meant for esoteric use, they were never widely publicized.

The statements of the Āgamas are not meant to be accepted merely on faith; they are to be verified in actual experience. We may take them on faith as working knowledge in the beginning, but the goal is to experience them for ourselves. In the Upaniṣadic tradition also, hearing the truth from the teacher (*śruti* or *śravaṇa*) is only the beginning. The next step is contemplation, or pondering over the teaching (*mati* or *manana*), and finally there is meditation, or the process of realization (*nididhyāsana*), which leads to higher experience (*anubhūti*).

The encounter with a foreign country is analogous to this process of verifying Āgamic truth. Suppose one has never been to a certain foreign country. Some people who claim to have been to that country give one a description of it. One also looks at books written about the country, based on descriptions given by people who have visited it. In the beginning one will have to accept what is written there. But, if one wishes to verify the truth of the record, one can do so. Of course, one will have to fulfill the prerequisites — acquiring the necessary passport and visa, saving money, booking passage, and finally taking the journey. Then one can see the new country with one's own eyes.

Similarly, we can verify the truth of the Āgamic record. Of course, we will have to satisfy the necessary prerequisites. We will have to do *sādhanā* and purify our consciousness; only then can we attain the intuitive Āgamic state of consciousness and see the truth with our own eyes.

Even in science, the process of verification has its own prerequisites. We cannot see scientific truth with the naked eye; we have to have the help of scientific instruments. Moreover, a naive layman cannot successfully verify the scientific statements; he or she has to undergo scientific training to some extent at least. Then alone will he or she be able to verify the findings. Similarly, the Āgamic truth cannot be verified without undergoing the *sādhanā* necessary for the unfolding of higher consciousness. If empiricists demand that the Āgamic truth be accessible to our ordinary untrained and impure consciousness, they are asking too much. And if for lack of that they reject the Āgamic claim as mere speculation, their attitude is dogmatic, illogical, and unscientific. The true scientist may have an attitude of doubt, not an attitude of rejection.

Tantra claims that the truth it espouses is verifiable, for it can actually be perceived. The *Kulārṇava Tantra* says, "Perception is the proof accepted by all beings. Those who argue against the truth are defeated by the strength of the perceptibility of the truth. Who knows about the unseen? The true philosophy is that which gives tangible results."[27] And, therefore, "Kaulism (Tantrism) stands proved because it gives tangible results."[28]

It is relevant here to refer to the criticism of Indian philosophy given by some occidental scholars to the effect that Indian philosophy is dogmatic because it is based on scripture. In answer to this I would point out that Indian philosophy is based on scripture for two reasons. First, the Indian philosophers knew perhaps from the very beginning that reality, or the ontological truth, is inaccessible to our ordinary knowledge, a truism that Hume and Kant pointed out as late as the 18th century. If reality is beyond our reach, but we still want to have a picture of reality, then we have to resort to the revelation of scripture. The words of those who are believed to have acquired higher knowledge and thus know reality are our only resource if we want to have a picture of reality. Otherwise all our thinking about reality will be mere speculation.

Second, recourse to scripture is not mere faith, as this scripture is taken as the recorded experience of the seers. Moreover, there is the possibility that the scripture can be verified in our actual experience, and there is a tradition of yogins and siddhas doing so in their lives. Knowing that reason or ordinary understanding cannot know reality and that there is a tradition of higher experience called *śruti* or *āgama*, it is natural for the Indian philosopher to make this higher experience the basic source of philosophy.

In a nutshell, the truth of the Āgamic tradition of spiritual realization, or Self-realization as it is called, is not just a possibility; there is a strong case for its probability. There is in India a long, continuous, and still-living tradition of Self-realization. Following are the points that suggest the truth of this tradition: (a) There have been people, the Upaniṣadic and Āgamic seers for example, who have claimed to have achieved complete Self-realization. (b) They have not said that they alone can have it and that others are simply to accept their insight on faith; they have declared that anyone can have it, and that in fact everyone has the potential to have it. (c) They have sought out the ways and means of achieving full Self-realization and have made them public for others to follow. (d) It is not that others have not tried it; in fact, there is a long line of seers, saints, and yogins who have followed the path and have confirmed the truth. (e) Even in modern times there is no dearth of such persons. Ramakrishna Paramahansa, Vijayakrishna Goswami, Lahiri Mahashaya, Shirdi Sai Baba, Nityananda of Ganeshpuri, Ramana Maharshi, Sri Aurobindo, and many others can be cited as examples. (f) The only people who reject the principle are those who have neither given due thought to it nor tried to verify the truth of it. Those who have followed the path have confirmed the truth; those who deny it have never tried it. (g) Finally, the theory of Self-realization holds out the promise that anyone can try it and see the truth of it for him- or herself. We can verify the truth of Self-realization in our own lives and see the truth for ourselves. We can be sure that no risk is involved.

OBJECTIONS TO ĀGAMA-PRAMĀṆA

Certain objections challenge the authenticity of higher experience. I will take the questions one by one. The Cārvāka would question, first, whether the so-called higher experience is a fraud and, because so many people are involved in it in an organized way, a case of mass deception.[29] In answer to this, I will refer to the internal and external evidence of its objectivity and authenticity. The internal evidence is that there is a self-contradiction in reaching Self-realization, on the one hand, and deceiving others, on the other hand. The psychology of cheating demands that there be others whom one considers different from oneself. One can cheat only those whom one considers not to be part of oneself. But a Self-realized person feels that everybody belongs to him or her; he or she is full of love for everyone. Who is cheated there? Only the person him- or herself, which is meaningless. Moreover, the realized person has no personal desires to fulfill; such a person has no motive for cheating others. If one has no selfish desires, under what circumstances would one cheat others?

The lives of the Buddha, Christ, and so on exemplify the truth of selfless love. Even those who are merely on the path toward Self-realization exemplify the same truth. Such people can be found in all times and places, though not in great numbers. Their actual behavior guarantees that there is no cheating involved. The sublimity of their characters, the inner calm of their minds, and the deep sense of self-satisfaction and fulfillment they possess show that they must have had that inner experience. Moreover, had they been cheats, they would have been exposed. Cheats, after some time, *are* exposed.

Hence, the claim of Self-realization is not a fraud. Of course, there is no logical guarantee of this. It is logically possible that the whole thing is fake; but, then, it is equally possible that it is all true. Although it cannot be proved, it cannot be disproved either. The possibility that it is true cannot be ruled out.

There are impostors and pseudo-Tantrists who, pretending to have attained the higher experience, cheat others. Such people arouse suspicion about the higher experience. Such people have always existed, and they can be found even now. But the presence of impostors does not disprove the truth of the higher experience. Their presence simply means that some false cases also prosper in the name of truth.

Moreover, the Āgamist would say, "Come and test for yourself; in testing no risk like nose-cutting is involved." It is true that the Āgamic claim can be proved or disproved only by testing it. It is open to test; if one has doubts, let one test it. The test does not involve risk; it requires moral and spiritual purification that is otherwise desirable anyway. There is a lineage of spiritual seekers who have tested and subsequently confirmed it. Those who reject it have never tested it, they reject it without duly verifying it. In fact, they are predisposed to reject it. Those who have tested it have confirmed it. The sincere seekers who really follow the path find truth in the Āgamic claim.

Another objection might come from the psychologist or the psychoanalyst. The psychoanalyst might point out that the so-called higher experience or Self-realization might not be a case of *consciously* deceiving others, but it could well be a case of unconscious self-deception. The so-called person of Self-realization might be a paranoid or hysterical personality; what is called higher experience might just be an abnormal or hysterical mood of his or her mind, and he or she could be under a permanent illusion of having had a higher experience. To put the question in simple terms, What is the guarantee that the so-called higher experience is not a mere illusion? In answer to this I can point out two things. First, higher experience, or

Self-realization, carries its own clarity and guarantee. It is not a denial of reason; in fact, it is higher reason. Our rational knowledge, which arises in our consciousness, does not require any proof, for it is self-illumined or self-proved. The Āgamic experience is all the more reliable, for it is a clearer expression of consciousness. The ordinary reason on which we rely is but a partial expression of the higher consciousness. Second, in Self-realization there is no possibility of illusion, as it is the realization not of an object but of the subject itself. In the case of an illusion or of a dream, what is false is the dream object, not the dreamer. Abhinavagupta says, "In the case of illusory perception, the knowing part is not false, for the knowing (together with the knower) is not falsified or contradicted (even when the illusion is dispelled); what is projected in consciousness as an object — that alone is false, for that alone is contradicted later on."[30] That is, the dreamer (subject) is true even after the dream is cancelled. The subject-consciousness is thus never false.[31] The higher experience is just the experience of the Self, or the Subject (Ātman), so there is no question of its being false. What is experienced as an object — say, as a perceptible form of some Deity — may be false. It is stated in the Upaniṣads that what is apprehended as an object of thought or perceived as an object of the senses is not Brahman; Brahman is that Subject by whose light the mind and sense organs function.[32]

I do not mean to rule out the possibility that the higher experience is an abnormality; however, the possibility of its being a genuine and healthy experience also exists. The Āgamist would say that the higher experience, which is a state of "being in oneself," is a sign of mental health, not mental abnormality. In fact, *svastha*, the Sanskrit term meaning "one who is healthy," refers to one who is established in the Self (*svasmin sthitaḥ*). Of course, it is true that there are abnormal persons suffering from psychoneuroses who claim to have had higher experience. Such people are certainly laboring under an illusion. But, again, the presence of such abnormal persons does not falsify the truth of the genuine experience.

The esoteric Āgamic experience should not be confused with the abnormal consciousness of the psychoneurotic.

The esoteric experience must also be distinguished from the abnormal experience aroused by drugs. Drugs may excite the nerves, and this may result in abnormal ideations and hallucinations. Such an experience is transitory — it lasts only as long as the traces of the drug remain. The esoteric Āgamic experience, on the contrary, results from a permanent state of consciousness, free from hallucinations and illusory ideations. The most significant characteristic of the Āgamic experience is its absolute clarity. In the drug-aroused consciousness one may be confused, but in the higher experience one is perfectly clear. The drug experience is largely akin to dreams, but the Āgamic experience is like the waking state.

A question might also arise about the variety of the forms of expression of the higher experience. One might for example ask, Why are there different and sometimes conflicting versions of the so-called higher experience? It is actually asked, "If Kapila is omniscient, what is the proof that Sugata (Buddha) is not? And, if both are omniscient, why is there a difference of opinion between the two?"[33] Does it not suggest a lack of objectivity?

In answer to the above, I will admit that the differences exist. There is, however, a valid explanation for them. The person who has attained the higher experience has arrived at that stage of experience by means of a particular language and culture. It is natural, therefore, that the expression of that experience be shaped by that particular language and culture. Because language and cultures vary, the expression of higher experience varies — not in its esoteric meaning, but in exoteric form. Second, one seer might emphasize a different aspect of the same experience, the different emphases arising out of the demand of the particular time and place to which he or she belongs. The Veda declares, "The Truth is one, but the wise speak of it in many ways."[34] Third, he or she may speak differently according to the different levels of listeners. The same truth can be expressed in different and sometimes apparently conflicting ways in order to suit the mental capability of different people. This is called *adhikārībheda.* I have already pointed out that there has been a very strong consideration of *adhikārībheda* in the Indian tradition. Fourth, there may be statements in the Āgama which are not self-contradictory, but the hearer may take them that way because of his or her misunderstanding and misinterpreting them. There may be — and in fact there is — a lot of misinterpretation on the part of laymen, philosophers, and scholars as well.

THE LIMITS OF KNOWLEDGE

We have already seen that there are two types of knowledge: ordinary knowledge, which we all normally possess, and revealed knowledge, which is received from the seers. Ordinary knowledge has limits. It reveals only the knowing consciousness, which is called the self and what it perceives (*ābhāsa*). I have already discussed the self-revelatory character of the self; the knowledge of sense-datum (*ābhāsa*) is also self-illumined.

Beyond the knowing self and that which is perceived, nothing can be known by ordinary knowledge. Tantra is clear on this point. Though the self is seen by ordinar y knowledge, its real identity as Śiva is not seen.[35] Ordinary knowledge is limited to the epistemological nature of the self — that is, to the knowing unity of consciousness. It cannot reveal the ontological nature of the self; it cannot determine whether the self is an entity — soul, Śiva, or a product of the body — or a mere principle of knowing. That this self is Śiva is revealed by Āgamic knowledge, not by ordinary knowledge. The recognition (*pratyabhijñā*) of the real identity of the self is only provided by Āgamic knowledge.

"Cogito ergo sum" and similar arguments prove the existence of the epistemological self only. Descartes mistook this for the ontological Self. Critics later showed that the workings of the rational processes indicate the existence of a knowing principle, but do not prove that this knowing principle is an entity, or soul. Only Āgamic knowledge can establish that this principle is indeed a soul, or Śiva.

By means of ordinary knowledge we cannot know Śiva, or matter either. What we "see" as matter is just the appearance (*ābhāsa*) of matter. We can at the most say that the world appears to us; we cannot be certain whether it is a real material world or a dream world projected by some mind. It should be made clear in this context that if the realist's position (that the world is real or material) cannot be known, the idealist's position (that the world is false or a mental projection) cannot be known either; we cannot know whether the world is true or false. The Tantrist idealist accepts the world as false (or as an ideal projection) not on the basis of ordinary knowledge, but on the basis of Āgamic knowledge.

By means of ordinary knowledge we also cannot know the existence of other selves. We can infer other selves on the basis of the bodily movements supposedly belonging to them, but we cannot be logically sure, for the bodily activities may be mere appearances in a dream. In other words, we cannot step out of the solipsism of the knowing self merely on the basis of ordinary knowledge. The Tantrist accepts the existence of other selves, again on the basis of Āgamic knowledge. Of course, the independent existence of other selves is indicated or suggested by inference, but this can be confirmed only by Āgamic knowledge.

Thus we see that the entire ontology of Tantrism is based on Āgamic knowledge. If we do not use Āgamic knowledge, proceeding merely on the basis of ordinary knowledge, we are bound to lapse into solipsism. Our ordinary knowledge cannot take us beyond the knowing self and the *ābhāsas*. Without Āgamic knowledge we cannot break through our metaphysical confinement; we remain ever skeptic or agnostic.

WHAT IS HIGHER EXPERIENCE?

What is this so-called higher experience? So far, I have only referred to it without revealing what it is. The question may be phrased thus: What is the nature of this experience? What is its mode and what is its content?

In answer to the above question I might point out that it is difficult to understand the nature of the higher experience unless one has experienced it. Still, we can try to form some idea of this experience on the basis of the account provided by the seers and yogins. I will discuss it in detail later in the context of Self-recognition (*pratyabhijñā*), or Self-realization, and kuṇḍalinī yoga. Here a brief treatment must suffice.

People tend to grasp the higher experience in various ways and refer to it by diverse names such as "mystical," "occult," "supernatural," "esoteric," and so on. But although the higher experience possesses characteristics denoted by all these terms, it can be accurately labelled with none of them. It is not mystical, if mystical is understood in the sense of something beyond reason, because we can have an understanding of it. It can be subjected to rational and logical analysis. The term *occult* is generally used to mean something that cannot be explained by the ordinary laws of nature. The higher experience is perfectly natural, so it cannot be called occult. Of course, it is in accordance with the *higher* laws of nature. Many higher scientific laws of nature are not known to the layman. Such scientific knowledge might be seen as occult, but the scientist knows that it is not occult. Similarly, the concept of higher experience may not be clear to the ordinary mind, but that is no reason to call it "occult." Tantrism, which is based on that experience, is therefore not occultism.

Similarly, higher experience is not supernatural, as it is a perfectly natural state of consciousness. Again, of course, it is a higher or deeper state of consciousness. In fact, it is extremely natural, because it is our real nature.

When we attain higher experience, it is not that we cultivate it anew; it is already there — latent or hidden or covered — and now it is uncovered. It is like removing the curtain from the face of a brilliant light, or like freeing a caged lion of its fetters so that the "lion-ness" of the lion fully comes to the fore. That is why it is paradoxically called the "getting of the gotten" (prāptasya prāptiḥ).

If the term *esoteric* is used to mean something profound and related to the deeper laws of life, then higher experience is certainly esoteric. But if *esoteric* is used to mean something that is secret and confined to a specially initiated circle — something that cannot be known and discussed publicly — then it is not esoteric. There is nothing secret about it, just as there is nothing secret about the higher scientific knowledge discovered by advanced science.

The terms used in the Tantric literature to denote this experience are *pratyabhijñā* or *ātma-pratyabhijñā* ("Self-recognition" or "Self-realization"), *ātma-jñāna* ("knowledge of the Self"), *Śivānubhūti* ("experience of Śivahood or Divinity"), and *mukti* or *mokṣa* ("liberation"). For want of a better English substitute, I am using the phrase higher experience; this is just to differentiate it from ordinary empirical experience.

In order to understand the nature of higher experience we must first understand the Tantric theory of *pratibhā*, or *prātibha jñāna*. Even at the ordinary stage of knowledge we find two sources of knowledge. One is what is called empirical knowledge, which is acquired through the sense organs. The other is what is called intuitive knowledge, which ensues directly from reason without the use of the sense organs. This type of knowledge comes into play in the formal sciences like Mathematics and Logic. Intuition (*aparokṣa-jñāna*) is actually the *mode* of knowing wherein there is no mediation (*parokṣatā*) between the knower (*jñātā*) and the known (*jñeya*). For example, one's reason or intellect (*buddhi*) directly apprehends mathematical truth without the mediation of the sense organs, therefore, this knowledge is intuitive or "immediate" (without mediation — *aparokṣa*). Empirical knowledge, on the other hand, is "mediate" (*parokṣa*), for we know the sensory object only through the sense organ. What is called *pratyakṣa-jñāna*, or perception—the knowledge of a table, for example—is really mediate knowledge (*parokṣa-jñāna*), for there is the mediation of the sense organ between the knower and the object of knowledge.

It is obvious that intuitive, or immediate, (*aparokṣa*) knowledge is not acquired through the sense organs or through any other mediation. It comes directly and spontaneously from reason, consciousness, or the Self itself. This is *pratibhā. Pratibhā* is the epistemological situation wherein knowledge originates not from any external medium but from the knowing consciousness itself, as in the case of logic and mathematics. *Prātibha-jñāna* is the intuitive, or immediate, knowledge that emanates from reason or consciousness itself like an inner flash, without depending upon scripture or a teacher. [36] The main thing is that *prātibha* knowledge — mathematical or logical knowledge, for example — is not acquired but innate. To use Kantian terminology, empirical knowledge is *a posteriori*, or based on sense-experience; *pratibha*, or intuitive knowledge, is *a priori*, or independent of sense experience — that is, comes from reason itself.

The scientist may think that the intuitive *a priori* method yields only purely "formal" or analytic, knowledge, as in logic and mathematics, and cannot furnish "real," or synthetic, knowledge, as in physics. The scientist would say we cannot intuitively know, for example, what exists in the world; "real" or "synthetic" knowledge can be obtained only through the sense organs. In answer I might point out that there are certain real things that we do know intuitively. For example, we are intuitively aware of ourselves and our knowledge, or our thinking. The Self and its knowledge is self-luminous (*svaprakāśa*), as I pointed out earlier. To say that something is self-luminous, or self-evident, is to say that it is intuitively known. Consciousness and its contents, which are detailed by descriptive phenomenology, are actually known intuitively and not empirically, as they are self-evident. Unlike the formal truths of logic and mathematics, they are real.

Not only that, it is also possible to know intuitively or immediately —without mediation — even objects of the world that are ordinarily known through the mediation of the sense organs. The Tantra points out that an advanced yogin can intuitively know the "real" objects of the world. In yogic perception, or "clairvoyance," there is no mediation by the senses between the knower and the known. The yogin, without using the sense organs, can cognize remote objects and events; he or she can also know the past and the future. However, the extent of this type of knowledge depends upon the freedom from impurity attained by the yogin. So, the yogin can intuitively "see" or know reality. This intuitive faculty, or phenomenon, can be called higher intuition or higher *pratibhā*. Psychic research in the West, even if it does not conclusively prove the existence of psychic phenomena, does point out the probability of intuitive knowledge of reality, as in the case of clairvoyance and so on.

Stretching the above possibility further and knowing that we intuitively know certain "real" things like consciousness and its contents, it would be quite reasonable to believe, as the Tantra claims, that even ultimate Reality can be known by higher intuition, or (*pratibhā*). This implies that there are hierarchical grades of intuition.[37] It is possible that by doing yogic self-purification (*sādhanā*), one can unfold from within oneself the higher forms of intuitive awareness (*pratibhā*). Hierarchical levels of the knowledge of reality are proportionately related to the hierarchical levels of the unfolding of *pratibhā*.

I have already mentioned the intuitive or immediate (*aparokṣa*) mode of knowing. The mode of higher experience is intuitive or immediate. This implies that higher experience is not acquired through the mediation of the sense organs but self-revealed; spontaneously revealed from within one's own consciousness. And the more one's consciousness is cleared of impurity, the more the higher knowledge reveals itself. Higher experience is *pratibhā*-knowledge, and *pratibhā* is linked with the purification of consciousness.

As for the content of higher experience—it is Consciousness itself. Since at its deeper level Consciousness (Self) contains the entire Reality according to Tantric metaphysics, including the

Reality of the world, within its bosom, the deeper Reality or Being of the world can also be considered the content of higher experience.[38] We have already seen that the self, or consciousness, becomes the content of intuitive experience. If it is true that the ordinary, or surface, self is the content of ordinary intuitive experience, then it can be equally true that the Higher Self is the content of higher intuitive experience. In Tantric metaphysics God is accepted not as a Being that is "other," but as one's own Higher Self. Therefore, God, as Higher Self, is also the content of higher experience.

Higher experience is not cut off from ordinary experience.[39] In fact, what I am calling "higher experience" is also the reality underlying ordinary experience; it is therefore immanently present in every experience. All ordinary experience is the lower manifestation of the same higher experience, or higher consciousness. It is consciousness that knows in the case of all knowledge, including sense experience, and, in this sense, consciousness is the underlying reality of all knowledge. This consciousness, the Tantra points out, comes from a deeper source which we call the Higher Self. Illumination, knowledge, or experience is the very nature of the Self, just as physical illumination is the very nature of the sun. It is the illumining power of the Self that makes any knowledge possible. The Upaniṣads clearly state that Brahman is not "knowable" by or accessible to the mind, or sense organs, yet at the same time the mind and sense organs function by the power of the Self.[40] The Upaniṣads further say that when "that" is illumined, everything is illumined, and everything is illumined with the light of that.[41]

The "light," or the illumining power of the Self, operates not only in the higher experience of Reality but also brings success in the mundane professional world. Professional success comes largely from the power of initiative, the power of visualizing new possibilities. If we analyze the psychology of initiative, we find that initiative does not come as a result of effortful thinking or vigorous willing, but as a flash or as a spontaneous movement of the will. Indian spiritual psychology would add here that the source of this too is the Self. The phenomenon of spontaneous initiative is called *pratibhā* in the Indian tradition. *Pratibhā* works both in cognitive and connative ways. When a research scientist, for example, works on the data in his or her laboratory it is not the knowledge of the data itself but the sudden flash of inspiration in the mind of the scientist that leads to the discovery. This sudden flash of ideas is *pratibhā*. *Pratibhā* figures in the success of a medical doctor or a lawyer. Every scientist may have the same amount of data to work on, or every doctor or lawyer may have the same amount of knowledge, yet success embraces those who have *prathibā*, which comes from the same spiritual source. The same is true in the case of other professionals, too. "Thus, what doesn't *pratibhā*-knowledge make one achieve, for everything is accomplished with *pratibhā* knowledge."[42] Or, "*Pratibhā* fulfills all desires."[43]

THE VALIDITY OF KNOWLEDGE

The validity (*prāmāṇya*) of knowledge is a much disputed topic in Indian philosophy. Some systems hold that knowledge is validated or invalidated by external sources; they believe in the extrinsic validity of knowledge (*parataḥ prāmāṇya*). Others believe in its intrinsic validity (*svataḥ prāmāṇya*); they hold that knowledge by itself is valid, and it is only invalidated by external knowledge. The Tantric systems, especially Kashmir Śaivism, advocate the theory of the intrinsic validity of knowledge (*svataḥ-prāmāṇyavāda*). The Nyāya advocates the theory of extrinsic validity (*parataḥprāmāṇyavāda*). It contends that knowledge by itself is neutral — it is neither true nor false. It is proved true or false by another knowledge — pragmatic knowledge, which is external to the original knowledge. Take, for example, the knowledge of a chair. When one first perceives a chair, the knowledge "this is a chair" is neither true nor false. In order to ascertain its validity one puts the chair to a pragmatic test by sitting in it. If the chair holds, it means the chair works or, in technical terms, the chair has pragmatic value (*arthakriyā* or *samvādipravṛtti*). This means the chair is real, and, subsequently, the knowledge of the chair is valid.

In the case of a mirage, however, at first one sees waves of water floating above a sandy desert in the summer season. When this knowledge is tested, the apparent waves do not satisfy the pragmatic test — they do not feel wet to the touch, nor do they quench the thirst. They have no pragmatic value (*arthakriyā*), and, therefore, they are illusory. Hence the knowledge of the waves of water is not valid — it is an illusion.

According to the realist (*parataḥprāmāṇyavādin*), *arthakriyā* is the test of the reality of a thing. The realist's logic is that it is possible for a thing to have *arthakriyā* only when the thing is real; an illusory thing cannot have *arthakriyā.* If the chair is illusory, it cannot hold one; one will fall down when one tries to sit in it. Mirage water does not quench one's thirst. If the thing is real, the knowledge of that thing is valid (*yathārtha* or *prāmāṇika*); if it is not so, the knowledge is otherwise (*ayathārtha* or *aprāmāṇika*).

Thus, according to the *parataḥprāmānyavādin*, knowledge of a thing is proved to be true or false by a second knowledge that tests the *arthakriyā* of that thing. This knowledge of *arthakriyā* is external to the original knowledge in question. Therefore, validity of a knowledge comes from outside that knowledge.

Those who subscribe to the intrinsic validity of knowledge, such as Abhinavagupta, do not accept the above theory. In criticism of the theory two things may be pointed out. First, it involves the fallacy of *infinite regress.* If knowledge by itself is neutral and has to be validated by an external knowledge, then the external knowledge, which itself is neutral by virtue of being knowledge, requires a third knowledge in order to be validated; the third knowledge requires a fourth one, and so on *ad infinitum.* Knowledge cannot be validated in this way. This means that the theory of the extrinsic validity of knowledge is self-contradictory. If knowledge is not valid in itself, it cannot be validated by any amount of external knowledge.

Second, the idealist Tantrist, such as the Kashmir Śaivite, would point out that pragmatic reality (*arthakriyākāritva*), in which the Nyāya realist puts so much store, is not the test of truth. An analysis of cases of illusion can easily reveal that the illusory objects also have pragmatic value (*arthakriyā*). The very meaning of illusion is that it is unreal, yet it is *arthakriyākārī* ("having pragmatic reality, or appearing as real"). If it does not *appear as real* — in other words, if it is not *arthakriyākārī* — it is not illusion at all; it is mere nothing (*asat*). An illusory object has the same amount of *arthakriyā* that a real thing has. The dream experience, for example, although being illusory, has one hundred percent *arthakriyā* — the dream world appears to be fully real. If I "see" a chair in a dream, and sit in it in order to test its pragmatic value, will it not hold me? The dream chair will pass the pragmatic test.

The realist perhaps thinks that the first knowledge, which he or she regards as neutral, is of one order and the second knowledge, which tests the truth of the first one, is of another order, one possessing more strength. But this is, the idealist would point out, a sheer misunderstanding; in fact, the two belong to the same order. Both are sense data; that is, both present themselves to the consciousness. How can one sense datum test the truth of another sense datum? How can one convict pass judgment on another convict? Abhinavagupta says, "The appearance of pragmatic value (*arthakriyā*) is just another appearance, and so the presence of pragmatic value (*arthakriyākāritva*) is not the reality of things."[44]

In Western philosophy the criticism of the correspondence theory of truth proposed by the coherence theorist is more or less the same in substance as the criticism of the theory of external validity by those who subscribe to the theory of intrinsic validity. Correspondence theory is akin to the theory of external validity. According to correspondence theory, if the knowledge of a thing corresponds to the thing itself, then the knowledge is valid, and, therefore, correspondence between knowledge and the thing is the test of truth. While criticizing Locke, who is an advocate of correspondence theory, Berkeley points out that correspondence can be accepted as the test of truth only when both terms of correspondence, that is *knowledge* on the one hand, and the *thing* on the other hand are known. Our epistemological access is confined to one term — the knowledge or "idea" — only; we do not and cannot know the thing itself. Whenever we approach a thing in order to know it in itself, we can know it only as it appears to us, we cannot know it as it is in itself; its nature *in itself* may be different from how it *appears* to us, as occurs in an illusion or dream. In other words, we *cannot* know the thing; we can know only one of the two terms — only knowledge, or what is called *idea* or *appearance* or *sense datum.* Therefore, we cannot know whether our knowledge corresponds to the thing or not. Correspondence, therefore, is an untenable theory.

If the validity of knowledge cannot be known externally (*parataḥ*), what then is the test of validity? The advocate of intrinsic validity holds that knowledge is valid by itself. "Validity arises by itself and is known by itself" is the general motto of the intrinsic validity theorist. According to Abhinavagupta, who is an adherent of this current of thought, all knowledge should be regarded as valid *as long as it is not contradicted by another knowledge.* Non-contradiction (*bādhābhāva*), or coherence, therefore, is the test of validity.[45] Dream experience, for example, is true as long as it is not contradicted by waking experience. As long as we are in a dream, one knowledge coheres with, or is not contradicted by, another knowledge; therefore it is taken to be valid. It is only when we wake up that the dream knowledge becomes false, because the waking knowledge now contradicts the dream knowledge. Therefore the "invalidity" (*aprāmāṇya*), or falsification of knowledge, is brought about by contradiction (*bādha*).[46] This is analogous to saying that a particular athlete is the champion as long as he or she is not defeated by another athlete. To be champion means to be undefeated.

In defense of the coherence theory, or of the theory of intrinsic validity, one can say that if correspondence cannot be known, or if knowledge cannot be validated by external sources, what else is the test of truth? The only way is to regard knowledge as valid as long as it is coherent or uncontradicted. Even the pragmatic test (*artha-kriyākāritva*) is really another way of confirming the coherence. When by the pragmatic test it is revealed that the thing in question — the chair, for instance — has pragmatic value, it simply means that the knowledge of the chair is coherent. In the case of the mirage the waves of water are taken to be false, because they are contradicted by fresh knowledge. The point is that even the external validity theorist who applies the pragmatic test is indirectly applying the coherence theory without knowing it. Everyone consciously or unconsciously uses the same criterion. Abhinavagupta says, "This coherence (*bādhya-bādhaka-bhāva*), which is used in order to distinguish truth and falsity, is the life of all our behavior."[47]

If we view the theory of intrinsic validity (*svataḥprāmāṇyavāda*) from the perspective of idealistic metaphysics, it appears to be all the more significant.[48] According to the idealistic view of knowledge, there is not much difference between knowledge and reality; what is known as real is nothing but the appearance of consciousness, matter being non-existent. Therefore what one knows is itself reality. This means that illusion or dream also has epistemic reality; the illusion is real as long as it persists. Advaita Vedānta also accepts the illusory (*prātibhāsika*) and the phenomenal (*vyāvahārika*) as relatively real. Here too the logic is that the reality of the known (*jñeya*) consists in its being known or perceived. (In the words of Berkeley, "esse est percipi.") If the reality of what one knows depends upon one's knowing it, then knowledge is intrinsically valid.

We should not be misled into thinking that if, according to the idealistic theory, knowledge itself is reality, then there is no difference between subjective illusion and objective knowledge. Every idealism, especially Kashmir Śaivism, accepts grades or levels of the *ideal* reality. What is called the objective world is the self-projection, not of the individual consciousness (*aṇu* or *paśu*), but of the Cosmic Consciousness, Śiva. It is the ordinary illusion that is a creation of the individual consciousness. Therefore to the individual the knowledge of the world of appearance is as objective and real as anything. As far as the epistemological distinction between the illusory and the real is concerned, there is no difference between the realist and the idealist; the illusory and the real are the two levels of reality, or consciousness.

It should be added here that in Tantrism the ontology of the world of appearance is not accepted on the basis of ordinary knowledge, nor is it speculative metaphysics; it is accepted on the basis of Āgama knowledge. Through our ordinary experience we can know only that the world *appears* before us; we cannot know whether it is false (mere appearance) or true (material reality).

THE TRIKA THEORY OF ERROR

The question of the validity of knowledge is related to the question of illusion or error. Therefore it is pertinent to consider the Tantric theory of illusion. In the systems of Indian philosophy the theory of error (*khyātivāda*) of a particular system is based on the ontological position that the system holds. An independent and neutral analysis of illusion is rarely to be found. We can broadly classify the Indian theories of error under two headings — realistic and idealistic. The distinction is obviously based on metaphysical considerations.

The realist does not accept illusion. Rāmānuja, for example, would say that all knowledge is true; there is no illusion at all. The important thing is that not only does realism not accept the world-as-illusion, it does not even accept ordinary empirical illusion like the famous rope-snake. The reason why the realist does not accept even ordinary illusion is, it seems, that if even one case of illusion becomes established, then at least the possibility of the world's being illusory will have to be accepted. The realist wants to deny this possibility. So realism maintains that illusion does not exist at all; the so-called illusory object is a real thing. In the case of the rope-snake illusion, for example, the knowledge of the snake is real; it has somehow or other gotten mixed up with the knowledge of the rope. As to how the knowledge of the snake gets mixed with the knowledge of the rope, every realistic system has its own explanation.

The Nyāya-Vaiśeṣika, for example, says that the snake that we perceive in the rope *does* exist — elsewhere (*anyathā*). It has come here by way of what is called *jñānalakṣaṇa pratyakṣa* — one knowledge hitching a ride on another — therefore, the knowledge of the snake is really a case of the knowledge of the object located elsewhere (*anyathākhyāti*). Rāmānuja would say that the snake is actually present in the rope — everything is present in everything (*pañcīkaraṇa*). The snake already implicitly present in the rope is now explicitly presented to consciousness. So the knowledge of the snake in the rope is a case of perceiving the real snake (*sat-khyāti* or *yathārtha-khyāti*). The Mīmāṁsā explains the case of error as non-apprehension (*akhyāti*) of the distinction between two knowledges. In the knowledge of the rope-snake there are actually two knowledges — the knowledge of the snake coming from memory, and the knowledge of the rope resulting from perception; the error is due to the non-cognition of the distinction between the two (*akhyātivāda* or *vivekākhyāti*).

In all the realistic explanations of error an attempt has been made to show that what is called error is really knowledge — it has a corresponding object; the only thing is that it has gotten mixed up with something else — say the rope — in the present instance. In criticism of the realistic theory of error the idealist would point out that what the realist misses, perhaps deliberately, is the fact that the illusory is identified with the real; the illusory takes the place of the real. The snake replaces the rope. That I "see" or know the snake is a fact. It is also true that there is no snake there — it is the rope. There may be a real snake elsewhere, but *this* snake that I "see" is certainly not there. *This* snake is a mental projection, a subjective creation, not an objective reality. The realist is ingenuous in not accepting the subjective element in the case of illusion, but his contrivance is futile, as the subjective element is absolutely clear —

illusion cannot be explained without this. The realist is trying to confuse the issue, bringing in far-fetched unrealistic explanations. We can doubt the illusoriness of the world, but there can be no doubt in empirical cases of illusion like the rope-snake or the dream object. How can we deny that what we "see" in a dream is an "ideal" projection of our mind?

The explanation of error given by all the idealistic systems is more or less the same in substance: they all accept illusion as subjective creation having only epistemic reality. Of course, they use different languages emphasizing different aspects of illusion. The Buddhist (Vijñānavādin) would say that the snake that we "perceive" in the rope does not exist in the rope; it is, in fact, in the subject or the self and is projected onto the rope. The knowledge of the snake, therefore, is a case of knowing the ideal projection of one's own self (*ātma-khyāti*). Advaita Vedānta maintains that illusion comes under a third category, the category of the false (*mithyā*), which differs from the accepted dual categories of real (*sat*) and unreal (*asat*). The rope-snake is not real, yet it appears; therefore it cannot be described either as *sat* or as *asat* (*anirvacanīya-khyāti*).

Abhinavagupta points out as spokesman for Kashmir Śaivism that the illusory cannot be said to be wholly false, as it is not mere nothing — it is a projection or an actual ideal creation of consciousness. That the illusory, such as the rope-snake, is a material entity independent of the knowing self is an incomplete (*apūrṇa*) view of the rope-snake; the complete view is that it is an ideal projection of consciousness (the self or the subject). Illusion, therefore, is a case of partial or incomplete knowledge (*apūrṇa-khyāti*).[49] Of course, illusion is a case of ignorance (*akhyāti* or *ajñāna*) but ignorance itself is not construed negatively. The literal meaning of *ajñāna* ("ignorance") is the absence of *jñāna* ("knowledge"). But illusion is obviously not the absence of knowledge (jñānābhāva), it is really wrong knowledge.[50] Wrong knowledge means incomplete or imperfect knowledge (*apūrṇa-jñāna*).[51] In the *Tantrāloka*, ignorance (*ajñāna*) is defined as the incomplete knowledge of the object.[52] When one "sees" the snake in the rope, it is not the absence of knowledge, for one is actually "seeing" the snake. However, one does not know the snake in its reality; therefore, one's knowledge of the snake is incomplete. The reality of the snake is that it is a projection (*ābhāsa*) of one's mind. When one comes to know that the snake is not an independent material object but a projection (*ābhāsa*) of one's mind, then one knows the full truth, and one's knowledge of the snake is complete, or perfect, (*pūrṇa*). The same is true in the case of the dream object. To know the dream object — say, a tiger — as an independent object different from one's consciousness, is an incomplete, or imperfect, knowledge of the dream tiger. This is illusion, but to know it to be an ideal projection of one's own consciousness and, therefore, not different from oneself, is to have complete, or perfect, knowledge of the same.

The Tantric theory of error, *apūrṇakhyāti*, although substantially not different from the *ātmakhyāti* of Buddhism or the *anirvacanīyakhyāti* of Advaita Vedānta, seems to have deeper insight as far as the real nature of illusion or the ontology of illusion is concerned. The illusory is generally taken to be nothing; therefore, it is not granted any ontological status at all. Tantra, however, holds that the illusory is not mere nothing; it is an appearance, or projection (*ābhāsa*), of consciousness. Without consciousness, or mind, projecting or appearing as the illusory object, there can be no illusion. This means the illusory object is true as an appearance of consciousness — the appearance *as appearance* is quite real. The illusory object is false only in the sense that it is not an independent material thing; as the projected "ideal" appearance it is not false. A motion picture, for example, is illusory only in the sense that what we see on the screen are not real objects. That they are images projected from the film reel cannot be denied. What we see on the screen is true as a photographic reflection. The same is true in the case of dreams and other cases of illusion. The dream world is a projection, or appearance, of consciousness; as the process of appearance it is true.

It is in this sense that Abhinavagupta calls the *ābhāsa* ("appearance") real. He does not mean that the appearance is the copy of a real material entity; what he means is that the appearance is a self-projected reflection in consciousness, and as *such* it is true. He does not grant to the illusory object any ontological status in the sense of its being a material entity. For him, too, the illusory is purely epistemic. But the epistemic itself is ontological in the sense that it is a real process of projecting ideal appearances. The appearance, therefore, is false in one sense — in the sense of being a material object — and true in another sense — in the sense of being a reflection or appearance. This is why Plato maintains that the world of shadows (appearance) partakes in reality (the world of ideas). The shadow *as shadow*, or the reflection *as reflection*, is real.

The ultimate object of the theory of *apūrṇa-khyāti*, as of any theory of error, is to serve the ontological purpose of determining the status of knowledge of the world. The world is an appearance of consciousness. Of course the world of appearances is not a creation of individual consciousness; it is the projection of the Cosmic Consciousness, Śiva. To the individual mind it appears objective and real. The individual illusion, like the rope-snake, dream, and so on, is an illusion within a greater illusion; it is "like a dream within a dream, or like a boil in the goitre."[53]

Like ordinary illusion, the illusion of the world is also an incomplete knowledge, as the world is not known in its entirety. In reality the world is a projection, ideal appearance, or ideational activity (*vimarśa*) of the Cosmic Consciousness, Śiva, and as such it is substantially not different from Śiva. When the world is known as Śiva, then the knowledge of the world is complete. Even failing this, the knowledge of the world is not completely false; the knowledge of the world is only partial, or incomplete.

From the point of view of the spiritual seeker, the sense of duality (*dvaita-prathā*) is the real ignorance or illusion. In reality the world is an ideal manifestation or self-projection of our own higher Self, which is the Absolute, or Śiva. The individual beings are ourselves, but we wrongly consider them to be different from us. We are really the Absolute, embracing everything within our fold. However, ignorant as we are of our real nature, we confine ourselves to a limited self (*aṇu* or *paśu*) — the individual self — cutting ourselves off from the rest of the world, which is really us. This apprehension of duality is the real illusion or ignorance.[54] When we rise up to Śiva-consciousness and realize that we are one with the entire universe, then our knowledge of ourselves and the world is complete or perfect (*pūrṇajñāna*).[55] The nearer we proceed to the goal and the more comprehensive our attitude becomes, the more complete our knowledge is and the more it relieves us from *saṁsāra* ("the round of existence").[56]

3

Absolute Consciousness (Śiva-Śakti)

Part I — Śiva

ŚIVA AS THE FIRST PERSON

In Kashmir Śaivism, as in Advaita Vedānta, the inquiry about Ultimate Reality starts not with the third person, as if Siva or Brahman were "out there" but with the first person, with Śiva "here" — within one as one's own higher self. Actually the inquiry is "Who am I?" or "What is my real nature?" This question ultimately leads to the position that one's real or deeper nature is Śiva or Brahman. It follows that describing the nature of Śiva means describing the nature of one's own real self and vice-versa. Thus Kashmir Śaivism is an *Ātma-śāstra* (inquiry into the Self). That is why the object of this particular discipline is the "recognition" of the real self, or "Self-realization" (*Pratyabhijñā* or *Ātma-pratyabhijñā*).

The above statement is illustrated in the second verse of the *Īśvara-pratyabhijñā-kārikā*, which affirms "Maheśvara (Śiva) lies as my own self (*svātmā*) and it is proved in the very beginning (*ādisiddha*) as myself who is the 'doer' (*kartā*) and the 'knower' (*jñātā*)."[1] If one has to locate Śiva, one can point to oneself, as one is an example of the entity, or substance, called Śiva. The entity called Śiva is really "consciousness" (*citi*, or *saṁvit*), and apart from one's body, one is an example of that consciousness, albeit an impure one.

This implies that one is of two types or one's nature is two-fold. One aspect is the surface nature or surface self, which is imperfect or limited (*aṇu* or *paśu*), bound by spiritual impurities (*mala*); and the other is the deeper, or the higher Self, which is perfect, infinite, and pure. Thus there is a surface, or "lower" self, and a deeper or "higher" self — or a lower "I" and a higher "I." When the word *śiva* is used to mean a substance or entity, it includes the *paśu*, or the lower self, because the *paśu*, the impure individual consciousness, is essentially one with Śiva.[2] But when the word *śiva* is used to denote its pure and cosmic form, it excludes the *paśu*. This position can be explained with the help of the analogy of the ocean and the waves. From the point of view of substance, the wave is nothing but water, which the ocean is also, and in this sense the wave can be considered to be the ocean itself. But since the wave is limited or individualized water, whereas the ocean is the underlying limitless expansion of water, the word *ocean* may also exclude the waves.[3] Another analogy would be that of a brilliant light that, when passed through a curtain, becomes dim and tainted with impurity.

The point is that when the texts expound the nature of Śiva, one should not thereby understand that Śiva is something different from oneself that stands "over there" as a third person; rather, one should think of Śiva in the first person — as "myself" (of course, my *higher* self). In other words, Śiva is the self.[4] In my treatment, Śiva as pure Cosmic Consciousness, like the ocean in the analogy, is referred to as the Self with a capital "S," whereas Śiva as the limited individual consciousness, like the wave in the analogy, is referred to as the self with a small "s."

ŚIVA IS THE ABSOLUTE

The Meaning of "Absolute"

The chief characteristic of Śiva, or the Self, is that Śiva is the Absolute. "Absolute" is a term in Western philosophy, but it is used in Indian philosophy to describe the nature of Ultimate Reality. The term *absolute* has two related meanings. Primarily it means that which is independent, or that which exists and is sustained by itself and does not require anything else to support it. This is in contrast with the term relative, which stands for that which depends upon some other. The Indian equivalents of the terms *absolute* and *relative* are *nirapekṣa* and *sāpekṣa*, respectively.

Śiva (the Self) exists by itself; it does not require anything else to support it. Thus it is *anapekṣa*, or *nirapekṣa.*[5] It is without *apekṣā*, or dependence; it is the Absolute. Such a thing would naturally be *aja* ("unborn") and *anādi* [6] ("beginningless"). The world, on the contrary, is relative (*sāpekṣa*), for it depends upon Śiva both for its existence and for its sustenance.

Śiva is absolute not only by being existent but also by being known. Awareness, or knowledge (*jñāna*), is the very nature of Śiva[7] for Śiva is Consciousness. Insentient matter (*jaḍa*) cannot know, whereas it is natural for consciousness to know. And consciousness not only knows other things but also knows itself; it is self-illumined (*svaprakāśa*). Thus Śiva is both self-existent and self-illumined, or self-known.[8]

The secondary meaning of the term *absolute* is that which covers or pervades all. In other words, the Absolute is that for which there is no "other"; everything is "that" itself. This meaning of *absolute* also applies to Śiva. Everything in existence can be called Śiva, for everything in the universe is a self-manifestation or extension (*prasāra*) of Śiva. What appears to be insentient matter and, therefore, a substance separate from Consciousness, is a self-projected appearance (*ābhāsa*) or emanation (*unmeṣa*) of Consciousness.[9] Thus, there is no duality.

The second quality of the Absolute, which is non-duality, is a natural corollary of its first and primary quality — independence or freedom. If there were a reality other than Śiva, this reality would naturally put a limit to the absoluteness of Śiva; the independence or freedom of Śiva would be barred by this other reality. In order to remain truly independent, Śiva must be non-dual also, and Śiva, in fact, *is* non-dual.[10] Thus Śiva is absolute in both senses of the word: (a) Śiva is perfectly independent, and (b) Śiva is the non-dual reality extending to everything in the universe.

The Problem of the Identity of Śiva With the World

What follows from the above contention is that Śiva is the only reality — one without a second. This conception of non-dual reality raises certain logical problems. If Śiva is the only reality, then what about the world, which is obviously not Śiva? Is it not real? If non-duality is the truth, then what is the ontological status of the world of duality that we quite obviously see around us? In other words, what is the relation of the absolute (Śiva) with the relative (world)?

In order to know the answer to the above questions we have to understand the meaning of non-duality. Non-duality does not mean the absence of apparent duality; what it means is that one and the same reality appears in different forms. When the mind, or consciousness, for example, projects a whole world of diversity in a dream, the projected dream world, although appearing to be different, is in reality the dreamer himself, or consciousness itself, because the dream objects are nothing but ideas or thoughts projected as things. In the same way, the world is a manifestation or projection of Śiva.[11] I will discuss this issue in detail in Chapter 5. Here it should suffice to say that since the world is a manifestation of Śiva, the world is substantially one with Śiva.[12] In other words, the world of duality is also Śiva appearing in different forms. This is the position that every Absolutist is bound to take.

Moreover, the world of duality is not only substantially one with Śiva but is also the free expression, or free manifestation, of Śiva. The non-dual (Śiva), out of *līlā* ("sportive activity"), freely manifests itself in the form of the world.[13] Thus duality is the free self-expression of the non-dual, and as such, is not inconsistent with the non-dual.

The Mādhyamika may object here that the world has characteristics contrary to that of Śiva, and that which has opposing characteristics cannot be one (*yo' sau viruddhadharmādhyāsavān nāsau ekaḥ*). Śiva is subject (*jñātā*), the world is object (*jñeya*); Śiva is consciousness, but the world is matter; Śiva is one, the world is manifold; and so on. Therefore, the world cannot be said to be one with Śiva.

This objection based on the logic of contradiction, put by the Mādhyamika, can be raised not only against Kashmir Śaivism but against any system of philosophy that accepts the identity of the one and the many. Some philosophers try to answer the logic of contradiction with the help of the logic of contrariness. But the Kashmir Śaiva philosopher has a simple answer. He or she would say that it is within the power of consciousness to project itself in a form apparently opposite to itself. The proof of this is found in our own experience — in dreams, for example. In the dream, consciousness becomes or appears as matter; the subject becomes the object; the one becomes many. In a dream, consciousness becomes what appears to be the opposite of consciousness, yet we know that the dream world is one with the dreamer. Dreaming is an experience or a phenomenon or a situation. The Mādhyamika cannot deny its reality. We have to use some language to express the dream situation, and the language of non-duality is not out of place. It is perfectly all right to say that the dream world is one with the dreamer.

In an ordinary dream the dreamer is ignorant; he does not know the truth that the dream is his own manifestation. Moreover, the dreamer does not freely create the dream. But the cosmic "dream" of Creation is different. The Creator, Śiva, freely projects the world out of Himself[14] and He also knows that the world is His own creation. To use the language of cause and effect, Śiva is both the material cause (*upādāna*) and the efficient cause (*nimitta*) of the world.[15] Since Creation is substantially one with the Creator, we can very well say that the two are identical. The Mādhyamika should have no objection to this language. In fact, he himself uses this language when he says that *saṁsāra* and *nirvāṇa* are one.

Śiva is Pure Unity (Non-Dual)

The problem of how the relative, or the world, can be related to the Absolute, Śiva, is the same as the problem of how difference can be related to Unity, or how determinations can be related to the Indeterminate. The answer is the same for all, as the same logic operates in all three cases. The relative, the many, or the determinate is the free manifestation of the Absolute, the One, or the Indeterminate. I have already discussed this in earlier sections of this chapter. It need not be repeated here. Here I will simply state the position taken by Kashmir Śaivism and differentiate it from that of other philosophies.

The Absolute (Śiva) in Himself (or Itself) is devoid of all variety (all forms, differences or determinations), yet all variety comes out of Him. He is compared to the liquid present in the egg of a peacock (*mayūrāṇḍarasavat*), which in itself is colorless (devoid of variety), yet all the colors of the peacock's plumes come out of it.

It should be noted here that the analogy of the egg or of the seed (*bīja*),[16] so frequently mentioned in the texts, should not lead us to think that the variety (of forms or determinations) is potentially contained in Śiva (the Absolute) and that Śiva is bound to actualize the world of variety. In the case of the seed, the tree is potentially contained in the seed and the seed is bound to actualize in the form of a tree. The seed cannot, for example, refuse to evolve into a tree if all the conditions for its evolution are provided. Thus, the seed is not free — neither free to actualize in a way different from what is potentially or genetically fixed, nor free not to actualize at all. But this is not true in the case of Śiva.[17] Śiva is free to manifest the way He likes; He is also free to not manifest at all.

The analogy of the seed or of the egg should thus not be stretched too far. The analogy is used to show that there is no variety in Śiva and yet all the variety of the world comes out of Him. It is not used to show that Śiva is bound to manifest that variety. We may use language to the effect that the world is potentially contained in Śiva, but the "potentiality" is not like the genetic fruits already present in the seed. The world is not present in Śiva, not even potentially as in the case of the tree potentially present in the seed. For Śiva, potentiality means the power or capacity to manifest; it does not mean the world is present in Śiva in seed form. Manifestation of the world is an act of absolute freedom on the part of Śiva. There is nothing of the world in Śiva; the world comes out all new. Creation is *spanda* — a free and spontaneous act without any determining factor from within or without.[18]

Thus we can see that the Absolute of Kashmir Śaivism is pure unity, not unity-in-difference. The Absolute of Hegel and the Brahman of Rāmānuja are unity-in-difference. There the world of difference is contained in the Absolute as the parts of a whole. Moreover, as the world of difference is potentially contained in the Absolute of Hegel (and of Rāmānuja), just like the tree in a seed, the evolution of the Absolute cannot be called a free act. Unity (the

Absolute) cannot but evolve into difference (the world). But in Kashmir Śaivism the Unity (Śiva) is free to manifest or not to manifest into difference. Here Creation is not "evolution," as in the case of the evolution of a seed into a tree, but a free extension (*prasāra*).[19]

In the Śaiva tradition itself, the three philosophies of (a) pure unity, (b) unity-in-difference, and (c) difference, all exist. Śaiva Siddhānta, a southern school of Śaivism, accepts three realities — Śiva, or God (*pati*), the individual soul (*paśu*), and matter (*pāśa*). Therefore it is a philosophy of difference. Vīra Śaivism, another school of southern Śaivism, accepts one reality, Śiva, but Śiva is qualified by Śakti, which is the power, or principle of the manifestation of the world. Vīra Śaivism is qualified monism — Śiva qualified by Śakti (*śaktiviśiṣṭādvaita*).

In Kashmir Śaivism, however, Śakti is not an attribute, or quality, of Śiva, but the very nature of Śiva. Śakti is Śiva and Śiva is Śakti. The truth is that here the Ultimate Reality, Consciousness, which is called Śiva or Parama-Śiva, is conceived of as dynamic and the very dynamism of Śiva is called Śakti. In other words, Consciousness is seen as energy or force, and thus it is called *śakti*. There is only one reality — call it Śiva or call it Śakti.[20] Therefore Kashmir Śaivism is a philosophy of pure unity.

Advaita Vedānta and Mādhyamika Buddhism are also absolutisms and philosophies of unity. The Brahman of Advaita Vedānta is pure unity, the one-without-a-second (*ekamevādvitīyam*). So is the *śūnya* of the Mādhyamika. (However, the Mādhyamika negatively calls the reality *advaya*, or "non-dual," rather than *ekam* — "one"; the very term *śūnya* has a negative connotation.) Although these two systems of philosophy are, in this sense, similar to Kashmir Śaivism, yet they differ from it in so far as the relation between Ultimate Reality and the world is concerned. The world is relative, determinate, and made of difference (duality). Ultimate Reality, on the contary, is absolute, indeterminate, and pure unity (non-dual). So every Absolutist, in order to preserve his or her Absolutism, is bound to explain the existence of the world of duality vis-à-vis the non-dual Reality. They have to answer the question, How can the Absolute and the relative, or Unity and difference, or the Indeterminate and the determinate, be related?

Advaita Vedānta and Mādhyamika Buddhism answer the question in one way, and Kashmir Śaivism does so in a slightly different way. Advaita Vedānta and Mādhyamika Buddhism maintain that the world of duality — (*prapañca*) as they call it — is illusion, a superimposition (*adhyāsa*) on Reality, caused by ignorance (*advidyā*), like the "rope-snake" (*rajju-sarpa*). In the rope-snake illusion, we "see" the snake, but it is really a rope; the so-called snake is a product of ignorance. The "snake" has only epistemic reality; it has no ontological status. Similarly, what we see as the world is really Brahman, or *śūnya* (or *nirvāṇa*), the world being merely an appearance of Brahman. We superimpose the illusory world on Brahman out of ignorance, just as we superimpose the "snake" on the rope. The point is that Brahman alone is real, the world is not. What exists, like the rope, is Brahman or *nirvāṇa*, and what appears as the world is just an illusion like the "snake." Thus, Advaita Vedānta and Mādhyamika Buddhism protect the unity of Reality by depriving the world of its independent and separate reality; the reality of *saṁsāra* ("the world") is *nirvāṇa* or Brahman, just as the reality of the illusory snake is the rope.

The above explanation is all right logically, but there is one problem with it. In the rope-snake analogy, the rope lies neutral and passive and the "snake" is superimposed on it from outside. The rope itself does not create the illusory snake; the "snake" is created by something or somebody else. This means there is a reality other than the rope, and this leads to the acceptance of a duality. Given this, can the analogy of the rope-snake be fully applied to Brahman? The Advaitins, especially the scholastic Advaitins, seem to apply the analogy in full, for they maintain that Brahman is inactive, that Brahman lies neutral like the rope and that the world is superimposed on Brahman due to *avidyā* ("ignorance"), with Brahman not actively creating the world-illusion but passively allowing Itself to be the ground for the superimposition. If Brahman is conceived of as inactive (*niṣkriya*), lying passive and neutral like the rope, and the illusion of the world is superimposed on it, then this means there is a machinery or agency other than Brahman, and this other agency is responsible for the creation and superimposition on Brahman of the illusion of the world. This clearly means there are two realities — Reality is not non-dual. This creates grave inconsistencies in the above-mentioned system and hits at the very backbone of Advaita Vedānta.

Kashmir Śaivism steers clear of the above difficulty by maintaining that the world, although an *ābhāsa*, or appearance, of Śiva, is not a superimposition on Śiva from outside but a self-creation or self-projection of Śiva. Śiva is not inactive; unlike the Brahman of the Advaitic scholiast, Śiva is vibrant with spontaneous activity, technically called *kriyā*, *spanda*, or *vimarśa*. This dynamism of Śiva is also called Śakti. Thus the world is a spontaneous creation of Śiva Himself.[21] If the Advaitin retorts that the superimposition on Brahman is not from outside but from within, as there is no reality other than Brahman, then Kashmir Śaivism says that this implies dynamism, or activity, in Brahman and that Brahman therefore cannot be accepted as *niṣkriya* ("inactive"). This would bring the Advaita Vedāntic position nearer to that of Kashmir Śaivism.

The Question of the "Will-Absolute"

Since the world is a free creation of the Absolute (Śiva), some scholars, using the phraseology of K. C. Bhattacharya, have made an interesting categorization of the Absolute of Kashmir Śaivism as the "Will-Absolute."[22] Professor Bhattacharya has created a very useful language for the categorization of the Absolutes of different systems. He has discerned three major types of Absolute: Knowledge-Absolute, Will-Absolute, and Feeling-Absolute, obviously based on the three mental faculties of cognition, conation, and affection. In this system of categorization, the Absolute of Advaita Vedānta and Mādhyamika Buddhism is taken to be Knowledge-Absolute, whereas that of Kashmir Śaivism is taken as Will-Absolute.

Since Consciousness, or the Absolute, in Kashmir Śaivism is seen as energy or force and since, therefore, it is dynamism or activity (*kriyā-Śakti*), it can aptly be called "Will." "Doing" is primarily "willing"; all conscious or sentient activity originates from willing. The world also is created out of the Will of Śiva; so Creation is volitional. The entire Tantric tradition emphasizes the *śakti-rūpatā*, or the activistic nature of consciousness, and since the activity of Consciousness is primarily of a volitional nature, the *citi* or *samvit*, (Consciousness) is called "Will" (*icchā*, or *saṅkalpa*).

It is true that the Will aspect seems to be predominant in the Absolute of Kashmir Śaivism, and therefore Kashmir Śaivism may be called Will-Absolutism; but we should not lose sight of the equal status of the knowledge aspect accepted in Kashmir Śaivism. As far as Advaita Vedānta is concerned, the Absolute is pure knower (*jñātā*) and not doer (*kartā*); therefore Brahman has what is called "freedom-from" and not "freedom-to." But the Absolute of Kashmir Śaivism is both *jñāna* ("knowledge") and *kriyā* ("activity"), Śiva and Śakti, or *prakāśa* and *vimarśa*, combined in one. It has both "freedom-from" and "freedom-to." Therefore, it is more appropriate to call the Absolute of Kashmir Śaivism a Knowledge-Will-Absolute. Those who categorize Śiva as purely a Will-Absolute actually try to see Kashmir Śaivism in contrast with Advaita Vedānta, but this position is not always accurate.

ŚIVA IS INDETERMINATE

The Meaning of "Indeterminate"

Just as the Brahman of Advaita Vedānta is conceived of as indeterminate (*nirguṇa*, *nirvikalpa*, or *nirviśeṣa*), and the Śūnya of the Mādhyamika is beyond all four categories of understanding (*catuṣkoṭi-vinirmukta*), so also is the Śiva of Kashmir Śaivism. Śiva is called *anuttara*,[23] which means both indeterminate and transcendent — that which transcends the categories of understanding, and that which, being the highest reality, transcends all the *tattvas* (categories of reality). Śiva is also called *nirvikalpa* ("without *vikalpa*, or categories of understanding") and *nirviśeṣa* ("with *viśeṣaṇa*, or qualification"). In other words, Śiva is seen as indeterminate.

What does it mean to be indeterminate? The term *indeterminate* has an epistemological as well as an ontological meaning. Epistemologically it means *that* which cannot be "determined," "grasped," or "judged" by understanding, reason, or intellect. Whatever we grasp through our understanding is called *vikalpa* or *guṇa* ("determination," "predication," or "qualification"). Something that cannot be so grasped or determined is called *nirvikalpa*, *nirviśeṣ*a, or *nirguṇa*.[24]

But why does the intellect not grasp that which is "indeterminate?" Because that thing does not possess those qualities that our intellect is equipped to grasp. Ontologically, *vikalpa*, *viśeṣa*, or *guṇa* means the qualities that can be grasped by our understanding. Likewise, the ontological meaning of "indeterminate" is that it does not possess the qualities that can be grasped by our understanding. It is obvious that the epistemological meaning and the ontological meaning of the term "indeterminate" go together.

Śiva is Beyond the Categories of Understanding

We are able to perceive or grasp the things of the world because they possess qualities that can be perceived or grasped. But could there be a thing that does not have such qualities and therefore could not be perceived, grasped, or even thought of? The Naiyāyika and Rāmānuja maintain that there is no such thing. The Naiyāyika would say that everything is knowable (*sarvam jñeyam*) and, therefore everything is describable (*sarvam abhidheyam*). Likewise, Rāmānuja would say that it is possible to at least conceive of or understand everything, if not to actually perceive it. To be existent and not be conceived of is a contradiction in terms he would say. Therefore *nirguṇa* ("indeterminate") is a meaningless term according to Rāmānuja. Rāmānuja accepts Brahman as fully determinate (*saguṇa* or *aśeṣakalyāṇaguṇa-saṁpanna*) and rejects the indeterminate Brahman of Śaṅkara.

Advaita Vedānta, Mādhyamika Buddhism, and Kashmir Śaivism, on the contrary, accept the possibility of indetermination and further accept that their Absolute is indeterminate. In answer to Nyāya and Rāmānuja, it can well be demonstrated through the analysis of our understanding and experience that there is the possibility of a thing's being indeterminate. If a person thinks that the mind, understanding, intellect, or reason is capable of knowing and conceiving of everything, that person is wrong. The mind is endowed with very limited categories of understanding. A child, for example, cannot understand many things that a grownup can simply because the child does not have the categories for understanding them. A three- or four-year-old child cannot understand what *marriage* is. The child can understand eating sweets or having fun because the child has the categories for understanding these things. A slightly more grown-up child can understand friendship between a boy and a girl because the category of understanding friendship has developed in that child. Although a marriage ceremony may contain some element of each of the above examples — eating sweets, having fun, and even friendship between the couple — none of these categories grasps the actual meaning of marriage.[25]

Even in sensory perception, the object of one sense organ cannot be perceived by the other sense organs. The eyes, for example, cannot perceive fragrance; only the nose can do that. The nose cannot perceive color; the eyes alone can do that. This is because each sense organ has a particular category of perception that cannot be extended to the realm of other sense organs.

Similarly, the intellect, mind, thought, understanding, or reason as a whole has limited categories of understanding; it is not possible for it to know everything. There might well be something that is beyond the grasp of the intellect — a Reality that cannot be determined by the categories of intellect. The contention of Nyāya, or of Rāmānuja, that there can be nothing indeterminate, is not tenable.

Ultimate Reality, Parama-Śiva, is, in fact, beyond the grasp of thought or reason. It cannot be characterized or defined. The best definition of Śiva, Utpaladeva says, is that it is untouched by all definitions.[26] Abhinavagupta, the grand-disciple of Utpaladeva, maintains that all our attempts to conceptualize Śiva are futile, for Śiva always eludes our grasp.[27] What we take to be Śiva, is really the Śiva of our own understanding; it is not Śiva in Itself. I can only understand Śiva in my own way, not in the way in which Śiva exists. To use Kantian terminology, Śiva is the thing-in-itself that always eludes our understanding, while we remain confined to the thing as it appears to us.

Abhinavagupta, while delineating the thirty-six *tattvas* (categories of reality) of his system, maintains that Ultimate Reality (Parama-Śiva) is the thirty-seventh;[28] if we conceive of reality as comprised of thirty-seven *tattvas*, then Ultimate Reality will be the thirty-eighth,[29] and so on. The point is that Reality (Parama-Śiva) will always be beyond our grasp.

That Reality is beyond the grasp of thought or reason is not a new idea put forth by Abhinavagupta; it is the age-old wisdom of the Indian tradition. The Upaniṣads declare that speech and mind have no access to Reality.[30] The Upaniṣads further state in a paradoxical way that Reality "is known to one who does not know it, and one who knows, does not know it; it is not known to the knowledgeable, and is known to those who are devoid of knowledge."[31] The point is that Reality cannot be "known" or grasped by thought; therefore intellectual knowledge is futile. The silence of the Buddha is well-known. All the mystic seers have expressed a similar view.

The Indian tradition does not believe in the competence of reason in the apprehension of Reality.

This does not mean that Brahman (or Śiva) — the Reality that the Vedas and the Tantras speak of — is not known at all, otherwise how would the statements about Brahman be possible? The point is that Śiva (Brahman), the Ultimate Reality, is not known by *reason* (intellect, or thought) but by what we might call "higher experience," which is supra-intellectual, or supra-rational — an experience which is believed to be actually had by the seers. (I have already discussed the possibility of such an experience in Chapter 2). The knowledge of Ultimate Reality that we find in the scriptures (Vedas and Tantras) is based not upon ordinary reason but upon the (alleged) higher experience.

The Role of Philosophy

If Reality eludes our understanding, then the question arises, What is the use of philosophy? Philosophy involves thought or reason. Abhinavagupta himself has done a lot of philosophizing. But what is the use of all this, if no philosophy can delineate Reality in its true colors?

In answer to the above question, Abhinavagupta would say that although Reality is beyond the grasp of thought or reason, reason apprehends Reality in its own way. Reason has its own laws, which it applies to Reality. For example, reason can admit Reality in a consistent and logical way only. Philosophy, which is the product of reason, employs logic as its tool, examining other theories on a logical basis.

Reason is itself a manifestation of ultimate Reality, so it has the full right to demand Reality to condescend to the level of reason and reveal itself in a way in which reason can understand it. There is also no harm in this. The philosopher is fully aware that the Reality that his reason is manipulating is the Reality of reason and not the

Reality-in-itself. This is what philosophy can, and should, do. In order to have the best philosophy, the philosopher will have to use logic, argumentation, and so on. Moreover, Abhinavagupta takes philosophy to be a spiritual discipline. The conception of Reality one holds, even if incomplete, does not hinder one's spiritual advancement. In the same way, one may love a person who is quite different from what one idealizes him or her to be, and yet the love and devotion one feels may be of value to oneself. Similarly, one should not bother about what Śiva, or Reality, in itself is; the sole concern should be that one's understanding of Śiva is consistent in one's own way. That in itself would be of value. It is important that one's mind is satisfied, and that one has a clear understanding of Reality in one's own way. This is a pre-requisite of spiritual advancement. Hence for Abhinavagupta the intellectual knowledge of Reality is of value.[32]

The question may be raised here: if one's own conception of Reality is what is desired, then every conception is subjective (and true in its own way); there is no use in objective reasoning and no sense in criticism and evaluation of others' thought. In answer to this, I would point out that when we say that we know Reality in our own way, we do not mean here the subjective reason or understanding that differs from person to person — we mean the objective reason that is universal. Looked at in the Kantian way, reason is an objective epistemological reality; it has its own objective categories of grasping, or knowing, anything. As far as Reality-in-itself is concerned, reason or understanding has no access. But the moment Reality is reflected in reason — that is, when reason apprehends Reality, in its own way, of course — reason starts working upon it (Reality) applying its logic, which is universal and objective. Reason is fully competent here. Reason can meaningfully criticize and evaluate rational conceptions of Reality. Abhinavagupta himself indulges in criticism of other philosophical positions.

Reconciling Determinations With the Indeterminate

As the Absolute is completely independent and free from limitation, the logic of the Absolute demands that the Absolute must be above all determinations. When one characterizes Śiva by saying "Śiva is this," or "Śiva is that," one limits Him with the qualifications ascribed to Him and thus makes Him appear finite. Śiva is free to appear in the way described, He is free to appear in some other way, and He is also free not to appear at all.

Śiva is not exhausted in any appearance and stands beyond all appearances. To characterize Śiva in one's own way is to deny Him other possibilities. Spinoza has rightly said that God cannot be determined, as "all determination is negation." The same position is held by Advaita Vedānta. Brahman cannot be determined; the moment we try to grasp Brahman, it becomes Īśvara, the personal God. All descriptions of Brahman are really descriptions of Īśvara, as Īśvara alone can be an object of our thought.

The logic of the freedom of the Absolute also demands that Śiva can manifest in any form — say, for example, in the form of the world. Śiva should be able to appear in any form He likes. If Śiva is only transcendent — that is beyond appearances — and is not also free to manifest, then Śiva is not completely free. Śiva not only has the "freedom-from" that the Brahman of Advaita Vedānta has, but He also has the "freedom-to" appear in different forms.

Abhinavagupta emphasizes not only the "freedom-from" but also the "freedom-to" aspect of Reality. "Freedom-from" means that Śiva is untouched or unaffected by world appearances, as He transcends all appearance. Appearances do not bind Śiva or effect any change in Him.[33] But the "freedom-from" alone is not the whole truth; it is only half the picture. Unless there is also "freedom-to," the freedom of the Absolute cannot be complete. "Freedom" implies the ability to act. If Śiva is not free to act, He is then really limited;

Śiva becomes just like the bound individual. Of course, activity is not a necessity for Śiva; Śiva is not obliged to act.[34] He is free not to act, but He is free also to act. Moreover, if there is no "freedom-to" in Śiva, then the existence of the world cannot be accounted for. The world will either be an independent reality as it is in Sāṁkhya, or it will have to be regarded as the free activity of the Absolute. No Absolutism can afford to give independent status to the world, and therefore no Absolutism can afford to deny "freedom-to" in the Absolute.

The Indeterminate is both "free-from" and also "free-to;" that is, it is free from determinations and also free to accept determinations. As for the determinations, however, they necessarily require the Indeterminate for their existence. The Indeterminate can be without determinations, but the determinations cannot exist without the Indeterminate. The reason for this is simple. If there are several determinations, or forms, of one and the same person, it means that the person him- or herself is different from and beyond the forms. If he or she is tied to one form, how can he or she assume other forms? The fact that a person adopts different personalities in drama shows that the person him- or herself is different from, and independent of, those personalities. Only that which has no form or determination of its own can adopt different forms or determinations. Light has no color of its own, therefore it can assume different colors when passing through various colored glasses. Similarly, water has no shape of its own, therefore it can adopt different shapes according to the various containers in which it is placed. Śiva has no forms or determinations of His own and therefore can adopt as many forms as He likes.[35]

In the above analogies the factors responsible for variety are external, whereas in the case of Śiva they, too, are self-created or self-projected. Variety (*vaicitrya*) is the free manifestation of Śiva.[36]

Thus, it is quite logical to think that Śiva is beyond all thought and yet appears to us, albeit in a modified way, through the medium of thought. Our reach is only up to Śiva as He appears to us, not to

Śiva in Himself. There is no contradiction in Śiva's being beyond thought, on the one hand, and assuming a form that befits our understanding, on the other hand.

The Problem of Communication

If mind has no access to Reality, and Reality is beyond thought, then the question arises: is there no means other than thought or reason to reach Reality and know about it? The Vedic and the Āgamic seers and other saints and yogins are believed to have had access to Reality. If so, what means did they use to know Reality? Reason and sense-perception are the only means of knowledge we ordinarily have. But there is also a higher or deeper way of knowing, symbolized by the mystic "third eye," which has access to Reality. The symbolic "third eye" is pictured as open in the case of Śiva and Śakti. The "third eye" lies dormant in us and can be awakened through spiritual *sādhanā.* The yogins and seers are believed to have achieved this. The Vedic and the Āgamic seers knew Reality through higher experience, not by reason or sense perception. The Upaniṣads and the Āgamas record the experience of the seers, and that is the source of our information about Reality.

Even if Reality is known through higher experience, how can the person of higher experience communicate his or her experience to the person who stands at the level of reason only, since reason cannot conceive of Reality? How can the supra-rational, or supramental, experience be translated into the language of mind, or reason? In the Upaniṣads and the Āgamas we find the description of Reality in the language of reason. This means that either Reality is knowable by reason and therefore describable, or all the descriptions found in the scriptures are false and meaningless.

The resolution to the above dilemma is a little complicated. It is true that Reality cannot be known and described in terms of reason, yet the description found in the scriptures is not meaningless — it serves the purpose of indirectly hinting at Reality. It is like the analogy of the moon on the branch (*śākhā-candra-nyāya*). When a child asks an adult where the moon is, the person may point to the branch of a tree and say, "Look, the moon is there on the branch." The child turns to the branches and is able to see the moon shining behind them. Here it is obvious that the statement, "The moon is there on the branch," is not correct, for the moon cannot be on the branch. Yet this statement serves a very useful purpose; it serves as a pointer to the moon and helps the child turn his or her attention to the moon and ultimately see the moon with his or her own eyes. Similarly, the scriptural description of Reality is not quite correct, as Reality cannot be described in our language; yet the description serves as a pointer to Reality, so that we turn our attention to Reality, do the requisite *sādhanā* for attaining it, and finally know it through higher experience. The means may be false, yet it can lead to the truth. Bhartṛhari says in this context, "Treading the path of falsehood, one reaches the truth."[37]

There can be three stages of the description of Reality. The first stage is that of silence. In fact, since Reality cannot be described, the best description of Reality is silence. Buddha took this position. The Upaniṣads and the Āgamas also refer to silence. But if someone presses for a description, then the best description is a negative one, that is, saying what Reality is *not*. Mādhyamika Buddhism adopts this position and describes Reality negatively by saying that Reality is *śūnya*, devoid of all that we conceive. The Upaniṣads describe Reality as *neti, neti*, ("not this, not this"). The Āgamas also declare Reality to be *anuttara*, ("transcending thought"), and Abhinavagupta naturally takes the same position.[38] Negative description is thus the second stage of describing Reality. But, like silence, the negative description also means nothing, as it gives no idea about what Reality is, and thus there is a demand for a positive description. The pupil presses the teacher for a positive account, and the Upaniṣadic teacher, although knowing full well that the positive description would be only approximate, declares that Reality is *sat-cit-ānanda*, ("existence-consciousness-bliss"). The Āgamas do the same; they even add one more thing to the description — *kriyā*, or *spanda*, ("spontaneous activity").[39]

In the history of Buddhism, the three stages of the description of Reality are found at three places. Buddha confined himself to the first stage, silence, and did not speak about Reality at all. The Mādhyamika Śūnyavāda adopts the second stage and describes Reality negatively (*śūnya*). The Yogācāra Vijñānavāda comes down to the third stage, positive description, and describes Reality as Consciousness (*vijñapti* or *vijñāna*). In the Upaniṣads and Āgamas, however, all three stages of the description of Reality are found together. This is perhaps because the teacher is conscious of the necessity of making the pupil aware of all three stages.

The third stage, the stage of the positive description of Reality, is in the realm of reason, and as we have already pointed out, this is not the true description of Reality; it is imperfect or only approximate. But this by no means diminishes the utility of the rational description of Reality, for the description, although not fully true, serves as the pointer to Reality. At *our* level we can grasp Reality in the rational way only. This is the level of philosophy. Philosophy certainly serves as a pointer to Reality and it indirectly and gradually leads to Reality by inspiring us to pursue practical *sādhanā*, which directly leads to the attainment of Reality.

ŚIVA IS THE SUBJECT-CONSCIOUSNESS

Since Reality is Consciousness, it is obvious that Reality is the Self, or the subject. The difference between consciousness and matter (*jaḍa*) is that matter does not "know" but "is known" by consciousness, whereas consciousness "knows." Naturally, therefore, insentient matter is the object that is the "known," whereas consciousness is the "knower." Consciousness always remains the subject, or the knower, and never becomes the object, or the known.[40] It is always addressed in the first person as "I," and never in the second or third person as "thou" or "it."[41]

It is self-contradictory to think that consciousness, which by its very nature is the subject, or the "knower," can become the object. How can "I" become the object of my knowledge? If I make myself an object of my knowledge and say "this is I," then I am not the "this" but the one who is knowing. Trying to know myself as an object is like trying to see my eyes. The eyes will always be the "seer," they can never be the "seen." If I point to the reflection of my eyes in a mirror or try to detach my eye as an object and say "This is my eye," that reflection or detached "eye" is not the true eye; what is seeing the reflection or seeing the detached eye is the real eye. The moment the eyes become the object, they cease to be the eyes. Similarly, Consciousness or the Self will cease to be the Self the moment it becomes an object. Reality, which is the Self by virtue of being consciousness, is the subject and *not* the object.

Though the subject cannot become the object, yet in our experience of dreaming we find that the subject does become the object also. But a careful analysis of the dream experience will show that there, too "I" am the "seer" or the one who is dreaming, not the "seen" or what is dreamt. Still, it is true that the dream object is my own projection and therefore it is true that it is "I" who have become the dream object also. This aspect of dream experience clearly shows three things, namely, (a) that the subject can project, or become the object, (b) that the projected object is substantially one with the subject, as the substance or the material of the dream object is nothing but consciousness, and (c) that the subject, even after self-projecting the dream object, remains the subject as the "seer" of the dream.

Thus dream experience reveals the very important and significant truth that the subject, while remaining very much the subject, becomes or projects the object also. There is really no contradiction between the logical truth that the Self or subject ceases to be the Self if it becomes the object, on the one hand, and the fact that the subject does become the object in a dream, on the other hand. With reference to dreams, the object is said to be one with the subject not in the sense that the "seen" is the "seer," but in the sense that the substance of the dream object is the same consciousness that is the substance of the subject also. The dream object is made not of material substance but of mind or consciousness. The dream object is not "real" but "ideal." It is made of ideas, or mental substance, which is nothing but Consciousness. The object is the reflection, or projection, of the subject and therefore substantially one with the subject. Of course, in the sense of being the "knower," and not in the sense of substance or material, the subject remains the subject even in the dream and never becomes the object. Thus, it is perfectly all right to say that the subject remains the subject and yet, at the same time, becomes the object also.

We can now understand the Kashmir Śaiva position, without self-contradiction, that Śiva is the subject-consciousness (*ātman*) and that Śiva at the same time also becomes, or projects out of Itself, the world, which is the object. Śiva as consciousness is the Self (*ātman*) and thus is the individual self (*paśu* or *aṇu*), and in this sense the two are one. The difference between the two is not with regard to the substance, as both are Consciousness and therefore the Self, but the difference is with regard to purity and impurity.[42] The individual self, or individual consciousness, is impure and finite, whereas Śiva, the Universal Self, is pure and infinite.[43] In this sense the individual can be called the lower self and Śiva the higher Self.

Thus the individual subjects, or souls, are limited expressions of the Universal Subject. The relation between the two can be said to be analogous to that between the ocean and its waves,[44] light and its rays,[45] or fire and its sparks. A further, more appropriate analogy would be that of a brilliant light and its rays passing through a curtain and, as a result, becoming impure and limited.

SELF-CONSCIOUSNESS IN ŚIVA

The Self-consciousness of Śiva, or pure Self, is a significant point in Kashmir Śaivism. The *kriyā* principle explains the self-consciousness in the absolutely non-dual Self. The Advaita Vedāntic logic of self-consciousness pertains to the awareness of the not-self. According to Advaita, one can be aware of oneself only when one is aware of, or encounters, the not-I. Self-consciousness, therefore, is essentially based on the distinction of the Self from the not-self. Brahman, which is a state of pure non-duality and which has no "other" to encounter, can have no self-consciousness. The objection of Advaita, therefore, is that either Śiva admits of duality, or if Śiva is purely non-dual, there can be no self-consciousness in Śiva.

It may be pointed out in response that awareness of the not-self is neither the only, nor a necessary, condition for self-consciousness; there is another explanation as well. The category of "not-I" becomes necessary only when one has to distinguish oneself from others. When one merely has to know of one's own existence and has no need to differentiate oneself from others, one need not be aware of others. What then would be the occasion for being aware of oneself? The explanation is *kriyā*. Self-consciousness is an activity of Consciousness, something like an eternal rippling in the ocean of Consciousness. And this is possible even when the non-dual Self alone exists. This natural effulgence or vibration (*spanda*) of Consciousness makes It aware of Itself.[46]

Self-consciousness, (*ahaṁ-vimarśa*), is the first and foremost activity (*kriyā* or *spanda*) of Consciousness. It is the very nature of Consciousness, or Śiva, and therefore it is eternal (*nitya*), whereas the triad of will-knowledge-action (*icchā-jñāna-kriyā*), which pertains to the creation of the world, is the free manifestation of Śiva. Self-consciousness is the natural activity of Consciousness just as self-illumination is the very nature of light.[47]

The Advaitin may again say that the very awareness of "I" implies the awareness of the not-I, as "I" is a relative term like "son" or "father" — to know a person as a son is also to know him as being fathered by someone. In answer it may be pointed out that the term "I" actually has two uses — the relative and the absolute. It is only in the relative use, that is, when one has to differentiate oneself from others and say, "I am not this or that," that the awareness of the not-self is implied. But in the absolute use of "I" when one has merely to know of one's own existence and simply say, "I am," there need not be a not-I. Logically it is quite possible to be aware of oneself, as in the case of Śiva, without others.[48] It is logically possible to have an absolute use of the term "I."

The point is that the awareness of the not-self is not the only logic of self-consciousness; there could well be an alternative logic. In the Tantric tradition we find an alternative logic of self-consciousness, namely, the logic of *kriyā*. When one is ill, in order to become healthy one need not necessarily take medicine; there may be alternatives to medicine — for instance, yogic exercise.

The Advaitin does not accept *kriyā* ("spontaneous activity") in Brahman. In the absence of duality in Brahman, therefore, the Advaitin reduces Brahman to a state absolutely devoid of self-consciousness. That is why the Advaitin is very fond of using the analogy of sleep.

The Tantrist would further respond to the Advaita Vedāntin that if Brahman, or Consciousness, is deprived of activity and self-consciousness, then It loses Its real beauty and becomes no better than unconscious matter. It seems funny to think that the Self, fully awake, could be devoid of self-consciousness. It seems contradictory that knowledge of Brahman is self-knowledge (*ātma-jñāna*), yet there is no self-consciousness. In the absence of self-consciousness, Brahman becomes like physical light that is self-illumined but not self-conscious. Brahman becomes, in the words of Radhakrishnan, "a bloodless Absolute dark with the excess of light."[49] To quote Radhakrishnan again, "The Absolute of Śaṅkara, rigid, motionless, and totally lacking in initiative or influence, cannot call forth our worship. Like the Taj Mahal, which is unconscious of the admiration it arouses, the Absolute remains indifferent to the fear and love of its worshippers, and for all those who regard the goal of religion as the goal of philosophy — to know the real — Śaṅkara's view seems to be a finished example of learned error."[50]

Considered from the axiological and spiritual point of view, the Absolute devoid of *kriyā* and self-consciousness becomes unintelligible. There can be no experience of joy (*ānanda*) without self-consciousness, nor can there even be joy itself, as joy is the inner *kriyā* or *spanda* of Consciousness. One may remark in this context that when we experience deep joy we forget ourselves and hence there is no self-consciousness in deep bliss. But what we forget in the experience of deep bliss is the ego — the individual self which differentiates oneself from others. In fact, we cannot experience deep bliss without dissolving the ego sense, for ego is the obstruction to the flow of joy, but this does not mean that there is no self-consciousness. Joy is not an entity but an experience. Experience means awareness, and in every awareness self-consciousness is present in one form or another. When one experiences deep joy, one is aware of it; later on one remembers it and says, "I experienced deep joy." Had there been no self-consciousness in the experience of joy, one would not have been able to remember experiencing it. Of course, in the experience of deep joy, the consciousness of ego (the differentiating principle) is not present, but consciousness of the self (the sentient existence) is very much present.

One begins to wonder if an Absolute that is unconscious of itself can be a value of life, much less the highest value, and whether such an Absolute is what is described in the Upaniṣads. In the Upaniṣads the axiological and spiritual interest is supreme; the emphasis is on Brahman as bliss, and Brahman is time and again said to be the highest value of life. But in Advaita Scholasticism, the epistemological and ontological interest seems to reign supreme; the spiritual aspect becomes auxiliary. The Upaniṣadic Brahman in the hands of the Advaita Scholiasts, perhaps with the single exception of Vidyāraṇya, seems to lose its axiological significance. The reason why the Advaita Scholiasts do not see the difficulty in an ice-like cold Brahman and remain quite satisfied and unperturbed with the notion of a "motionless" Brahman devoid of Self-consciousness, is, it seems, that they do not seriously consider the issue from the axiological point of view. This is an injustice to the Upaniṣadic Brahman; such a frigid and abstract view of the Absolute is really un-Upaniṣadic. The Upaniṣads present a living philosophy. To use the terminology of the Existentialist, the Upaniṣadic philosophy is "praxis;" it is "authentic" throughout. There are occasions when Upaniṣadic thought becomes abstruse and abstract, but the running thread of authenticity is never lost. However, when we come to the Scholiast, we find much of the authenticity is lost; it no longer remains a living philosophy. Some of the scholastic texts, such as the *Khaṇḍana-Khaṇḍakhādya* of Śrī Harṣa, are authored with the explicit purpose of sharpening the intellect in order to defeat the opponent in polemics.[51] Even the Sāṁkhya system, though mainly negativistic in approach, is "praxis;" but scholastic Advaita seems to be otherwise. Āgamic philosophy, on the other hand, is mainly a "praxis."[52]

A further objection may be raised from the Advaita Vedāntic side that self-consciousness is a determination (*vikalpa*), and that there can be no determination in the indeterminate (*nirvikalpa*) Śiva-Consciousness. In answer the Tantrist points out that the mere "I am," or self-consciousness, is not a *vikalpa*. It becomes a *vikalpa* only when one says "I am *this*" or "I am *that*." "I am" is the state of the pure subject without any predicate. Grammatically speaking, "subject" is that about which something is said or predicated, and "predicate" is what is said about the subject. "I am" is not a description or predication, for it does not say *what* one is. When one says "I am," one has not limited oneself by any determination, for one has not said what one is; one could be anything.[53]

ŚIVA AS THE ABSOLUTE PERSON

There is a logical connection between being self-conscious and being a person, as the very meaning of personality is self-consciousness. "One is a person" does not necessarily mean that one has a physical form, for one can be a person even without a body. God in many religions — Judaism, Christianity, Islam and some denominations of Hinduism, for example — is conceived of as a person, formless — God is seen as pure Spirit with no body or matter. The Divine Person can be without form (*nirākāra*) as well as with form (*sākāra*); form is not a necessary qualification of being a person.[54] What is it, then, that makes one a person? The answer is self-consciousness. A person is a self-conscious being. This implies that only a sentient being can be a person; insentient things such as material objects cannot be persons.

There are systems of philosophy that conceive of Ultimate Reality or God as a person, but generally they also accept realities other than God — their position is that of dualism or qualified monism. On the other hand, there are philosophies that conceive of Reality as the all-pervading non-dual Absolute, and therefore Reality, according to them, is impersonal. The Brahman of Advaita Vedānta and the Śūnya of Mādhyamika Buddhism are impersonal. The Advaitin, for example, may argue that the all-pervading consciousness cannot be taken as a person, for ascribing personality to Reality means putting a limitation on Reality. The Reality or God of the dualist does not have absoluteness or pure unity, while the Reality of non-dualists such as the Advaita Vedāntin and the Mādhyamika Buddhist has no personality.

The position of Kashmir Śaivism differs from both of these. The ultimate Reality (Śiva) of Kashmir Śaivism is the pure non-dual Absolute, and yet Śiva is a person — the Absolute Person. The Advaitin may question the compatibility of personality with Absoluteness. He may argue that claiming that Śiva is a person means Śiva is limited to one particular form and is cut off from the rest of the universe. In other words, personality pre-supposes duality. In answer to this I could point out that the same argument is advanced against the compatibility of self-consciousness with Absoluteness. As we have already seen, self-consciousness is very much possible in the absolutely non-dual Śiva.

Śiva is a Person because Śiva has self-consciousness. The self-consciousness of Śiva is not like the limited "I-consciousness" of the individual in which one differentiates oneself from others. The Divine "I" is the absolute or perfect "I" which incorporates everything within its bosom.[55] When Śiva is completely alone — the one without a second — even then self-consciousness means being in oneself.[56] Even in the state of the pure non-duality of Śiva, self-consciousness is possible by virtue of the natural inner dynamism (*kriyā*, *vimarśa*, *spanda*, or *śakti*) of Śiva.[57]

Self-consciousness is the natural dynamism of the non-dual Śiva-consciousness; it is its "eternal vibration" (*nitya-spanda*).[58] This is the state of the pure "I am." When Śiva, out of His freedom, spontaneously manifests Himself as the world, the "I am" becomes "I am this." "This," or the object, exists only when the world arises, but "I am" is always there, irrespective of Creation.

Here it should be made clear that personality is not the same as individuality. Individuality is the sense of the ego, which is limited and which differentiates the "I" from the rest of the world. Individuality has two characteristics: namely, (a) self-consciousness and (b) differentiation of oneself from others. But self-consciousness alone means personality. It may or may not adopt individuality, which has the sense of differentiation as its exclusive characteristic. When personality or self-consciousness also adopts the sense of differentiation of oneself from others, then it becomes individuality. But it need not do so. There can be self-consciousness as the awareness of one's own existence without the awareness of others. Personality is thus wider than individuality, which may or may not be part of personality.

ŚIVA IS PERFECTION

Perfection (*pūrṇatva*), freedom (*svātantrya*), indefinitude (*bhūmā*), and bliss (*ānanda*)—these four terms are all used to describe Śiva in the Tantras and Brahman in the Upaniṣads, and if we analyze the meaning of these terms, we will find that they all mean virtually the same thing.

The Self or Śiva is perfect by nature.[59] What does perfection mean? Some people think that in order to be perfect, Reality has to have everything in it, both good and bad. But there is no numerical sense in perfection. To say that Reality or Śiva is perfect does not mean that Śiva contains everything numerically or quantitatively. Perfection means that Śiva lacks nothing — there is no want in Śiva. Thus perfection is a state of complete fulfillment or enrichment. It is the state in which all desires are fulfilled; therefore it is a desireless state. Abhinavagupta calls the state of perfection *nirāśansa*, which means desireless. This is not inconsistent with the position that Śiva wills the creation of the world, for Creation is *spanda*, or a spontaneous overflow of the joy of Śiva, and not the outcome of any desire to fulfill some lack or want.

Perfection also implies that only the desirable is present, which goes against that idea that perfection should encompass everything. To admit to undesirable or bad things would mean imperfection. To be imperfect means to be limited or finite. One cannot do or be everything that one wants to be; there are limitations, or checks, on one. It is obvious that one can be fully happy only when one is able to do or be whatever one wants to, only when there are no limitations on one. Suffering means there is something one does not want that is present, or one cannot accomplish a desired goal. This means one is in the predicament of being limited, or finite, and happiness lies in becoming limitless, or infinite. The *Chāndogya Upaniṣad* says, "That which is the infinite (*bhūmā*); there lies happiness (*sukha*); there is no happiness in the finite (*alpa*)."[60]

If one is imperfect or limited it further implies that one is not free. Again, happiness (*ānanda*) requires that one be free, that there be no sanction or compulsion on one, either from within or from without. That is why freedom (*svātantrya*) is said to be the power of happiness (*ānanda-śakti*). Kashmir Śaivism emphasizes the freedom of Śiva;[61] freedom is seen as the very nature of Śiva.

Thus we see that happiness or bliss lies in perfection, infinitude, and freedom. In fact, all four terms — perfection, infinitude, freedom, and happiness — mean virtually the same thing. So, Śiva may be called perfect, infinite, free, or blissful — it all means the same.

There is a significant point that should be mentioned in this context. The notion of perfection demands that Śiva, or God, be good. A "bad" God is no God at all. To be bad is to be imperfect morally and spiritually. This point has been fully understood and emphasized in the Tantric tradition. That is why Reality (Consciousness, Self, or God) is termed "Śiva," which means "good," "benign," or "noble." It implies the meaning of the terms piety, nobility, uprightness, love, kindness, righteousness, and compassion all in one.

Here it should also be made clear that the "goodness" of Śiva is not what is technically called ethical or moral goodness, but spiritual goodness, which naturally includes within itself the merits of moral goodness also. Morality is naturally present in spirituality. Śiva by His very nature is good. He does not become good by a deliberate act — but goodness naturally or spontaneously overflows in Him. A moral act is not spontaneous; it is done by a deliberate effort. Moreover, there is the sense of one's being the agent or the doer of the moral act. The ego sense is involved. This may also generate a feeling of pride in being moral. But in spirituality there is no ego sense; goodness flows naturally or spontaneously.

Moreover, in "moral" consciousness we find a dichotomy between what is called the good (*śreya*) and the pleasant (*preya*). One may have to choose the good at the cost of the pleasant. But in "spiritual" consciousness this dichotomy simply does not exist; in spirituality there is a natural synthesis of the good and the pleasant, or Truth and Beauty. What is good (*śiva*) is also pleasant (*ānanda*). Thus spirituality is better than morality, which is normally taken to be the highest value, for spirituality naturally incorporates within itself the merits of morality minus the demerits. The word "spiritual," that is, pertaining to spirit, is used because egoless and spontaneous goodness is taken to be the very nature of the pure "Spirit." Śiva is pure Spirit or pure Consciousness.

Part II — Śakti[1]

THE NATURE OF ŚAKTI

According to the Advaita Vedāntic interpretation of the Upaniṣads, Ultimate Reality, which is Consciousness or the Self, is pure knowledge (*jñāna*). It is static, so to say, as it is devoid of all activity (*niṣkriya*). It is also devoid of self-consciousness; as there is no duality in it, the Self has no not-self to contend with. According to the Āgamic tradition, on the contrary, Consciousness (*citi* or *saṁvit*) is knowledge (*jñāna*) and activity (*kriyā*) in one. Śiva, or the Self, is actually Śiva and Śakti, *jñāna* and *kriyā*, or *prakāśa* and *vimarśa* in one.[2] Śiva and Śakti are *two* only by connotation; by denotation they are one and the same. Śiva, or Consciousness, is conceived of as dynamic, and the very dynamism of Śiva is called Śakti, or *kriyā*. A current of water is water and current both in one. The current, or flow, is not a separate entity, it is just water that is flowing. The word *flow* is used simply to connote the state of the water, namely its fluidity. The entity denoted by the two words *water* and *flow* is one and the same; yet we can meaningfully use two words. The linguistic usage may create the illusion that there are two corresponding entities. But all words do not denote entities. The same is true in the case of Śiva and Śakti. The word *Śakti* is used simply to connote the nature of Śiva, or Consciousness; activity or dynamism (*spanda*) is the nature of Śiva, and Śakti is just the name given to this dynamism. Śakti therefore is nothing but the nature of Śiva. The symbolism of Śiva-Śakti cannot and should not be taken literally.

The symbol of Ardhanārīśvara is meant to suggest the unity of Śiva and Śakti. In the symbol the male (Śiva) and the female (Śakti) are not *two* persons; they are a single person who is both man and woman, or Śiva and Śakti. The symbolism of Ardhanārīśvara seen in the stone images and paintings, however, is not a perfect one, because in the symbol one side is Śiva and the other side Śakti. But there is no such partition in Reality. The whole of Reality is Śiva, and the whole of it is Śakti as well. However, we face limitations in the artistic media when Reality is to be expressed in symbol. A stone can only be carved half and half to depict both man and woman in the same figure. One technique that might more closely convey the concept of two persons in one are the pictures that when looked at from one angle show one scene, and when looked at from the opposite side, show another. The symbol of Ardhanārīśvara, if pictured using this technique, would be a better symbol of Reality.

The key concept of the Āgamic philosophy is the *kriyā*[3] or Śakti principle, which distinguishes Tantric philosophy from other systems of thought, especially from Advaita Vedānta.[4] All other points of distinction in Tantric philosophy can be derived from this single concept. Since the *kriyā* of Śiva is not mechanical or determined activity, it is called *svātantrya* ("freedom").

In order to understand the exact nature of *kriyā*, it must be distinguished, on the one hand, from ethical action that is voluntary and effortful, and on the other hand, from automatic activity that is mechanical and determined. While performing volitional or ethical action, one has to exert one's will or make an effort. This is not *kriyā*, as *kriyā* is effortless activity; it is spontaneous, natural, or automatic, so to say. At the same time it is not automatic reflex action, nor like the mechanical activity of a robot, nor the obsessional behavior of a psycho-neurotic; all these activities are determined, not free. In *kriyā* there is freedom; one is not bound to perform the activity; one simply allows the activity to flow. The activity is perfectly in tune with oneself. One can, if one likes, check or dismiss the whole process. *Kriyā*, therefore, has both the merits of freedom and effortlessness. It is, therefore, called spontaneity (*spanda*). *Spanda*, or *kriyā*, may be called a kind of natural activity, free and spontaneous.[5]

We may find examples of actual experiences in our ordinary life where we can have some inkling of *kriyā*. These examples, however, are not instances of pure *kriyā*, but they can help us to understand the idea of *kriyā*. Take the example of joy. When we are extremely joyful, jubilant activities like singing, dancing, and so on may automatically flow from us. Or, when we happen to meet, after a long period of separation, someone who is very dear to us, we may spontaneously perform certain joyful activities in his or her welcome. When a child plays, it has no motive; it is quite natural for a child to play. This does not mean that the act of playing is mechanical or determined; it is free and spontaneous on the part of the child. It does not result from some lack or want in the child; it ensues from the joy and fullness of the child. The child's free play is a replica of the creation of the world out of the joy of the Absolute. A child's natural playing, free and spontaneous, is an example of *kriyā*, although not a perfect one. *Kriyā* activities are not willfully done. They spring forth automatically, yet we feel free while doing them or, rather, allowing them to occur through us. There is no compulsion on our part, for the activity is not forced on us either from external factors or from internal ones like urges and instincts. It is not that we engage in the activity against our will, as in the case of obsessional neuroses.

The reason that pure examples of *kriyā* are not found in our ordinary life is, according to Tantra, that in ordinary experience the flow of pure *kriyā* is obstructed and defiled by what is called *mala* ("dirt" or "ignorance"). The moment one is perfectly freed from *mala*, one finds oneself exhibiting perfect currents of pure *kriyā*. In actual life there is partial *kriyā* because there is partial freedom or partial perfection.[6] Pure *kriyā* is possible only in the state of perfection that is found in the life of a *jīvanmukta.*

In Advaita Vedānta and allied systems there is no distinction between *kriyā* and *karma.*[7] For the Advaitin all *kriyā* seems to be nothing but *karma*, which is volitional or ethical action. The Tantric philosophers, however, are very careful in using the words *kriyā* and *karma.* They never equate the two. In fact, they, like all other Indian philosophers, hold that what is called *karma* is bondage; as such it cannot occur with *jñāna* ("knowledge"). This differentiation of *kriyā* from *karma* is a unique contribution of the Tantric tradition. The Advaitin does not care to take into account such an important aspect of our actual experience.

COMPATIBILITY OF ŚAKTI (KRIYĀ) WITH ŚIVA (JÑĀNA)

The Advaita Scholiast may question the compatibility of *kriyā* and *jñāna.* The Advaitin would say that if Śiva, or the Self, is considered perfect, then there can be no *kriyā* in Śiva. *Kriyā*, or *karma* as the Advaitin would understand it, is a mark of imperfection—we perform action only when there is some want or lack that we want to fulfill. In answer to this it may be pointed out that this objection is valid only with regard to the voluntary action that we call *karma.* It is not valid with regard to *kriyā*, which is spontaneous and natural activity. It is natural in the sense that it is not caused by any motive and there is no exertion of the will. Even Gauḍapāda, an Advaitin, accepts this position when he, explaining Creation, says, "This (Creation) is the very nature of the Lord; what shall a perfect Being desire."[8] The Advaitin may still ask, "If in Śiva there is no need, incentive, or motive for doing anything, what shall account for His doings?" In answer we would say that this is accounted for by the freedom (*svātantrya*) of Śiva. Śiva need not do and yet He does. Śiva is not compelled to do; neither is Śiva compelled not to do.

If one wants an explanation for Śiva's activity, we would say that when Consciousness is free and full it naturally overflows in creative activity. This does not mean that Śiva is acting all the time. Śiva is free to act, but also free to withhold all activity and sit in silence in Himself enjoying the inner bliss of his nature (*svarūpāmarśana*). It is natural for a child to burst into playing, but this does not mean that the child plays twenty-four hours a day. *Kriyā*, therefore, can go with the state of desirelessness, or perfection. We would say, on the contrary, that *kriyā*, or spontaneous activity, is possible only when we, even to some extent, attain the state of desirelessness. This statement is substantiated by cases in actual experience. For example, we feel like playing, singing, or doing anything of the kind only when we are relatively free and full.[9] When we are burdened with cares and anxieties, we do not feel like doing so. All true artistic creativity spontaneously emanates from the freedom and fullness of the artist. Artistic creativity is an example, although an imperfect one, of *kriyā*. The Upaniṣads also adopt this position when they declare, "All these things spring forth from the Bliss itself."[10]

The point is that the desireless, perfect state of Consciousness need not be devoid of activity. It is quite possible that one is free from all compulsion, desire, and motive, yet sparks of joyful activity spring forth from oneself. This is exactly what is meant by *līlā*, ("play" or "sport") in the Tantric tradition, and by *mauja* ("free expression of joyful activity") in the Sufi mystic tradition. It is the unity of both the freedoms—"freedom-from" and "freedom-to." The Advaitic Scholiast seems to accept "freedom-from" and reject "freedom-to," as the Advaitin finds "freedom-to" incompatible with "freedom-from." The Advaitin would be justified only if "freedom-to" is construed in terms of motivated volitional ethical action (*karma*). But if "freedom-to" is understood in the sense of *kriyā* under reference, the two freedoms—"freedom from" and "freedom to" are quite compatible.

The second objection to the concept of the compatibility of *kriyā* and *jñāna* is that the natures of *jñāna* and *kriyā* are such that the two are opposed to each other. *Jñāna* is a passive state and, therefore, it cannot go with *kriyā*, or activity, which is diametrically opposed to the state of passivity. Moreover, action is subjective (*puruṣatantra*), while knowledge is objective (*vastutantra*). They are opposed to each other like light and darkness, as it were. How can these two contradictory ideas go together? In answer to the above objection it may be pointed out that this applies, again, to *karma* and not to *kriyā*. *Kriyā* is a state of both realization and activity. In *kriyā* one is not a doer in the effortful sense, as the activity flows automatically and there is no exertion of will. The state of *kriyā* may be expressed in a paradoxical statement like "passive activity," "actionless activity," or "relaxed activity."[11] Such activity is quite compatible with *jñāna*.

In India there is an age-old tradition of "passive activity." The *Bhagavad-Gītā* refers to this kind of activity in more than one place when it says, "While indulging in activity, he does nothing."[12] "I am the doer of it, yet take me not to be the doer."[13] "The Karmayogin, while performing all activity, knows that he is doing nothing,"[14] and so on. The *Yogavāśiṣṭha* also refers to the same when it says, "Having artificial willing outside, but inside having no willing at all, move in this world, O Rāghava, being a non-doer within and a doer without."[15] Or, "Move, O Rāghava, being heated (in activity) without and cool within."[16] The mystic saint-poet Kabir says, "All activity is done by me, yet I am away from action."[17]

The fact that *kriyā* is subjective does not disqualify *kriyā* from being a consort of *jñāna*. Being subjective simply means that one is free in doing. But why on earth should this be contradictory to *jñāna*? There can be a contradiction between the two only in the sense that *kriyā*, or *karma* as the Advaitin would take it, is a sign of imperfection, whereas *jñāna* is a state of perfection. We have already met this objection by showing that *kriyā* is different from *karma*.[18]

Kriyā ("activity") ordinarily involves *krama* ("sequence" or "succession").[19] Activity is usually a series of movements, one after the other. This further involves *kāla* ("time"). There can be no sequence without time; it is also true that there can be no time without sequence. In fact, sequence and time are one and the same; the very sense of "one after the other" is time.[20]

Although sequence (*krama*) seems to be the very nature of activity (*kriyā*), this is true in the case of ordinary activity (*laukika kriyā*) only; it does not apply to the eternal activity of the Lord.[21] There is no time in Ultimate Reality and thus there is no sequence there.[22] Śiva is *akrama* ("without sequence"). Therefore, the *kriyā* of the Śiva level is also *akrama*, or non-sequential.

Here a very serious objection may be raised. How can there be non-sequential activity? Abhinavagupta in the introduction to verse 2.1.2 of the *Īśvarapratyabhijñā-kārikā*, himself raises this objection, representing the *pūrvapakṣin*, when he says, "Sequence is the very nature of *kriyā* ("activity"), but there is no *krama* ("sequence") in the Lord devoid of time, and so there can be no activity (*kriyā*) in Him (Śiva)."[23] In response, however, Abhinavagupta says, "Just as sequence is not possible in the Lord (Śiva), so sequence is not possible in His activity either."[24]

But to be fair to the opponent, what Abhinavagupta says in his answer is just the statement of a position and not an explanation or justification of that position. To say that "since Śiva is *akrama*, the *kriyā* of Śiva is also *akrama*" is no answer to the objection that there can be no activity in the non-sequential state of Śiva-consciousness. If activity (*kriyā*) is without sequence (*krama*), it is not activity at all. To call it activity is a misnomer; in fact, "non-sequential activity" (*akrama-kriyā*) is a contradiction in terms. Maintaining the notion of *akrama-kriyā* is like arguing that "ordinary fire is hot, but divine fire is not hot." If the so-called divine fire is not hot, it is not fire at all; calling it fire is a contradiction in terms. The basic question of the opponent is how the existence of non-sequential activity is at all possible. The argument of the opponent tends to rule out the very possibility of *akrama-kriyā.*

Though Abhinavagupta has not explicitly answered the above objection by showing or proving the possibility of non-sequential activity, the answer is implicitly present in his position.[25] Reality is Consciousness (*cinmaya*)[26] and the activity of Consciousness would naturally be of the form of thinking (*vimarśa*) or willing (*kriyā*). In physical activity there is sequence (*krama*),[27] but in the activity of Consciousness, that is, in thinking or willing, there need not be *krama.* For example, if we had to construct a building, we would first construct the foundation, then the plinth, the walls, the roof, and so on, placing the bricks one by one. But if we had to construct the building with the mind, or consciousness, we could imagine the entire building at once. The activity here is not sequential, for we do not have to mentally lay the bricks one by one.

To use the example given by Abhinavagupta himself, the physical activity of cooking has different steps.[28] Moreover, the different steps are determined according to the laws of cause and effect. But there is no such determination in the activity within consciousness; we can freely think or mentally create all the steps of the cooking process, even all at once.[29] Sequence in activity is logically related to the determinism of cause and effect. Freedom (*svātantrya*) and sequence-less activity (*akrama-kriyā*) are also logically related. In physical activity we cannot by-pass the successive steps of the activity at will, as they are causally related. But in the case of the activity of consciousness, we can think or create the different steps at will, so the activity need not have sequence.[30] Freedom is the unique characteristic of Consciousness; Consciousness does not depend upon anything else for its activity. Naturally, therefore, it can have sequence-less activity.[31]

Moreover, even in the realm of physical activity, there are examples of non-sequential activity (*akrama-kriyā*). For instance, if one presses a cushion with one's leg and continues holding the leg against the cushion and not removing it, then this is an activity in which there is no sequence, for there are no gaps within the activity as a whole; the activity of pressing the cushion is a single act in continuity.[32]

The opponent may further object that even if it is granted that there is non-sequential activity, the activity still involves time, as continuity of activity is in time. Since time comes at a lower stage of creation, and there is no time in the Ultimate, Śiva, there can be no activity in timeless Śiva. In answer to this, I will point out two things. First, the epistemological constitution of our ordinary consciousness is such that we cannot but conceive of anything as being or happening in time; time is a necessary condition of our thinking. Though Reality, or Śiva, is timeless (*akāla*), when we try to conceive of it, we have to use the category of time. When we try to picture the "Timeless" (*akāla*), we conceive of it only as "Eternal Time" (*mahākāla*). So the *kriyā* of Śiva is timeless, yet we can conceive of it only as an indivisible continuity of time. This is a limitation of our thinking.

Second, just as it is possible to conceive of a non-sequential activity, so is it possible to conceive of a non-sequential time, or a "timeless time."[33] This would be something like the "timeless duration" posited by the followers of T. H. Green and Henry Bergson. This paradoxical "timeless time," or "timeless duration," is not a self-contradictory notion but a possibility that suggests the idea of continuity without sequence or break. This "time" would be equated with Śakti or *kriyā* itself.

ŚIVA-ŚAKTI RELATIONSHIP

I have already explained that Śiva and Śakti are not two realities or even two parts of one reality—the relation between the two is that of identity. As to the question of why, then, we use two separate words *Śiva* and *Śakti*, which suggests that there are two, I have already explained that the difference between the two is merely connotative, not denotative. The words connote two characteristics of one reality, but denote one and the same reality. Śiva is conceived of as dynamic, and the very dynamism of Śiva is called Śakti.

Although the relation of Śiva and Śakti is one of identity, in the texts we find allegorical references to Śiva-Śakti, which may suggest that the relationship is that of unity-in-difference, or even that of difference. The Tantras are full of allegory, symbol, and poetic expression. If one is not familiar with the tradition, one may be misled. There are three types of allegorical description, which may suggest the three following concepts of the relationship of Śiva and Śakti. (a) Śiva and Śakti are pictured as spouses or as a couple in love.[34] This suggests that Śiva and Śakti are two existing in harmony, which implies a duality of entity. (b) Śiva and Śakti are also known as Śaktimāna and Śakti. Śiva as Śaktimāna ("the possessor of Śakti or power") suggests a substance-quality relationship. Śiva is the substance and Śakti is its quality, the power possessed by Śiva.[35] (c) Śiva and Śakti are also said to be identical, the difference being just in name.[36] Following the line of thought expressed in Kashmir Śaivism, it becomes obvious that, out of the above three alternatives, the third one is the real position of Kashmir Śaivism. Reality is one and the same, whether it is called Śiva or Śakti. As to why, then, the other types of description are given in the texts, the answer is simple. These descriptions are symbolic and poetic, they are not meant to be taken literally. The identity of Śiva and Śakti may well be described allegorically using dualistic language.

Abhinavagupta makes it clear by explicitly referring to the *Vaiśeṣika* philosophy of Kaṇāda that in the philosophy of Śiva, or Kashmir Śaivism, Śakti is not a quality (*dharma*) and therefore it does not have any substratum (*āśraya*).[37] In the notion of a substance-quality relationship, the substance is the substratum that holds the qualities, and the qualities *reside* in it or are held by it. This further implies that there is a difference between the substance and the quality. But this is not the case in Kashmir Śaivism. Here Śakti is not a quality of Śiva; Śakti *is* Śiva. It is said in the *Tantrāloka* that if Śakti is different from Śiva, even in the sense of being the quality that resides in Śiva, then the statement made in the Trika tradition, that Śiva (or Śakti) alone exists[38] would be meaningless.

Thus the term *Śiva-Śakti-Sāmarasya* used to denote the unity of Śiva and Śakti, does *not* imply that Śiva and Śakti are *two* existing in harmony. The reality denoted by the two terms is one and the same, whether it is called Śiva or Śakti.

KINDS OF ŚAKTI

When the question of the kinds of Śakti is raised, the first question that may be asked is whether Śakti is one or many. Śakti has many different functions and is given a separate name for each role she plays. This may give the idea that there are many *śaktis* instead of one.

In answer to the above question we would point out that Śakti is really one, it is called many only with reference to the different results or ends it achieves.[39] For example, the burning power of fire and the cooking power of fire are *two* only with regard to the different results produced by them. As far as the power (*śakti*) itself is concerned, there is no difference between the burning and cooking powers.[40] Śakti, the power of Śiva, manifests itself in different forms of activity. There is really no pluralism of Śakti, nor does the non-dualism of Śiva diminish by any means.[41] Śiva is free to act as He likes, and the *śaktis* termed variously *icchā*, *jñāna*, *kriyā*, and so on, are the manifestations of His freedom (*svātantrya*) which is *the* Śakti.[42] Śakti really means "freedom" or "freedom to act" and this one Śakti is expressed in different forms of activity.

In Kashmir Śaivism as in the Tantric tradition in general, there are five denominations of Śakti classified into four hierarchical grades that correlate with the four stages of *Vāk-śakti* ("Speech- or Word-power"). These five denominations are *cit*, *ānanda*, *icchā*, *jñāna*, and *kriyā*. *Cit* and *ānanda* belong to the first stage of *Vāk-śakti*, which is really not a stage at all, as it is the transcendent level of Ultimate Consciousness where there is no world or Creation. These two are the correlates of the transcendent categories (*tattvas*) Śiva and Śakti. Since Śiva and Śakti are not two realities but one, the two belong to the same level. Naturally, therefore, *cit-śakti* and *ānanda-śakti* also belong to the same transcendent level (*para* or *parā*). Since this is the transcendent stage of Consciousness where there is no duality — the process of Creation having not begun — it is the stage of pure unity. Hence, it is the stage of pure *aham*, the pure subject or the "I am," not the stage of *ahamidam* ("I am this"), as the "this," the object, or the world, has not yet arisen.

The other three *śaktis* — *icchā*, *jñāna*, and *kriyā* — which are lower than *cit* and *ānanda* and which are placed in hierarchical order, are related to the process of Creation. Hence they arise only when the process of Creation begins. (See chart below).

Cit-śakti is the power of awareness, illumination, or knowledge. The difference between consciousness and insentient matter (*jaḍa*) is that insentient matter does not "know" whereas consciousness "knows." Here "knowledge" is used not in the sense of knowledge of any specific object, but in the general sense of awareness or illumination.[43]

Ānanda-śakti is the bliss that is naturally present in Śiva. It is said to be the very nature of the Self, which means that for Śiva joy is not caused by any exterior thing as is the case with the bound individual, but exists in Śiva by itself. Śiva is made of joy, as it were. To use an analogy, the light of the moon is not its own light; it is borrowed from the sun. Light is not the nature of the moon. But in the case of the sun the light is not borrowed from anything else; light is the very nature of the sun. Light flows from the sun by itself. Similarly, bliss flows naturally from the Self, as bliss constitutes the Self.

Bliss implies freedom. That is why *ānanda-śakti* is defined as *svātantrya*, or "freedom." Suffering means one is bound by limitations; one needs or wants something that is not within one's power to achieve. Conversely, happiness means one attains whatever one

Śakti	Tattva	Vak	Degree of Differentiation			Experient
Cit-Ānanda	Śiva-Śakti	Parā	Aham ("I am")	Pure unity	Pure subject or pure self (without object-consciousness)	Śiva-pramātā
Icchā	Sadāśiva	Paśyantī	Ahamidam ("I am this")	Unity-in-difference (difference in the potential form — āsūtraṇa)	The subject just emitting the object	Mantra-Maheśvara-pramātā
Jñāna	Īśvara	Madhyamā	Idamaham ("This I am")	Unity-in-difference (difference more manifest as ideation — Vimarśa)	The subject fully ideating the object	Mantreśvara-pramātā
Kriyā	Sadvidyā	Vaikharī	Ahañca idañca ("I am and this is")	Unity-in-difference (difference fully manifest as appearance — Ābhāsa)	The subject externally projecting the object as ābhāsa	Mantra-pramātā

The Stages of Śakti

wants; there is no gap between one's wishing and the wish being fulfilled. *Ānanda* means there are no limitations in one's way; one is perfectly free.

The reason why *ānanda* is called *ānanda-śakti* is that *śakti* means dynamism, and *ānanda* is dynamic. The Tantric tradition had the significant insight that *ānanda* or "joy," is really *kriyā* or *spanda*. *Ānanda* is not a static state of consciousness. Rather, it is a flow of Consciousness. This flow may be an inward motion, a flow within Consciousness itself. This may sometimes express itself in the outward flow of creative activity. When we are in a state of inner contentment and are not doing anything, even then there is an inward, silent flow of Consciousness. This particular state of *ānanda* is symbolically expressed in the smile of Lord Śaṅkara in the Śāmbhavī mudrā. The outward flow of *ānanda* is expressed in the form of the cosmic dance of creation, the symbolic dance (*nṛtya*) of Śiva Naṭarāja. *Ānanda* in any form is *kriyā*. That is why *ānanda* is called *ānanda-śakti*.

The triad of *icchā-jñāna-kriyā* describes the process of creation. *Icchā* means the will to create. When Śiva desires[44] to create the world, or manifest Himself in the form of the world, this is *icchā*. *Icchā* is the first spark (*camatkāra*)[45] of the creational activity in Śiva.

It should be noted here that in the case of Śiva, *icchā* is not like ordinary volition in which we have to exert our will or make an effort; *icchā* in Śiva arises spontaneously and effortlessly (*anāyāsa*). The will here is spontaneous will.

After the will to create the world arises in the mind of Śiva, the next step is that of the ideation (*jñāna*) of the world. The full mental[46] picture of what is to be created comes to the mind of Śiva. Since in this stage the world remains an idea or mental image in Śiva, it is called *jñāna*. In this case *jñāna* does not mean awareness, or illumination, that is the nature of Consciousness. It means idea or ideation. Since an idea in the mind is nothing but *jñāna*, it is called *jñāna*.[47]

After the mental picture (*jñāna*) of the would-be created world becomes complete in the mind of Śiva, the next step is that of externally projecting the world as appearance (*ābhāsa*). This is called *kriyā*, which means the external activity of creation.[48] In the case of ordinary creation, such as the creation of a pot by a potter, the creation is a physical or material one. But in the case of Śiva there is no material creation; the world is created or projected as a reflection, or *ābhāsa* ("appearance"), like the reflection in a mirror. Since the reflection in a mirror is not just an idea (*jñāna*) of the mind but an actual appearance (*ābhāsa*) outside the mind, it can be called external or even physical. Thus, *kriyā* is the externalization or physicalization of the idea (*jñāna*). *Kriyā* in this sense does not mean the *vimarśa* that is the nature of *prakāśa* or Śiva; it means a particular step in creation, the last step—external projection.

There is sometimes a misunderstanding regarding the meaning of *icchā-jñāna-kriyā*. Non-specialists sometimes understand it as "knowing-willing-feeling," which are the three faculties of the mind. But this is a gross misunderstanding of the terms. *Icchā*, *jñāna*, and *kriyā* are the three hierarchical steps of creation, which are found in any kind of creation. When an architect constructs a building, he or she first wills to construct it. This is *icchā*. Then the entire picture or idea of the would-be building forms in his or her mind; the building is erected in the form of a clear idea. This is *jñāna*. Then the architect actually constructs the building—the building comes into physical existence. This is *kriyā*. In the creation of the universe, too, the Lord first wills to create (*icchā*); then the entire picture of the would-be universe clearly forms in Śiva-consciousness as ideation (*jñāna*); finally the Lord actually creates the universe by bringing it into visible existence (*kriyā*).

It should also be noted that the terms *jñāna* and *kriyā* are not used here in the general sense of illumination and dynamism (*prakāśa* and *vimarśa*), which are the connotations of Śiva and Śakti. They are used here in the special sense of steps of creation. When anything to be created forms as an idea in the mind, it is *jñāna*, and when it is actually created as an external reality, it is *kriyā*. *Jñāna* is the internal or mental creation of anything; *kriyā* is the external or physical creation of the same.

THE TWO LEVELS OF ŚAKTI

The manifestation of the world, or the *idam* ("this"), is the freedom (*svātantrya*) of the *aham* ("I") or the Absolute. There is a misunderstanding of the Tantric position that Creation is a logical implication or necessary outcome of Śiva or Śakti. This misunderstanding is based on Tantric statements to the effect that the world is the nature (*svabhāva*) of Śiva-Śakti or that Śiva, out of His sport (*līlā*), again and again creates, preserves, and destroys the world (*carīkarti barībharti sañjarīharti līlayā*).[49]

The Tantric statement that Creation is the nature of Śiva or *parāśakti* is made in the same way that we say that playing is the nature of a child. This does not mean that playing is a necessity or compulsion for the child or that the child plays all day long. It simply means that there is no cause or motive for the play—it is just natural for the child to play. It does not contradict the fact that the act of playing is the freedom of the child. We can very well say, on the one hand, that playing is the freedom of the child, and, on the other hand, that playing is the nature of the child. When it is said that creation is the nature of Śiva, it simply means that for creation there is no motive or cause on the part of Śiva; creation arises out of His free sportive nature[50] and Śiva always creates out of His freedom.

If we take Creation to be a necessary act of Śiva or Śakti, it will go against the concept of freedom (*svātantrya*) that is basic to Tantrism. Moreover, the Tantras declare Creation to be the freedom (*svātantrya*) of Śiva in unequivocal terms. Furthermore Śiva, or Śiva-Śakti, is basically regarded as transcendent (*anuttara*). Śiva cannot be transcendent if Creation is a compulsion for Him.

The misunderstanding that the act of creation is necessary for Śiva arises from overlooking the distinction between *śakti* and *svarūpa-śakti*. In the Tantric tradition *cit* and *ānanda* are said to be the nature (*svarūpa* or *svarūpa-śakti*), whereas the triad of *icchā-jñāna-kriyā*, which pertains to the creation of the world, is said to be power (*śakti*) but not *svarūpa-śakti*. *Cit* and *ānanda* are *svarūpa*, but the triad of *icchā-jñāna-kriyā*, or the Creation of the world, is not *svarūpa* in the technical sense of *svarūpa-lakṣaṇa*. Creation is based only on the freedom of the Lord.[51] He may enact the cosmic function of creation, maintenance, and so on forever, for some time, or not at all.

In Tantrism, because the world is said to be Śakti or *kriyā*, and because Śakti or *kriyā* is said to be the nature of Śiva, the world should be regarded as the nature of Śiva. But what is overlooked here is the truth that only *cit-ānanda*, not all Śakti, is the nature (*svarūpa*) of Śiva. *Icchā-jñāna-kriyā*, which results in Creation, is not the *svarūpa* in the technical sense. The activity (*kriyā*) that is at the *svarūpa* level (*cit-ānanda*), and that is illumined in itself, is only *aham* ("I am").[52] It is not *ahamidam* ("I am this"), which comes only at the level of Creation (*icchā-jñāna-kriyā*). *Aham* or Self-consciousness, therefore, is said to be the eternal activity or eternal dynamism (*nitya-kriyā* or *nitya-spanda*) of Consciousness. The free act of Creation may also be said to be eternal or even innate (*svarūpa*) in the sense that Śiva freely performs the cosmic functions of creation, and so on. Creation is not a necessity to Śiva; it is a manifestation of His freedom (*svātantrya*). It is meaningless to say that Śiva may not be *cit-ānanda*, for Śiva is nothing but *cit-ānanda*. However, it is perfectly meaningful to say that Śiva *may not* create the world. Creation completely depends upon the will of Śiva.

SYNONYMS AND SYMBOLS OF ŚAKTI

We find in the Tantras, and also in Abhinavagupta, various synonyms for Śakti. As synonyms they all denote the same Śakti. But different synonyms are used in order to emphasize various aspects or characteristics of Śakti. Each synonym of Śakti carries a particular connotation that refers to a particular characteristic, aspect, or facet of Śakti. So, every synonym is significant.

There are four or five major synonyms for Śakti—*Śakti*, *kriyā*, *vimarśa*, *spanda*, and *svātantrya*. Śakti literally means "power," "force," or "energy." It is the potentiality of all activity. Even when there is no actual activity, there is the potentiality or the capacity for activity. Śakti basically means potentiality. When this potentiality actualizes or becomes manifest in actual activity, it is called *kriyā*. *Kriyā* is function, movement, flow, or actual dynamism. Consciousness is dynamic, so *kriyā* is the very nature of Consciousness. Since Consciousness is a potential power, force, or energy that actualizes in activity, it is called Śakti. If Śakti is potentiality, *kriyā* is actuality.

This *kriyā* ("activity") is not physical activity, but activity in consciousness — mental activity, so to speak; thus it is called *vimarśa* ("thinking"). According to the idealistic Kashmir Śaivism system, there is no physical reality or matter; there is only Consciousness (*citi* or *saṁvit*). Naturally, therefore, the activity of Consciousness is not physical activity; the activity of Consciousness takes the form of thinking (*vimarśa*). *Vimarśa* or *āmarśa* literally means "thinking." Since the activity of Consciousness is of the thinking type, it is called *vimarśa*. *Vimarśa* is used to suggest that the activity of Śiva is not physical. Even at the *paśu* level activity is not physical, for the world is a mental projection or appearance of consciousness, as in a dream. In a dream, what appears as physical or bodily activity is really the thinking of the mind. So *kriyā* is also *jñāna*.[53]

Kriyā is also called *svātantrya* because the activity (*kriyā*) of Śiva is not bound or conditioned but is completely free. Generally, compulsion for doing something can come from two sides. First, there may be external circumstances that compel the doer to act in a particular way. Second, there may be inner urges and desires that compel action. But in the case of Śiva, there is no conditioning or compulsion from within or from without. Śiva is perfectly free (*svatantra*) to act or not to act, or to act in the way He wishes. Śiva is a state of complete "freedom-to." So, the activity of Śiva can aptly be called *svātantrya* ("freedom").

Kriyā, again, is not the effortful voluntary action that we perform by exerting our will but is spontaneous activity, so it is called *spanda. Spanda* means the free and automatic vibration of activity; in other words, it means spontaneity. Spontaneous activity is different from what is called *karma* ("effortful voluntary activity"). The word *spanda* carries the sense of both freedom and spontaneity, the sense of being automatic or effortless. Thus *spanda* is the most perfect term for the activity of Śiva.

In the Tantric texts, Śakti is described through symbols. One characteristic of the Tantric tradition is that there is a very rich and effective symbolism found therein. The significance of symbol, and also of myth, is that it appeals to the heart or feeling and thereby works a powerful effect on the spiritual aspirant. Tantrism is a spiritual discipline, so it aims at mobilizing the heart of the spiritual seeker (*sādhaka*). This is most effectively done through symbols, myths, and allegories.

Śakti is symbolized as a woman or the mother. The *jñāna* aspect of Consciousness is symbolized as Śāṅkara (male) and the *kriyā* aspect as Pārvatī (female). In the Buddhist Tantric tradition, however, the *jñāna* aspect is seen as female and the *kriyā* aspect as male. Perhaps the Buddhists think that activity is the sign of masculinity. In Hindu Tantra the reason for accepting the female as the symbol of Śakti may be the following: Of a child's two parents, the father is associated with reason or intellect that guides, disciplines, and admonishes (and so on) the children, whereas the mother is primarily conceived of as all love and affection for the children. So the mother is associated with the heart, which is the seat of emotions and feelings. It is obvious that the power to act comes from the emotions, the heart, and not from reason, the head. Reason or intellect controls the activity, but the actual activity ensues from the emotional aspect of the personality. Thus it is understandable why the mother or woman, the person of heart, is made the symbol of Śakti.

The mother symbol, Pārvatī or Umā, taken to be the consort of Śaṅkara, is expressed in the various forms of Durgā, Caṇḍī, Kālī, Lakṣmī, and so on. The multiple arms of Durgā may be taken as symbolic of multiple facets of activity or Śakti. Triguṇa-śakti, or the triad of Sarasvatī, Lakṣmī, and Kālī, which are the different forms of Durgā/Pārvatī, may be taken as a symbol of the triad of *icchā-jñāna-kriyā*, or the triad of sāttvic, rājasic, and tāmasic forces of our minds. All the sāttvic, rājasic, and tāmasic tendencies are forces, or *śaktis*, and as such can be mobilized towards spiritual advancement. Sarasvatī is said to be formed of sāttva, so she symbolizes the sāttvika qualities; Mahālakṣmi and Mahākālī symbolize the rājasic and the tāmasic qualities respectively. They may also be taken as symbols of *icchā-jñāna-kriyā*: Mahāsarasvatī symbolizing the subtle creation of the world in the form of will; Mahālakṣmi the comparatively more active and more manifest form of creation as ideation or *jñāna*; and Mahākālī the grossest and the most manifest form of creation as the external world.

In the left-handed (*vāma* or *kaula*) Tantric tradition, Śakti is worshipped through sexual union, a means given by Nature. There, Śakti is taken as Bhairavī, who is in eternal sexual union with Bhairava (Śiva). She is also called Tripurā, Tripurā-bhairavī, Tripurasundarī, or simply Sundarī ("the beautiful"), Vāmā ("the better half"), or Ṣoḍaśī ("the damsel of sixteen years"). The Divine Śakti is worshipped as a very beautiful goddess who is Sarveśvarī ("the queen of all").

The Yogic name for Śakti is *kuṇḍalinī* ("the serpent power"). Tantrism is a yogic tradition employing yogic symbols for the Power of Consciousness. *Kuṇḍalinī* literally means "female serpent." Since Śakti is symbolized as a woman and since the word *śakti* is grammatically feminine, all the symbols of Śakti are naturally in the female gender. This serpent is said to be seated in the human body at the base of the spine beneath the genitals. The serpent is the unconscious symbol of libido or sex energy. Libido is perhaps the most primal and important form of energy, which when sublimated, expresses itself in the form of love, devotion to God (*bhakti*), aesthetic creativity, and so on. So the serpent is an appropriate symbol for the primal energy working in our personality. *Kuṇḍalinī* is said to be lying half asleep, which means that the *citi-śakti* is already working in our personality, although not fully. The *śakti* can be awakened or aroused to work with its full force.

Kuṇḍalinī is really the Power of Consciousness (*citi-śakti*), which is working in us at different levels. At the biological level the *citi-śakti*, or *kuṇḍalinī* as it is symbolically called, is working in the form of the vital energy (*prāṇa-śakti*) and is called *prāṇa-kuṇḍalinī.* At the mental level the same *citi-śakti /kuṇḍalinī* works in the form of mental activity and is called *nāda-kuṇḍalinī* or *Śakti-kuṇḍalinī.* At the spiritual level *kuṇḍalinī* works in the form of spiritual enlightenment and is called *bodha-kuṇḍalinī* or *parā-kuṇḍalinī*, which means the highest *kuṇḍalinī.*[54]

ŚAKTI AS VĀK ("SPEECH")

Śakti in the Tantric tradition is conceived of as *vāk* ("speech" or "word") with its four levels of *parā*, *paśyantī*, *madhyamā*, and *vaikharī.* The entire Creation is taken to be the manifestation of *vāk.*[55]

4

The Process of Creation

THE THEORY OF CAUSATION

We have already seen that in a metaphysical Absolutism it is logically necessary to regard the world as substantially one with the ultimate reality, the Absolute. Kashmir Śaivism, like Advaita Vedānta, is an Absolutism, and thus here the world is regarded as a manifestation or extension (*prasāra*) of Śiva, which is the Absolute. Therefore the world is, in substance, one with Śiva. There is nothing in the universe that is other than Śiva.[1]

The absolutist theory of Creation implies a theory of causation in which the cause (*kārana*) and the effect (*kārya*) are regarded to be substantially one. According to Kashmir Śaivism, the world is the effect and Śiva, the absolute Consciousness, is the cause[2] and the two are substantially one, since the substance out of which the world is created is nothing but Śiva Himself.[3] Therefore the theory of causation accepted in Kashmir Śaivism is Satkāryavāda, which means the effect is not created out of nothing as an absolutely new existent, but is created out of the cause, which is its substance. Kashmir Śaivism accepts the Advaita Vedāntic and the Mādhyamika logic that nothing can come out of nothing. If, for example, a potter wants to create a pitcher, he or she will need clay as the material from which to make it; or if a mason has to erect a building, he or she will need bricks, mortar, and so on, with which to construct the building.

Absolute Consciousness or Śiva is the material out of which the world is created. So, Śiva is the material cause of the world. In the case of a potter's making a pitcher, the potter is the maker or what is technically called the efficient cause, and differs from the clay which is the material cause of the pitcher. But in the case of Śiva's creating the world, Śiva is both the material cause and the efficient cause of the world. Śiva creates the world not out of some external material but out of Himself.[4] In other words, Śiva Himself becomes the world. This is what is meant by saying that the world is a manifestation or extension of Śiva.[5]

But how can the world, which seems to be made of matter, come out of Śiva, which is Consciousness? Or, if Consciousness becomes matter, does Consciousness not become a different substance? The problem in the first place is that Consciousness cannot become matter, a substance totally different from Consciousness. Second, even if it is granted that Consciousness becomes matter, then the problem is that the world, made of matter, becomes a different substance, and we therefore cannot say that the world is substantially one with Consciousness or Śiva.

Perhaps this is the reason that the Sāṁkhya system, appreciating the above logic, maintains that the world of matter comes out of a material substance, which is *prakṛti*, and not from Consciousness, which is *puruṣa*. Advaita Vedānta also accepts the above-mentioned logic but moves in a different direction. Advaita Vedānta accepts the world as illusion (*mithyā*), which in turn means that the world is a mental projection like that in a dream or in the case of the rope-snake illusion. This solves the problem, as the world no longer remains a material substance but becomes Consciousness, for the dream object or the rope-snake is not real but ideal. It is made of the idea of the mind, the idea being substantially one with Consciousness. Even if the Upaniṣads do not clearly advocate Māyāvāda — the theory that the world is illusory — there is a rationale to the demand of Śaṅkarācārya that the world must be regarded as illusion in order to understand the statements of the Upaniṣads consistently. For example, the Upaniṣadic position that Brahman is Conscious-ness and that "all this is Brahman" (*sarvaṁ khalu idaṁ brahma*) can be understood consistently only when "all this" (the world) is taken to be illusory, for only then does the world substantially become one with Consciousness.

Kashmir Śaivism adopts almost the same position. The world, according to Kashmir Śaivism, is a conscious self-projection of Śiva-Consciousness.[6] As such, the world is made not of matter but of Consciousness; it is not a "real" but an "ideal" projection of Consciousness. However, Kashmir Śaivism differs from Advaita Vedānta in so far as the world, according to Kashmir Śaivism, is an active self-projection of Śiva, whereas according to Advaita Vedānta, it is a superimposition (*adhyāsa*) on Brahman and Brahman lies neutral.

Thus we see that while creating or becoming the world, Śiva-Consciousness does not become matter; it remains the same substance — Consciousness — for the substance of the "ideal" projection is Consciousness.[7] It is thus perfectly legitimate to say that the seemingly "material" world comes out of Consciousness, and that, while this is happening, Consciousness does not become a different substance.

What follows from the above position, and what is accepted in Kashmir Śaivism, is that the world is not a real transformation (*pariṇāma*) of Consciousness. Pariṇāmavāda is a sub-category of Satkāryavāda, and it means that the cause really or materially becomes the effect, as in the case of milk becoming curd. According to Rāmānuja, the world is a real transformation of Brahman (Brahma-pariṇāmavāda). So also, according to Sāṁkhya, the world is a *pariṇāma*, but it is the *pariṇāma* of the material principle, *prakṛti* (Prakṛti-pariṇāmavāda). But according to Advaita Vedānta and Kashmir Śaivism, the world is not a real transformation but a false manifestation of Brahman or Śiva. In Advaita Vedānta the false manifestation is called *vivarta*, and the world is the *vivarta* of Brahman

(Brahma-vivartavāda). In Kashmir Śaivism, however, the false manifestation is called *ābhāsa*, and the world is the *ābhāsa* of Śiva (Ābhāsavāda). Both *vivarta* and *ābhāsa* mean appearance or false manifestation — illusion. But according to the Vivartavāda of Advaita Vedānta, the illusory world is a superimposition on Brahman like the rope-snake, whereas, according to the Ābhāsavāda of Kashmir Śaivism, the illusory world is a free self-projection of Śiva like the creation of a yogi or a psychic magician.[8] Thus Vivartavāda and Ābhāsavāda fall on the same side opposite Pariṇāmavāda. Vivartavāda and Ābhāsavāda, on the one hand, and Pariṇāmavāda, on the other hand, are the two different sub-categories or sub-divisions of Satkāryavāda.

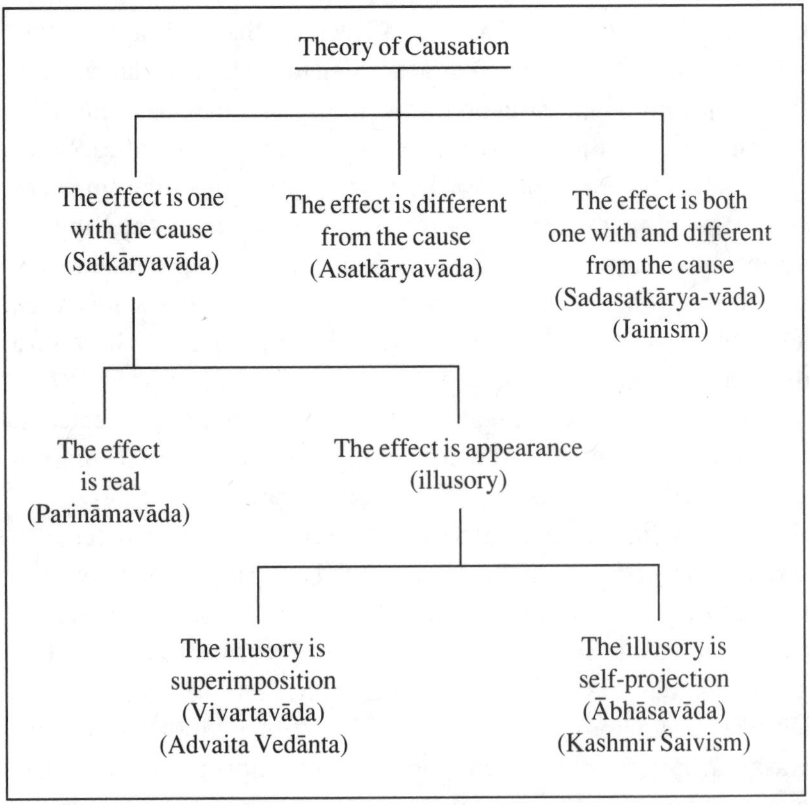

Theory of Causation

THE FIVE-FOLD COSMIC FUNCTIONS

Creation in Kashmir Śaivism, and in Indian philosophy in general, is seen as cyclic, not linear. The three states of creation (*sṛṣṭi*), preservation (*sthiti*), and dissolution (*saṁhṛti*) move in a cycle. Śiva again and again creates, preserves, and destroys the world.[9]

These three cosmic functions of the Divine Person are accepted by all systems of Indian philosophy that accept the world as Creation. Kashmir Śaivism, as Tantrism in general, accepts two additional functions. These are concealment (*nigraha*) and grace (*anugraha*).[10] When Śiva manifests Himself in the form of sentient individual souls (*paśus*) and insentient things of the world, He conceals His real nature, which is pure knowledge and pure bliss (*cidānanda*), and becomes limited and ignorant people and things.[11] This is part of His *līlā* or "sportive activity." The individual souls are not able to see the real form of Śiva because their vision is obstructed by impurity; Śiva conceals His identity from them. This is "concealment" or "bondage" (*nigraha*). But Śiva also liberates the souls by removing the obstruction or impurity; He actually creates the opportunity for the souls to work out their liberation. This is called "grace" (*anugraha*). The five-fold cosmic function (*pañcakṛtya*) of Śiva is thus the five actions of creation (*sṛṣṭi*), preservation (*sthiti*), dissolution (*saṁhṛti*), concealment (*nigraha*), and grace (*anugraha*).[12]

One may ask the question here, Why dissolution? If the world is created only to finally be destroyed, why is it created at all? The cyclic functions of creation and dissolution appear to be like the whimsical acts of a wanton child. But, dissolution does have a profound purpose. It is actually designed to give rest to the souls who become tired after moving through several rounds of birth and death. Considered from the point of view of the souls, the world is created to provide them with proper circumstances and opportunities for working out their salvation with the maturation of impurities (*mala-paripāka*). The soul goes on working for the same object knowingly or unknowingly. Since the soul toils in life, it is quite natural that it becomes tired and in need of rest. The state of dissolution is meant to provide this rest.

Thus creation and dissolution taken together are the cycle of work and rest. But this is not the only cycle of work and rest; there are two more such cycles, one of which is shorter than the other. The shortest is the one-day cycle, consisting of one day and one night, in which the individual soul (*paśu*) works during the day and sleeps or takes rest during the night. The day is created for working and the night for sleeping or resting.[13] In other words, the day is the state of creation and night is the state of dissolution. This is the one-day cycle of creation and dissolution — the shortest one — meant for work and rest.

The second cycle of creation and dissolution, or work and rest, which is comparatively longer, is that of life and death. After working for the whole life, the soul becomes tired and so it is retired in death. Just as sleep during the night is a temporary state of retirement, and the individual again wakes up with increased vigor to work during the day, so also death is a state of retirement and rest — of course, for a longer period. The soul awakes after this longer period of rest into another life with renewed vigor and power to act.

The third and longest cycle of creation and dissolution, or work and rest, is the cycle of cosmic creation and dissolution. In the cosmic dissolution the entire world is dissolved and all the souls collectively lie in a state of rest. When Creation starts again, the sleeping souls wake up to start their journey in the new Creation.

Thus we see that dissolution is quite meaningful, as it provides rest, which is a necessary step in the work and advancement of souls.

Dissolution is the state of sleep and rest for the souls, but for Śiva it may not be the same. It seems unreasonable to think that Śiva becomes tired and therefore sleeps or takes rest. We may say so allegorically. In Christian theology it is maintained that God did the activity of creating the world for six days, and on the seventh day, the Sabbath, He rested. Similarly, we can say that Śiva takes rest, but that would be only symbolic or allegorical. For Śiva, dissolution is what is called *nimeṣa. Nimeṣa* literally means "closing the eyes."[14] But again, *nimeṣa* does not mean that Śiva actually sleeps. It only means that Śiva turns His attention from external activity inward.

Creation is said to be Śiva's *unmeṣa*, literally, "opening the eyes." Both terms — *unmeṣa* and *nimeṣa* — are used symbolically. Kashmir Śaivism is an idealistic system. The world, according to it, is an external self-projection of Śiva-Consciousness. Thus Creation may be considered the opening of Śiva's eyes. When Śiva "thinks" or "ideates" the world, or "opens up His eyes," the world comes into existence. The existence of the world depends upon Śiva's "seeing" just as the existence of the dream world depends upon our "seeing" the dream. When Śiva stops seeing the world of appearance, the world is dissolved.

Hence, *nimeṣa* does not mean that Śiva actually sleeps; it only means that the Śiva-Consciousness is interiorized.[15] The *nimeṣa* of external Consciousness is really the *unmeṣa* of internal Consciousness. *Unmeṣa* is the exteriorization of Consciousness and *nimeṣa* its interiorization.

GENERAL QUESTIONS REGARDING CREATION

There are some general questions that are relevant to a clear understanding of the nature of Creation according to Kashmir Śaivism. For example, it may be asked: Why does Śiva create the world? How is Creation related to the Creator? Why does Creation not affect the Creator? How can the changing world be logically reconciled with the changeless Reality (Śiva) of which it is said to be an outcome? How can the presence of evil and suffering in the world be explained, especially when Creation is said to have sprung forth from a Reality that is nothing but goodness and bliss? The way in which Kashmir Śaivism answers these questions determines the nature of Creation as conceived therein. We will consider the questions one by one.

The first and foremost question is the why of Creation. This question is important especially since Śiva, the Creator, is conceived of as a perfect Being that has no want or lack. We perform action in order to fulfill some want or lack in us. Why should a perfect Being who lacks nothing do *anything*, not to speak of the gigantic work of Creation? The Advaita Vedāntic scholiast argues that there can be no active creation on the part of Brahman, for Brahman lacks nothing. Therefore, Creation should be regarded as a superimposition on Brahman due to ignorance (*avidyā*). The Upaniṣadic sentences describing Brahman as creating the world should be regarded as myths (*ākhyāyikā*), the Advaitin would therefore suggest.

Kashmir Śaivism has a definite answer to this question. Creation is not an effortful voluntary act of Śiva in order to fulfill some want or lack; Creation is the spontaneous activity (*spanda*) of Śiva. We have already discussed the concept of *spanda* or *kriyā*; it need not be repeated here. Here it must suffice to say that it is the nature of bliss (*ānanda*) to freely overflow in spontaneous activity — creation is such an activity. It is the emanation (*sphuraṇa*), or the natural effulgence (*vijṛmbhā*), of Śiva.[16] It is the sportive activity (*līlā*) which freely and spontaneously emanates from the state of joy; it is the spontaneous and blissful dance of Naṭarāja (dancing Śiva). Naṭarāja is the most appropriate symbol of Śiva as Creator, suggesting that Creation is not *for ānanda* but *from ānanda.* It is not that Śiva does not already have *ānanda* and in order to get it initiates the sportive activity of Creation. In fact, Śiva is already full of *ānanda* and the fullness of *ānanda* freely overflows in the joyful activity of Creation.

We have already made it clear that the activity of Creation is not a necessity for Śiva, nor an automatic activity of the mechanical type, but a completely free activity that has the merit of both freedom and effortlessness, or spontaneity.

As far as the question of the relation of Creation to Creator is concerned, it has already been discussed in the chapter on Śakti; we need not repeat the material here. Let it suffice to say that Creation is a free activity of Śiva; the relation between the Creator and

Creation is that of a free actor and his or her free act. If the question is not about the relation of the *act* of Creation, but the relation of the things or objects of Creation with Śiva, then we could say the relation is that of identity, for the world is substantially one with Śiva-Consciousness.[17] But this identity is the identity of substance, not the identity of form or function. The world is different from Śiva in form — Śiva is pure consciousness and the world is the *ābhāsa* ("appearance") of Śiva-Consciousness.[18] The individual soul is also identical with Śiva in so far as its substance is concerned, for the soul is made of the same substance — Consciousness. But the individual soul (*paśu*) is different from Śiva in so far as the individual is limited and tainted with impurity (*mala*). Thus the Creation, consisting of sentient individuals and insentient matter, is identical with Śiva in substance but different from Śiva in form and function.

The answer to the question of why Śiva is not affected by His creation is that he has complete freedom (*svātantrya*). Śiva is affected neither by the act of Creation nor by the things and events of Creation (the world). The reason He is not affected is His freedom — both "freedom-to" and "freedom-from." He is not affected by His own act of Creation because it is His free act. Nothing from within or from without compels Him to create; He has perfect "freedom-to" — the freedom to act; what He does, He does freely. If He had to act in a bound way, under compulsion, then of course He would be affected. But that is not the case; nothing can touch His freedom.[19]

Śiva is not affected by the things or events of the world because, although the world is His manifestation, He is beyond the world. When Śiva becomes the world, it is not that Śiva no longer remains Śiva or that Śiva is lost and He now becomes the world, as, for example, when milk becomes curd. When milk becomes curd, the milk is lost and only curd remains; the milk is completely affected by the creation of the curd. But in the case of Śiva's becoming the world, Śiva remains Śiva and also becomes the world.

When an actor takes part in a drama, he or she remains him- or herself and also becomes the character in the drama. The actor freely assumes the character. The actor does not really change; he or she is not affected by the drama. Similarly, Śiva is not affected by Creation, which is His free drama, so to speak. Although the world has come out of Śiva, Śiva remains fully Śiva (in Himself); in this sense Śiva is different from and transcendent to the world. If the opponent (*pūrvapakṣin*) presses the point that the individual soul (*paśu*) is nothing but Śiva, and since the individual is affected, Śiva also is affected, we would answer that Śiva in the form of the individual is affected, but Śiva in the form of Śiva is not affected. Śiva as Śiva is different from Śiva as individual. In Absolutism the unity between the two is that of substance, not of form and function. Absolutism does not mean that the duality of form and the duality of function between Śiva and the world is denied.

We have already answered the question of how the changing and determinate world comes out of the changeless and indeterminate Absolute by pointing out that the changeless and indeterminate Absolute can freely express itself, or freely adopt the changing determinations.

The question of evil and suffering will be addressed in Chapter 6.

CREATION AS VĀK ("SPEECH")

One of the significant points of the Tantric treatment of Śakti is the conception of Śakti as *Vāk* ("speech") and Creation as the manifestation of *Vāk*.[20] *Vāk*, or *Vāk-śakti*, is said to have four hierarchical levels or stages — *parā*, *paśyantī*, *madhyamā*, and *vaikharī* — which are actually the correlates of the different levels of Creation. The first one, *parā*, is the transcendent level beyond all Creation, and the remaining three are the three natural stages of Creation.[21]

In the philosophical tradition of the Grammarian (*vaiyākaraṇa*), Ultimate Reality, Brahman, is conceived of as "word" (*śabda*, or *śabda-brahma*), and the world is conceived of as the creation of *śabda*. Bhartṛhari, in his *Vākyapadīyam*, puts forth the view that the world is an apparent creation (*vivarta*) of Śabda-brahma. Somānanda, the father of the Pratyabhijñā school of Kashmir Śaivism, in his *Śivadṛṣṭi*, however, criticizes the Grammarian. Somānanda's point is that if *Śabda* is understood as a reality different from and independent of Consciousness (*cit*), it is incapable of creating the world; it can create the world only if it is understood as not different from Consciousness or Śiva. Therefore Consciousness (*cit*), and not śabda ("word"), should be regarded as the ultimate principle of Creation. Moreover, Somānanda thinks that the Grammarian, who starts with the level of *paśyantī*, has no concept of *parā* ("the transcendent"), which as the source of all Creation, is a logical necessity. However this criticism by Somānanda does not really apply to the Grammarian, for the Grammarian implicitly, if not explicitly, accepts *śabda* as not different from Consciousness (Śiva). Moreover, the Grammarian implicitly accepts the transcendental state (*parā*, or *parapaśyantī*), which is the matrix of everything. However the main purpose of the Grammarian is to explain the process of Creation, and as a matter of fact, the process of Creation, as in Kashmir Śaivism, starts with *paśyantī*. Somānanda seems to have missed the intention of the Grammarian. Abhinavagupta, however, correctly understands and appreciates Bhartṛhari. Kashmir Śaivism may be taken as the metaphysical version of the linguistic philosophy of Bhartṛhari, and the philosophy of Bhartṛhari may be taken as the linguistic version of Kashmir Śaivism.

It is significant to note why Śakti is called "speech" (*vāk*) in the Tantric tradition. In order to understand why Śakti is called "speech," we must first understand why Śakti is called *vimarśa* ("thinking" or "ideation"). Idealism is the prominent tone of the Tantras; according to them, Consciousness alone is the Reality. Matter does not exist; what is known as matter is really the appearance (*ābhāsa*) or projection of Consciousness. Since matter is non-existent, there is no material activity; all activity is activity in Consciousness or "mental" activity. Activity in Consciousness means "thinking" or "ideation" which is the literal meaning of the word *vimarśa*. Furthermore, according to Tantrism all thinking is carried out in language; we cannot think without using language.[22] And since language in its express form is phonetical, it is called *vāk* ("speech"), *nāda* ("sound"), or *śabda* ("word"). Abhinavagupta says that *śabda* is the very life of *vimarśa*,[23] meaning that *vimarśa* ("thinking") cannot take place without *śabda* ("language").

Since the world is a manifestation of *śakti* or *citi* (Consciousness) and since *śakti* is understood as *vāk* ("speech" or "word"), it is understandable that the world is the manifestation of *vāk*.[24] The world is a result of the spontaneous flutter or dynamism (*spanda*) of Consciousness (Śiva), and all dynamism of Consciousness is in language (*vāk*). *Vāk* ("speech") may not be articulate at the higher levels of *madhyamā*, *paśyantī*, and *parā*; it becomes articulate at the gross *vaikharī* level only. Thinking is *silent* talking, and therefore *vāk* at the higher levels may be in the form of inner speech or speech without articulation.[25] When it is said that Creation is caused by *śabda*, what is meant by *śabda* is not articulate sound but the inner Consciousness that is expressing itself in language (*śabdātmaka*). Of course, articulate sound is the grossest manifestation of *vāk* and is called *vaikharī vāk*.

Parā, which is Ultimate Consciousness, is independent; it is the Absolute. It is the source of Creation and yet is itself beyond Creation. It is quite logical that the source from which the world comes should itself be independent of the world. That is why it is called the *parā* ("the transcendent"). This *parā-vāk*, which is also a state of freedom (*svātantrya*), freely manifests the lower forms of *paśyantī*, *madhyamā*, and *vaikharī* and is immanently present in them as their very ground. Thus the *parā* is both transcendent to and immanent in them; without the *parā* as their underlying reality, they would become non-illumined and therefore non-existent.[26] *Parā-vāk* is itself independent, but the stages of *paśyantī* and so forth are dependent on *parā-vāk*.

In the *parā* state the Self alone exists; Creation has not taken place. There is only *aham* (the Self or "I"); there is no *idam* (the object). *Parā*, therefore, is the level of pure unity in which there is no difference. It is one without a second. Considered from the point of view of the thirty-six categories (*tattvas*), *parā* is the ultimate Śiva-Śakti, which is the source of all Creation and which in itself is above all Creation. Considered from the point of view of *śakti*, *parā* is *cit-ānanda*, which is the nature of Reality.

It should be clearly understood that *parā-vāk*, or *parā-śakti*, is identical to *Parama-śiva*. If *Parā-śakti* is taken to denote a reality different from *Parama-śiva*, it would be a gross misunderstanding of the Tantric position. Śiva, or Consciousness, is conceived of as a force or dynamic power (*śakti* or *spanda*), and the very dynamism of Śiva is called Śakti. Śakti, therefore, is synonymous with Śiva; it is a way of understanding Śiva (Consciousness) as force or sentient energy. So, call it Śiva or call it Śakti, the Reality is the same.[27] Utpaladeva says that Absolute Consciousness (*citi*) whose nature is "thinking" or ideational dynamism (*pratyavamarśa*), is the *parā-vāk* that is independent.[28]

Parā is the state of Self-consciousness (*aham* or "I am") without consciousness of the object (*ahamidam* or "I am this"). Here, the question of the consciousness of the world does not arise as there is no world — the world has not arisen in any form whatsoever. There is only *aham* (the "I," the Self, or the subject)[29] and no *idam* (the "this," the not-self, or the object). This is the absolute "I" (*pūrṇāham* or *pūrṇāhantā*), as it is not related to or dependent on consciousness of the "thou" or the object.

When *parā-śakti* or *parā-vāk* wills the creation of the world, it becomes *paśyantī*. The *paśyantī* state is compared to the swelling (*ucchūnatā*) of a seed, which is the first step in the creation of a tree. In the swelling, the seed becomes "inclined" (*unmukha*) towards manifesting itself in the form of a tree, the tree still being mere potential in this stage. Similarly, in the *paśyantī* state the world is in potential form, as this is simply the state of willing to create and not of actually creating the world. When the Upaniṣads say of Brahman that "He willed (or desired) 'Let myself become many and procreate'"[30], this is actually the *paśyantī* state of Brahman. So in terms of the five powers of Śiva (*pañcaśaktis*), *paśyantī* is the *icchā* ("will"), the first step in the triad of *icchā-jñāna-kriyā* that is the actual process of Creation. That is why in the hierarchy of the *tattvas*, *paśyantī* is the state of *Sadāśiva*; *Sadāśiva* just wills (*icchā*) to create.[31]

Considered from the point of view of unity and difference, *paśyantī* is the state of "unity-in-difference" (*ahamidam* — "I am this"). The succeeding states of *madhyamā* and *vaikharī* are also states of "unity-in-difference." The difference among the three states is based on the progressively greater actualization of the difference within the unity itself. In the *paśyantī* state the difference is the least proclaimed, in the *madhyamā* it becomes more proclaimed as it is more actualized, and in the *vaikharī* the difference is fully actualized or externalized. The *paśyantī* state is analogous to the undifferentiated fluid in the egg of a peacock, where the variety of the colored plumes of the peacock is fully submerged in the undifferentiated unity of the egg, yet the difference is potentially contained therein. In this state the desired object exists just in the form of initial consciousness.[32] The distinction between the word (*vācaka*) and the object (*vācya*) has not yet arisen; the two exist in undifferentiated form.[33] The consciousness of the object (*idam*) has sprouted, but it still lies undifferentiated from the subject (*aham*).

Madhyamā is the second step in the process of creation. This state of *vāk*, or Consciousness, is grosser, or lower, than that of the *paśyantī* and subtler, or higher, than that of the *vaikharī*. That is why it is called *madhyamā*, which literally means "the middle one." In this state the world is more manifest than in the *paśyantī* state.

Considered from the point of view of the five powers of Śiva, *madhyamā* is the state of *jñāna* ("ideation"). Here the would-be world is a clear idea. It no longer remains in the form of the will to create, but it still remains an idea and has not yet become the actual physical reality, which comes in the *kriyā*-state.[34] From the point of view of the *tattvas*, *madhyamā* is the *Īśvara-tattva*, which is the correlate of *jñāna* in the triad of *icchā-jñāna-kriyā*. This is the state of what is called *idamaham* ("this I am"). This is also within the general framework of unity-in-difference, but here there is an emphasis on the difference (*idam* or "this") as the difference is more manifest. The subject fully ideates the object, the object being contained in the subject as an idea. *Paśyantī* is the beginning of difference (*bheda*) whereas *madhyamā* is the full awareness of difference, although within oneself.[35]

Vaikharī is the grossest manifestation of *vāk-śakti.* In this state the world is fully actualized; it no longer remains an "ideation" (*vimarśa*, or *jñāna*) as in the *madhyamā* state, but becomes actual or external reality. Considered from the point of view of the five-fold acts of Śiva, *vaikharī* is *kriyā*, which is the actual Creation as the physical world. According to the realistic interpretation of *vaikharī*, or *kriyā*, the world that is created externally is a real or material entity. But according to the idealistic interpretation, which is held by Tantrism in general and Kashmir Śaivism in particular, the world manifested at the level of *vaikharī*, or *kriyā*, is an appearance (*ābhāsa*), not a material reality. At the *madhyamā* level the world is "ideation" (*vimarśa*, or *jñāna*), and at the *vaikharī* or *kriyā* level, it is "appearance" (*ābhāsa*). The difference between "ideation" and "appearance" is that "ideation" means the conceiving of or thinking of anything within the "mind" or consciousness as a mere idea or image, whereas "appearance" is the actual projection (although false), as in the case of a hallucination, dream, or reflection in a mirror. In "ideation" a thing is merely imagined, but in "appearance" the thing actually appears, like a dream object or the reflection in a mirror.

Of course, in the case of a hallucination or dream we are in ignorance — we do not know that it is merely appearance. Śiva, however, knows that His creation is just an appearance and not a material entity. His creation is more like that of a yogi or a magician who creates false appearances and at the same time is fully aware that the created things are false. Or it is like a motion picture, which is a false projection. We know that it is false, yet we see and enjoy it.

Considered from the angle of the *tattvas*, *vaikharī* is the *sad-vidyā-tattva.* In the *sad-vidyā* state the world is fully actualized or externalized. The object comes out of the subject and stands as if on par with the subject.[36] That is why it is the state of "I am and this is" (*aham ca idam ca*). The difference is fully proclaimed — so much so that it seems to be independent of the unity that is the knower (the subject). But although it appears as independent of the knowing Self, the Self (Śiva) is aware that it is not different from Him.

The four levels of *vāk-śakti* can also be understood purely in terms of the spoken word. It should be clear that the word (*śabda*) does not exist in itself without the thing (*artha*)[37] indicated by the word. Whenever we speak a word, we have the thing that is the meaning of the word in our mind. The process of the word and meaning is a sentient process — a process of consciousness. Therefore, this process must originate from consciousness and proceed in-and-through consciousness. Ultimate Consciousness, which is the source of this process and which itself is independent of this process, is *parā-vāk.* When, in the *parā* state, the will to speak or express an *artha* arises, it becomes *paśyantī.* Here only the will to speak the *artha* exists, the full picture or idea of the *artha* has not yet arisen — it is the beginning of speech. In *madhyamā* the idea or the picture of the *artha* becomes fully clear, but it is still within the mind or consciousness of the speaker; it is only "ideated" (*vimarśana*). In *vaikharī-vāk* the word (*śabda*) expressing the *artha* is articulated and becomes audible sound. Up to the *madhyamā* level the word remains a thought-form; it is only at the *vaikharī* level that the word becomes articulate sound.[38]

It should also be noted that when the *parā* manifests itself in the form of *paśyantī*, and so on, the *parā* is not exhausted. The *parā* remains in itself and at the same time manifests the lower levels; it never loses its absolute nature. In other words, the lower levels are the extension (*prasāra*) or free manifestation (*sphuraṇa*) of the *Parā-śakti* itself. The Goddess says, "I myself remain as the same Goddess Parā-Vāk, unaffected by differentiations.[39]

The five hierarchical categories of *Śiva-Śakti*,[40] *Sadāśiva*, *Īśvara*, and *Sadvidyā*, classified under the four correlate levels of *Vāk-śakti*, are said to be pure categories (*śuddhādhvā*). They are pure because the sense of non-duality is never forsaken even at the lowest level of the *sad-vidyā-tattva*. *Parā-śakti*, although manifesting Herself in duality, is always aware that the duality is Her own manifestation and that She is ever the non-dual Absolute Reality.

The four hierarchical levels of *vāk-śakti* can be likened to the different procreative stages of a mother. When the mother has not yet conceived and is completely in herself, this is the *parā* state. When she just conceives (the stage of fertilization), this is like *paśyantī*. When the fetus attains the full form but is still within the womb, this is like *madhyamā*. Finally, when the mother gives birth to the baby, that is, when the baby comes out of the womb, this is like *vaikharī*. The cosmic Mother (*parā-śakti* or *parā-vāk*) conceives the world in the form of willing or *icchā* (*paśyantī*); she develops the conception into a full-fledged fetus within the womb of Consciousness in the form of ideation or *jñāna*[41] (*madhyamā*); and finally she actually gives birth to the world in the form of *kriyā* (*vaikharī*).

Even after giving birth to the child, and even after the child's appearing as different from her, the mother fully knows that the child is her own and is not different from her. Similarly, the Cosmic Mother is aware of the non-duality even after projecting the world outside, which remains in Her fold.

The following chart may be of some help in viewing the four levels of the *Vāk-śakti*.

THE PURE CATEGORIES

The first five categories (*tattvas*), namely, *Śiva*, *Śakti*, *Sadāśiva*, *Īśvara*, and *Sadvidyā* are called the "pure categories" (*śuddhādhvā*). Why are they called "pure" categories and what is the meaning of "pure" (*śuddha*)? In Tantrism (Kashmir Śaivism) the criterion of purity versus impurity is the sense of unity (*abheda-bhāva* or

Śakti	Tattva	Vak	Degree of Differentiation			Experient
Cit-Ānanda	Śiva-Śakti	Parā	Aham ("I am")	Pure unity	Pure subject or pure self (without object-consciousness)	Śiva-pramātā
Icchā	Sadāśiva	Paśyantī	Ahamidam ("I am this")	Unity-in-difference (difference in the potential form — āsūtraṇa)	The subject just emitting the object	Mantra-Maheśvara-pramātā
Jñāna	Īśvara	Madhyamā	Idamaham ("This I am")	Unity-in-difference (difference more manifest as ideation — Vimarśa)	The subject fully ideating the object	Mantreśvara-pramātā
Kriyā	Sadvidyā	Vaikharī	Ahañca idañca ("I am and this is")	Unity-in-difference (difference fully manifest as appearance — Ābhāsa)	The subject externally projecting the object as ābhāsa	Mantra-pramātā

Chart of Pure Manifestation (Śuddhādhvā)

abheda-buddhi) as opposed to duality or difference (*bheda-bhāva* or *bheda-buddhi*). When one sees or feels difference or disunity, when one takes oneself not to be one with others or feels that the world and other individuals are "other" to one, then one is in the state of impurity. Ignorance (*ajñāna*) is impurity, and ignorance itself means the sense of duality or otherness. Abhinavagupta says that it is the sense of duality (*dvaita-prathā*) that is ignorance, and it is *this* that creates bondage.[42] This is what is meant by impurity.

Similarly, the sense of unity (*abheda-bhāva* or *abheda-buddhi*) is knowledge (*jñāna*). It is this that liberates. In the state of *jñāna*, one feels one's unity with all, one feels that all are oneself. The sense of otherness is gone. Selfishness is ignorance, and universal love is knowledge.

The sense of unity (*abheda-bhāva*, or *abheda-buddhi*) is knowledge, and this is what "pure" (*śuddha*) means.[43] In a dream, although the dream world is the dreamer's own projection and therefore one with the dreamer, he or she is suffering from ignorance and takes the dream world to be other than him- or herself. But when one imagines or consciously projects some object, one is aware that the object is one's own projection and therefore not "other" than oneself.

In the state of *śuddhādhvā* the Śiva-consciousness, although projecting the world as "this" (*idam*), is aware that the "this" is His own projection and therefore one with Him. The opponent may say that the very presence of "this," or the object, is due to ignorance and is thus an impurity. But this is really not so. The mere presence of *idam* is not due to ignorance; the *idam* may be the result not of ignorance but of conscious self-projection. Ignorance is in the sense that the *idam* is different from oneself, as happens in a dream. One sees, for example, one's face reflected in a mirror. It is true that one actually sees the reflection, but one is also aware that what one sees is the reflection of one's own face that, therefore, is not different from or independent of one's face. The act of seeing the reflection does not bind one.

Similarly the *idam* exists in all five stages of *śuddhādhvā*, but Śiva knows that the *idam* is His own reflection and is therefore not different from Him. So Śiva does not become impure. Utpaladeva says that one who knows that "all this is my own glory" remains pure Śiva even in the face of the *idam.*[44] In the process of Creation, it is only when Consciousness is tainted by *māyā* and becomes the ignorant *puruṣa*, or individual soul, that the impurity comes into play and the *puruṣa* takes the *idam*, or the world, to be other than itself. Thus all thirty-one categories after the five categories of *śuddhādhvā* belong to the *aśuddhādhvā*, or impure category.

MĀYĀ

Māyā is the starting point of impure (*aśuddha*) creation. It is *māyā* that is responsible for impurity. *Māyā* generates the five sheaths of limitation, *pañca-kañcukas*, which bind the pure universal nature of Consciousness and make it the limited *puruṣa* or *paśu. Māyā* is the matrix of the *pañca-kañcukas.* Mother Māyā together with her five progeny (the *pañca-kañcukas*) creates bondage for the soul.

Māyā is the principle of limitation. The universal Consciousness becomes the *paśu* ("the bound soul") or *aṇu* ("the limited soul") due to *māyā*[45]; the all-pervading Consciousness adopts limited individuality and differentiates itself from others. Differentiation is possible only when Consciousness becomes limited to one particular individuality. So the principle of limitation is the principle of differentiation. Thus it is *māyā*, the principle of limitation, that makes Śiva (Consciousness) the *paśu.* The *paśutva* (fettered individuality) of the *paśu* is due to *māyā.*

On the part of Śiva, this act of limitation is part of the sportive activity (*līlā*) of Creation.[46] Śiva enjoys Himself by becoming the bound *paśu.*[47] One may object here that Śiva's *līlā* of becoming a bound *paśu* seems whimsical and cynical on Śiva's part. Moreover, what joy does Śiva derive from becoming a bound person, and is Śiva not affected by this queer act of befooling Himself?

In answer to the above question it should be made clear in the first place that Śiva, while becoming the bound *paśu*, fully remains Śiva; the nature of Śiva remains intact. Śiva remains Śiva and, in addition, becomes the bound soul. It is not that Śiva, in the process of becoming the *paśu*, is lost, as when milk is transformed into curd. In this process, the Śivahood of Śiva is never lost. Śiva Himself is not affected by the process.

Moreover, Śiva is really play-acting in becoming the *paśu*. His activity may be likened to that of an actor in a drama. We *do* enjoy ourselves in play-acting. If we really become bound, then we are *not* play-acting, and the result is suffering. But if we deliberately and freely pretend to be a fool, as an actor does, then this is play-acting, a thing of joy that does not bind the actor. Moreover, the actor knows full well that he or she has not really become whatever his or her role is in the drama. Similarly Śiva, the Cosmic Actor, play-acts in the form of bound souls but is Himself not bound by this.

A further issue may be raised here. Becoming the bound soul may be play-acting on the part of Śiva and therefore not cause Him any problem, but as far as the bound soul is concerned, he or she is suffering. The poor *paśu* pays for the enjoyment of Śiva! It should be made clear that the case of Śiva's becoming the bound soul is slightly different from what happens in the analogy of the actor. In the case of an actor in a drama, the assumed persona does not existentially become separate from the actor; therefore there is no issue of a separate person. But in the case of Śiva becoming a *paśu*, the *paśu* attains a separate individuality and an existence apart from Śiva. The separation of *paśu* from Śiva is an existential fact. So, Creation may be play-acting on the part of Śiva, but for the *paśu* it is a cruel and tortuous game.

Becoming the ignorant *paśu* is itself not the cause of suffering. Ignorance may be the necessary cause of suffering, like fire is the cause of smoke, but ignorance itself is not the sufficient cause of suffering, just as the fire itself is not the sufficient cause of smoke. It is only when we add wet fuel to the fire that the fire becomes the sufficient cause for creating smoke. Similarly, ignorance becomes the sufficient cause for creating suffering only when we add the abuse or misuse of our free will to it. It is the abuse of our free will — that is, the abuse of our powers initiated by the choice of our free will — that is responsible for suffering.

Nature made fire for the good purposes of cooking and heating, not to create smoke, but we create smoke by adding wet fuel to the fire. Electricity is generated for useful purposes, but it also causes electrocution due to human error. Similarly, ignorance was created for enjoyment, not to cause suffering. This is exemplified in the case of a child. The child is ignorant, but is quite happy and plays joyfully, for it has not added the abuse of free will to its ignorance. The grown-up abuses his or her free will and creates suffering for him- or herself according to the Law of Karma.

Śiva, the cosmic Gamesmaster, has initiated the game of Creation, not for evil and suffering, but for goodness and joy. If the players (the *paśus*) did not violate the rules of the game, the game would go on merrily. But the players are not like robots, they have free will through which they freely misuse their powers. A hockey player, for example, instead of striking the ball, swings his stick at the head of his co-player; then he is bound to be punished. The Gamesmaster does not want His players to commit crimes and suffer in consequence, but the players do it of their own accord.

The *māyā* of Kashmir Śaivism is different from the *māyā* of Śaiva Siddhānta, the dualistic southern school of Śaivism, which accepts three realities — *pati* (Śiva), *paśu* (the individual soul), and *pāśa* (the bondage that is also called *māyā*). *Māyā* in Śaiva Siddhānta is, like the *prakṛti* of Sāṁkhya, a material principle that forms the material cause of the world. *Māyā* is matter, which has objective reality separate from Śiva. But in Kashmir Śaivism there is no material reality; *māyā* is just the principle or *śakti* ("power") of self-limitation,[48] and as such, is not separate from Śiva. The *māyā* of Kashmir Śaivism and the *māyā* of Śaiva Siddhānta are thus very different. The only similarity is that in both systems *māyā* binds the soul, that is why it is called *pāśa* (the binding principle) in both systems.

The *māyā* of Kashmir Śaivism is nearer to that of Advaita Vedānta than to that of Śaiva Siddhānta. In Advaita Vedānta, too, *māyā*, unlike the *prakṛti* of Sāṁkhya, is not a real material entity and is not separate from Brahman. It is the power (*śakti*) of Brahman, which is why it is also called *māyā-śakti* or *avidyā-śakti* ("the power of ignorance or nescience"). The *māyā* of Advaita Vedānta also functions as the principle of limitation or bondage of the soul.

The *māyā* of Kashmir Śaivism is different from that of Advaita Vedānta in one respect. *Māyā* in Kashmir Śaivism is the principle of self-projection and self-limitation, as Śiva Himself freely projects the world. But in Advaita Vedānta, *māyā* is the principle of superimposition; the world-illusion is superimposed on Brahman automatically, while Brahman lies passive and neutral like the rope in the rope-snake illusion. Brahman does not actively create the illusion of the world but passively allows the illusion to be superimposed on it. But the Śiva of Kashmir Śaivism freely creates the illusion Himself. If the world-illusion is taken as a superimposition *on* Brahman and not a self-projection *of* Brahman, then this means that there is a separate reality that is responsible for the superimposition and is thus separate from Brahman.

THE FIVE SHEATHS

It is obvious that although *māyā* is the sportive principle of self-limitation in the case of Śiva, it is the principle of bondage in the case of the individual soul (*paśu*). *Māyā* binds (or limits or covers) the soul with five sub-principles or factors which are her own creation, her own progeny. They are called "five" (*pañca*) "sheaths" (*kañcuka*). Here the term *kañcuka* is used in a symbolic or allegorical way. *Kañcuka* literally means "clothing" or "cloak." It also means the outer skin of a snake that the snake casts off periodically.

Thus *kañcuka* actually means covering or sheath in which the soul is kept bound. The sheaths are said to be five in number. These five sheaths are called *vidyā*, *kalā*, *rāga*, *niyati*, and *kāla*. Sometimes *māyā* is included along with the five sheaths, increasing their number to six.[49]

1. Vidyā

Vidyā is the power of knowledge (*jñāna-śakti*) under limitation. It is the understanding of oneself as the limited knower. *Vidyā* literally means "knowledge." *Vidyā* also appears in the fifth category of the *śuddhādhvā*. But there it is called *sad-vidyā* or *śuddha-vidyā* ("pure knowledge"). There it is called pure because there is no sense of duality. It is not limited knowledge, as it does not limit Consciousness to a particular individuality. But *vidyā* as a *kañcuka* is called *asad-vidyā* or *aśuddha-vidyā* ("impure knowledge"). This is impure knowledge because of the sense of duality. One knows the object (the world) to be different from or other than oneself. One takes the world to be "other" because one limits oneself to a particular individuality and thereby cuts oneself off from the rest of the world. The result is that one is not the true knower, as one does not know the truth that the entire world is one's own projection.[50]

2. Kalā

Just as in *vidyā* one's power of knowledge (*jñāna-śakti*) becomes limited, in *kalā* one's power of activity (*kriyā-śakti*) becomes limited. *Kalā* is the limited or bound *kriyā-śakti* where one takes oneself to be the limited doer.[51] Again, like *vidyā*, the term *kalā* is also used for the pure and free activity (*kriyā*, *śakti*, or *spanda*), which is in the very nature of Ultimate Consciousness (Śiva). There, of course, it is the *śuddha kalā*. But *kalā* as a *kañcuka* is *aśuddha* ("impure") *kalā*. In the state of *kalā* one performs effortful voluntary action — *karma* — that belongs to the ethical realm of vice and virtue (*pāpa* and *puṇya*), and not to the spiritual realm of spontaneous activity where morality is naturally synthesized with the joyful sportive activity of the Self. *Karma* is technically different from *kriyā*; *karma* belongs to the ethical realm, whereas *kriyā* belongs to the spiritual one. In the state of pure *kalā*, which is the state of *kriyā*, one is perfect and joyful sportive activity naturally emanates from one. But in the state of impure *kalā*, as in the *kañcuka*, one takes oneself to be imperfect, to be lacking something, and tends to perform action in order to fulfill the lack.

3. Rāga

Rāga means attachment to or clinging to something. The opposite of *rāga* is *dveṣa*, which means aversion to or antipathy towards something. *Rāga* and *dveṣa* really represent one and the same state of mind. When I like something, I develop a sense of attachment to that thing; when I dislike something, I develop an aversion to it. *Rāga* and *dveṣa* indicate the same attitude of mind — liking what is pleasant and disliking what is painful. Since *dveṣa* is actually the negative *rāga*, it is not mentioned or counted separately; otherwise *rāga* would be known as *rāga-dveṣa*.

As is true in the case of *vidyā* and *kalā*, *rāga* arises out of the sense of imperfection resulting in differentiation of oneself from the rest of the world. The psychology of *rāga* is that one desires only that which one does not have; there is no question of desiring what one already possesses. *Rāga* ("attachment") means desiring what does not belong to one.[52] When, in the state of perfection, one feels that everything belongs to one, and therefore everything will naturally always remain with one, there is no question of attachment.

It also follows from the above that *rāga* is possible only when one is bound by *niyati* ("determinism" or "cause and effect"). One longs for something only when one thinks that one cannot obtain it simply by willing it, because it depends upon the cause-effect determinism of Nature. But when, after attaining Śivahood, one becomes free from this determinism and knows that everything depends upon one's own will, then one no longer longs for, or is attached to, anything. *Rāga* co-exists with *niyati*;[53] there is no *rāga* in the state of freedom from *niyati*.

From the analysis of *rāga*, it follows that what is called *sarvātma-bhāva* ("the feeling of unity with all"), or *viśva-prema* ("universal love"), is the cure for *rāga* ("attachment"). Love is different from attachment. Sometimes the word "love" (*prema* in Sanskrit and Hindi) is used in the sense of "like," as, for example, when one says, "I love *rasagulla*" (a Bengali sweet). But this is a loose use of the word. Love is the opposite of selfishness. In selfishness, one sees others as outside of oneself and uses or exploits others to one's own ends. But in love, one considers others as part of oneself and desires their welfare as much as one's own. In *rāga*, the person to whom one is attached is not the end; one is oneself the end, and since the person gives one pleasure, one clings to it and does not want to part with it. The happiness of that person is not one's goal; one's own happiness is the goal. Thus *rāga* is a subtle form of selfishness.

What is technically called *dvaita-bhāvanā*[54] ("the sense of duality") is nothing but selfishness, in plain words, and what is called *advaita-bhāvanā* ("the sense of unity with all") is nothing but universal love, which gives us immense satisfaction and joy unmatched by the meager pleasure that we obtain in the state of *rāga*. It is this *advaita-bhāvanā* ("love") that cures us of *rāga* and leads us to our freedom. In Kashmir Śaivism, as also in the Upaniṣads, the *sādhanā* ("spiritual practice") of *advaita-bhāvanā* is emphasized.

4. Niyati

Niyati[55] means determinism, which is the opposite of freedom. The predicament of the individual soul (*paśu*) is that what the soul wants to achieve or has to achieve is not achieved simply by willing; the individual has to follow the law of cause and effect. For example, if we want to become healthy, we have to fulfill the conditions of health — suitable food, good climate, exercise, medicine, and so on. Health is the effect and in order to attain this effect, we have to abide by its cause. The effect will not be attained merely by willing. Similarly, if the cause has taken place, I cannot evade the effect. For example, if you put your finger into a fire (cause), you cannot avoid burning it (effect). This law of cause and effect operates in life and the world. This is called *niyati* ("determinism"). *Niyati* is a binding factor; it binds the *paśu.*

Śiva-Consciousness is not bound by *niyati.* In order to create an effect, Śiva does not have to abide by the cause; He can create the effect simply by willing it. Similarly, He can avoid the effect even if the cause exists. Śiva is beyond cause and effect. Moreover, the causal relation that we find between the things of the world is the free creation of Śiva. Why should a particular cause produce a particular effect? This is because it is so willed by Śiva. Śiva wills the law of cause and effect that operates in Nature.[56]

Another form of *niyati* is the law of *karma* that binds the *paśu.* The *paśu* is bound to reap the moral fruit of his action, good or bad. Action is the cause and the fruit that results is the effect. The law of *karma* is thus really the law of cause and effect operating in the moral realm. The law of *karma* is willed into existence and controlled by Śiva, and again, Śiva Himself is beyond the law of *karma.* The same becomes true in the case of one who attains *mukti* ("liberation") or Śiva-realization.[57]

Some people construe *niyati* as "space" (*deśa*), probably in order to use this word side by side with *kāla* ("time"), which is the fifth *kañcuka.* But this is a misunderstanding. "Space" in Sanskrit is *deśa* or *dik*, not *niyati. Niyati*, which means determinism or cause and effect, in the physical as well as in the moral realm,[58] can have no direct connection with space. "Space" is indeed a binding factor like time, but that is no reason to construe *niyati* as "space."

5. Kāla

The fifth *kañcuka* is *kāla* ("time"). In some of the realistic systems of philosophy like Nyāya-Vaiśeṣika, Jainism, and so on, *kāla* is conceived of as an independent reality, a substance. But in an idealistic system like Kashmir Śaivism, time is understood as an attribute of Consciousness — a way of thinking, so to speak. Even if we leave aside ontological considerations and try to understand time purely in an epistemological way, as Kant did, we find that time is not a thing or an actual reality, but an *a priori* conditioning of our knowing or thinking. We cannot think without time. Whenever we know or think something, we know it as being or happening in time. We cannot understand anything as not being in time. Even when we have to understand the "timeless" (*akāla*), we can understand it only as "eternal time" (*mahākāla*).

Time (*kāla*) is the sense of before and after (*pūrvāpara*). This is what is called sequence (*krama*). *Kāla* is one with *krama*.[59] It exists in the form of past, present, and future. We divide time into fragments — minutes, hours, days, months, years, and so on. Although time is ordinarily understood as divided into segments according to a sequence of events, time can also be understood as one continuum, an eternal flow. For example, when there are no particular events, even then time in itself goes on.

What is important about time is that it does not exist by itself, for it is not a thing; it exists only in our consciousness and conditions the consciousness in such a way that consciousness cannot think but in time. In this sense time (*kāla*) is a *kañcuka*, a factor that binds the consciousness.

But as is true with all *kañcukas*, *kāla* is a sheath which conditions the ordinary consciousness only. In Śiva-Consciousness there is no *kāla*. Time, which is just a way of thinking, is a free manifestation of Śiva (pure Consciousness), but Śiva himself is beyond time. In Śiva-Consciousness there is no thinking in terms of past-present-future; there is no sense of time at all.[60] That is why Śiva is called *akāla* (the "timeless").

Space (*deśa* or *dik*), like time (*kāla*), is a way of thinking that conditions our consciousness, and as such it should also be included in the *kañcukas*. The reason it is not might be that space is not as important as time. Or, space should be understood as already paired with time, and therefore included in the notion of time.[61]

THE INDIVIDUAL SOUL (PURUṢA)

We have already seen that *māyā* together with its *kañcukas* makes Consciousness limited or individualized. This limited or individualized consciousness is called *puruṣa*.[62] We have also discussed the notion that for Śiva, becoming the limited soul (*puruṣa*, *paśu*, or *aṇu*) is a sportive activity (*līlā*), and this sportive act of limitation does not bind Śiva.

Puruṣa is limited consciousness and therefore it is called *aṇu*. The term *aṇu* is used in the sense of "atom" in some other systems of Indian philosophy, such as Nyāya-Vaiśeṣika. The primary meaning of the word *aṇu* is "small" or "infinitesimal in size."[63] The atom is called *aṇu* because it is the smallest particle of matter. In the Tantric tradition, however, the word *aṇu* is used to mean "limited." The idea is that Consciousness becomes "small" because of the limitation it takes on — *māyā* limits Consciousness and makes it "small."[64] This limitation serves as bondage for the *puruṣa*. As the bound soul, the *puruṣa* is called "animal" (*paśu*) because the ordinary animal is bound by a rope or chain as well as its own instincts and the conditioning of certain behavior patterns. The word "animal" has thus become the symbol for the bound state.

At the stage of *puruṣa*, Consciousness enters into the realm of duality. Up to the stage of *sadvidyā*, Consciousness, which is the subject or *aham*, although projecting the object or *idam* from itself, retains its sense of unity or non-duality, as it knows that the *idam* is its own projection. That is why the categories up to *sadvidyā* are called "pure" categories (*śuddhādhvā*). But at the *puruṣa* stage, the sense of non-duality is lost; the soul (the subject) takes the object to be really different from itself. There is a bifurcation of the subject and the object. Now the subject does not take the object to be just *ābhāsa* ("appearance" or "reflection"), but takes it to be a real thing made of matter. At the stage of *sadvidyā* the bifurcation of the subject and the object also exists, but at that stage the subject knows that the object is not a real, material thing but an *ābhāsa*, and it also knows that the *ābhāsa* is its own projection or manifestation.

Thus, the point of difference between the stage of *sadvidyā* and that of *puruṣa* is that in *sadvidyā* the unity is not lost, as the object in that stage is self-projected *ābhāsa*; whereas in the stage of *puruṣa* the unity is lost, as the object becomes a real material thing and therefore becomes separated from the subject. The bifurcation of the subject and the object becomes a real one in *puruṣa*. The object becomes real not in the sense of being a material object, as even then it really remains the *ābhāsa* of consciousness and therefore one with the subject,[65] but it becomes real in the sense that it appears real to the subject. So the relation of *puruṣa* (the subject) with the object is that of duality or difference; the object is separated from the subject.

Although the *puruṣa* of Kashmir Śaivism appears to be quite similar to that of Sāṁkhya, the two are different in so far as their real nature is concerned. The similarities are the following: (a) at the level of the material world, both systems accept the plurality of *puruṣas*, as there are many individual souls acting in the world; (b) the *puruṣa* is different from the world of matter; and (c) in its present state the *puruṣa* is in bondage — bound or veiled by *māyā*, which is also the principle of materiality (like *prakṛti*).

But the differences between the Sāṁkhya and Kashmir Śaiva conceptions of *puruṣa* are very significant. According to Kashmir Śaivism, although there are many *puruṣas*, they are like the many rays coming out of and connected with one and the same light, which has become many while passing through different individualities. The individual *puruṣas* are connected with the one higher *puruṣa* (Śiva), and are therefore ultimately one. In Sāṁkhya, however, the plurality of *puruṣas* is ultimate; there is no *parama-puruṣa*, like Brahman or Śiva, with which they can be linked up. Again, although at the surface level the *puruṣa* of Kashmir Śaivism is separate from *prakṛti* ("the world"), at its deeper level of existence it is one with *prakṛti*; *prakṛti* is its own *śakti* ("power") and its own extension (*prasāra*) or manifestation. But in Sāṁkhya, the *puruṣa* is ultimately different and separate from *prakṛti*. Moreover, in both systems, the *puruṣa* attains *mukti* ("liberation") by freeing itself from bondage; but according to Kashmir Śaivism, the *puruṣa* in the state of *mukti* becomes one with Śiva, the cosmic Self, whereas according to Sāṁkhya, there is no merger into or becoming one with a higher Self (*paramātman*), for there is no such thing as a higher Self.

One can note here that at the practical level of worldly existence, where *puruṣa* is bound by *māyā*, there is practically no difference between the *puruṣa* of Kashmir Śaivism and that of Sāṁkhya, the difference being only in their real nature at the ultimate level. However, this difference in the nature of the Ultimate makes a lot of difference in the pursuit of *mokṣa* and also at the level of worldly activity.

THE TWENTY-FOUR MATERIAL CATEGORIES

Māyā causes Consciousness to divide itself into two — the subject (*puruṣa*) on the one hand and the object (*prakṛti*) on the other. As Sāṁkhya does, we can classify the entire world into two categories or two principles — the principle of consciousness (*puruṣa*) and the principle of materiality (*prakṛti*). These two categories apparently seem to be two different substances, opposite in nature. But the two are manifestations of one and the same substance or reality — pure Consciousness (Śiva). It is Śiva, the ultimate Consciousness, that becomes both *puruṣa* (the subject) and *prakṛti* (the object). Thus both *puruṣa* and *prakṛti* are manifestations of Śiva.

The world of matter, according to Kashmir Śaivism, is an *ābhāsa* ("appearance," "reflection," or "projection") of Consciousness. The so-called matter is really Consciousness — objectified, solidified, coagulated Consciousness. Matter is "Consciousness fallen asleep" as Sri Aurobindo puts it. In Sāṁkhya we find a dichotomy between *puruṣa* (Consciousness) and *prakṛti* (matter), and the two ultimately fall apart. But in Kashmir Śaivism there is no dichotomy between the two, the two are really one substance. *Puruṣa* is not the "conquerer" of nature (*prakṛti*), for Nature is not his enemy; in fact, Nature is himself — it is his own *śakti* ("power") or the manifestation of his own deeper Self.

In the time of Newton, science maintained a gap between matter and energy. Modern science has bridged this gap — matter is coagulated or solidified energy, and energy is evaporated matter, so to speak. But science is not yet able to bridge the gap between Consciousness and matter; science does not even accept Consciousness as an entity. Biology, the science of life, accepts Consciousness only as a function of the body — a cerebral activity. In the future history of science, a time may come when Consciousness is accepted as a reality and the gap between Consciousness and matter is bridged. Tantrism, the yogic science of ancient India, believed in this. In fact the Tantric seers, who could be called spiritual scientists, discovered the reality of Spirit or Consciousness, and the unity of Consciousness with Nature.

The twenty-four material categories of Sāṁkhya are not ontologically related to Consciousness (*puruṣa*); *prakṛti* is the independent primordial substance (*pradhāna*) from which the rest of the twenty-three categories follow. The difference between Kashmir Śaivism and Sāṁkhya regarding the conception of *prakṛti* and what evolves from it is the following: (a) in Sāṁkhya, *prakṛti* is real, that is, made of matter, independent of the knowing consciousness. In Kashmir Śaivism, *prakṛti* is appearance (*ābhāsa*), although an active self-projection, of Consciousness. (b) In Sāṁkhya, *prakṛti* is an independent reality; there is no lord or controller of *prakṛti*. In Kashmir Śaivism, *prakṛti* is dependent on Śiva; *prakṛti* is the manifestation or creation of Śiva. (c) In Sāṁkhya, *prakṛti* and *puruṣa* are dichotomous and opposite in nature, although *prakṛti* is said to be working for the liberation of *puruṣa.* In Kashmir Śaivism the two are in perfect harmony, *prakṛti* being the consort of *puruṣa* as it were.

Apart from the above-mentioned basic differences, *prakṛti* and its twenty-three derivatives are enumerated and defined in almost the same way as in Sāṁkhya. From *prakṛti*, the matrix of the material world, first evolves the triad of *buddhi* (or *mahat*), *ahaṁkāra*, and *manas*, which is something like a subtle internal organ or minute apparatus through which Consciousness (*puruṣa*) performs the acts of knowing (cognition), willing (conation), and feeling affection. *Buddhi* [66] ("intellect") is responsible for knowing, *ahaṁkāra* for willing, and *manas* for feeling. The three together are sometimes called *citta*, sometimes *antaḥkaraṇa* ("internal organ"), and sometimes the term *manas* is used to denote all three — *manas*, *buddhi*, and *ahaṁkāra.*[67]

The word *manas* is sometimes translated into English as "mind," but "mind" as a term of Western philosophy means something quite different from *manas.* "Mind" in Western philosophy is primarily used for the knowing consciousness — what is called self or soul — *puruṣa* in Indian philosophy — therefore, mind is not material. *Manas*, however, is material — it evolves from *prakṛti*, a subtle evolution of matter, of course. *Manas* is a special concept of the Indian tradition that is not found in the West. Indian philosophers conceived of a subtle organ, which is made of subtle matter, a subtle apparatus that evolves out of the material *prakṛti*, through which Consciousness performs the mental functions. This subtle organ or apparatus is called *manas* and includes *buddhi* and *ahaṁkāra.*

The idea of conceiving of an organ or organs for mental functions perhaps came from reflecting upon the function of the sense organs (*indriyas*). The self or consciousness perceives through the sense organs. For example, it sees through the eyes, hears through the ears, and so on. These sense organs are material but, of course, subtler than the gross flesh of the body. If there is some defect in a sense organ, the self cannot perceive. It might have occurred to the Indian thinkers that just as the *indriyas*, which are material, are organs or apparatuses through which the self (consciousness) perceives, there should be subtler organs through which the self performs the subtler mental functions of thinking (or knowing, willing, and feeling). For this they conceived of *manas*, through which the self performs thinking — thinking being the general term for all mental activity -- or they conceived of *manas*, *buddhi*, and *ahaṁkāra* as the respective organs of feeling, knowing, and willing.

The Western philosopher would perhaps say that the mind or the self thinks or performs the mental activities like knowing, willing, and so on, all by itself and that there is no need of conceiving of an extra mental organ for that. The biologist, of course, locates different brain centers for different mental activities. But this is a purely physical conception of consciousness; the mind, or consciousness, is not an independent reality that works through the brain; the mind itself is a product and activity of the brain. Mind is a product of matter. Indian psychology, however, conceives of the "mind," in the sense of consciousness or self, as an independent reality working through the apparatus of the brain.

Considering the fact that there are sense organs that serve as apparatuses for different types of perception and there are subtle brain centers that play important roles in mental functions, it is quite reasonable to think that there are even subtler organs, like *manas*, *buddhi*, and *ahaṁkāra*, that serve as subtle apparatuses for the mental functions like thinking (or knowing, willing, and feeling). To accept the mind (consciousness or the self) as an independent reality, and to further accept mental apparatuses for the workings of the mind, is a legitimate hypothesis accepted in Indian psychology.

From the triad of *manas-buddhi-ahaṁkāra*, the five motor organs and the five sense organs evolve. The five motor organs are *vāk* (the organ of speech), *pāṇi* (the hand, the organ of work), *pāda* (the foot, the organ of locomotion), *pāyu* (the anus, the organ of excretion), and *upastha* (the sex-organ). The five sensory organs are *ghrāṇa* (the nose, the olfactory organ), *rasanā* (the tongue, the organ of taste), *cakṣu* (the eye, the visual organ), *tvak* (the skin, the tactual organ), and *śrotra* (the ear, the auditory organ). This is the obvious and universally acceptable classification of motor and sensory organs that are mentioned because they are important stages in the evolution of earthly existence.

It should be noted here that the motor or sensory organs are not the visible external limbs of the gross body that is part of the *pañca-mahābhūta* ("five gross elements"); they are subtle functionaries that are situated in their respective external limbs. The eye, for example, is not just made of the *mahābhūtas* or "gross elements"; it is the subtle organ that functions through the retina and so on. Similarly, the motor organ that is called "hand" (*pāṇi*) is not just flesh and bones, which are the gross elements constituting the body; it is the subtle organ that works through the aggregation of muscles and bones that we normally call the hand. When this subtle organ becomes diseased, the working of the organ becomes faulty even when the external gross limb is very much intact.

From the subtler elements that constitute the five sensory organs evolve what are called the *pañca-tanmātra*, the five subtle elements. They are *gandha* ("odor"), *rasa* ("taste"), *rūpa* ("color"), *sparśa* ("touch"), and *śabda* ("sound"). The olfactory organ (*ghrāṇa*) is related to *gandha-tanmātra* ("odor"); the organ of taste (*rasanā*) to *rasa-tanmātra* ("taste"); the visual organ (*cakṣu*) to *rūpa-tanmātra* ("color"); the tactual organ (*tvak*) to *sparśa-tanmātra* ("touch"); and the auditory organ (*śrotra*) to *śabda-tanmātra* ("sound").

The *tanmātra* is the intermediary between the sense organ and the external object (*mahābhūta*). A particular sense organ is able to grasp its particular object because there is something in common between the two. The eye, for example, is able to grasp color because the subtle element of color (*rūpa-tanmātra*) is present in the eye as well as in the object. The sense organ falls on the side of the subjective and the gross elements on the side of the objective. The *tanmātra* joins the two and it has the characteristics of both — the subjective and the objective.

From the five *tanmātras*[68] ("subtle elements") evolve the five gross elements (*pañca-mahābhūta*).[69] The *pañca-mahābhūtas* are *pṛthvi* ("earth"), *ap* or *jala* ("water"), *tejas* or *agni* ("fire"), *vāyu* ("air"), and *ākāśa* ("ether"). *Pṛthvi* ("earth") is related to *gandha-tanmātra* ("odor"); *ap* or *jala* ("water") to *rasa-tanmātra* ("taste"); *tejas* or *agni* to *rūpa-tanmātra* ("color"); *vāyu* ("air") to *sparśa-tanmātra* ("touch"); and *ākāśa* ("ether") to *śabda-tanmātra* ("sound").[70]

The intimate relation of the sense organ (*jñānendriya*), through the subtle element (*tanmātra*), to the gross element (*mahābhūta*) becomes obvious when we analyze our perceptual experience. But when we view it from the angle of idealistic metaphysics, the relationship becomes all the more clear. According to idealistic metaphysics (that is, Kashmir Śaivism), the gross element (*mahābhūta*) is the projection or appearance (*ābhāsa*) of Consciousness. As such, the *mahābhūta* must depend upon our "seeing" it.[71] Hence, it is quite appropriate to maintain that the objective *mahābhūta* comes out of the subjective element that is present in the sense organ. And since the subjective, in the process of becoming the objective, must pass through an intermediary that connects the two, it is also quite appropriate, even warranted, that the *tanmātra*, which is an intermediary between the subjective and the objective, should be conceived of. Thus the causal relationship between the sense organ and the *mahābhūta* through the *tanmātra* is quite understandable.

It should be noted here that the above position should not be interpreted in favor of Subjective Idealism, which Kashmir Śaivism is not. Kashmir Śaivism is Absolute Idealism, which maintains that the world is a projection of the cosmic Śiva-Consciousness. But since the projected world of *ābhāsa* has perceptual existence only, it must evolve from the perceptual elements which are present in the sense organs.

Though the language of the five gross elements (*pañca-mahābhūta*) that is used for understanding and classifying all the material elements (*tattvas*) appears to be crude and primitive, it is quite relevant even now. The ancient Indian thinkers classified all the material elements into five categories. Science has discovered more than a hundred elements. Almost all the traditional *mahābhūtas* are found to be compounds of various elements. For example, water is a compound of hydrogen and oxygen (H_2O), air is a compound of oxygen, nitrogen, and so forth. What we call earth (*pṛthvī*) is itself a mixture of a hundred elements. All the elements can be conveniently classified under the five general categories of *mahābhūtas* on the basis of the similarity and unification of elements. It would be more convenient to talk about the elements in ordinary language in terms of the five gross elements (*pañca-mahābhūta*) than in terms of the hundred-plus elements. Of course for specific scientific purposes, the language of *mahābhūta* would not work; but for ordinary purposes it is sufficient.

The five gross elements are placed in a hierarchical order from the more gross to the less gross. An element's place in the hierarchy is based on the number of sense organs capable of perceiving it. *Pṛthvī* ("earth") is the grossest of all the *mahābhūtas*, for it can be perceived by the maximum number of senses (touched, seen, tasted, and smelled). Water is less gross; it can be touched, seen and tasted. Fire is still less gross; it can be touched and seen. Air can be grasped only through touch (*sparśa*). Ether (*ākāśa*) is the least gross, for it can be grasped by none of the sense organs; in fact, *ākāśa* is not perceived but inferred on the basis of sound, which is the characteristic of *ākāśa*. The reason the materialist (*Cārvāka*) does not accept the fifth element *ākāśa* ("ether") is that *ākāśa* is accepted on the basis of inference, not on the basis of perception, which alone is accepted by the *Cārvāka*.

DISCUSSION OF THE CATEGORIZATION

A question is sometimes raised that since Kashmir Śaivism accepts thirty-six *tattvas* ("realities" or "categories"), it must be a pluralistic system. The acceptance of as many as thirty-six *tattvas* is seen as going against the monism of Kashmir Śaivism. This question is obviously naive, for the so-called *tattvas* are not independent realities. They are all manifestations of one and the same Reality, the Śiva-Consciousness that is the unity of Śiva-Śakti. The single reality that is Śiva-Śakti (or dynamic Consciousness) extends or manifests itself into the form of the world, and the process of one becoming many is described in thirty-six hierarchical and successive steps or stages. Thus Reality itself is one and not thirty-six; the thirty-six categories are merely a convenient way of describing the process of manifestation (Creation).

The process of Creation involves succession (*krama*), as is suggested by the thirty-six categories; but Śiva-consciousness, which is the matrix of the world of succession, is itself *akrama* ("without succession or sequence"). From the point of view of Śiva-Consciousness, Creation is without succession and really without difference,[72] for Creation is not a physical or material activity but is creation within Consciousness. When we imagine or construct in our mind the successive and changing steps of the creation of something, our consciousness itself does not undergo succession nor does it really change. So the *akrama* (Śiva), although giving birth to the *krama* (Creation) always remains the *Akrama*; therefore it can be said that Śiva is both *Krama* (Creation) and *Akrama* (beyond Creation). In his *Śivastotrāvalī*, Utpaladeva, the grand-teacher of Abhinavagupta, brings out this position in poetic perfection. In one of his verses he says, "I bow to Śambhu (Śiva) who is the world, and is beyond the world."[73]

In this context it should be noted that the picture of Reality presented through the thirty-six categories is Reality as grasped or understood by reason or the intellect. It is not Reality *in itself.* The thirty-six categories become the object of thought or the known (*vedya*), and whatever becomes the object of thought is not Śiva, as Śiva (the Self) is always the knower not the known. So Śiva (Reality) presented in the form of the thirty-six categories is the Reality of *our* understanding, not Reality in itself, which is beyond our grasp. That is why Abhinavagupta says that the real Śiva,

Parama-Śiva as it is called, is the thirty-seventh category.[74] And if we include Parama-Śiva within the categories and have thirty-seven categories, then Parama-Śiva would be the thirty-eighth[75] and so on. The point is that Parama-Śiva will always elude our understanding, for when grasped by the mind, it becomes known as an object, and Parama-Śiva (the Self) is the knower (*vettā*) not the known (*vedya*). This idea is made abundantly clear in the Upaniṣads also.[76]

As far as the number of categories is concerned, thirty-six is not a hard and fast number; the total can be more or less. But the given number is perhaps the most convenient way of enumerating the categories. At the grossest level the elements are understandably classified into five. The external elements are related to the sense organs that perceive them. So it is natural that the five gross elements have, as their correlates, the five sense organs that are given by Nature. It is also natural that there should be intermediaries that conjoin the sense organs and the gross elements (*mahābhūtas*). Hence the five *tanmātras.* The five motor organs given by Nature are as important for individual existence as the five sense organs.

Above these twenty categories, it is reasonable to accept the three categories of the subtle organs of knowing, willing, and feeling (*buddhi, manas,* and *ahaṁkāra*). The matrix of all material categories is *prakṛti;* this *prakṛti* is the twenty-fourth. Acceptance of consciousness is indispensable, hence *puruṣa* is the twenty-fifth category. In fact the sentient mind, or consciousness, and insentient matter constitute the entire earthly existence.

Kashmir Śaivism does not stop with these twenty-five categories, as Sāṁkhya does. The true nature of *puruṣa* is different from its present bound state, and it is necessary to enumerate the factors that contribute to its bondage. Hence the six categories of *māyā* and its five *kañcukas.* It is also obvious that since Kashmir Śaivism is an Absolutistic system, it will not stop with the resulting thirty-one categories that constitute the realm of duality. Five more categories are thus accepted. These are the categories of unity from which the categories of difference emerge.

The categories of unity, which are called "pure" categories (*śuddhādhvā*), must be five in number. The first two categories, Śiva and Śakti, are ultimate. Unlike Advaita Vedānta, which accepts an Absolute (Brahman) that is only illumination or knowledge (*jñāna*), Kashmir Śaivism includes Śakti or dynamism (*kriyā*) within the Absolute. At the ultimate level then, there is not just Śiva but Śiva-Śakti. When this ultimate Reality (Śiva-Śakti) creates the world, it naturally passes through the three stages of *Sadāśiva*, *Īśvara*, and *Sadvidyā*, which are the correlates of *icchā*, *jñāna*, and *kriyā*. The triad *icchā-jñāna-kriyā* is involved in every act of creation.

The five "pure" categories (*śuddhāddhvā*) and the thirty-one "impure" categories (*aśuddhādhvā*) together constitute the entire Reality. As can be seen, every step in the process of Creation, from ultimate Consciousness to the gross elements, is more or less necessary. Hence the justification of accepting the thirty-six categories of Creation.

It is obvious that the process of Creation goes from unity to difference. It is also natural that when unity becomes or manifests difference, it (unity) has to pass through the stage of unity-in-difference. Śiva-Śakti, the ultimate conceivable level of Consciousness, is the state of pure unity (*abheda*). It is the state of the pure subject or the pure "I am" (*aham*). The object, or the "this" (*idam*), is simply not there, as Creation has not yet started. The remaining three "pure" categories (*Sadāśiva*, *Īśvara*, and *Sadvidyā*) are the stages of unity-in-difference. When Śiva-Śakti freely wills the creation of the world, it successively becomes *Sadāśiva*, *Īśvara*, and *Sadvidyā*, which are the correlates of *icchā*, *jñāna*, and *kriyā*.

In order to finally manifest the stage of difference, the state of unity-in-difference has to pass through these successive stages in which the difference becomes increasingly manifest, although it is held by unity throughout. In the *Sadāśiva* (*icchā*) stage, the difference (*idam*) has just sprouted. It (the difference) is in the form of the will to create the "this." This is technically called the stage of *ahamidam* or "I am this," the "this" being in the nebulous stage. In the *Īśvara* (*jñāna*) stage, the difference (*idam*) becomes more manifest, as it comes out in the form of a complete mental picture or ideation of the object to be created (the world). It is called the stage of *idamaham* or "this I am," the "this" being fully evolved but still in the mental stage of ideation. In the *Sadvidyā* (*kriyā*) stage, the difference becomes the most manifest as it emerges as external *ābhāsa* ("appearance") or *pratibimba* ("reflection"). This is called the stage of *ahañca idañca* or "I am and this is," the "this" being externally projected as *ābhāsa* but still held by the unity of "*aham.*"

The above-mentioned stages are the three essential successive stages of unity-in-difference, as they are involved in every act of creation in the form of *icchā-jñāna-kriyā.* To accept the three stages of unity-in-difference is the insight of Tantrism. The remaining thirty-one categories that form the *aśuddhādhvā*, or "impure" categories, belong to the realm of difference, as here the sense of unity is lost. Thus, Śiva-Śakti is unity or pure unity; *Sadāśiva*, *Īśvara*, and *Sadvidyā* are unity-in-difference; and the other thirty-one categories, from *māyā* to *pañcamahābhūta*, are difference (*bheda*).

It is also obvious that the process of Creation moves from the subtle to the gross. Consciousness can be called subtle (*sūkṣma*) and matter gross (*sthūla*). Creation moves from Consciousness to matter. Even in the evolution of the material categories of *prakṛti*, the movement is from subtle matter to gross matter. Thus Creation is from unity to difference, from subject to object (*aham* to *idam*), from Consciousness to matter, from internal to external, from subtle to gross, from higher to lower.

Dissolution naturally occurs in reverse order. The gross is dissolved into the subtle, the *idam* into *aham*, matter into Consciousness, the external into the internal, difference into unity, the lower into the higher. The gross *mahābhūta* is dissolved into the subtler *tanmātra*, the *tanmātra* into still subtler elements, and so on. Finally everything is dissolved into the ultimate Śiva-Śakti from whence everything had originally emerged.

Thus goes the process of creation and dissolution, which is part of the eternal sportive activity (*līlā* or *krīdā*) of Absolute Consciousness (Śiva, the Self) and in His very nature. That it is the nature of Śiva means that it is not caused by any motive — for motive would suggest some want or lack in Śiva — but is the natural overflow or emanation of the bliss (*ānanda*) of Śiva. But this does not mean that Śiva cannot check the process or that it will go on for ever even if Śiva does not want it. Śiva can dismiss the whole process and refrain from creating the world if He so desires. Creation is completely an expression of the freedom (*svātantrya*) of Śiva. So, Śiva can be *with* or *without* Creation. Utpaladeva says, "I bow to Śiva who causes the world to come into existence and who also contradicts (dissolves) it, who takes the form of the world and who also remains without the world."[77]

5

The Theory of Appearance (Ābhāsavāda)

In India the Yogācāra Vijñānavāda (Buddhism) is considered idealism; the very name of the system, *vijñānavāda*, means "idealism." Kashmir Śaivism is another idealistic system of Indian philosophy. But whereas in Yogācāra Vijñānavāda there is also a clear tradition of subjective idealism (*dṛṣṭi-sṛṣṭi-vāda*) and it is a matter of controversy whether Vijñānavāda is subjective idealism or absolute idealism (*sṛṣṭi-dṛṣṭi-vāda*), Kashmir Śaivism is absolute idealism as it clearly maintains that the world is an "ideal" projection, not of the individual self, but of the cosmic Self, Śiva. If "idealism" is taken as a "speculative" philosophy, Kashmir Śaivism is not that; the idealism of Kashmir Śaivism is quite different from Hegelian idealism, which is purely speculative. Kashmir Śaivism is nearer to the idealism of Plato or even more, that of Plotinus, where idealism is based more on mystic experience than on speculation. The Kashmir Śaiva idealism is actually based on the higher experience of the seers and yogins; it is the "tradition of experience" (*anubhava-sampradāya*), as Abhinavagupta puts it.[1]

The world, according to Kashmir Śaivism, is not a material reality but a reality in Consciousness.[2] It is not subjective, for it is not the projection of an individual mind. It is objective but not material. To be objective and to be material are two different things. The world can be fully objective and yet made of Consciousness (Spirit) and not matter. Consciousness itself is an objective reality.

THE MEANING OF ĀBHĀSA

The world is what is called *ābhāsa*. The meaning of the word *ābhāsa* is "appearance," that which appears (*ābhāsate*). *Ābhāsa* is also called *pratibimba* ("reflection"), which is quite helpful in understanding the meaning of *ābhāsa*. *Ābhāsa*, or *pratibimba*, is for example, what is reflected in a mirror — say the face. When one sees one's face in a mirror, the actual face is the archetype (*bimba*) and what is reflected in the mirror is *ābhāsa* or *pratibimba*, ("appearance" or "reflection").

In one sense, the reflection is one with the archetype, but in another sense it is different.[3] The reflection is one with the archetype in the sense that it is not a different substance or reality; in reality it is nothing but the archetype. It is the reflection *of* the archetype, not a reality in itself. In the case of Śiva's projecting the world as appearance or reflection, Śiva-Consciousness is the archetype of the world as well as the mirror in which the world is reflected. The reflection differs from the archetype in that the reflection is a reflection and the archetype an archetype; the reflection itself is *not* the archetype. What happens to the reflection of the face in the mirror may not happen to the face itself. For example, if the reflection in the mirror is hit by a stone, the mirror may shatter but the actual face is not harmed.

Again the reflection (*pratibimba*) is in one sense unreal and in another sense real. It is unreal in the sense that it is not what it appears to be. For example, the reflection of the face in the mirror looks like the face, but it is really not the face made of flesh and blood. It is just a reflection. What is real is the actual face (*bimba*) and not the reflection (*pratibimba*) which is just an appearance (*ābhāsa*). But the *pratibimba* (*ābhāsa*) is real in the sense that it actually appears and is not simply imagined. You actually see it outside yourself; you do not just imagine it in your mind. The reflection *as reflection* or *as appearance* is quite real. Or to use another example, the photograph of a person is not real (if by "real" we mean the person himself or herself), but *as photo* it is real and it is also used for real purposes like fixing it on an identity card or passport.

In order to understand the meaning of *ābhāsa* ("appearance") it is necessary to distinguish it from what is called *vimarśa. Vimarśa* literally means "thinking;" the word *vimarśa* is used for mental activity or "ideation" in the mind. As such, *vimarśa* is something that goes on inside the mind and does not appear outside it. But *ābhāsa* is an external projection that can be grasped by the sense organs. *Ābhāsa* therefore is not a mere idea in the mind but an actual appearance reflected outside the mind. For example, when one imagines one's face in one's mind, it is *vimarśa*, as it is just a thought, but when one sees the reflection of one's face in a mirror, it is *ābhāsa*, as it is an actual appearance.

To enumerate the three states of *vimarśa*, *ābhāsa*, and the real object: when one remembers a loved one, it is *vimarśa*, as the person is in one's mind; it is a form of thinking (*vimarśa*). When one sees a photograph of the person or sees the reflection of that person in a mirror, that is *ābhāsa*, as it is not the person him- or herself. When one sees the person in flesh and blood, this is the object, as it is the real archetype (*bimba*). The *bimba* in itself is the object; the *bimba* when reflected in a mirror as *pratibimba* and the *bimba* when reflected in the mind as an idea or thought, becomes *vimarśa*.

Thus we can see that *ābhāsa* is objective but not material. The reflection in the mirror is objective because it exists as reflection, and it can be seen. But the reflection (*pratibimba*) is not material because it is not the real object; it is just a reflection or mere appearance. The *bimba* is material, for it is made of actual matter. But the reflection in the mirror is not made of matter; it is the appearance of matter, not matter itself. We can paradoxically say that it is a thing and yet not a thing. It is a thing because it is seen, and in that sense it is objective; it is also not a thing because it is just the reflection or appearance of the real thing.

With the meaning of *ābhāsa* discussed above, it is now possible to understand the ontological status of the world according to Kashmir Śaivism. The world is *ābhāsa* projected or reflected in the mirror of cosmic Consciousness. Abhinavagupta explains this position with the help of the analogy of the reflection in a mirror — his favorite analogy. "Just as earth, water, etc. are reflected in a clean mirror without being mixed, so also the entire world of objects appears together in the one Lord Consciousness."[4] "The Lord appropriates the entire world to Himself, (reflecting the world) in the mirror of His Consciousness, and in this way He has pure ubiquity."[5] "This entire world of 'many-ness' appears in the Self (Consciousness) like a reflection (*pratibimba*), and the Self is the lord of the entire reflected world."[6]

Abhinavagupta is also aware of the limitation of this analogy in conveying Reality faithfully.[7] The analogy has two shortcomings as a representation of Śiva-Consciousness reflecting the world. For one, the reflection appears in the passive mirror from an object (*bimba*) that stands outside the mirror; it is not one with the mirror. For another, the mirror is not aware of the reflection, as the mirror is an insentient thing (*jaḍa*). But in the case of the world being reflected in Śiva-Consciousness, Consciousness (the Self or Śiva) is the *bimba* (the world) that is reflected and Consciousness is also the mirror in which the world is reflected. Unlike the passive mirror, which receives reflections from outside, Consciousness actively creates its own reflections. In other words, if Consciousness is taken as a mirror, it should be a creative "mirror" that projects or creates reflections from within itself. There is nothing except Consciousness, and there is nothing outside of Consciousness which could be reflected in Consciousness; Consciousness self-projects or self-manifests the reflections (the world).[8]

Moreover, unlike the insentient mirror that is unaware of the reflection, Consciousness (the Self or Śiva) is fully aware of the process of reflection going on within It. In fact, Consciousness enjoys Itself by reflecting within Itself the world that It freely creates from within Itself.

THE EPISTEMOLOGY OF ĀBHĀSAVĀDA

It may be asked, what is the proof for Ābhāsavāda, the theory that the world is appearance? The final proof of anything is the cognition (experience or knowledge) of that thing; we can be sure of a phenomenon only when we know or cognize it. The question arises: how do we know that the world is appearance? What is the epistemological ground for the theory of world-as-appearance (Ābhāsavāda)?

Epistemology does not contradict Ābhāsavāda. There is no epistemological ground on which we can reject Ābhāsavāda as a theory. Logically and epistemologically, the theory of world-as-appearance cannot be disproved. Of course it cannot be proved either, but the point is that the logical possibility of the theory definitely exists.

The general arguments given in criticism of Realism and in favor of Idealism are given by Abhinavagupta also. The language of the arguments may be slightly different, but the content is almost the same. But what Abhinavagupta has to add, and what makes his position unique, is that Ābhāsavāda is based on the actual experience of the seers and yogins.

In order to establish idealism (Ābhāsavāda), Abhinavagupta starts with the criticism of Realism. This he does in the *Vimarśinī* and also in the *Tantrāloka*. Realism means that the object that we perceive is real. This means that the object exists in its own right independent of being perceived by a knower. The object does not come into existence by virtue of its being seen, as happens in dreams, but it exists even if one does not see it. The object exists first; our knowledge of it comes later. This can happen only when the object is made not of mind or consciousness but of matter, which is an independent substance. The secondary meaning of "real" is "material."

Idealism, on the contrary, means that the object that we perceive depends upon our seeing it — *esse est percipi*, in the words of Berkeley. The object comes into existence when it is perceived, as occurs in a dream. The "seeing" or "perceiving" comes first, the object comes later. This can be true only when the object is made not of matter, but of mind, consciousness, or thought, as in the case of the dream object. The object is thus not "real" but "ideal" — made of thought. According to Idealism, Consciousness is the only reality, and what appears as matter is the projection or appearance (*ābhāsa*) of Consciousness as its reflection in a mirror or as things in a dream.[9]

The main argument of the Realist, put simply, is that the world is real because it appears to be real. The table, the chair, and the whole world appear quite real. In technical terms, the object is real because it has pragmatic value (*artha-kriyā-kāritva*) or correspondence (*saṁvādi-pravṛtti*). If the object is real it is expected to fulfill certain pragmatic demands. For example, a chair should be felt when we touch it; it should hold us when we sit in it, and so on. If it passes the pragmatic test, then it is real. If it does not pass the pragmatic test, it is illusory, like a mirage. In the summer season one sees from some distance waves of water over a sandy desert. When one goes near in order to touch the water and quench one's thirst, one's expectations are not met. One realizes that what appeared to be water was only a mirage — an illusion. For the Realist, *arthakriyā* is the test of truth, and the world is real because it has *arthakriyā* or pragmatic value.

We have already seen that *arthakriyā* is not, in fact, the test of truth. Here it must suffice to say that *arthakriyā* is equally present in the illusory object as, for example, the dream object. An illusion, by its very definition, is something that is not real yet appears to be real. It appears to have *arthakriyā*. The dream chair is an appearance, and the chair holds you when you sit in it in the dream. This act of supporting your weight is just as much an appearance as the chair itself. *Arthakriyā* is thus another appearance; it cannot prove the reality of the object.[10] The Realist is thus not able to establish his or her case. Had Nature not given us the experience of dreams or other cases of illusion, we would have dogmatically believed that what *appears* to be real *is* real; we would never have suspected that what appears to be real could also be false. Epistemologically speaking, the dream is our eye-opener, it opens up the possibility of the world's being an appearance.

Abhinavagupta, as a typical Idealist, argues that the knowledge of the object, that is, the things of the world, depends on knowledge itself. The object is *jñāna-sāpekṣa* ("related to, or dependent upon, knowledge"). Whenever the object comes to be known by the mind, it is known as knowledge, not as a material thing. We know it as it appears to us, not as it is in itself.[11] As Kant would put it, we only have access to the appearance; we have no access to reality or the thing-in-itself. This is what is meant by *sahopalambha-niyama* of the Buddhist. The object always comes (*upalambha*) *with* (*saha*) knowledge (that is, *as* knowledge), it does not come independently; it is always dependent on knowledge. So how can we know it in itself? We cannot know the thing itself, we can only know the knowledge of the thing. For us, the "known" is also knowledge (appearance), as we do not see the "known" independent of the knowledge.[12]

Abhinavagupta, therefore, points out that when we know the world, the world comes to our mind as reflection (*pratibimba*). It cannot be otherwise, for objects enter the mind or consciousness only as something mental or ideational, they cannot enter into the mind as material things. For example, the physical table cannot enter into the mind; what enters the mind is the impression, appearance, reflection, or knowledge of the table. The mind can grasp only the appearance (*ābhāsa*) or the reflection (*pratibimba*) not the *bimba* or the thing itself.

It is true that the mind can contain only *pratibimba* ("reflection"), but the fact is that an actual object is needed in order to produce the reflection in the mind. It is true that the mirror can contain only the *pratibimba*, the *bimba* itself cannot enter into the mirror. But is it not true that the reflection in the mirror occurs only when there is an object outside the mirror? A camera can receive only film; a person enters the camera only as an image made of light and shade. While the solid human being made of flesh and blood cannot enter the camera, it is also true that the camera records the image of a person only when somebody poses before the camera.

Abhinavagupta himself raises this question, speaking for his opponent (*pūrvapakṣa*), asking, "How can there be *pratibimba* in the absence of *bimba*?"[13] The answer he gives is that in our actual experience we find that there is *pratibimba* even without *bimba*,[14] as in a dream. The tiger that we "see" in a dream is not standing before us as the *bimba*; the dream tiger is merely a *pratibimba* created or projected from within the mind, not reflected from an outside *bimba*. There is no real tiger as an outside object.[15]

The objection that there can be no *pratibimba* without *bimba* would be valid only if the mind is a passive thing like the material mirror that passively receives *pratibimba* only from outside itself. But the mind is an active and creative thing; it can create *pratibimba* from within itself without *bimba*, as it does in a dream. Some people naively argue that the tiger that we see in a dream is real because the same tiger is seen at the zoo or in the jungle; they forget that the tiger that we "see" in a dream is not the tiger of the zoo, it is a mental tiger projected as *ābhāsa*. *Bimba* does not mean just anything existing anywhere; it means an object that stands before one like the face before the mirror. The tiger from the zoo is not the *bimba* here, as it does not stand before one to be reflected in or grasped by the mind. It is thus perfectly valid to hold that there can be *pratibimba* even without *bimba*; the mind is capable of projecting or creating *pratibimba* by itself.[16]

In the Modern period of Western philosophy, Locke raised the question of the content of knowledge. It became clear to him that the mind cannot know the actual things of the world, for the things themselves cannot enter into the mind; the mind can know only what he calls "ideas." By "ideas" Locke does not mean a concept in the mind but what appears before the sense organs. The mind can receive only mental things — ideas, images, or reflections — not things or "substances." We can understand Locke's position by bringing in the analogy of the mirror or the camera. The mirror can grasp only the reflection, not the thing itself, just as the camera can receive only images, not people. Similarly the mind, which is analogous to the mirror or the camera, can grasp only the "ideas," the appearances, or reflections. Locke concludes that the mind can know or perceive only ideas, it cannot know things or substances.

But Locke, realist as he is, further argues that there must be external things that cause the ideas or which reflect into the mind in the form of ideas. This is the argument that there must be *bimba* in order to create *pratibimba.* Locke contends that although we do not know or see the real things, we must accept by logical implication, the existence of a real world that causes ideas or reflections in the mind. Berkeley, the idealist, refutes the argument of Locke by showing that the mind is creative; it can create ideas without a real and material world, as is obvious in the example of the dream. Berkeley maintains that the existence of things depends upon our perception; the things exist when we see them (*esse est percipi*).

A question remains: while the dream object — say a tiger — is false or mere appearance and is the projection of the *idea* of a tiger, from where did the idea of the tiger come? It came from seeing a real tiger in a zoo or the jungle. The real tiger exists not in a dream but in the actual world. To use the analogy of the cinema, what we see on the screen is a moving picture projected from the film reel in the projector. The images on the screen are not real. The world may be like a motion picture and the film reel from where it is projected may be in our mind in the form of ideas. But the film itself is prepared by shooting real scenes in which real men and women have acted. So it originally comes from a real world. This is the argument that Aristotle used against Plato's theory of ideas, the "argument of a third world." Aristotle argued that even if we accept the present world as a shadow projected from the world of ideas, we have to accept a third world from which the world of ideas is copied.

The usual answer given to the above question is that it is not necessary that the ideas be copied from some real world; the ideas may be inherently present in Consciousness. It is quite possible that Consciousness alone exists, and exists with its ideas naturally and inherently present in it. Abhinavagupta would only add that ideas being inherent in Consciousness does not make for any kind of necessity in Consciousness. The ideas are present in Consciousness not as a deterministic potentiality, similar to the way that information exists in the gene or the seed, but as the freedom of Consciousness. Consciousness freely creates the ideas as *vimarśa* ("thinking") and projects them as *ābhāsa* ("appearance").[17] That the ideas are inherent means only that they have not come from outside.[18]

If the realist still maintains that Consciousness cannot have ideas of its own accord, the idealist can counter that just as matter has its own forms, Consciousness has its own ideas. It is obvious that matter has a variety of forms. Suppose the realist who believes in the existence of matter is asked where the "forms" of matter come from? The realist would obviously answer that the forms came from nowhere, they are inherent in the matter itself. The idealist would then retort that if matter can have its inherent forms, why can Consciousness not have its inherent ideas, which are the inherent forms of Consciousness? Plato actually calls the ideas "forms," and his Theory of Ideas is also called the "Theory of Forms." If it is valid to maintain that forms are inherent in matter, it is also valid to maintain that ideas are inherent in Consciousness.

Thus we see that the position of the idealist is logically tenable; Ābhāsavāda (Idealism) is a logically plausible theory. But this does not mean that the idealist succeeds in disproving the position of the realist, thereby proving his or her own position. What the idealist succeeds in doing is not demolishing the realist's position; all that he or she succeeds in showing is that the realist cannot establish his or her case. The realist stands suspect, but this does not mean that realism is proved to be wrong. The same is true of the idealist. Hume sides with Berkeley when Berkeley declares, against Locke, that the existence of matter cannot be proved, but Hume also demonstrates, against Berkeley, that the idealist's position cannot be proved either.

If we analyze the position of idealism (Ābhāsavāda) from the point of view of a neutral critic, we will find that logically and epistemologically Ābhāsavāda can neither be proved nor disproved. It is beyond the capacity of our ordinary understanding to know the reality of what appears to us as the world. At most we can say that something is appearing before us that seems to be real, but whether it is a mere appearance or there is a real material world behind it cannot be determined. What appears to us may not be real, but it may also be very real. Ābhāsavāda cannot be proved by ordinary knowledge; from the point of view of ordinary knowledge, it is just a possibility.

Abhinavagupta would accept that Ābhāsavāda cannot be proved on the ground of ordinary knowledge. But he would add that Ābhāsavāda is accepted on the basis of *āgamic* knowledge. *Āgamic* knowledge is the higher experience of the seers and yogins. It is they who have experienced the world as *ābhāsa*. The Āgama (Tantra), which is the record of such experience, declares that Śiva appears (*ābhāsate*) in the form of the world. Those who attain *mukti* ("liberation" or "Self-realization") and reach the level of Śiva know that the world is a free appearance of Śiva (the Self).

Moreover the yogic phenomena bespeak the validity of Ābhāsavāda. Tantrism believes in yogic phenomena, as Tantrism is a yogic tradition. An advanced yogin has the power to materialize things — to create them out of nothing.[19] Creating things out of nothing means creating them out of will or by thought. The yogin is able to create the thing out of thought because the thing is really the thought in concrete appearance. The yogin is able to materialize or dematerialize the things of the world because these things are concretized thought, or materialized Consciousness. In India and in Tibet such yogins have existed in all times; they exist even now. Of course there are many tricksters, but there are also genuine yogins who can transform Consciousness into matter (materialization) and matter into Consciousness (dematerialization). There have been yogins who are reported to have disappeared by dematerializing the body, and have re-appeared at some other place, by re-materializing the body. If such phenomena are true, and they have every probability of being true, then this suggests that the gap between Consciousness and matter is not real and that so-called matter is the concretized appearance of Consciousness.

Thus, we can say that Ābhāsavāda is not just a logically possible theory but is even a probable theory. Āgamic knowledge supports it, and yogic experience is heavily tilted in its favor. The proof of a theory can be twofold. First, it should be logically and rationally explained and shown to be possible. Second, it should be corroborated by experience. We have already seen that the Ābhāsavāda theory is logically possible and rationally explainable. As far as corroboration by experience is concerned, yogic experience strongly supports it, if not fully proving its validity.

ĀBHĀSAVĀDA AS AN ONTOLOGICAL THEORY

We have already seen that epistemology prepares the ground for the theory of appearance (Ābhāsavāda) as an ontological theory. Kashmir Śaivism presents the ontology of appearance (*ābhāsa*). According to Kashmir Śaivism, Consciousness (*samvit* or *citi*), which is called Śiva, is the only reality; there is no matter. This Consciousness (Spirit or Self) *appears* as the material world.[20] The so-called matter is a projection or reflection (*pratibimba*) of Consciousness,[21] like the reflection in a mirror.[22]

Consciousness projects or reflects the world *from* itself, *by* itself, and *within* itself. Consciousness is thus unlike the mirror, which is different from the thing or the archetype (*bimba*) that is reflected in it. Consciousness is both the reflected *bimba* and the mirror in which the *bimba* is reflected. In fact Consciousness is the *bimba*, the mirror, *and* the reflection (*pratibimba*). It is the *bimba*, as It Itself is reflected or projected; there is no reality other than Consciousness, or outside of Consciousness, that could be reflected in Consciousness. It is also the ground or substratum upon or within which the reflection takes place. That is, it is the "mirror" in which the world is reflected.[23] The reflection is also Consciousness, for it is Consciousness that has manifested the reflection. The *pratibimba* ("reflection") is the representation of Consciousness, and the representation is one with the thing represented,[24] as it is the representation *of* Consciousness, just as the reflection in the mirror is the reflection *of* the face, or the photograph is the photograph *of* the person. In that sense the reflection (*pratibimba*) is one with the thing reflected (*bimba*).

So, the world is ideal (made of "ideas") or Consciousness, not real or material. As such, it is one with Consciousness,[25] as it is made of Consciousness, not of matter. A mental projection is one with the mind (consciousness), for the stuff of which the projection is made is the mind or consciousness itself.[26]

Apart from the analogy of reflection in a mirror, the analogy of the dream[27] is usually given to explain the position that the world is appearance and that it is one with Consciousness. The dream, which is a universal phenomenon, is not merely an analogy but also an example of consciousness appearing as things. Consciousness creates or projects out of itself a whole world in dream. The dream object or dream world is substantially nothing but Consciousness itself; in the dream, Consciousness becomes the dreamer as well as the dream object. The world is also a big dream — the cosmic dream of Śiva-Consciousness.

But the "dream" of Śiva is basically different from the dream of the individual soul (*paśu*). It is different in two important respects. First, in the dream of the individual self, the individual forgets that he or she is dreaming; he or she takes the dream to be a real experience. This means that the mind is under an illusion; therefore, although the dream world is the individual's own creation, he or she is not aware of this truth. Second, the individual is not free in creating the dream world. The dream is the creation of the individual's subconscious mind; he or she cannot choose to "see" the dream the way he or she likes. Sometimes dreams occur quite contrary to our liking, as in the case of a nightmare. But Śiva's dream is free from both these defects of ordinary dreams. First, Śiva does not suffer from ignorance or illusion; Śiva knows fully well that the world is His dream, or that the world-as-appearance is His own conscious creation or projection and therefore one with Him. The world is the *conscious* dream of Śiva. Second, Śiva's dream is not bound or determined by unconscious forces; Śiva freely creates his dream. Śiva is free to project the dream world the way He likes.

The analogy of the ordinary dream thus does not completely fit in the case of Śiva. The dream analogy is only used to suggest that just as the dream world is a creation, or projection, of our own consciousness, the world is an appearance or projection of Śiva-Consciousness.[28] The phenomenon of imagination is free from the two defects of dream. The imagined thing is our free creation and we are also aware of the truth that it is our own creation. But the imagined thing is just an idea in our mind in the form of thinking (*vimarśa*); it does not become an actual reflection (*pratibimba*) or appearance (*ābhāsa*). So imagination cannot be used as an analogy. The world is not merely an idea (*vimarśa*) in the mind of Śiva; Śiva actually sees the world as a tangible appearance in form and color, just as we see the reflection in a mirror. The reflection in the mirror is not a mere idea, but an appearance; it is also not a real thing, as it is mere reflection. We see it in the mirror and yet we know that it is mere appearance. Śiva's dream is something like that.

The analogy of the dream should also not give the impression that the world is false and valueless (*tuccha*) like a dream. The dream analogy is used to show that the so-called material world is a manifestation of Consciousness just as the dream world is the manifestation of individual consciousness. The dream analogy is used by the idealist (Ābhāsavādin) and the illusionist (Māyāvādin) alike, but with different intentions. The Advaitin and the Mādhyamika are not idealists in the technical sense of the term; they would also not like to be called idealists. They are illusionists (Māyāvādins), since according to them the world is not an extension of Consciousness (Reality), but a superimposition on it and thus totally false. But the theory of appearance (Ābhāsavāda) of Kashmir Śaivism is an idealism that maintains that the appearance (*ābhāsa*), although "ideal" (made of "idea" or non-material and in that sense false), is true or real as an appearance of Consciousness. That is why Abhinavagupta calls the appearance or the dream real (*satya*). The dream world is not mere nothing; it is an "ideal" reality (made of "idea," or made of mind or consciousness). In Kashmir Śaivism the dream is taken as an "ideal" reality, not as an illusion.

Since the world is a dream, not of the individual mind but of the Śiva mind, it becomes clear that Kashmir Śaivism is an absolute idealism. According to the subjective idealist (*dṛṣṭi-sṛṣṭi-vādin*), there may be only the individual souls and no cosmic or universal mind, like God or the Higher Self, and the world is accepted as the projection of their individual minds. Kashmir Śaivism accepts a cosmic mind or cosmic Self, called Śiva, and maintains that the world of appearance is a projection or creation of this Śiva-mind, not of the individual mind. Therefore, for the individual mind, the world is objective reality. For Śiva, the world may be a subjective reality, although an external appearance and not a mere idea or conception, for it is the creation of the Śiva-mind. It is not so for the individual (*paśu*).

This absolute idealism answers some very serious objections from the realist. The realist may, for example, suggest that if the world is a dream, it should vanish with deep sleep or with the death of the dreamer (the individual soul). But the world persists even when one is in deep sleep or when one dies. Moreover, if the world is a dream, it should vary with different dreamers, every dreamer "seeing" his or her own dream differently from that of others. But we all see the same world, which means that it is not a dream at all. Kashmir Śaivism would answer both these objections by saying that the world is the "dream" not of the individual mind but of Śiva. Since the world is the projection of one and the same Śiva-mind, all individual souls see the same world.

Moreover, the world of appearance persists even after the disappearance of the individual minds, because it is the creation of the cosmic mind (Śiva) and not of the individual mind (*paśu*). Individuals may come and go, but the world goes on forever. Of course, when Śiva dismisses the process of projecting the world by "closing the eyes" (*nimeṣa*), the world of appearance is dissolved. The dream world comes into existence when Śiva "sees" or projects it, and thus Creation is called the *unmeṣa* ("opening of the eyes") of Śiva. The world of appearance is dissolved when Śiva stops "seeing" it; the Dissolution is thus called the *nimeṣa* ("closing of the eyes") of Śiva.

The subjective idealist also answers these questions in his own way, of course. Subjective idealism says that the world *does* disappear when nobody sees it, as the existence of the world depends upon its being seen by someone. The world exists in the eyes of the seer (*dṛṣṭi-sṛṣṭi*), and it is projected outside when the seer opens up his or her eyes (*ātma-khyāti*). When the seer shuts his or her eyes, his or her world disappears. There is no proof that the world exists even when nobody sees it, the subjective idealist would argue. He or she would further maintain that all individuals see the same world because the idea of the world, or the film reel of the world, is the same in all minds; the same idea is common to all. As far as the coherence and cohesion among different individuals is concerned, the coordination is due to a "pre-established harmony," as Leibnitz, a subjective idealist, puts it. The theistic idealist, like Leibnitz, would say that the harmony is established by God, and the atheistic idealist, like the Buddhist, would say that the harmony is established by Nature.

Subjective idealism is no doubt a logically possible theory, and it *does* answer the questions of the realist. However, the subjective idealist seems to answer those questions with some strain, bringing in far-fetched theories for explanation, whereas the absolute idealist answers the questions more easily by accepting the world of appearance as the creation of a cosmic Consciousness (Śiva or God) and not of the individual soul.

Since the world of appearance is created through the freedom of Śiva, the appearance is *not* already determined, as occurs in the case of a seed or gene. The tree is already potentially present in the seed, and the seed will evolve according to the genetic prescription already present in the seed. Moreover, the seed cannot refuse to grow if and when the conditions necessary for the growth of the seed are presented. But Śiva has no such determinism. Śiva is free to extend or expand Himself in any way He Likes; Śiva is also free not to expand at all if He so chooses. This marks the difference between Kashmir Śaiva idealism and Hegelian idealism. In the Hegelian position, the future steps of evolution of the Absolute are already potentially given in the Absolute, and the Absolute is bound to evolve, and to evolve in the way already fixed. But the Absolute of Kashmir Śaivism enjoys perfect freedom.[29] The second point of difference between the two systems, which is logically related to the first point of difference, is that the Hegelian Absolute is a "unity-in-difference," difference being inherent in the unity, not the free expression of unity, whereas the Absolute of Kashmir Śaivism is pure unity, and difference is the free expression of the unity.[30]

According to Advaita Vedānta too, the world is appearance. There the appearance is technically called *vivarta* and the theory of appearance is called *vivartavāda.* The ontological status of the world in both the Ābhāsavāda of Kashmir Śaivism and the Vivartavāda of Advaita Vedānta is the same — the world is appearance and therefore not real or material. But there is an important difference between the two. According to Vivartavāda, the world illusion is a superimposition (*adhyāsa*) on Reality (Brahman or the Self) like the rope-snake. But according to the Ābhāsavāda of Kashmir Śaivism, the world of appearance is a self-projection or self-manifestation of Śiva (Brahman). Śiva-consciousness, dynamic by its very nature, actively creates the world of appearance out of Itself; the world of appearance is not superimposed on Śiva from outside. Creation is an activity — the free activity — of Śiva; it is the dance of Naṭarāja. But the Brahman of Advaita Vedānta does not and cannot create the world as appearance, as Brahman is inactive and neutral; it can only serve as the ground upon which the world illusion is imposed — it can only allow itself to be mistaken for the world. The Brahman of Advaita Vedānta has "freedom-from" as it is unaffected by the world of appearance, but not "freedom-to" as it cannot actively create the world of appearance. The Śiva of Kashmir Śaivism has both "freedom-from" and "freedom-to," as it actively and freely creates the world as appearance and is also unaffected by this creation of the world. *Ābhāsa* ("appearance") is thus the free self-extension or self-expansion (*svarūpa-prasāra*) of Śiva, whereas *vivarta* (*adhyāsa* or "superimposition") is the limitation and obstruction of Brahman.

THE SENSE IN WHICH ĀBHĀSA IS CALLED REAL

Although the word *ābhāsa* means something illusory, Abhinavagupta also calls the *ābhāsa* "real" (*satya*).[31] Some people naively think that since Abhinavagupta calls the appearance real, he is involved in a contradiction, as the very word *appearance* means what is not real. A careful analysis of the position of Abhinavagupta reveals that the sense in which he calls *ābhāsa* true or real (*satya*) is logically warranted, and the special contribution of Abhinavagupta lies in pointing out that sense.

At the very start it should be made clear that when Abhinavagupta calls the *ābhāsa* real, he never means to suggest that the *ābhāsa* is a real material thing and not an illusory appearance. Abhinavagupta does not accept the existence of matter; he is clearly an idealist. He explicitly refutes the position of the realist in his *Vimarśinī* and elsewhere and demonstrates that the object is not real but only an appearance. He even uses the classical analogies and examples of appearance like the dream,[32] rope-snake,[33] and so on, that are used in Advaita Vedānta, and calls the world "illusion" (*bhrama*),[34] "unreal" (*niḥsatya*),[35] or "false" (*mithyā*).[36] He says, "The world does not really exist, what is then the question of the bondage of the person? . . . This is illusion like the rope-snake or the shadow-ghost caused by false attachment . . . ."[37]

Abhinavagupta does not grant ontological reality to the world like that of a real material thing. As in Advaita Vedānta, so for Abhinavagupta, the reality of the world is purely epistemic; the world exists in knowledge or consciousness, as the world is nothing but the appearance (*ābhāsa*) of Consciousness. But Abhinavagupta would further say that there is a sense in which the *ābhāsa* can be, and should be, called real. There are three senses in which we can do so.

(a) If appearance is to be taken as a thing made of matter, it is unreal; but appearance *as appearance*, or as a projection of consciousness, is real. For example, a tiger "seen" in a dream is not real in the sense that the dream tiger is not a real thing made of flesh and blood. But the dream tiger as a mental projection, a projection of consciousness, is true. In the example of a motion picture, what we see on the screen as men and women are really not flesh and blood people, but just shadows or images, and in this sense they are not real. But are they not real in the sense that they are actual shadows or images? It is very much true that what we see on the screen is a "picture" projected from the film reel. Being a "picture" is its reality. As actual men and women, the film is not real, but as a picture it is real.

In the context of the illusory object, what people generally forget is that the illusory is not *asat* ("unreal") like the "son of a barren woman." Unlike this non-existent child, it is not merely an idea of the mind; it actually appears and *as appearance* is not true as a real thing (*bimba*), but as a reflection (*pratibimba*), it is true. What is false in the dream is the dream object that the dreamer took to be a real thing. But the dream as an experience or as a mental projection is not false. The Upaniṣads say that the knowing (*dṛṣṭi*) of the knower (*draṣṭā*) never becomes false.[38] The knowing or the "seeing" of the seer in the dream, although "seeing" not real things but appearances, is true. When we wake up from a dream, what becomes false is the dream world that we mistook as real, not the fact that we "saw" a dream. The dream is a fact or phenomenon — the phenomenon of consciousness projecting appearances; as such it is true.

What some of the Advaitins seem to forget is that from the real (*pāramārthika*) point of view, the world is appearance or illusory (*mithyā*), not mere nothing (*asat*) like the barren woman's son. It is a fact that the world appears, and since it appears, it cannot be mere nothing (*asat*); it must at the least be appearance. Nobody can deny the hard fact that the world appears. If we analyze the structure of an illusory appearance, we find that it appears only when it is projected from some mind or consciousness and as a projection of consciousness, it is true or real. Even when the world is an illusory appearance, it is real as the projection of consciousness, or as a process of illusory experience within consciousness; we have to accept that a process of appearance is going on in the bosom of Reality.

(b) The second sense in which the *ābhāsa* is said to be real is that the *ābhāsa* is an active self-projection or self-creation of Consciousness, not a superimposition on it. If the world as appearance is taken as a superimposition on Reality (Brahman) and not as a self-projection of Brahman, then that implies that there is a principle or reality independent of, and separate from, Brahman that is responsible for the superimposition of the world of appearance on Brahman. This would mean accepting two realities and foresaking non-dualism. The only way to preserve the non-duality of Brahman would be to maintain that the world as appearance is a self-projection of Brahman, for in that case there would be no need of accepting anything other than Brahman to create the world.

Kashmir Śaivism accepts that the world is a self-projection of Śiva. That means the world as appearance is an active creation of Śiva — an activity of Śiva. As an activity of Śiva it is real. It does not matter whether Śiva is creating false appearances or real things. Even when Śiva creates false appearances, it is a positive activity within the mind of Śiva, and as such it is true.

(c) The third sense in which *ābhāsa* is understood as real is the aesthetic sense. *Ābhāsa* has aesthetic value and is meant to be enjoyed by the perceiver (*pramātā*) who has an aesthetic identification (*sādhāraṇikaraṇa*) with the *ābhāsas*. This point will become clear with the help of the analogy of a drama. When we watch a drama, we know that the drama is not a real life event but just a fiction or a false enactment on the stage. We also know that the characters that appear on the stage are not real but are forms artifically adopted by the actors. In a word, we know that the drama is a false event; at the same time we also enjoy it. In watching the drama, we establish what is called *sādhāraṇikaraṇa*, which means aesthetic identification with the characters and their enactment. This helps us enjoy the drama. Thus, though the drama is false, it has aesthetic value. In fact, drama means an enactment which is artificial and false; it cannot be a drama if it is a real event. The beauty of the drama is that we do enjoy it. In that sense drama is real.

The same is true of play (*krīḍā* or *līlā*). Play activity is not real work; in fact, play cannot be play if it is work. The very distinguishing point between work and play is that work is real and play is false. But still the play is real *as play*. The play is real as an act of enjoyment.

Similarly, Creation or the world as appearance is the sportive activity (*krīḍā* or *līlā*) of Śiva, the blissful dance of the Naṭarāja, and is meant to be taken by the individual soul (*paśu*) in the same spirit. Tantric *sādhanā* aims at making the entire life a playful activity. We have already seen that Creation is a spontaneous overflow of the bliss (*ānanda*) of Śiva in the form of self-projection as the world of appearance; as such it is meant to be enjoyed. It is not a superimposition on Śiva, meant to be rejected.

This marks the difference between Līlāvāda and Māyāvāda. According to Mādhyamika Buddhism and Advaita Vedānta, the world is *māyā* ("false"), created out of ignorance (*avidyā*) and superimposed on Reality. Naturally therefore, if we want to attain Reality, we have to reject the superimposition (*adhyāsa*) that is an obstruction to Reality. But according to Kashmir Śaivism and other Tantric systems, the world is not a superimposition on Śiva due to *avidyā*, but a self-projection or self-expansion (*svarūpa-prasāra*) of Śiva in bliss (*ānanda*). As such, it is not an obstruction or bondage, and therefore, there is no question of rejecting it. The world is not the obstruction or bondage — what is bondage is the ego, selfishness, and sense of duality or otherness (*dvaita-prathā*) which are indeed to be rejected in order to attain Self-realization, or the realization of Reality. Thus we see that Māyāvāda and Līlāvāda are ontologically not different, but axiologically the two are very much different, even contrary to each other. As far as the ontological status of the world is concerned, the world is false or appearance, according to Līlāvāda as well as Māyāvāda, for Creation cannot be play (*līlā*) unless it is false. But the axiological attitude towards the world of appearance is different from that of the Māyāvādin. Here the attitude is not one of rejection but one of acceptance and enjoyment. The initial meaning of the word *māyā*, and the one that is accepted by the Līlāvādin, is the false magical creation (*indrajāla*) of a magician, which is purely an appearance and not a reality. But the Līlāvādin would ask, why reject the magic show? Magic is meant for enjoyment. The Lord is the greatest magician, and His magic (false or apparent creation) is to be enjoyed.

Appearance (*ābhāsa*) is thus ontologically false (as it is just appearance and not reality), but axiologically it is real. *It becomes a value.* The Māyāvādin, the Advaitin, or Mādhyamika Buddhist, would not attach axiological importance to the world of appearance. He or she would argue that since the world is appearance and not reality, it is utterly valueless (*tuccha*), and therefore it has to be ultimately rejected. The attitude of the Māyāvādin towards the world is negative both ontologically and axiologically. The Līlāvādin, however, has a very positive attitude towards the world of appearance, accepting it as a value, although he or she knows that ontologically it is false.

That the world is ontologically false means only that it is the appearance (*ābhāsa*) or the reflection (*pratibimba*) of Consciousness and not a material reality. That is, the world is made of Consciousness and not of matter. It does not mean that the world is nothing, or that the world is a superimposition on Reality, or that it has no place in Reality. The world as appearance is a self-expression or self-expansion of Reality (Consciousness).

So the world is a freely-adopted appearance, or a free self-manifestation, of Reality. As such, it is part of Reality, but a freely-adopted part of Reality, not a necessary part of Reality, as we find in the philosophy of Hegel and Rāmānuja. In this sense the world of appearance is even ontologically real. By calling it ontologically real, I do not mean that it is an independent reality made of matter, all I mean is that the world of appearance is a free manifestation of Reality (Consciousness or Śiva), and as such it has a place in Reality or it is part of Reality. If Śiva appears as the world, the world of appearance is the appearance of Śiva. As such it is the freely-adopted form of Śiva. Both Śiva and the world of appearance are real — Śiva is real as Śiva and the world of appearance is real as the appearance of Śiva, just as an actor in a drama is real as an actual person and the role he or she adopts is real as the role in the drama. Appearance is not mere nothing; it is something — it is the *appearance* of Reality in the form of the world.

THE THEORY OF APPEARANCE (ĀBHĀSAVĀDA) AS THE THEORY OF FREEDOM (SVĀTANTRYAVĀDA)

Ābhāsavāda ("the theory of appearance") can also be called Svātantryavāda ("the theory of freedom"), as appearing in the form of the world is the free expression of Śiva. Freedom is the very nature of Consciousness, just as knowledge (illumination) is. Knowledge distinguishes consciousness from insentient matter (*jaḍa*); consciousness knows and matter does not know. Freedom is another distinguishing factor. Consciousness is free and matter is not free.[39]

Many systems of Indian philosophy — Sāṃkhya and Advaita Vedānta, for example — duly emphasize the knowledge (awareness) aspect of Consciousness, symbolically called *prakāśa* ("light" or "illumination"), but they overlook the freedom aspect. Kashmir Śaivism fully appreciates the aspect of freedom (*svātantrya*), which is as significant a characteristic of Consciousness as knowledge (awareness) is. The concept of freedom in conjunction with knowledge is the unique contribution of Kashmir Śaivism.[40]

Svātantrya ("freedom") is also called *vimarśa*, and *vimarśa* is understood along with *prakāśa*. *Vimarśa* is also called *śakti* ("power," "force," or "potentiality"), *kriyā* ("activity"), or *spanda* ("spontaneity"), just as *prakāśa* is also called Śiva or *jñāna* ("awareness" or "knowledge"). Consciousness in Kashmir Śaivism is understood as *prakāśa-vimarśa*, Śiva-Śakti, or *jñāna-kriyā* — two in one. *Svātantrya* ("freedom"), *śakti* ("potentiality" or "power"), *vimarśa* ("ideation" or "thinking"), *kriyā* ("activity"), and *spanda* ("spontaneity") are synonyms that emphasize different connotations of one and the same characteristic of Consciousness, juxtaposed with the other characteristic called Śiva, *prakāśa*, or *jñāna*.

If freedom is the very nature of consciousness, why does consciousness appear to be bound? The same question can be asked about awareness (knowledge) also — if awareness is the nature of consciousness, why is it absent in the state of deep sleep? The answer in both cases is the same: consciousness is veiled or obstructed; therefore its freedom, and also the illumination, is veiled. To use an analogy, illumination is the very nature of the sun, but when the sun is obstructed by clouds, the light seems to be absent. When the obstruction is removed, the light is revealed. The more the obstruction is cleared, the brighter is the light. Similarly, when the impurity is removed from consciousness, its natural freedom comes to the fore and begins to function. The amount of freedom is proportionate to the removal of impurity. In the state of Śiva, consciousness is completely pure, and thus Śiva-Consciousness is completely free.

Even in its limited form as the individual soul (*paśu*) which is a "mini-Śiva," consciousness does have some amount of freedom, although its world of freedom becomes limited.[41] The *paśu* exhibits its freedom even in this limited state, and performs all of the five functions (*pañcakṛtya*) of Śiva, although in a limited way.[42] The individual is like a caged lion, which, though caged, expresses its freedom by roaring through the bars of the cage. The individual consciousness is fettered, but the very fact that it struggles to come out of its fetters suggests that its essential nature is freedom. At present the individual self may not succeed in breaking the fetters, but the fact that it feels that it is in fetters and refuses to remain content with its fettered state means that freedom is part of its nature. The refusal to be content with determinism is itself suggestive of freedom.

It is true that the individual consciousness of a human is determined by the factors existing within and without; but it cannot be true that the individual is completely determined. Complete determinism can be true only in the case of insentient matter. It cannot be true in the case of consciousness. Freedom exists to the extent that consciousness is expressed. In the lower species, consciousness is far less manifest; therefore there is more determinism. But in the case of human beings, where consciousness is more clearly expressed, there is far less determinism. Freedom goes hand-in-hand with consciousness — less consciousness, less freedom; more consciousness, more freedom.

This freedom is not only "freedom-from" but also "freedom-to." According to Mādhyamika Buddhism and Advaita Vedānta, Reality (Śūnya or Brahman) is "freedom-from," as it is unaffected by the process of appearance. But it has no "freedom-to." It cannot create the world as appearance because it is inactive (*niṣkriya*) and neutral. The world of appearance is superimposed on it due to *avidyā* ("ignorance"). The freedom to act is simply not present in Reality, for Reality, or Consciousness, is not conceived of as a dynamic force that has activity (*kriyā*), but is seen as a passive observer (*draṣṭā*).

Freedom cannot be complete if it is only "freedom-from" and not "freedom-to." The very meaning of freedom is "freedom-to" — freedom to act. Consciousness, though having knowledge or awareness as its nature, cannot be called free unless it has the freedom to act,[43] as the freedom of activity is the very definition of freedom.[44] Kashmir Śaivism sees in Consciousness a freedom (*svātantrya*, *vimarśa*, *parāmarśa*, *kriyā*, or *spanda*) that means free activity. Śiva-Consciousness is both "freedom-from" and "freedom-to." "Freedom-to" does not imply the voluntary and effortful action (*karma*) that arises out of some lack or want. This type of action differs from *kriyā*, which is free, spontaneous activity.

A truly free action is one that has no motive whatsoever. When we want or lack nothing or we have nothing to achieve, and we still act, that is a state of free activity. It is activity not conditioned or determined by anything. The Lord in the *Gītā* says, "I have on earth nothing to do and nothing to achieve or accomplish (as I am ever full), and yet I perform action."[45] But is such an activity possible? Is there no contradiction in motiveless activity? Such an activity is very much possible, and it is also free from the contradiction of motiveless action.

When we live fully in joy (*ānanda*), playful activity spontaneously and naturally emanates from this state. *Ānanda* naturally overflows or spontaneously expresses itself in the form of joyful activity, like singing, dancing, or playing. The beauty of such activity is that we do not exert our will or make an effort, yet the activity automatically, spontaneously, and effortlessly happens according to our will. There is also perfect freedom in the activity, for it does not go against our will, nor is there any compulsion — we can also dismiss it if we like. This type of activity is what is called *spanda*, or *kriyā*. *Kriyā* is the spontaneous overflow of joy in the state of perfection. Creation is an activity of Śiva that spontaneously emanates from His joy; it is the dance of Naṭarāja. The Upaniṣads also say that Creation springs forth from the *ānanda* (that is Brahman).[46] The remarkable thing is that Creation is said to be *from ānanda*, not *for ānanda*, suggesting that Creation takes place not to fulfill any lack of *ānanda*, but that *ānanda* itself overflows in the form of creative activity.

It is also obvious that duality is the free expression of non-dual Consciousness. The world as appearance consists of duality. The non-dual Śiva freely expresses or projects Himself in the duality of the world as appearance;[47] to appear as many is the freedom of Reality (Śiva), which is one.[48] Abhinavagupta offers his salutations to Śiva who out of His freedom "first projects the world of duality as the *pūrvapakṣa*, and then takes it back to the *uttarapakṣa* of unity."[49]

We have already seen that the analogy of the seed (*bīja*) or that of the fluid in the egg of a peacock (*mayūrāṇḍarasa*) should not be taken to mean that duality or difference is inherently present in Śiva as potentiality, that is, necessity. What it means is that there is no duality in Śiva at all, and yet all duality comes out of Śiva, just as the colorful variety of the peacock's feathers comes out of the colorless and non-differentiated fluid of the egg. In the case of the seed, manifestation of variety is not the free expression of the seed — the seed is genetically conditioned to manifest variety. But in the case of Śiva, manifestation of variety is the free expression of Śiva, which is pure unity. Whatever Śiva does or in whatever form He appears, it is the expression of the complete freedom of Śiva. Śiva has the power and freedom to do even the most difficult and unimaginable things, and that is His glory.[50] When He projects the wondrous world of appearance, He does so not out of any compulsion, but out of His free will.[51]

THE THEORY OF ILLUSION

It may be true that the world is an appearance and not real in the sense of being a material object, but it is also true that to the bound *puruṣa* or *paśu* it appears to be real. The *paśu* takes the world not as mere appearance (*ābhāsa*) or reflection (*pratibimba*) but as a real material thing or substance. Why does this happen? Obviously, the explanation is that the mind of the *paśu* is illusioned; out of ignorance he or she perceives the world as a material reality. This means there should be a clear-cut theory of illusion to explain the phenomenon of mistaken reality.

The Māyāvādin (that is, the Mādhyamika Buddhist or the Advaita Vedāntin) has a clear-cut theory to explain why we see the world as real although it is false, or merely appearance. The Māyāvādin explains the situation by accepting two levels of truth. One level is that of the noumenon (reality) and the other is that of the phenomenon (appearance). In Mādhyamika Buddhism these are called *paramārtha-satya* and *saṁvṛti-satya*;[52] in Advaita Vedānta they are called *paramārtha* and *vyavahāra*. From the point of view of reality (*paramārtha-satya*), the world is false; it is really Brahman, or *nirvāṇa*, mistaken for the world, or *saṁsāra*. In the case of the rope-snake illusion (*rajju-sarpa*), the snake exists only from the point of view of the illusion itself. In reality there is no snake; it is really a rope. Or in a dream, the dream world is real as long as we are dreaming, but in reality — that is, from the point of view of the waking state — the dream world is false, as it is merely epistemic and not material. Similarly, as long as we are in *vyavahāra*, or *saṁvṛti*, which is the state of illusion, the world is real for us. But from the point of view of the real truth (*paramārtha*), the world is false.

There is also a substate of illusion, the subjective illusion caused by the individual mind, within the objective world illusion. Dreams and other subjective illusions like the rope-snake come under this category. It is called *pratibhāsa* in Advaita Vedānta and *parikalpita* in Buddhism. Abhinavagupta also accepts the existence of this substate and says, "In the state of *Māyā*, all is illusion; but even there, there is a sub-illusion like a dream within a dream or like a boil on a goitre."[53]

Abhinavagupta does accept a theory of illusion, which is called *apūrṇakhyāti*. *Māyā*, together with its five cloaks (*pañca-kañcuka*), is responsible for the illusion. Under the influence of *māyā* the individual soul (*puruṣa* or *paśu*) perceives the world as real, although in reality the world is mere appearance. But Abhinavagupta does not make an explicit distinction between *vyavahāra* and *paramārtha* the way the Māyāvādin does. Without this distinction between *vyavahāra* and *paramārtha*, we cannot explain why the world, although mere appearance, appears as real. Advaita Vedānta and Mādhyamika Buddhism, which do make the distinction between *vyavahāra* and *parmārtha*, can be said to complement Kashmir Śaivism in this particular respect.

There may be two reasons why the distinction between two levels of truth is not made in Kashmir Śaivism, in spite of the fact that Kashmir Śaivism accepts the world as appearance. First, unlike Advaita Vedānta and Buddhism, Kashmir Śaivism does not have a long history. Vedānta and Buddhism developed over more than a thousand years; there was enough time for the systems to reach their fullness. The tenets of the Advaitic system of Śaṅkarācārya, for example, were fleshed out by the post-Śaṅkarite philosophers up to Niścaladāsa in modern times. But the history of Kashmir Śaivism goes back not more than three hundred years before Abhinavagupta and it virtually stops with him. After Abhinavagupta, no important philosopher came to make explicit the implicit points and fill in the gaps in his philosophy.

Second, the de-emphasis on the distinction between *vyavahāra* and *paramārtha* may have a reason that is perhaps more valid and is due to the special cast of Kashmir Śaivism. The Kashmir Śaiva philosophers perhaps deliberately do not emphasize the distinction between *vyavahāra* and *paramārtha* because it may lead to an erosion of the positive attitude towards the world, and give the impression that the world is ultimately unreal (*tuccha*) and therefore to be finally rejected. This is what happened in the case of scholastic Advaita Vedānta and Mādhyamika Buddhism. These systems caused a negative attitude towards life and the world in their followers. The pursuit of *mokṣa* was divorced from worldly pursuits, including the work of socio-political upliftment. It was a great pity that the Upaniṣadic ideal of life-fulfillment was interpreted in the most negativistic way to the effect that even social and cultural work was considered a hindrance to the attainment of *mokṣa.* The result was that many of the best minds of India turned their backs on the work of social upliftment, and the society was left to its own fate, led by selfish, egotistic, and ignorant people.

Kashmir Śaivism, however, took notice of the fact that what is called appearance is the manifestation of Consciousness, and as such it is not unreal at all. What is unreal is the belief that the world is an independent reality made of matter. This is what is suggested by the theory of illusion called *apūrṇakhyāti* that is accepted in Kashmir Śaivism. The world is not completely false, as it is one with Consciousness as an appearance or manifestation of Consciousness. What is false is its independence and materiality. So when we take the world to be real, that is, made of an independent reality called matter, then this is wrong knowledge; it is wrong because it is a partial or incomplete (*apūrṇa*) view of reality (*apūrṇakhyāti*).[54] But when we view it as the appearance of Consciousness, then we have the complete view; this is right knowledge.[55] The world is not completely false; it is part of Reality as the manifestation, or appearance, of Reality. This is what Plato meant when he said that the "world of shadow" partakes of Reality.

Moreover, the distinction between *vyavahāra* and *paramārtha* has also led to an undesirable situation caused not by the theory itself but by some Advaitins who misuse the theory. Some Advaitins abuse the theory to justify behavior that goes against Advaitic philosophy, saying that what is true in *paramārtha* may not be true in *vyavahāra*. For example, almost all the scholastic pandits of Advaita Vedānta believe in castism and untouchability. This is quite incongruous with the Vedantic philosophy that all beings are really one's own Self (Brahman). The "pandit" justifies this behavior by saying that unity is true in *paramārtha*, but in *vyavahāra*, difference is true.[56]

Of course hypocrisy, or discrepancy of behavior, is to be found among the Tantrists also. Many pseudo-Tantrists take to the Kaula-*sādhanā* of the *pañca-makāra* (the five "M's," including *maithuna* or sexual intercourse) just for material enjoyment but pretend to be Kaula *sādhakas*. Many non-Tantric practices go in the name of Tantrism. There is the need to correctly interpret Tantrism, just as there is the need to correctly interpret Māyāvāda.

The distinction between *paramārtha* and *vyavahāra*, two levels of reality, is logically true and Abhinavagupta accepts it in spirit. But he is also conscious of the fact that the Māyāvādin overlooks the important truth that the world of appearance is a positive manifestation of Brahman and takes the all-integrating philosophy of the Upaniṣads to the logical absurdity of utter negativism. Abhinavagupta, as a true Tantrist, never talks in negative terms, and he emphasizes the truth that the world of appearance is real as the appearance of Śiva.

6

The Problem of Evil

When dealing with the question of evil, the student of Kashmir Śaivism faces a problem. In the texts of the system one does not find explicit reference to the question, much less discussion of the subject. Hence, at first glance there seems to be no clear indication of the exact position of Kashmir Śaivism on the problem of evil. However, the lack of a clear treatment of the problem in the texts does not mean that Kashmir Śaivism does not have a well-defined position with regard to the problem of evil or that the philosophers of this school were not clear in their minds on this issue.

Of course, Kashmir Śaivism has a clear-cut stand on the problem of evil, and in spite of the absence of explicit textual treatment, we can logically work out the explanation of evil from the fundamental position of this school. The basic standpoint of the system can be pressed to successfully yield reasonable conclusions about its position on evil. This approach is the only way to get at the problem of evil within the general framework of Kashmir Śaivism.

THE PRESENCE OF EVIL

The presence of evil in the world is an obvious fact. The optimist may refuse to recognize the presence of evil, but this flies in the face of the facts. The optimist's statement, "Everything is good and wisely put," may have some significance, but it is contradicted by the facts, the presense of sin and suffering being so conspicuous. Lord Buddha took notice of the fact of suffering (*duḥkha-satya*); suffering is the first truth in his four Noble Truths. However, it may be a kind of extremism to hold the view that everything in this world ultimately leads to suffering (*sarvam duḥkham*); the balanced view is that the world is the seat of both suffering and happiness. Nobody can deny, however, that suffering is a prominent presence in the world.

Evil is present in the world chiefly in two forms, (a) sorrow, or suffering (*duḥkha*) and (b) moral evil, or what is called sin (*pāpa*). These two are present in various forms. Bodily suffering in the form of disease, pain, and so on; mental suffering in the form of agony, anxiety, want, bereavement, and so on; and spiritual suffering in the form of want of love, discontentment, absence of inner peace, and so on — these are known by almost everyone. Some sorrows, like old age and death, are normally the destiny of all beings. Buddha used the phrase "old age and death" (*jarā-maraṇa*) as the symbol of the suffering of life. There is suffering that results from the deliberate actions of others, for instance injury, murder, exploitation, war, and so on; there is also suffering that results from natural calamities like earthquakes, floods, epidemics, and so on.

The second form of evil — moral evil or sin (*pāpa*) — is the most irritating phenomenon. This can be found all over the world in varying degrees. This is a phenomenon for which people can be held entirely responsible, for it results from their own free choice — from their abuse of their free will. There may be instigating factors — internal and external — that may be held partially responsible for the commission of sin, but ultimately it is free will that makes the choice and determines the sinful activity. It is sin that poses the real problem.

THE PROBLEM

Since evil, whether in the form of suffering or in the form of sin, is present in the world, the question naturally arises, why does evil exist? Explaining the presence of evil is tantamount to giving a solution to the problem of evil.

The Naturalist would explain the existence of evil by contending that both good and evil are products of Nature. Both the materialistic and the spiritualistic forms of Naturalism trace the origin of evil in Nature. Spiritualistic Naturalism holds that evil is present in the underdeveloped state of the human psyche. It signifies the lower stage of evolution; it is completely overcome in the higher stage. If evil is part of Nature or reality, even at a lower stage, then the problem of the explanation of evil is solved. Naturalism is a perfectly plausible position.

Naturalism is one possible solution, but the issue is not that simple for adherents of theistic systems that have an omniscient, omnipotent, good, and free God. Those who believe in God naturally conceive of Him as Almighty and All-knowing. God is also seen as all goodness; He loves His creatures and is kind to them. With the existence of such a God why is there evil? It is not that God cannot remove evil; He is omnipotent. One cannot say that God does not know that there is evil in the world, for He is omniscient. Nor can it be said that though God knows that there is evil in the world, and though He *can* remove it, He does not want to do so; this would go against His nature as good, kind, and loving. The most prominent aspect of the concept of God is His goodness, His love for creatures expressed in His willingness to do good for them. If God wills the eradication of evil from the world, what could prevent it? It does not stand to reason that God is kind enough to allow Satan (evil) to remain in His Kingdom. It would be unreasonable on the part of a just God to permit Satan to vitiate His creation. In the face of the naked evil prevalent in the world, one may be justified in rejecting the very existence of God. The presence of evil in the world is one of the most powerful arguments against the existence of God.

Some people accept the existence of God but are forced to reject the idea of His eternal goodness as they realize the crushing weight of evil. They put the blame entirely on God.[1] Even some of the devotees of God take Him to task for permitting evil such as genocide.[2] Mass persecution of innocent people is not an evil of a particular time only; it is often repeated in history from ancient times.

God's permitting the existence of this type of evil leads to the logical conclusion that God is a tyrant and a sadist. It would be more logical to reject the very existence of God than to conceive of God as a whimsical and sadistic tyrant permitting enormous evil in the world.

In a system like Kashmir Śaivism the problem of evil becomes all the more prominent, for the incompatibility of evil with the creation of Śiva becomes conspicuous. In Kashmir Śaivism, creation is conceived of as the spontaneous outcome of the bliss (*ānanda*) of Śiva; it is the sportive activity (*līlā*) of the Lord, the cosmic dance of Naṭarāja. Moreover, Śiva, which literally means "the good" or "the benign," is just the opposite of evil. Here the question arises, if Creation is the blissful play of "the benign," where do sin and suffering come from? Evil is incongruous with a world of *līlā*. If the world is an active creation of Śiva and if everything comes out of Śiva, then evil should also be regarded as the creation of Śiva, which makes for a self-contradictory position.

In the dualistic, theistic systems God becomes relatively free from the responsibility of evil. In Śaiva Siddhānta, the southern dualistic school of Śaivism for example, evil has its roots in *māyā*, which is an independent and beginningless reality, co-existent with

Śiva. The souls (*paśus*) are covered with a beginningless ignorance, or spiritual dirt (*mala*). Śiva has not created ignorance; ignorance or *mala* is already present in *māyā*. Śiva is always good to the individual beings (*jīva*); in fact, Śiva acts to help the *jīva* come out of ignorance. The sole purpose of Creation is to free the soul. In Śaiva Siddhānta, therefore, Śiva is not directly to blame for evil. In a monism or absolutism like Kashmir Śaivism, however, God appears to be directly responsible for the evil in the world. Here *māyā* is not an independent entity. Unlike the *māyā* of Śaiva Siddhānta and the *prakṛti* of Sāṁkhya, *māyā* in Kashmir Śaivism is the very power (*śakti*) of Śiva. *Māyā* does not function independently. Moreover, it is Śiva who has created ignorance, or it is Śiva who has, as part of His *līlā*, become the ignorant *paśu*.[3] The process of bondage and liberation is the play of Śiva.[4] With such a metaphysical position what immediately occurs to the student of Kashmir Śaivism is that it is Śiva, and not the *paśu*, who should be held responsible for evil.

It is true that in Kashmir Śaivism there appears, at first sight, to be a case against God as far as evil is concerned, and the problem of evil becomes so prominent that it seems to shake the basic structure of the system. However, this does not mean that in this system there is no explanation of evil or that the explanation is not a reasonable one. Kashmir Śaivism gives a satisfactory explanation of evil to those who examine the system patiently and refrain from hasty judgments. Of course, it is quite understandable that a rational person should, in the face of evil, reject the very existence of God; it would be childish to ignore the towering problem of evil. However, it would be equally irrational to summarily dismiss, on that account, the existence of God or the divine governance of the world. If one merely sees evil in the world and concludes that the Divine does not exist, this is too hasty a conclusion. It is unreasonable to pass judgment without analyzing the situation in its entirety and working out the possibilities of satisfactory explanations for the existence of evil.

FREE WILL AND MORAL EVIL

The seed of the explanation of evil can be found in the theory of *svātantrya* ("freedom") that is one of the basic presuppositions of Kashmir Śaivism. Śiva is free, and the individual soul, as a kind of "mini-Śiva," is also free, though in a limited sense. The individual has free choice and free will; he or she fully exercizes this choice and expresses this freedom in his or her behavior within this limited realm.[5] Of course, besides being limited, the freedom of the individual is different from that of Śiva in an important respect. Śiva being absolutely free from ignorance (*ajñāna*) or spiritual impurity (*mala*), has no possibility of being tempted towards evil, whereas the *paśu*, who is ignorant, can abuse freedom and choose to commit evil.

That the activities of the individual are not completely determined — that one is free within a limited sphere — is a truism that is vouchsafed by experience. There are certain ideologies that highlight the factors determining man's behavior, from which they conclude that man is a determined being. Of course it is true that the activities of man are highly determined, but this is only half the truth; the other half consists of his freedom. Man finds himself in the peculiar predicament of being largely determined by forces beyond his control, but at the same time he is aware of his freedom, too. Man is a combination of freedom and determinism, but freedom is unique to him and that is where his essence lies.[6]

To some extent God, or Śiva, does not interfere in the individual's freedom. According to the Līlāvāda of Kashmir Śaivism, Śiva creates the world for sport. Śiva, without changing His essential nature, also becomes the ignorant individual (*jīva* or *paśu*) as part of His *līlā*. The *paśu* thus becomes different from Śiva. Śiva employs these individual souls — his own manifestations — as actors or partners in His big game of Creation. Śiva is the master of the game, and the individual souls take part in it. The point to note here is that Śiva does not intend that His play be vitiated by evil or that the players (the individual souls) violate the rules of the game. But the players are not robots — they have free will. Their behavior is unpredictable.

Sometimes the players abuse their free will and violate the rules of the game, which they have the option to do, even if it is against the will of the gamesmaster. As a result, they are scolded and punished, and they suffer. The play becomes tainted with undesirable events that were not in the game plan. The gamesmaster is not to blame for this evil; the entire responsibility for it goes to the players who abuse their freedom. A hockey player, for example, is supposed to use the hockey stick to strike the ball, not the leg or the head of a fellow player. Instead of striking the ball, however, the player strikes at the fellow player, severely violating the rules of the game. The gamesmaster does not condone this, and the offender is punished. Similarly, the Lord of the game of Creation does not intend that there be evil in the world, but evil creeps in entirely due to the individual souls. Naturally, therefore, the Lord introduced the machinery of the Law of Karma, which acts as executor of justice and corrector of evil.

The question may be asked here; knowing full well that the players can and will misuse their freedom, why does the Lord allow them the freedom to do so? The answer is that the Lord, of course, wants His creatures to follow the path of goodness and not to commit sin. At the same time He wants them to follow the path of goodness freely, not forcibly. He is like a father who wants his children to be good and noble, but who at the same time wants them to adopt goodness out of their own free choice. He may provide opportunities for the children to be inclined to choose goodness, but he never wants them to become machine-like. If God wills, the creatures forced by the will of God, cannot commit evil; but in that case they would be just like robots, choosing nothing for themselves. Their very individuality would be lost. The individual selves would then no longer remain "selves," but would become self-less machines. The Lord allows freedom of will to His creatures, not only because they would otherwise become like robots, which would mar the pleasure of the play, but also because it would be improper for the Lord to deprive the soul of its freedom. If the Lord proposes to deprive us of our freedom and make us just like robots, then we ourselves would object to this, for this would be tantamount to death. If we accept this proposal, it would be nothing short of committing suicide.

One may suggest that the Lord should allow freedom of choice only when one chooses the good, not when one chooses the bad. In answer we would say that this would really mean not allowing freedom of choice at all. If one is barred from choosing the bad and is allowed to choose only the good, this means that really there is no choice. The word "choice" is a misnomer here, and one is again, just like a robot.

There may be an important question — if the Lord allows one to choose to become bad in so far as one harms oneself and not others, so far so good; but why is it that the Lord allows one the freedom to harm others, and that, too, to the extent of killing or giving severe pain to others? Why does the Lord not check one who chooses to destroy others, just as the police arrest the person who is out to inflict pain on others? Why should the innocent suffer from the actions of one who abuses the power of free will? If the innocent suffers, does it not go against the justice of God and the divine Law of Karma?

In answer to the above question we would say that this involves the complicated working of the divine Law of Karma. The Law of Karma demands that no innocent should suffer, therefore one *does not* suffer at the hands of an offender *unless* one's own karma warrants the suffering. For example, a person may abuse his or her free will and try to harm someone, and by that act he or she may be liable to be punished, for he or she is committing a sin, but however he or she may try to harm the other person, that person will not be harmed unless he or she has already committed a sin and his or her own karma justifies the suffering. The divine governance is such that one's own previous karma, of this life or a past life, is adjusted against the suffering that one receives from an offender. In the divine governance it is ordained that the suffering of the so-called innocent at the hands of a tyrant becomes possible only when the previous karma ready for fructification (*prarābdha karma*) of the visibly innocent person is adjusted against the present suffering. This does not mean that the tyrant is exempt from punishment; he or she will have to suffer his or her own karma.

As a corollary of the above position, it follows that if the "innocent" is really innocent — that is, free of *prarābdha* karma — then any amount of effort on the part of the tyrant or the offender will fail. In the world it sometimes happens that several well-planned and well-organized attempts on the life of a person fail; at other times it happens that a person is killed in an insignificant attempt, even where there is no intention of murder. Such happenings can be explained by the above theory. Thus, even when the Lord allows freedom of will to a tyrant, there is no harm, for the efforts of the tyrant cannot succeed in violation of the Law of Karma. The Law of Karma reigns supreme.[7]

A further corollary follows from the above position. When a person attempts to offend someone, even when the offender does not succeed because the target has no past karma *prarābdha* to suffer, the offender still incurs sin as he or she has completed his or her part of the offense; therefore, he or she is liable to receive punishment. In order for an act to become a sin, or evil, it is not necessary that the act result in actual suffering on the part of the target, it is sufficient that the offender has made the attempt. Suffering depends on the previous karma of the sufferer, not on the efforts of the offender. Sin works the other way; sin depends on the efforts of the offender, not on the suffering of the person the offender sought to harm.

A further objection can be raised; if the Lord allows His creatures freedom of will, subject to abuse, it becomes obligatory on the part of the Lord to make it clear to the creatures what a good choice is and what a bad choice is and how He wants the creatures to exercise their will. In answer one could say that the Lord already does this. The Lord has arranged to teach the creature through two sources — external and internal. Holy scriptures and personal teachers (sages, bhaktas, yogins, and so on) are the external sources from which the creature can learn;[8] while the inner illumination and inner conscience of a person is the internal source. The creature, out of contempt arising from its false ego, may not pay heed to such teachings, but the Lord from His side is trying to enlighten the creature. In this respect it is the creature who is to blame, for it intentionally shuts its eyes and, out of egotism, does not want to see. The individual not only avoids learning from the external sources, but also turns a deaf ear to the voice of his or her own conscience. But if one sincerely intends to know and learn, one can easily and successfully do this; God is showering His instructions in abundance.

All the points discussed above are relevant only when we accept the premise of free will, which we can legitimately do in the case of humans, who are (partially) free and rational beings. But there are animals who have neither reason nor free will. They act instinctively. Many such animals, determined by their blind nature, act in a violent way and inflict injury on other beings. This happens especially in the case of the food-seeking animals; this is just their nature.[9] In such cases there is no question of the abuse of free will; animals have no free will. The violence takes place by dint of instinct. Now, the question arises — if violence in the animal kingdom is due to instinctive nature and not to free will, then the responsibility for the violence falls entirely upon God, who has made these animals that way. It is contrary to reason to think that it is the tiger, for example, who is to blame for killing the innocent cow; the blame goes to the one who has made the tiger and installed such a nature in that species. Moreover, what is the fault of the cow which falls prey to the carnivore? The naturalist will have no difficulty in explaining this situation, but what about the theist who accepts Nature as the creation of God?

To this problem the answer found in Hindu scriptures, which Kashmir Śaivism would also accept, is that animals fall in the category of *bhoga-yoni* ("species meant for reaping the fruits of actions"), not *karma-yoni* ("species meant for doing fresh action"). Thus the offender and the sufferer in the animal kingdom both belong to the *bhoga-yoni.* They are not evolved to the stage where it is possible to initiate action; they can only reap the results of action. According to the Hindu scriptures, the human species is the most evolved and only in this form is it possible to perform fresh action. It is believed that a person who performs very bad deeds may be given an animal form in his or her next birth; after working out his or her karma in that body, he or she may resume the human form in the following birth.

Moreover, it can be said that when Nature allows violence to occur in the animal kingdom, She has her own way of balancing the violence. For example, it may be that Nature reduces the pain of the inflicted creature to a minimum, or even neutralizes it completely. In the case of human beings we find that when pain becomes unbearable, the person becomes unconscious so that he or she can no longer feel the pain. This may happen in the animal kingdom from the beginning of the infliction of violence.

Animals are not *completely* devoid of free will. The activity of an animal may appear to be entirely involuntary, but still there may be some amount of free will. Perhaps this free will explains the difference in personal nature from one animal to another in the same species. In the case of small children, too, there is not a complete absence of free will. To the extent the animal or the child has will, it is responsible for its activity; to that extent it becomes responsible for its action and reaps the moral fruit acccording to the Law of Karma.

GOD AS THE REAL DOER

There is an important question regarding the agency of the individual self. Kashmir Śaivism clearly admits that God, or Śiva, is the real doer; the ego in itself is just a cipher. It is Śiva who does everything, but the ego appropriates the doing to itself. In other scriptural texts this idea is clearly expressed. "The Goddess, forcibly hypnotizing the minds of even wise persons, induces them to ignorant activity."[10] "All actions are actuated by the constituents (*guṇas*) of Nature (*prakṛti*); the individual out of egotism and ignorance thinks 'I am the doer.'"[11] "God resides in the heart of all beings, and moves them with His power of delusion, as if they were put in a revolving machine."[12] Religions of the world accept the supremacy of the divine will. "Not a leaf moves without the will of God."[13] Now the question arises; if God is the real doer and the individual will is only a camouflage, then the entire responsibility for evil falls on God, and the individual deserves complete exemption from the responsibility. How can the individual be held responsible if he or she is really not the doer?

In answer to the above question we would say that the paradoxical statement of the scriptures that God is the real doer does not really go against the responsibility of man for committing evil. The same scriptures make it clear that God does not induce anybody to commit sin; therefore He is not responsible.[14] The same texts that declare that everything is determined by the Divine will, in the same breath prescribe a path for people to follow, and then leave it to their own choice.[15] If God, and not man, is the doer, what sense is there in asking man to do something, such as perform good action? God will do it, for He is the doer; people need not bother with it. Moreover, if God is the doer, what is the sense in saying that people, and not God, are responsible for sin and that they have to reap the fruit of their actions? What I want to suggest here is that the statement that God is the real doer and that the individual ego is nothing, should be understood in a highly technical sense.

The technical sense to the above statement is twofold. First, it means that the power to act comes entirely from God; the ego in itself is absolutely powerless. God (Śiva) is the Higher Self (*paramātmā*) of all the individual selves or egos — just as the ocean is to the waves — supplying His powers to the ego. The ego is said to be a cipher, or zero, because like a zero that derives all its value from the digit that stands by its side, the ego in itself is valueless.[16] Of course, the choice to use or misuse God's power is the individual's. In the case of a student who is dependent on his or her parents, all the money that the student spends comes from the parents; the student has no money of his or her own. It can well be said that it is the parents, not the student, who are spending money. But the choice to spend the money in a good or bad way is the student's. He or she can choose to spend it in the right way; he or she can choose to spend it in the wrong way as well. So it is the student, not the parents, who is responsible for the misuse. Similarly, the power with which the individual acts is entirely God's; the individual has no power of his or her own for doing anything. In this sense it can be said that it is God, not the person, who is the doer. But the choice to use God's power in a good or bad way is the individual's, and so it is the individual, and not God, who is responsible for the misuse of powers, which is another name for evil or sin.

It is not that we understand the futility of the ego only when we accept God; the nothingness of the ego can be realized just by analyzing our ordinary experience, without bringing God into the picture at all. That the body and mind follow the dictates of the ego simply means that Nature cooperates with the ego; if and when Nature refuses to obey, the ego can do nothing. We think, for example, that the dexterity in our hands and the power of locomotion in our feet are ours and therefore, the hands and the feet are at our command; but when they become paralyzed, can we still successfully command them to work? Likewise, we think that the intelligence in our brain is our own and that we are very intelligent; but we are intelligent because Nature has given us intelligence. Nature has placed the faculties of mind at our command. If Nature, or God as the theist would put it, withdraws the powers, that is if the mind goes mad or the mental faculties are paralyzed, what can we do? We are thus not the real source of these powers; Nature, or God, is the source, and it is grace that these powers are vested in us.[17] We, out of false egotism and ignorance, credit the ownership to ourselves.

Even if we do not accept the existence of God, we have to accept the powerlessness and nothingness of ego. Buddhism, which is not a theistic philosophy, accepts this truth and advocates it even more forcefully than many theistic systems.[18]

The second sense in which the statement "God is the real doer" is made is that God sometimes really prompts or induces the individual to certain activity in order that the individual may reap the fruits of his or her actions. God is the master executor of the Law of Karma. He need not shunt the souls to heaven and hell in order for them to reap the fruits of their good and bad deeds; He may execute the fructification of deeds in this very life. When He so intends, He may directly or indirectly prompt people to choose to act in a certain way so that it ultimately leads them to happiness or sorrow as the case may be. It is in this very sense that it is said that the Goddess forcibly induces even the wise into ignorant activity.[19] Here God is the doer not merely in the sense that the capacity to act comes from Him, but also in the sense that He is the direct prompter of activity. In this case God is not prompting the person to commit fresh sins; He is simply driving him or her towards a situation in which the fruit of his or her past deeds can be reaped.

Thus we see that the statement that God is the real doer has a highly technical meaning. It primarily means that the entire capacity to act comes from God. It means that God is the direct prompter of man's activity in the sense that the Lord intends to bring people's deeds to fruition; it never means that the Lord incites humans to sinful activity. Of course, when the individual surrenders his or her own will to the Divine Will and chooses to abide by the will of the Lord, then the Lord may directly prompt the individual; but in that case the Lord would always make the individual do good deeds. Thus the Lord may become the direct prompter of people's actions (and in that sense He may be the doer in a literal sense) when the individual chooses to serve the Lord and become a medium for His activity — the activity of doing good to the world. This amounts to saying that when the individual follows his or her own will, he or she is subject to error; but when the individual surrenders to the Lord and allows the Lord to act through him or her, then there are no chances of error, for the Lord is perfect.[20]

It follows from the above that if all the individuals chose to follow the Divine Will and abide by the moral rules of Divine governance, there would be no evil in the world. It is theoretically possible that the world could be absolutely free from evil provided the individuals perfectly abide by the Lord. In fact, the Lord (Śiva) intends exactly this. He has initiated this great sport of Creation for joy and blissful playing, not for evil and suffering. If the individual players who are vitiating the Sport by the abuse of their free will choose to abide by the rules of the Sport and follow the benign will of the Sportsmaster, then there can be no evil and, therefore no suffering, and life in the world would always remain a blissful sport.

Thus the statement "God is the doer" means three things: (a) all power to act comes from God — the ego being a cipher — but the choice to use or abuse that power is the individual's; (b) God prompts the individual's actual action or decision when He has to provide happiness or suffering to the person according to his or her *karma*; and (c) when the individual (the lower self) completely surrenders to God (the Higher Self) and comes totally in line with God, then God Himself performs activity through that person and in this case only good actions are possible.

A further question may be asked here. It is already said that it is Śiva who, as part of His *līlā*, becomes the individual *paśu*. In the *Śiva-dṛṣṭi* it is said, "The Lord out of sport adopts the bodies that sin and suffer and live in hell. Just as an all-powerful king in a sportive mood takes to foot locomotion, so also the playful Lord sports in degraded bodies."[21] The question is: if it is the Lord who is sporting in the form of the sinful *paśus*, there is no question of free will on the part of the *paśu* and the responsibility of evil is the Lord's.

In answer to the above question we would suggest a statement such as this must be interpreted within the framework of Kashmir Śaivism if it is not to be confusing and misleading. We have already pointed out that when Śiva becomes the *paśu*, it is not that Śiva is lost and only the *paśu* remains, as happens in the case of milk becoming curd. Śiva completely remains Śiva, and at the same time also becomes the limited *paśu* — the individual as an extension, not a transformation, of Śiva. In this way a duality is created within Śiva — Śiva as *paśu* becomes different from the original Śiva. Creation of duality itself is part of the sport of the non-dual Śiva, and Śiva ever maintains His unity with the individuals, although the individuals become different from Śiva. From the point of view of Śiva there is no duality, for He feels one with the individuals, and yet the individuals, although essentially one with Him, existentially become different from Him. When the ocean manifests itself in the form of individualized waves, it remains one with them, yet the waves maintain their separate individuality. A mother giving birth to her children feels her unity with them, although the children have their separate existence. Similarly Śiva, manifesting in the form of independent individuals, never loses sight of His unity with them and yet they have their separate existence.

Although the *paśu* is essentially one with the Lord (*pati*) and although the Lord from *His* side is quite conscious of His unity with the *paśu*, yet the *paśu* enjoys a relatively separate and independent existence. This allowance for relative independence of the *paśu* may be part of the Lord's *līlā* or it may be His grace, but the fact remains that the individual is set free. He or she becomes independent of the Lord, just as a child becomes independent of its mother. Thus the *paśu* is endowed with free will, and is responsible for his or her choices. Since the *paśu* has separate and independent identity, the Lord is not responsible for the individual's deeds. Just as a mother, although enjoying herself in her children and feeling her complete unity with them, is not held responsible for the evil deeds they commit, so also the Divine Mother (Citi-śakti or Śiva), although feeling absolutely one with Her creatures and enjoying Herself in their form, is not responsible for the evil deeds of the creatures who commit evil of their own accord, by abusing their freedom of will.

IGNORANCE AS THE CAUSE OF EVIL

Almost all systems of Indian philosophy maintain that ignorance, or nescience, (*ajñāna* or *avidyā*) is the cause of bondage and evil. The *Gītā* says that knowledge is covered by ignorance and it is this that prompts the individual to commit evil.[22] Abhinavagupta himself says, "All the Scriptures declare that ignorance is the cause of bondage in *saṁsāra* and that knowledge is the cause of liberation."[23] Here ignorance is used not merely in the sense of intellectual ignorance (*bauddha ajñāna*) but also in the sense of the five sheaths of *māyā* (*pañcakañcuka*) that make up existential ignorance (*pauruṣa ajñāna*). It is further maintained that ignorance is not a creation of the individual soul; it is caused by the Lord. Atheistic philosophies such as Buddhism, Jainism, and Sāṁkhya do not maintain that ignorance is created by God, for they do not accept God; but they hold that ignorance is not created by the individual either, as it is a cosmic principle and is beginninglessly present of its own accord. That ignorance is the cause of evil and that it is not caused by the individual is found to be true in our experience also. If a person commits a theft, for example, it is because he or she has both the desire for money and the sense of duality — he or she considers the victim to be separate from him- or herself. Had there been no desire for money and had the thief considered the affected person to be his or her own self, he or she would not have committed the theft. Neither the desire for money nor the sense of duality, which are part of ignorance, are created by the thief; they already exist in him or her from birth. Similarly without the sexual impulse there could be no sex crimes. The sexual impulse is the cause of sex crime; but sex is not our own creation.

Now it may be suggested that if one commits evil out of ignorance, and if ignorance is not one's own creation, then one should not be held responsible for evil. It is Śiva, the creator of ignorance, that should be held responsible for evil. In answer we would point out that although ignorance is the cause of evil, ignorance itself is not a sufficient cause for the commission of evil. Ignorance is the necessary cause of evil but not its sufficient cause. It is like the case of fire and smoke. There can be no smoke without fire, so fire is the "necessary cause" of smoke. But fire in itself is not guaranteed to create smoke, there can be fire without smoke, as in the fire in a grate of charcoal or in an electric heater. Thus fire, while it is the "necessary cause" of smoke is not the "sufficient cause." In order to create smoke, wet fuel is needed in addition to the fire. The wet fuel then is the real cause of the smoke and, therefore it is the wet fuel and not the fire that should be held responsible for the smoke. In the case of ignorance and evil, ignorance is the "necessary cause" of evil, for if there is no ignorance, there can be no evil. But ignorance in itself is not sufficient for the creation of evil. What is needed in addition is the abuse of the free will. It is only when the individual chooses to abuse his or her powers that he or she commits evil. The sexual impulse, for example, does not itself cause the sex crime; it is only when the individual adds to sex the abuse of freedom that a crime is committed. Everyone has sexual impulses but not everyone commits sex crimes. Those who choose to restrain their impulses or choose to satisfy them in an accepted way do not commit sex crimes; only those who choose to gratify themselves in the wrong way commit a crime. The crime is due to the criminal's abuse of free will, not to the natural passion or the natural ignorance in him or her. All souls are ignorant and all have natural passions. Had ignorance or passion itself been the sufficient cause of evil, every person at all times would commit evil; but it is not so. One commits evil only when one chooses to do so. Therefore it is the abuse of free will that should be held responsible for sin, not ignorance. The responsibility for evil therefore lies with the individual who transgresses, not with God who has created ignorance.

The opponent may ask why Śiva has created ignorance, which serves as the ground of evil. In answer we could say that ignorance is created for a good purpose, not for causing evil. Śiva creates ignorance for the sake of *līlā*, for joy; if the abuse of free will is not added to ignorance, ignorance by itself serves that good purpose. The life of a small child is an example of this. The child is ignorant, but how happy it is! The child blooms with spontaneous joy. The faculty of free will has not yet developed in the small child; therefore there is no question of the abuse of free will. The ignorance of the child serves the good purpose of giving it playful joy. When the child grows up, develops free will, and chooses to abuse it, then alone does evil come. Ignorance and evil are not necessarily connected.

One may be a little confused here as to whether the spontaneous joy in the child is due to the natural *spanda* of Consciousness or is due to ignorance. Really the joy in the child is due to the *spanda* of Consciousness, and the simple ignorance free from the abuse of free will allows the *spanda* to manifest itself in the child. Mere ignorance, although limiting Consciousness, does not in itself go against bliss (*ānanda*), nor does it by itself cause evil. If ignorance is created by God (Śiva) and the creature is not responsible for it, God has no right to make the creature suffer due to ignorance. The creature does not suffer due to ignorance, it does so due to the abuse of its own free will. Ignorance of course is the creation of God, but abuse of free will by the creature is not God's creation; it is entirely a creation of the creature; thus the creature itself is responsible for it.

Thus we can say that ignorance is created by the Lord for a good purpose — so that the creatures should enjoy life in the world as sport or *līlā*. And they do enjoy it, provided it is not mixed with factors created by the creatures themselves. In the case of fire and smoke, fire was created not to produce smoke but to serve innumerable beneficial purposes; smoke is produced due to the addition of wet fuel to the fire. Electricity is generated not in order to cause electrocution but to provide immensely good services. We cannot say that because airplanes are sometimes involved in accidents and cause the loss of human lives that the airplane is not a good thing and that it was a mistake to invent and develop it. Similarly we cannot say that because ignorance causes evil too, it is unjust on the part of the Lord to create it. Ignorance can cause harm only when deliberate human immorality is added to it. Even then, according to the Law of Karma, the suffering is incurred not by the innocent others but by the immoral agent who must suffer for his or her ill deeds.

It should be clear that the acts done in the state of mere ignorance, devoid of the state of free will, cannot be covered by the category of morality — they are neither moral nor immoral. That is why the acts of infants or of animals are not considered immoral or sinful. The category of morality is only applied to those acts that are done through free will. Growing children, and some animals also, may have some amount of free will, and their acts will come under the moral category proportionate to the amount of free will they possess. To that extent, if they act wickedly they are liable to be punished. It is volition or free will, not ignorance, that turns an action to good or bad. Therefore it is the abuse of free will, not ignorance, that is the cause of suffering.

SUFFERING AND THE LAW OF KARMA

It may be clear from what we have discussed so far that it is man, not God, that is responsible for his evil acts; man is thus liable to be punished for those acts. Rational understanding demands that the good be rewarded and the evil have retribution. This is justice, and this justice is the least that is expected in the kingdom of God. Religions of the world vouch for this justice. "As you sow, so you reap" is the dictum accepted by them. In India this is called the Law of Karma. All the systems of Indian philosophy, except the Cārvāka, accept it. In order to accept the Law of Karma, it is not necessary to presuppose the existence of God; the Law of Karma can be accepted as an independent, objective law of existence. In fact, Buddhism, Jainism, Mimāṁsā, and so on accept it in this very form; they emphasize it even more than the theistic systems do. Buddhism declares, "One must reap the fruit of one's action, good or bad."[24]

Kashmir Śaivism accepts the Law of Karma as the other systems do, but the uniqueness of its approach to the Law of Karma lies in its emphasis on the freedom (*svātantrya*) of humanity. We have already stated that *svātantrya* ("freedom of consciousness") is the basic concept of Kashmir Śaivism; the individual self enjoys this freedom, though in a limited way. By putting emphasis on the free will of the individual, Kashmir Śaivism places the entire responsibility of evil on the individual; the Benign One (Śiva) is kept free from the responsibility. Some students of Kashmir Śaivism may think that because the entire Creation is the play of the Lord, evil is also part of His plan; but as I have already pointed out, this is an erroneous view of Kashmir Śaivism. Kashmir Śaivism cannot and does not accord the evil to Śiva, who is by His very nature good or benign.

Suffering, understood from the point of view of the Law of Karma, is meant for two things. First, it comes as punishment for the evil deeds done in the past; second, it is meant to correct or reform the individual. This implies that the Law of Karma is not a mechanical law but purposive. When a law is mechanical, it works blindly. But the Law of Karma is not like this. It has a definite purpose — to reform or correct. We find in our experience of the world that there are people who do not take to the right track without suffering. Suffering is a must for the correction of those who are wicked. It is suffering that hammers our ego and makes us realize the necessity of following the path of goodness. In this sense suffering is a great benefactor. Moreover, if we ourselves do not choose to make ourselves better and purer, suffering per force makes us become so and we attain a spiritually better state of consciousness, fit to be endowed with the higher gifts of life.

If we approach suffering from the above point of view, then God will not appear as a tyrant condoning the suffering of His creatures. Śaiva Siddhānta views suffering as the expression of God's love for His creatures. Just as a mother disciplines her child in order to correct it, so also the Divine Mother sanctions the suffering of Her creatures in order that they become righteous, good, and pure.[25] It is not for nothing that the creature is confronted with pain and suffering.

One thing may be mentioned in this context. The creature has to suffer not only for its doing evil but also for its being evil. The state of being is more important than the state of doing, for doing naturally results from being. One who is evil or bad by nature, although not actually doing any evil, is liable to be corrected. The very presence of an evil person, although he or she may not be doing anything wrong, is nauseating. Likewise a good person, even if he or she is not doing anything, is agreeable and desirable. The story of Martha and Mary in the Bible refers to the above distinction. Martha is in the state of doing, whereas Mary is in the state of being, and Christ prefers Mary to Martha. In Kashmir Śaivism too, in the hierarchy of means (*upāyas*), *śāmbhavopāya*, which correlates with the state of being is ranked higher than *kriyopāya* and *āṇavopāya*, which are states of doing (*āṇavopāya* involves the physical or external activity, and *kriyopāya* the mental or internal activity).[26]

The oft-advanced argument against the Law of Karma and against Providence is that there is an obvious violation of the law of distributive justice in the world. In the world the wicked may prosper and the virtuous may suffer.[27] In answer we would point out that the Law of Karma has an explanation for this apparent discrepancy based on the past deeds of the persons involved. We cannot deny the possibility of such an explanation. Moreover the phenomenon of the wicked being prosperous and the virtuous suffering needs to be analyzed more deeply and comprehensively.

In this connection we may refer to certain points that are generally ignored while presenting the above challenge. First, it may be that the "bad" are not all bad and the "good" are not all good. Second, the ultimate balance of sorrow or happiness may be in accordance with the vice or virtue of the person involved. That is, it may be that the sinful one is temporarily exalted and has to suffer in the long run, and the virtuous, in the long run, finds peace and happiness. Or it may be that in spite of his or her apparent prosperity, the sinful person has other kinds of sorrows and sufferings — material prosperity is not necessarily indicative of a happy and peaceful life.[28] Similarly we may find "poor" people who rejoice and make merry in a far more lively way than the rich. Third, the genuine cases where the virtuous are suffering and the sinful prospering involve past actions — past history that may go back even to previous births. According to the Law of Karma one is bound to repay one's debts and cash in one's credits. If a man has at present become virtuous, his past actions will not be ignored on that account.

We will discuss one by one the points mentioned above. As far as the question of vice and virtue is concerned, it is not easy to ascertain who is really sinful and who is really virtuous. It is only by peering into a person's inner life and by being intimately acquainted with him or her for quite some time that one can really ascertain whether he or she is good or bad. One who from a distance appears to be good and virtuous, may turn out to be otherwise when we come to know him or her well. Similarly the rascally looking person may have certain praiseworthy virtues and may behave more squarely and honestly than the so-called virtuous person.

We generally go by the traditional standards of morality accepted by society, or by the divine law of the scriptures and the religious pontiffs in making judgments regarding vice and virtue. We sometimes judge by the standard of our own intellect and conscience. But none of these standards is absolute. History has witnessed many acts of injustice and cruelty in the name of social justice and so-called divine law. The judgment based on the inner conscience is also not necessarily objective and impartial; what is called conscience or inner reason may be the result of the dispositions (*saṁskāras*) of the external standards that have entered into our inner mind. Our judgments of vice and virtue based on these standards thus may be quite erroneous.

Moreover the virtuous may be suffering from the very serious defect of ego. Sometimes the ego of the virtuous harms others much more than the behavior of the ordinary sinner does. The ego of a person works in the most subtle way and makes all his or her virtues ineffective. Ego harms both oneself and others. That is why it is said that the Lord does not tolerate even the smallest grain of ego in His devotee and tends to destroy it. The *purāṇas* are full of stories that narrate how the Lord destroys the ego of His devotee by making the devotee suffer. We can safely conclude that if a virtuous person has ego, that person is really not virtuous; egolessness is the condition of all virtue. It follows from this that one who follows the Lord and the path of righteousness egolessly will not be subjected to suffering; but if one does so with ego, one is liable to suffer. In fact, if one has ego one is really not following the path of the Lord.

The entire story of the *Mahābhārata* depicts in a very subtle and ingenious way how one is responsible for one's own suffering. This is seen in the case of every character of the epic; and the Lord (Kṛṣṇa) acts as an impartial executor of the divine law of justice. Many of the stories of Hindu mythology also depict this truth. In the famous stories of the war between the gods (*devas*) and the demons (*dānavas* or *asuras*), we find that the Lord intervenes to help the gods only after they have suffered for some time and have undergone sufficient purging. The Lord does not immediately incarnate to protect the good people (*sādhus*); first He allows the *sādhus* to suffer for some time.

The evil in one's character or actions is of two types. The first type is what is easily recognizable as immoral — theft, murder, rape, dishonesty, cheating, betrayal, ungratefulness, and so on. The opposite would be righteousness, honesty, integrity, truthfulness, and so on. The other type of evil, which is not easily recognizable, is ego. We may find a person who is very honest, upright, and so on, but who is at the same time very egotistic. The evil of ego inflicts unjustified pain on others as strongly as the evil of the first type. Nature, or the Law of Karma is thus bound to punish ego just as it is bound to punish immorality. It is quite natural that an egotistic person, although abiding by the laws of morality, must suffer just as an immoral person suffers. A really good person or a really virtuous one is someone who is free from both the evil of immorality and the evil of egotism. Such a good person would not suffer, as it would be contrary to the law of Nature or the Law of Karma that a really good person suffer.

Thus we see that most cases where the "virtuous" are found to be suffering and the "sinful" rejoicing can be explained by the fact that (a) the "virtuous" may not really be that virtuous nor the "sinful" that sinful, and (b) considering the total balance of happiness and suffering, the "happy" person may not really be that happy and the "suffering" person may not really be suffering that much.

Still there may be some cases where the person is really good or really virtuous yet the person is suffering, and on the contrary a really bad person may be very happy for the time being. Such cases can be explained only by bringing up the notion of past karma. Most karma is rewarded or punished in the same life; the "terrible" action (*utkaṭa karma*) may fructify in the same birth. But some karmas go on accumulating and fructify in future births.

Thus the theory of the Law of Karma also implies the theory of rebirth. The theory of the Law of Karma and rebirth gives rise to many questions, but this is not the place to discuss them all. Here we may simply note that rebirth is a possible phenomenon that cannot be disproved. It is a typically Indian belief, but others have cherished it as well. The ancient Greeks believed in rebirth. Some of the early Christian fathers also believed in the theory of rebirth — Origen, for example. It was only in the later centuries that the theory of rebirth was officially discarded by the Christian church. Nowadays there is a growing interest in the West in the phenomenon of rebirth.

As to the question of collective suffering or death caused by events like accidents, earthquakes, wars, and so on, we could say that an accident resulting in collective suffering is caused by the collective karma of the persons involved. The past action ready for fruition (*prārabdha*) of each person involved accumulates at one point and results in collective suffering.

The Law of Karma can also be transcended. Since the Law of Karma is not mechanical but purposive, we can transcend it by satisfying its purpose. The purpose of the Law of Karma is to purify the person or to make him or her good. When we become completely good and pure, we are exempted from the punishment, just as the punishment of a prisoner is reduced for good conduct. This is what is meant by "repentance" as mentioned in the Bible. Real, sincere repentance means inner reformation and the resolution not to commit crime again. Repentance means purification of heart.

Complete self-purification is achieved in a person when he or she totally surrenders to God or the Higher Self or turns completely in tune with the Self. Then he or she satisfies the purpose of the Law of Karma and it is fitting that his or her past karmas be forgiven or destroyed. The Upaniṣads declare that when one realizes the transcendent Self, one's karmas become ineffective.[29] The state of Self-realization, or *jñāna* ("enlightenment") is the state of complete self-purification. Accordingly the *Gītā* says, "Just as the burning fire reduces the fuel to ashes, so also the fire of *jñāna* ('knowledge' or 'enlightenment') burns all the karmas to ashes."[30] A saint or sage attains this state and therefore becomes free from karma. The mystic poet Kabir says "The saint is the heroic warrior who treads on the decree of karma and transcends it."[31] Tulsīdāsa makes the Lord say, "When the soul comes face to face with me, his karmas of innumerable births are destroyed."[32] Coming face to face with God means complete attunement with the Self; this in turn means complete self-purification, which leads to the transcendence of karma.

Thus we see that the law of the transcendence of karma is as significant as the Law of Karma itself. Kashmir Śaivism would emphasize the law of the transcendence of karma, because freedom from the Law of Karma suggests the freedom of the human who is consciousness, not matter, and whose true nature is freedom (*svātantrya*). Kashmir Śaivism emphasizes the potential freedom of man. The Law of Karma is determinism (*niyati*) and transcendence of this law is the freedom from determinism. The state of Self-realization (Śiva-realization) is the state of the transcendence of the Law of Karma and therefore the state of freedom.

THE PLACE OF EVIL IN LĪLĀVĀDA

From the explanation of evil given in the foregoing pages, it should be obvious that evil is not in the nature of Reality, and therefore it is not in the true nature of man. Evil is *caused* — caused by individuals' *deliberate misuse* of their free will. In other words, evil is accidental not natural. To use an analogy, when a piece of cloth accumulates dirt by its association with external factors, the cloth itself looks dirty, but the fact is that the dirt is not part and parcel of the cloth. Dirt is caused by external factors and it can be removed. The cloth by its very nature is clean. The dirt can easily be removed because dirt is not the nature of the cloth but it has incidentally accrued to the cloth. Similarly evil is not the nature of humanity; evil has accidentally cropped up due to people's deliberate abuse of their freedom.

It follows from the above position that evil can be eradicated from the world if we so choose. We have already seen that man, not God, is responsible for evil. We have also seen that people become or commit evil not out of any compulsion but out of their own free will. It is more than clear that God does not want people to commit evil. In fact He wants them to follow the path of goodness, and He makes every attempt to put them on the right track. The Law of Karma itself is one of the means that God uses for bringing people to the right path. It is true that God is omnipotent, but it would not be proper for God to interfere in man's freedom of will. Disallowing freedom of will to man would be tantamount to disallowing man's very existence; doing so would be unjust on the part of God.

Of course, it is obligatory on the part of God to make clear to humanity just what is good and what is bad. God does this quite efficiently. He calls on people in two ways — (a) from inside, as their inner conscience, and (b) from outside, as teacher, scripture, or even as *avatāra* ("incarnation"). But people, out of ego, pay heed neither to the inner voice of conscience nor to the external voice of the teacher. We do not hear the voice of God, not because He does not speak to us, but because we do not *want to hear* Him. We want to follow our own false ego. Vanity, or false ego, is the one thing not given by God; it is entirely humanity's. When it is said that everything comes out of Śiva (God), what is meant by "everything" is the natural things of the world, including people and their natural desires and capacities, not what is artifically created by humanity itself. Ego is created by humanity, not by Śiva; thus evil, which is the product of people's ego, is also created by humanity, not by Śiva.

Lord Kṛṣṇa in the *Gītā* apprises Arjuna of the right path to follow, but to follow or not is the free choice of Arjuna. Thus the Lord has to say in the end, "I have related to you the wisdom that is the secret of all secrets, and now after considering it fully, *do as you like.*"[33] God cannot forcibly put a person on the right path because doing that would mean not allowing the person his or her freedom and making him or her just like a robot, which in turn would mean denying the person his or her very existence. God can only tell or teach; to follow or not is the prerogative of humanity. God does *His* part; He teaches humanity about the truth and the right path. He also makes positive attempts to set people straight — for example, He calls to people in the form of the guru. He also rejoices in the "return of the prodigal son," but He cannot force the prodigal son to return, as this is the free choice of the son. That is why, in spite of all the efforts on the part of God, the world is not yet rid of evil.

But it also follows from the above position that if people chose not to abuse their freedom and to follow the path of goodness, no evil would remain in the world. Since evil depends entirely upon humankind, humans alone can check evil; and if they so choose, there will be no evil in the world. So it is theoretically possible for the world to become completely free from evil if humanity does *its* part. But since it all depends upon people's free choice, we cannot predict it, but the possibility exists. The hope lies with humanity, which *can* become good if it so chooses.

The purpose of Creation is joy (*ānanda*) and not suffering; the object of life is happiness. The world is created from joy and for joy. We are all meant to partake in this joy. The world is the cosmic stage for the drama of bliss. Śiva is the director (*sūtradhāra*) of this drama and we are all actors required to play our parts happily. The world is the playground for the cosmic game of happiness. Śiva is the grand Gamesmaster, and we, the players, are required to play in accordance with the rules of the game. But we violate the rules of the game against the will of the Gamesmaster. The Gamesmaster then has to punish us of course.

If the players (the individual souls) did not violate the rules of the game and followed the benign will of the Gamesmaster, there would be no evil and therefore no suffering in the world, and the grand game of Creation would go on merrily. Suffering is caused by the evil that we do and doing evil is the choice of the players who have free will. The Gamesmaster does not want us to do evil; but He also cannot nullify our existence by denying us free will. Therefore we players, and not the Gamesmaster, are responsible for the evil that is present in this grand game of Creation. The Gamesmaster loves His players and wants them to follow His way of goodness, but His constraint is that He cannot force the players to act according to His will. He cannot *Himself* act through the players unless the players allow Him to do so. God directly acts through the souls only if and when they freely give way and allow Him to act through them; to allow God to do so is the free choice of humanity. It is the players, not the Gamesmaster, who can make the sport of Creation free from evil.

7

The Concept of Pratyabhijñā ("Self-recognition")

PRATYABHIJÑĀ IS CENTRAL TO KASHMIR ŚAIVISM

The central issue of Tantra as interpreted by Kashmir Śaivism is the recognition (*pratyabhijñā*) of the Self. This is the beginning and the end of the Tantric pursuit. Tantra strives to answer the question "Who am I?" Am I nothing more than this psychophysical organism bound by its limitations, or am I an independent being, free from the limitation of the body and its environments, but accidentally captured within it for a time? Is freedom my true nature and if so how can I realize this freedom?

Even in our limited state of existence we feel partially free. In all our endeavors we strive, directly or indirectly, consciously or unconsciously, to free ourselves fully from our present state. Unfulfilled wants, disease, pain, and so on are ever-present limitations, but we strive endlessly to accomplish our desires, fulfill our wants, and gain mastery over our environment. In other words, we are always striving to overcome our limitations and become free.

This natural human endeavor suggests that our real nature is perfect freedom towards which we unconsciously push.[1]

Our dissatisfaction with our present state stems from its not being natural to us — we do not belong to this state. While a rat may be perfectly at home in a pile of refuse, we shrink from the stench and filth. It is not in our nature to be at home there. Similarly, we rebel against our present state of imperfection because our real nature is other than this. The emphasis of the Tantras is on knowing what this real nature is. While they may describe in detail the origin and nature of the world, the central focus of the texts is the recognition of the Self.

Although the Tantras describe in detail the process of Creation, the real problem for the *paśu*, or limited self, is not to know how the world is created, but to know what his or her real nature is. Of course, in a way it is necessary to know the origin and nature of the world, because we are related to it, and we cannot know ourselves without knowing the world. That is why the process of Creation is discussed. But the question is not to know the world for its own sake, but to know it in order to know the self. The main problem, then, is that of knowing the self.

It is reasonable to believe, as I have shown earlier in the chapter on epistemology, that the phenomenon of consciousness that appears at the surface level is just the tip of a bigger reality lying deeper in us, like the iceberg, only a tiny portion of which is visible above the surface, or like an artesian spring that is invisibly connected to a deeper and vaster underground water reserve. We are really not the poor self suffering from the limitations of life, growing in the state of "anguished freedom." We are really Śiva, a state of freedom from all limitations — a state of perfection and complete fulfillment.

The point is that our real identity is different from what it appears to be; what appears to be our identity is, in one word, a state of imperfection or limitation. But this is only a surface picture — the real picture is the state of complete freedom (*svātantrya*) or perfection. We know our existence, but we do not know our perfection, and so we do not behave like perfect beings.[2]

The problem is that we are not aware of our real identity. We exist, but we do not know who we really are. It is the Guru or the Āgama (or Śruti) that makes us aware of our real identity, that declares that we are really Śiva (or Brahman)[3] and also points out the way to realize our real identity (which is Śivahood).

The Upaniṣads also tend to make one have the *pratyabhijñā* ("recognition") of oneself. The *mahāvākyas* ("great sentences") of the Upaniṣads are *pratyabhijñā*-sentences, for they declare our real identity, which is Ātman or Brahman. The identity of the self as Brahman is revealed by the *mahāvākyas* in all three grammatical persons of the self — first, second, and third. *Ahaṁ brahmāsmi* ("I am Brahman") reveals the identity of the self in the first person (I); *tattvamasi* ("That thou art") does the same thing in the second person (thou); and *ayamātmā Brahma* ("This self is Brahman ") reveals the identity of the self in the third person (he, she, or it). The Upaniṣads suggest that the self in all its three persons is nothing but Brahman — I am Brahman (first person), you are Brahman (second person), and he, she or it is Brahman (third person). The self in every case is Brahman.

Tantra asserts that the real nature of the Self is Śiva, which is Pure Consciousness (*śuddha saṁvit*), the state of freedom and perfection. We are really Śiva, but we find ourselves in the state of a poor, limited being (*paśu*). Unaware of our real nature, we do not recognize that we are Śiva. The moment we have this realization, we are free. But is the situation really so simple? Is ignorance of the nature of the Self the only reason for the colossal misfortune that is human limitation? And is knowledge of the Self a miracle cure for this disease? According to Kashmir Śaivism the answer to these questions is yes. It remains to be seen, then, what the nature of this knowledge of the Self (*ātma-pratyabhijñā*) is and how it effects a transformation in the lives of those who gain it.

THE MEANING OF PRATYABHIJÑĀ

Pratyabhijñā (*pratyābhijñāna* or *abhijñā*) is usually translated into English as *recognition*. But the word *recognition* provides only a partial definition of the term. It implies the remembrance of something already known. For example, having met a person once, if you encounter him or her a second time you will know who the person is, remembering his or her appearance. This is *recognition*, or *pratyabhijñā* as it is commonly understood.[4] But what is meant by *pratyabhijñā* as technically used in Kashmir Śaivism is slightly different. Here it is not a matter of recognizing something that is already known, but of coming to know the identity of something that may never have been seen before, or may have been seen many times before but was not known. Knowledge of identity is the key to *pratyabhijñā* in Kashmir Śaivism. *Pratyabhijñā* is not synonymous with perception. In perception we take note of an object, but we may not be aware of its identity. Of course, *pratyabhijñā* does have the element of perception, for we can recognize a person only when we perceive him or her. However, perception itself is not *pratyabhijñā*; *pratyabhijñā* is the knowledge of the real identity of the person perceived. *Pratyabhijñā* is also different from memory, although the recognition of the Self (*ātma-pratyabhijñā*) is sometimes described metaphorically as remembrance.

Pratyabhijñā is different from memory also. In the case of remembering a thing, we do not perceive that thing, we simply reflect it in the mind; memory is the mental reproduction of something experienced in the past. But in *pratyabhijñā* we see the person and also recognize the person (know the real identity of that person). Of course, *ātmapratyabhijñā* ("recognition of the Self") is sometimes described as remembrance, for our present predicament is something like "forgetting" our real nature, and *pratyabhijñā* is naturally something like "remembering" it. But we should be careful to note here that forgetting our real nature is not an event in the history of our existence; it is not that in the beginning we knew our real nature and then later on forgot it. In fact, we are ignorant from the very beginning, like someone who is born blind as opposed to one who lost his or her sight later on. But although we are ignorant of our real nature from the very beginning, and sleeping in darkness, as it were, we can at any moment awaken into the light of knowledge — we can know our real nature. Remembrance in this case would then mean awakening to our real nature, not the recollection of some past thing.

Abhinavagupta gives two examples of *pratyabhijñā.* In one, the king of a country does not know a certain pandit. Another pandit, who is a member of the king's court, brings the unknown pandit to the king, introducing him and citing his qualifications. The king now knows the full identity of the new pandit. This is a case of *pratyabhijñā.*[5] The second example is that of a lady with a love-laden heart. She has developed the feeling of love for her betrothed, even though she has not yet met him. When he stands before her, she, not knowing who he is, sees him as no different than any other man. But when his identity is disclosed to her, she comes to know that this is no ordinary man but her beloved husband-to-be. The moment she knows his identity he becomes a source of enormous joy for her.[6] This is *pratyabhijñā* — recognition in the sense of coming to know the true identity of some person.

Similarly, the Self is a given in experience. We are aware of ourselves as entities. We see ourselves, but we do not recognize, that is, know the true identity of, ourselves.[7] Unfortunately, we take ourselves to be nothing more than limited individuals when our real identity is Śiva, the infinite. Through the agency of the guru or scripture we learn our true identity as Śiva. This awareness of the real identity of the Self is the *pratyabhijñā* ("recognition") of the Self.[8] To use the terms of Advaita Vedānta, the *that* is already given to us; but we mistake the *what* (the identity) of it. In the case of a rope-snake the *that* (the thing before one) is already given in one's experience, but one does not know that it is a rope; one takes it to be a snake. One does not really know *what* it is. But when one comes to know that it is rope, then it means that one has recognized the *that.*

From this analysis of the meaning of *pratyabhijñā* two things became clear. First, the thing recognized (*pratyabhijñāpita*) is not a new thing, created afresh; it already exists. In this sense it is already acquired (*prāpta*). Hence the paradox that *pratyabhijñā* is the getting of the gotten (*prāptasya prāptiḥ*). Second, it is a new event, although the thing recognized had already been in existence. The Self (Śiva) was already present, but we did not know this before; it was hidden from our sight. Only when the veil has been removed do we become aware of the real identity.[9] Thus *pratyabhijñā* is something new in the history of the *paśu.*

INTELLECTUAL KNOWLEDGE AND EXISTENTIAL KNOWLEDGE

One may ask here, can one attain Śivahood merely by knowing that one's real identity is Śiva? By learning the scriptures or hearing the guru one comes to know that one is Śiva, but this knowledge does not give one Śiva-realization; one remains the same bound *paśu.* Does *pratyabhijñā* mean the verbal or intellectual knowledge of one's identity, and if so, does this knowledge bring freedom? In answer to this we must refer to two types of ignorance and, subsequently, two types of knowledge or illumination mentioned by Abhinavagupta. One is called *bauddha* and the other is called *pauruṣa. Bauddha* ignorance means intellectual ignorance that can be removed by intellectual knowledge acquired from the scriptures. *Pauruṣa* ignorance means the ignorance that has gripped the entire person.[10] It is of the nature of spiritual impurity (*mala*)[11] or bondage. This ignorance cannot be removed by mere intellectual (*bauddha*) knowledge.[12] Only the practical initiation (*dīkṣā*) into the path of spiritual *sādhanā* and following the path sincerely can remove it.[13] When the scripture declares that liberation (*mokṣa*) can be attained by knowledge, we should construe knowledge as spiritual or existential (*pauruṣa*) knowledge, not intellectual (*bauddha*) knowledge.[14] Intellectual knowledge can give liberation only when the existential ignorance is removed; it cannot do so independently.[15] But existential (*pauruṣa*) knowledge independently and unconditionally brings liberation.[16]

However, this does not mean that intellectual knowledge is irrelevant. On the contrary, it is quite helpful and even necessary. It is the prerequisite for the advance in spiritual *sādhanā*. The intellect or understanding of the *sādhaka* ("spiritual practitioner") must be clear. The *sādhaka* should understand the philosophical position of his or her teacher, and his or her mind should be free from doubts. He or she should know intellectually that his or her real nature is Śiva, so that he or she may be induced to follow the practical path to realizing the same. Hence the importance of the scriptures, which convey intellectual understanding, cannot be ignored. It is also true that one can fully understand the meaning of the scriptures only when one's existential knowledge is to some extent awakened. The two knowledges, therefore, are mutually helpful. It is impossible to draw a sharp line between the two, as they are generally intermixed. When we say that *pratyabhijñā* is not intellectual knowledge, what we mean is that *pratyabhijñā* is not mere intellectual knowledge; existential knowledge is needed as well. And of the two, the existential knowledge is the more important.

Pratyabhijñā therefore is not the mere intellectual knowledge of Śiva, but the actual uncovering of the Self preceded by the removal of impurities (*mala*), especially *āṅava mala*, which is responsible for the individuation or limitation of the Self. Thus we can say that *pratyabhijñā* is the total spiritual transformation of the person.

If *pratyabhijñā* is said to be a transformation of personality, does this mean a literal transformation as in the case of milk changing into curd? No, the transformation is not meant literally; it is instead a purification. This purification is not of the Self or Consciousness Itself, for Consciousness in Itself is eternally pure. In spiritual transformation the Self does not change nor is anything added to it. Rather there is a removal of impurity or ignorance.[17] This results in a spiritual change in the person. In this sense purification itself can be called change or transformation. When the dirty cloth becomes pure by being washed, it is not transformed nor is anything added to it; there is simply the negative function of the dirt being removed. Nevertheless, can we say that the cloth remains the same? Does it not change from the impure state to the state of purity? Is the washing of the cloth merely a negative function? Is it not positive in the sense that the cloth attains its pure nature? Similarly, in spiritual transformation the Self attains its real nature, which is already pure and perfect.

We have seen above that *pratyabhijñā* is not verbal knowledge; it is an actual experience. We do not simply *know*, in the verbal sense, the Self, but we actually experience it. In Russellian terms, it is not knowledge by description but knowledge by acquaintance. It is the direct awareness or cognition of the Self. It can also be called illumination (*bodha*).

This point is stressed in the Upaniṣads also. There we find that *śravana* — the verbal communication that one is identified with Brahman — is not enough; *manana* ("contemplation") and *nididhyāsana* ("merging oneself in the Higher Self") must follow in order for *brahmajñāna* ("knowledge of Brahman") to dawn. *Brahmajñāna* is not mere verbal knowledge but an actual experience (*anubhava* or *anubhūti*). Hearing the word (*śruti* or *śravana*), followed by contemplation of it (*mati* or *manana*) leads to the actual experience (*anubhūti*) of Brahman. Thus it is said that when one knows Brahman, one becomes Brahman (*brahma veda brahmaiva bhavati*).[18]

The significance of the existential knowledge emphasized in Kashmir Śaivism is twofold. On the one hand, by emphasizing that knowledge of the Self is the actual removal of impurity, it corrects the common misunderstanding that Self-knowledge is just verbal or intellectual knowledge. On the other hand, it emphasizes that Self-knowledge is not a physical change but a change in consciousness — an actual removal of ignorance.

WHY PRATYABHIJÑĀ IS CALLED KNOWLEDGE

The question may be asked here, if *pratyabhijñā* virtually means the removal of *mala*, or spiritual transformation, why is it called *bodha* or *jñāna* ("knowledge")? In answer we may point out that *mala* is not like physical dirt; it is, in fact, of the nature of *ajñāna* ("ignorance"), which can be removed only by *jñāna* ("knowledge"). Take the example of a dream or illusion. When in a dream one "sees" one's hands and feet tied by thieves and one is subjected to torture, is this whole misfortune not because there is something wrong in one's mind? One is gripped by some kind of ignorance. When one becomes insane and forgets even one's identity, then this is, philosophically speaking, a case of ignorance. And this ignorance is such that it effects a practical change in the person; that is why it is called *pauruṣa* ("existential") ignorance. When one wakes up after the dream or one is cured of one's insanity, then this is a case of *jñāna* ("knowledge"). And again, this knowledge is such that it effects a practical change in the person in the opposite direction. Thus it is called *pauruṣa* knowledge.

Pratyabhijñā is called *jñāna* ("knowledge") because it is an awakening, enlightenment, or rising to a higher level of awareness or consciousness. *Jñāna* does not mean only objective knowledge in the form of *this* or *that*. It may also mean any kind of illumination. The translation of *jñāna* into the English word *knowledge* is liable to create some confusion, as the word knowledge is generally used in the sense of the objective knowledge of an object. *Jñāna*, of course, includes the same but it is not confined to that. The simple awareness, for example, that "I am" and not that "I am this" or "I am that" can also be called *jñāna*. The highest *jñāna*, according to

Tantra, is the awareness that one is all. This is called the perfect "I" (*pūrṇāhantā*).

If we understand the concept of *pratyabhijñā* in light of the idealistic metaphysics of Kashmir Śaivism, it will be still more clear that *pratyabhijñā* is *jñāna*. Kashmir Śaivism is an idealistic system that admits of no physical or material reality. Consciousness is the only reality; the reality of the world is epistemic or ideal (*ābhāsa*). There is therefore no physical or material transformation; all transformation is epistemic or mental (to use the word *mental* in the Western sense), just as the change from the dream state to the waking state is an epistemic change. In the *paśu* state one has forgotten oneself, just as one forgets oneself in a dream. Ignorance is a kind of primordial forgetfulness of one's real nature, and *pratyabhijñā* therefore is a kind of remembrance of the same. Ignorance can cause transformation of personality, and so, too, can knowledge. This can be seen in the case of a dream. In the dream state one becomes a different person, so to speak, and when one wakes up, one's previous existence is restored.

One may ask, is *pratyabhijñā* a knowledge qualitatively different from ordinary knowledge? *Pratyabhijñā* is certainly different from ordinary knowledge, but it is doubtful whether it would be appropriate to call it *qualitatively* different. If by qualitative difference what is meant is the transformation from one state of consciousness to another — just as the waking state is different from the dream — then there is no harm in calling it qualitatively different. But if we mean by it a mode of knowledge that is completely unknown to us, then it is not so. *Pratyabhijñā* is the immediate knowledge of the Self. We ordinarily have the immediate knowledge of ourselves and *pratyabhijñā* differs from it not in the mode, nor in the *thatness* of the content, but it differs only in the *whatness* of the content. In *pratyabhijñā* one knows oneself as the all-pervasive perfect Self (*pūrṇāham* or Śiva). Of course it differs in mode from objective knowledge like the knowledge of the *blue* and *yellow*. Blue (*nīla*) and yellow (*pīta*) are the classical examples of objects like the chair and the table or the pitcher and the cloth. The blue and the yellow, or the chair and the table, are known as objects in the subject-object duality, whereas the self is known in a self-illumined way (*svayamprakāśa*). As far as the mode is concerned, *pratyabhijñā*, although different from objective knowledge, is not different from the ordinary knowledge of the self. It differs only in the *what* of the content. In the ordinary knowledge of the self the *what* of the content (self) is *paśutva* or *aṇutva* ("the state of the person as limited self"), whereas in *pratyabhijñā* the *what* is *Śivatva* ("the state of the person as Śiva or the Infinite").

To regard oneself as different from what one really is, is ignorance. We are really one with all, but we regard others as different from ourselves; this is ignorance. Ignorance essentially consists of the distinction of the self from the rest of the world.[19] This duality is possible only when we confine ourselves to a particular limited individuality or ego (*aṇu*). We are unmindful of our all-embracing and infinite or perfect nature and take ourselves to be limited, finite beings, different from others. This is an imperfect understanding of ourselves. Ignorance is just this imperfect understanding of ourselves (*apūrṇakhyāti*).

If ignorance is to cut oneself off from the rest of the whole, then *jñāna* ("knowledge") is to embrace all within oneself, to regard oneself as one with all (*sarvātmā*). When we become one with all, then we realize our infinite or perfect nature. This is the perfect understanding of ourselves, or knowledge, which is contradistinguished from ignorance, or the imperfect understanding of oneself.

One may again ask here, how are we to understand our oneness with the all? We are physically different from others — how can this hard truth be obliterated? And if there is a state of consciousness where this unity is achieved, can it be shown to be there in actual experience? The answer is that this unity is quite apprehensible even by our common understanding. We can apprehend this unity in the experience of love. In love the duality vanishes, we become one with the person whom we love. And the deeper we enter into love, the more we realize this unity. Experience of love is the knowledge of unity. Of course our common experience of love is imperfect; normally we do not achieve it in its completeness. But it can be logically stretched to its fullness; we can conceive of a perfect and complete state of love where the duality has completely vanished. This could be the state of *pratyabhijñā.* Spiritually speaking, ignorance is nothing but selfishness or egoism, and *jñāna* is selflessness or love. *Pratyabhijñā* is nothing but the perfect all-embracing love. The Upaniṣads also speak of this unity with all.[20]

THE MODE AND CONTENT OF PRATYABHIJÑĀ

We have already seen that Self-recognition (*pratyabhijñā*) is a kind of knowledge. Now let us see what the mode or form of this knowledge is and what its content is. The mode of this knowledge is immediate or intuitive. This knowledge is that of the Self, and we know the Self directly or immediately, not through some mediation. Moreover the most remarkable thing is that here the knower and the known are one. The unity of the knower and the known is possible only in the case of the Self. One knows *oneself.* But again, one does not know oneself in the subject-object mode of knowing as the Nyāya maintains. Here the position of Kashmir Śaivism is completely one with Advaita Vedānta.[21] The Self is not the object of one's knowing as the table and the chair are; one knows oneself in a self-illumined (*svayamprakāśa*) way. The analogy of light is quite appropriate here. The light illumines objects and also illumines itself. But the mode of illumining itself is different from the mode of illumining the table. The light falls on the table and thus illumines it in the objective mode — the light is the subject and the table the object. But in order to illumine itself, the light does not turn back and fall upon itself. It does not make itself its object but is self-illumined. One need not bring another light to see that light. Similarly the Self does not make itself its own object but is self-illumined (*svayamprakāśa*).

What is the content of *pratyabhijñā* knowledge? Obviously the content is the Self Itself. *Pratyabhijñā* is a case of Self-knowledge or Self-realization (*ātma-pratyabhijñā*). Thus it is the immediate or intuitive experience of the Self. But there is a question here. One already has the immediate or intuitive experience of oneself, and there is nothing extra-ordinary about it. So how does *pratyabhijñā* differ from the ordinary experience of the Self? In respect to the mode of knowing, *pratyabhijñā* does not differ from the ordinary experience of the Self. It also does not differ as far as the content is concerned, for one "sees" the same Self. The difference occurs in the *reality* of the content. In *pratyabhijñā* we experience the Self at a deeper level, where everything is included within the Self. The ordinary experience is that of the lower self — the surface or false self — that is called *paśu*. *Pratyabhijñā* is the experience of the Higher Self — the Deeper or Real Self — that is called Śiva. The deeper we enter into the Self, the more we realize the external world as the reflection of the Self. There is a point where the entire multiplicity of the world becomes one with the Self. This is the state of the Self in perfect unity with all (*pūrṇāhantā*). It is the state of perfect freedom and bliss. We may call it mystic in the sense of being elusive to sense experience and discursive thought. But it is not mystic in the sense of being occult, for it is perfectly natural. The only difference is that it is the experience of the higher or deeper nature.

Since in Kashmir Śaivism the Self is the only Reality, *pratyabhijñā* can also be called the knowledge of Reality. Kashmir Śaivism is an absolute idealism. According to it, all that exists is the Absolute Self (Śiva). The entire world is a self-projection of the Self. So when one knows the Self through *pratyabhijñā*, one also knows the world as the projection (*ābhāsa*) or reflection (*pratibimba*) of oneself. Reality is nothing but the Self in its entirety. Therefore knowledge of the Self is the knowledge of the entire Reality. One who attains Self-realization (*ātma-pratyabhijñā*) becomes the knower of Reality and is called the "seer" of Reality (*tattva-draṣṭā* or *satya-draṣṭā*). The point is that *pratyabhijñā* is not only the knowledge of the Self, but it is also the knowledge of Reality, as the Self includes all of Reality within itself.

A very significant question can be asked here, how can we be sure that what we take to be the recognition of the Self is really so? What is the guarantee that an experience is really *pratyabhijñā*? In answer we could say that *pratyabhijñā* is a state of clear consciousness, even clearer than that associated with the reasoning faculty. If we ask what is the guarantee for reason, the answer would be that reason is its own guarantee. Reason is self-evident; it does not require any other thing to prove it. Reason judges and proves other things; it itself is self-proved. But what is this reason? Reason is clear consciousness and nothing else. It is consciousness that works in the form of reason. And if consciousness operates as clear reason, it is quite possible that consciousness works as even clearer reason in the state of *pratyabhijñā*.

The same consciousness that works in reason also works in *pratyabhijñā*, where it works even more clearly, as it is freed from impurities. Impurity (*mala*) serves as an obstruction to the clarity of consciousness. The greater the freedom from impurity, the clearer the consciousness is. *Pratyabhijñā*, which is a state of consciousness free from impurity, thus has clearer reason or understanding. Therefore, if reason is self-evident and requires no proof, this is even more true of *pratyabhijñā*. That is why those who attain *pratyabhijñā* have no doubt about it.

In the animal, the same consciousness is present but it is much more obstructed than in the case of human beings, and so its reason or understanding is not as clear as that of human beings. Similarly, consciousness or reason in ordinary human beings may be less clear than that of liberated persons who have *ātma-pratyabhijñā* ("Self-recognition" or "Self-realization"). The point is that *pratyabhijñā*-knowledge is by no means inferior to ordinary reason in terms of self-evidence and guarantee; it may even be superior in this respect.

This refers to the *pratibhā* theory of the Tantric tradition of Abhinavagupta, which we have already discussed. Here it must suffice to say that *pratibhā* is the opposite of acquired knowledge; it is self-present or self-evolved. Reason too is *pratibhā*, as the faculty of reason is not acquired but self-evolved from within; it is naturally present in man. The clarity and self-evidence that reason carries is not earned, learned, or acquired, but is inborn, innate,[22] or *pratibhā* ("pertaining to *pratibhā*"). We may have to make an effort in purifying the consciousness for clearing the path for *pratibhā* to flow — that is a different matter. But the *pratibhā* knowledge comes automatically or intuitively. The effort is in clearing the path for *pratibhā*, not in bringing or fetching it; *pratibhā* flows automatically when the path is clear.

The object of mentioning the *pratibhā* theory is to point out that *pratyabhijñā*-knowledge is really *pratibhā* knowledge, which brings with itself its evidence, clarity, and proof. Just as mathematical or logical knowledge, which is *pratibhā* knowledge, brings its evidence and clarity, so also does *pratyabhijñā*-knowledge.

Apart from being self-evident, *pratyabhijñā* has other benign characteristics also. The person of Self-realization (Self-recognition), in the Indian tradition, is called a *jñānī* ("wise one"). Here *jñāna* ("knowledge") is used not in the sense of ordinary knowledge about the things of the world, but knowledge of the profound spiritual truths of life. Moreover *jñāna* includes practical living with spiritual qualities. For example, one who is selfish and exploits others, being ignorant of the truth that the "others" are not really other to him or her, is called *ajña* ("ignorant"), and one who feels one's unity with all and loves all is said to be *jñānī* ("wise"). The reason the benign qualities of practical living are included in *jñāna* ("knowledge") is that the laws of life, or the laws of nature, are in favor of goodness and purity of heart. The wise person knows that one can be happy only when one is good and pure. Therefore the wise cannot become bad. There is a lot of truth in the Socratic dictum that knowledge is virtue.

Jñānī thus means both (a) one who knows the profound ethico-spiritual laws of life, and (b) one who lives the life of goodness and purity and has attained the state of universal love. This is the state of spiritual enlightenment. Spirituality consists in abolishing the selfish distinction between oneself and others; the dichotomy between the good of oneself and the good of others is gone, as happens in the state of true love. It is called *spiritual* because such is the very real nature of the *Spirit* (the Self or Consciousness); the Spirit is naturally endowed with such benign characteristics. *Ātma-pratyabhijñā* (Self-recognition or Self-realization) is a spiritual state — a state of enlightened and exalted consciousness.

The most significant point in the concept of *pratyabhijñā* is that the state of consciousness that is to be attained is already naturally there. It does not have to be created afresh; it is only veiled or covered by *māyā* [23] and we are thus not able to recognize it even when we see it (*dṛṣṭepyanupalakṣite*).[24] *Pratyabhijñā* is a process of uncovering or "dis-covering" (*āviṣkaraṇa*).[25] As such, it is a question of going back to our original nature or "turning our eyes inward"[26] — a reverse *pratīpa* movement, so to speak.[27] The Self, which is full and perfect by its very nature, is revealed in all its richness when the "veil" is removed.

The logic behind the above assertion is that we can easily become what we already potentially are. If we are not already potentially perfect or divine, it will be extremely difficult, if not impossible, to become so. Fortunately our real nature, currently hidden from us, is already divine. Divinity is our birthright; we are natural heirs to the throne of divinity. So it is a question of regaining what is already ours, becoming what we already are.

Pratyabhijñā is knowledge that is obtained directly by oneself; the guru or scripture serves only as an aid in this matter. The statement of the guru or of scripture helps one turn one's attention to one's real identity and "see" the Self. One's real identity is not accepted on mere faith in the word of the guru or of scripture, but is realized for oneself. This can be said to be analogous to accepting the correction in a mathematical sum made by a mathematics teacher. In contrast to the statements of a history teacher, which we cannot verify for ourselves, the truth of what the mathematics teacher says can be verified by us, as the mathematical truth is self-evident and the teacher merely brings it to our attention. Similarly when the guru points out our real identity, we can see it for ourselves. This is beautifully illustrated in the allegorical anecdote of *daśamastvamasi* ("Thou art the tenth") given in the Upanisads. When the tenth idiot asks the wise man, "Where is the tenth?" the wise man in answer points out, "Thou art the tenth!" Then the enlightened "idiot" is able to see for himself the truth that he is the tenth.[28] The point is that the guru or scripture helps turn ones attention to the Self, but the Self is known or experienced immediately or directly.

Of course in the beginning stage, when our consciousness is obstructed and tainted with spiritual impurity we cannot know ourselves as Śiva. In that stage we will have to accept the statement of the guru or scripture on faith as *āgama-pramāṇa*. But when the obstruction is cleared by the practice of spiritual *sādhanā* and existential knowledge is attained, we will have the direct experience (*anubhūti*) of ourselves as Śiva. Hearing from the teacher or scripture is only the starting point; it is followed by contemplation (*mati* or *manana*) accompanied by practical *sādhanā* (*nididhyāsana*), which finally leads to one's own experience (*anubhūti* or *anubhava*).

It is possible that Self-recognition (*pratyabhijñā*) may also dawn by itself, without the help of a teacher or scripture. Abhinavagupta, in line with Tantric tradition, accepts this position. It is said that knowledge can come from three sources — from teacher, from scripture, and from oneself.[29] Knowledge that comes automatically is called *prātibha-jñāna*. Abhinavagupta says that here one knows by oneself without depending upon scripture or teacher.[30] Such a person is called *saṁsiddha* ("one who has attained Self-realization by oneself").[31] Such self-discovered knowledge is called *sāṁsiddhika-jñāna*.[32]

Advaita Vedānta seems to think that Self-knowledge can only come from scripture or the teacher; it cannot arise spontaneously. According to Advaita Vedānta, the individual soul has been groping about in ignorance forever. Therefore how can the individual even know that it is in ignorance and that it really belongs to the world of light? To this, Kashmir Śaivism would say that of course others are benefitted when an enlightened person shows the light. Further, this is generally how realization is brought about. But this does not mean that light can never arise from within by itself. In fact, most of the enlightened people who have shown light to others have themselves attained light by their own efforts without the light's being shown to them from some other source. Light can shine from within oneself if and when the consciousness is purified and the inclination to purify oneself can come both from without and from within. History shows that there have been enlightened persons who were self-enlightened. They attained enlightenment by themselves without any substantial help from an external guru. Buddha, Christ, Rāmakrishna Paramahansa, Ramana Maharshi, Sri Aurobindo — all attained enlightenment by themselves. This does not mean that the guru has no importance. In fact, in Tantrism, the guru is of the utmost importance. But still, Tantrism does not rule out the possibility of self-enlightenment. In fact the real guru is within oneself. It is one's own higher Self. The external guru helps in recognizing this inner guru. The Buddha used to say, "Be *yourself* your lamp" (*attadīo bhava* or *ātmadīpo bhava*), "make yourself your shelter" (*attasaraṇā* or *ātmaśaraṇāḥ*), "don't take shelter in others" (nānyaśaraṇāḥ).

PRATYABHIJÑĀ IS THE DISSOLUTION OF THE EGO

We have seen that *pratyabhijñā* is the knowledge or realization of the Cosmic "I" or Śivahood. It follows then that *pratyabhijñā* is virtually the dissolution of the ego. Ego is the consciousness of the individual "I" as different or separate from others. It confines one to a particular body and mind and is thus the principle of differentiation and limitation. It can easily be seen that the ego stands as an obstruction to Śiva-realization. In fact the ego is the greatest obstruction. Śiva is the all-pervasive Self that is in perfect unity with all. Ego is just the opposite. It keeps one confined to a particular individuality. As long as the ego persists, one cannot realize one's Śivahood. It is only when one breaks out of the ego shell that one becomes one with the all-pervasive Self. The wave cannot become one with the ocean unless it surrenders its individuality. Therefore to preserve ego and attain Śivahood is a contradiction in terms. One cannot feel unity with all if one is captivated in a particular individuality.

The dissolution of ego should not be understood as the annihilation of the Self or as existential suicide. Egolessness does not mean the disappearance of the Self; it only means the disappearance of the limited form of individuality that the Self has adopted. When the wave surrenders its individuality, what is lost is not water but the particular form and name that the water had adopted. The wave becomes the ocean. In fact, the wave was already one with the ocean; its wavehood was accidental. Once the accidental state is removed, the wave attains its real nature, which is ocean. Similarly the individual shakes off its limited finite individuality and becomes the infinite Śiva. Or more correctly, the Self is already Śiva, its individuality being an adopted covering that, once gone, allows the Self to shine in the pristine purity of its Śivahood. Therefore there is no question of committing suicide. What appears to be self-immolation is really self-enrichment or self-fulfillment.

If *pratyabhijñā* is viewed as the dissolution of the ego, then it approaches the theistic conception of self-surrender. In theistic devotion (*bhakti*), the individual self (*jīva*) is required to surrender itself to God. But what is most significant in Tantric *sādhanā* is not God but the act of surrender itself. There can be surrender even without conceiving of a God to whom to surrender. In that case surrender is just the silencing or extinction (*nirvāṇa*) of the ego. In Buddhism we find self-surrender or self-renunciation without God. This can be called the surrender of the path of knowledge (*jñāna-mārga*), analogous to the surrender of the path of devotion (*bhakti-mārga*).

The *pratyabhijñā* system of Kashmir Śaivism does recognize the self-surrender of the path of devotion as genuinely beneficial. Other *sādhanās* are also accepted, as they indirectly tend towards the thinning of the ego. In fact, the degree of success of every *sādhanā* depends upon the degree of the effacement of the ego it directly or indirectly brings about.

It may be objected here that if there is no ego, then there is no person or Self. How can there be egoless personality or egoless Self? The ego is not a necessary characteristic of the Self. Ego is a relative condition that may or may not be present in the Self. When the Self is absolute and embraces all in its bosom, there is no question of ego there, for ego is only the limiting and differentiating factor. Ego comes at the limited state of the Self called *paśu* or *aṇu*. Ego is required only when the Self has to differentiate itself from others. The ego limits Consciousness to one particular individuality and thereby cuts it off from the rest of the world. This produces the "self" with a small "s." But when the Self feels its unity with all, then the smaller self becomes the bigger Self and the ego is virtually gone.

ŚIVA-PAŚU UNITY AS THE METAPHYSICAL GROUND OF PRATYABHIJÑĀ

It is logically appropriate, even logically necessary, that the concept of *pratyabhijñā* have as its metaphysical ground the concept of the unity of the individual and the Absolute. Tantra emphasizes again and again that the individual is nothing but Śiva; it is Śiva who has adopted the form of the individual.[33] If the individual is not already Śiva, it can never become Śiva. One cannot be "made" into Śiva. The wave can completely become one with the ocean because it is nothing but water. A different object, say a ship made of iron and wood, may go into the fathomless depths of the ocean. Yet it will not become one with it because it is made of a different material; it is not water. A spark of fire, because it is essentially fire, can take the form of a conflagration and burn a whole village, but a pebble, no matter how much it is fanned and fueled, cannot burn at all, simply because it is not already fire. Similarly, the individual becomes completely one with Śiva because substantially it is nothing but Śiva or Consciousness. The individual is different from Śiva only in that it has taken on a particular limited form, just as the wave is a particular limited form of the ocean. The moment the particular limited form is dissolved, the wave is completely one with the ocean and the individual is completely one with Śiva. The same logic is found in the Upaniṣads, where the *mahāvākyas* declare that the *jīva* is Brahman.

The *pratyabhijñā* philosophers go one step further in this regard. They say that the individual is not only substantially one with Śiva, but it also, even in its limited form, performs the same activities, on a smaller scale, that Śiva Himself performs. They mean to say that the individual is a mini-Śiva. Śiva performs the five cosmic actions (*pañcakṛtyas*) of creation, preservation, destruction, self-concealment (*nigraha*), and self-revelation, or grace (*anugraha*). The limited Śiva, or the individual, performs all these functions with regard to its own world.[34] The individual creates its own imaginary world when dreaming, sustains it for a time, and finally destroys it while waking up. It covers itself by assuming a new form, such as when acting in a drama, thereby apparently becoming something other than itself. Then it also uncovers itself and takes on its usual form.

The logic behind conceiving of the individual as a mini-Śiva is that if the individual is one with Śiva, the individual must enjoy, at least on a limited scale, the freedom that Śiva enjoys. Tantra emphasizes the freedom of the individual simply to show its divine heritage. The individual enacts or imitates the actions of Śiva and exercises its freedom whenever possible. The free activities of the otherwise bound individual remind us of its real nature, which is

Śivahood or Freedom. The individual is just like a caged lion declaring its freedom and might by roaring within the cage and trying to break out of the bars that hold it.

LEVELS OF PRATYABHIJÑĀ

Does Self-realization admit of degrees? Is it meaningful to say that A has more Self-realization than B? It can safely be said that there is no possibility of degrees of Self-realization, just as perfection does not admit of degrees. Just as it is meaningless to speak of more perfect or less perfect — one is either perfect or imperfect — so there is no such thing as less or more Self-realization. Either one has recognized the Self, or one is ignorant.

Still, it is possible to conceive of a hierarchy of those who aspire to the goal of Self-realization. The aspirants are like pilgrims journeying toward a shrine — at any given time some are far from the shrine, some near to it, some still nearer, and so on. In Self-realization, the hierarchy is based on one's ability to break out of one's ego and identify oneself with others. The more a person sees him- or herself in others, the more he or she widens his or her identity and realizes his or her true nature. It is not a question of identifying oneself with more persons or more things, but identifying oneself with others more deeply or intensely. Of course, the quantity is a factor; there is, finally, nobody and nothing that is not included in oneself. But the real question is how far one has penetrated the depth of unity.

In spiritual progress, the Tantras mention a hierarchy of seven grades of souls that are called the seven knowers (*sapta-pramātā*). They are *pralayākala*, *sakala*, *vijñānākala*, *mantra*, *mantreśvara*, *mantra-maheśvara*, and *Śiva*. The progress from the stage of *pralayākala* to that of *Śiva* may be considered the evolution of the Self from a narrower to a wider and fuller identity. The *Śiva-pramātā* is the highest stage, where the identity is achieved in its fullness.

The difference among the hierarchical stages of evolution of the soul can be understood in terms of purification of Self or removal of spiritual impurity (*mala*). The more the impurity is removed, the brighter the light of Consciousness shines from within the Self. Just as the brightness of the light of the sun or the moon is proportionate to the clarity of the sky, so also the brilliance of Consciousness is proportionate to the degree of self-purification.

Although Self-realization is the highest level of unity, it is implicitly present in all the lower stages. It is not that one experiences the joy of Self-realization only when one reaches the highest stage; the current of joy starts trickling from the very first step one takes on the path of Self-realization, and the nearer one draws to the Self, the more deeply one experiences the bliss of the Self.

It follows from the above discussion that there is some basis for admitting of a step by step approach to the deeper levels of our reality. Self-realization can be achieved in degrees. Even at the lowest level there is some degree of Self-realization, as the power of Consciousness (*citi-śakti* or *kuṇḍalinī* in the symbolic language of Tantric yoga) works in us in the form of the mental phenomena. Obviously, it is possible that in different people this Consciousness becomes manifest in varying degrees, either naturally or by the deliberate process of uncovering or unfolding the beauties of Consciousness. We can continue this process until we achieve the fullest manifestation of Consciousness — Self-realization, or spiritual attainment in the highest degree.

PRATYABHIJÑĀ AS THE GROUND OF ALL THE UPĀYAS

There is a related question — is Self-realization a means or an end? Sometimes Self-realization has been referred to as a means (*pratyabhijñopāya*). But if we consider the problem in view of the entire treatment of Self-realization in the Tantric tradition, we will understand that it is said to be a means (*upāya*) just by convention. In fact, Self-realization is the end of all the *sādhanās*. It stands at the highest reach. Self-realization is thus not a means to anything else;

it is an end in itself. It can be said to be an *upāya* only in the sense of being the ground of all the *upāyas.*

It should be noted here that in spiritual life the end and the means virtually become one. What is the end becomes the means for its own achievement. For example, the Self is the state of purity and goodness (*śivatā*), and the means for attaining the Self is to become pure and good. The Self is the state of universal love, and the means to realize the Self is to cultivate universal love. Similarly the Self is the state of egolessness, and the means for attaining this state is to surrender or dissolve the ego. If Self-realization is both the goal and the means to the goal, we can then realize the Self by becoming or practicing what the Self naturally is — unity, love, purity, goodness, egolessness, relaxation, peace, and so on.

What does it mean for Self-realization to be the ground of all the *upāyas*? It means that Self-realization is implicitly present in all the *upāyas.* This further means that the success of every method depends upon its capacity to effect Self-realization by dissolving the ego-sense. It should also be borne in mind that Self-realization cannot be effected as a new creation, as it is not the effect of a cause — it dawns of its own accord when the way is cleared. *Sādhanā* effects Self-realization in that it lets Self-realization shine by clearing the ground. A *sādhanā* is effective because it brings the light of Consciousness to the fore by purifying the self and thereby uncovering the light of the Self. And Self-realization means nothing but the unfolding or uncovering of the hidden Self. Self-realization is thus not one of the means (*upāyas*); it is *the upāya,* as it is the underlying reality of all the *upāyas.*

THE RELEVANCE OF BHAKTI IN PRATYABHIJÑĀ

A question may be asked, if the individual is one with Śiva or God, is it possible to talk meaningfully of *bhakti,* which presupposes a difference or duality between the devotee (*bhakta*) and

God? The answer is yes, as long as the individual retains its individualized consciousness and is thus differentiated from cosmic Consciousness, Śiva. When Śiva becomes the *paśu*, Śiva is not lost. Śiva remains Śiva and also becomes the *paśu*. When the *paśu* exists, Śiva also exists in His own right. The *paśu* is like the wave to Śiva's ocean. It is perfectly meaningful to talk of *bhakti*, for the individual is different from Śiva just as the wave is different from the ocean, although in essence the two are one. This position is clearly envisaged by Utpaladeva in his *Śivastotrāvalī*.

This position is appreciated also by the Advaitin, who is the champion advocate of Brahma-*jīva* unity. There is a lot of wisdom in the famous verse ascribed to Śaṅkara, which is addressed to God: "Though the difference between you and me does not exist at all, yet it is true that I am yours and not that you are mine; just as the wave belongs to the ocean and not that the ocean belongs to the wave."[35]

If *bhakti* presupposes difference, it also presupposes unity. There can be no bhakti without unity; there can be no love and no devotional relationship between two substantially different persons. In fact, what is required in *bhakti* is a real unity and an apparent difference between the devotee and God, which is quite possible in the Absolutist position. The object of love or devotion must really be one with the devotee and yet somehow different from him or her. The Absolutist analogies of the wave in the ocean and the spark (*sphuliṅga*) of the fire conform with this idea, for the wave, or the spark, is both one with the ocean, or the fire, and different as well. The difference persists as long as the *bhakta* does not attain Self-realization by shaking off his or her individuality. The culmination of *bhakti* is the merger of the devotee in God.

Thus, although one is Śiva or Śiva is one's self, yet it is meaningful to say that one is the lower self and Śiva is the higher Self, Śiva being the self of all selves (*sarvātmā* or *viśvātmā*), just as the ocean is to its waves. The difference between the higher Self (*Bhagavāna*) and the lower self (*bhakta*) persists only as long as the lower self is the individualized soul (*paśu*). In the final stage the lower self must merge into the higher Self and become completely one with It, just as the wave, by merging into the ocean, becomes completely one with it. Thus *bhakti*, which means surrendering or merging one's ego into the Lord, is enormously helpful in attaining Self-realization.

PRATYABHIJÑĀ ("SELF-RECOGNITION") AND APAROKṢĀNUBHŪTI ("DIRECT EXPERIENCE")

It would not be out of place to mention the comparative similarity between the Self-recognition (*pratyabhijñā*) of Kashmir Śaivism and the intuitive experience (*aparokṣānubhūti*) of Advaita Vedānta. In mode and also in content the two are one. The content of Advaita Vedānta's immediate or intuitive experience is the Self. One knows Brahman as oneself. One knows Brahman by being Brahman.[36] In fact the individual is already Brahman, though veiled by ignorance or *māyā*. And the intuitive experience of Advaita Vedānta is just the uncovering of this veil, thereby realizing that one is Brahman.

When the Upaniṣads declare, "That thou art," "I am Brahman," or "This self is Brahman," they are actually referring to *pratyabhijñā*. We are ignorant of our real identity, and the Upaniṣads disclose the same to us. The analogy of "Thou art the tenth" means the same. This saying, however, also suggests the mode of knowing, which is immediate (*aparokṣa*) experience (*anubhūti*).

The difference between the Self-realization of Kashmir Śaivism and the immediate intuitive experience of Advaita Vedānta lies in the conception of the real nature of the Self at the ultimate level[37] — the Self that is the content of this experience. According to Advaita Vedānta, the ultimate Self is inactive (*niṣkriya*), for all activity belongs to the lower principle, *māyā*, which is false. The Self is also devoid of Self-consciousness. But according to the Pratyabhijñā system, *śakti*, or dynamism, is the very nature of the Self (*śaktirūpa*). The Self is also Self-conscious.

If Self-recognition (*pratyabhijñā*) and direct experience (*aparokṣānubhūti*) are virtually the same, does the usage of the word *pratyabhijñā* have some advantage over the word *aparokṣānubhūti*? *Pratyabhijñā* suggests the content of experience in question — the emphasis is on *what* one knows. *Aparokṣānubhūti* does not suggest any such content. But *aparokṣānubhūti* has an advantage over *pratyabhijñā* in that it suggests the mode of the experience in question — the way in which one knows oneself is immediate (*aparokṣa*). The word *pratyabhijñā* gives no clue to the mode. The two words are thus mutually complementary, one suggesting the mode of the experience, the other its content.

There is another point of difference between the Pratyabhijñā system and Advaita Vedānta in this context. The Pratyabhijñā view emphasizes what one *is*, while the Advaita view emphasizes what one is *not*. The "I am Brahman" message of the Upaniṣads was, later on in the Advaitin's analysis, converted into the position that one is not the body, and so on. It was understood that unless one negates oneself as the body, mind, and so on, one cannot reach Brahman, because the false identification with the not-self is an obstruction to Brahman. Therefore, the question is one of uncovering or removing the obstruction. The Pratyabhijñā view, on the other hand, emphasizes that one is Śiva. Unless one knows oneself as Śiva, one cannot dissociate oneself from the body, and so on. Thus we see that while the Pratyabhijñā approach points to one's real nature, the Advaita view points to the extrinsic elements with which one has falsely identified oneself. The two approaches are therefore complementary.

8

Bondage and Liberation

THE MEANING OF BONDAGE

In the concept of liberation (*mokṣa*) two things are implied or logically presupposed.[1] First, there is a self, or soul, which attains *mokṣa*.[2] Second, this soul, or self, is in bondage, for only a bound person can become free. *Mokṣa* presupposes bondage.

We have already seen that Kashmir Śaivism accepts the existence of the self, evident as the doer (*kartā*) and knower (*jñātā*).[3] It is further maintained that this self is in bondage[4] and so it is not able to enjoy its real nature. Before we can understand *mokṣa*, it is necessary to know the nature of bondage.

Bondage is ignorance (*ajñāna*) — ignorance of one's real nature. This ignorance is of two types—*bauddha* and *pauruṣa*.[5] The word *ajñāna* although literally meaning "absence of knowledge," is used in the sense of "illusion," not the absence of knowledge but wrong knowledge. Wrong knowledge means incomplete or imperfect knowledge (*apūrṇa-jñāna*, or *apūrṇa-khyāti*)[6] — the incomplete knowledge of reality.[7]

A question may be asked here, even if ignorance is understood as wrong knowledge, how does this ignorance bind a person? Is ignorance so powerful that it can work existential change in a person to the extent that one becomes a different — changes from Śiva to *paśu*? The answer is yes. The power of ignorance to bring about change in the personality is evident in the dream state. When a king in a dream finds himself deprived of his kingdom and roaming as a beggar suffering from hunger and so on, no real physical change has occurred. What has happened is that there is something wrong in the king's mind. He takes himself to be a suffering beggar, and he does suffer in the dream but when the king wakes up, and his mind is corrected, he changes back from the beggar to the king.

The wrong apprehension changes reality, for all practical purposes. The proverb "as we think so we are" can be understood all the more clearly in an idealistic system like Kashmir Śaivism, where consciousness, or thought, itself is the reality. There is not much difference between imagination and reality. This is the dynamic at work when a yogin effects physical change with the power of thought (*mantra*).

We are a bound soul because we mistake ourselves for a bound soul. But of course, this is not an intellectual misapprehension (*bauddha ajñāna*), but an existential one (*pauruṣa ajñāna*) — as occurs in a dream. Dream ignorance is not mere intellectual ignorance. But at the same time, the change in the dream is not a physical change; it is just a change in the mental state or consciousness. So although there is a virtual change of personality in the dream, it is just due to ignorance, which is related to the mind, not matter.

It should also be noted that the bondage of consciousness cannot be of the material type; it can only be of the mental type. The nature of ignorance (illusion) is wrong thinking or wrong knowing. In this sense, the bondage of consciousness is not a "real" or "material" bondage; it is bondage in the form of wrong thinking. Of course, the language used to express bondage is the language of matter. "Bondage," "covering," "obstruction," "dirt," (*mala*) — these are all terms that apply to the material world, symbolically applied to Consciousness in order to denote spiritual impurity. And the spiritual impurity itself is merely wrong thinking, which is the characteristic of a deluded mind.

It is clear that bondage is ignorance or wrong knowledge, but what is the nature of this wrong knowledge? The answer is "duality" (*dvaita-prathā*) — the sense of duality or otherness — the sense that the people and objects of the world are different from or other than oneself. Abhinavagupta says that the sense of duality is the real ignorance, and it is this that really binds.[8] Non-duality is the awareness that all are oneself or belong to one; it is the sense of one's unity with all,[9] the state of universal love. What differentiates one from the totality is the ego, which is the sense of being limited to one particular individuality, which one calls "me." Ego results in taking one's own person alone to be oneself and seeing the rest of the world as "other." This is another name for selfishness. This is the ignorance or illusion that binds. It is like the case of the mother who, by an unfortunate turn of events, was separated from her children. When her children are at last brought before her, she does not know that they are her own children and takes them to be "other" than her. The great discovery made by the Tantric and Upaniṣadic seers is that the entire universe is one with the Self, oneself, but ignorance keeps us unaware of this all-fulfilling truth.

THE CONCEPT OF MALA ("IMPURITY")

It becomes clear from the above treatment of ignorance that ignorance is not a negative state but is something positive — a positive state of wrong knowledge. Wrong knowledge is itself really a state of spiritual impurity (*aśuddhi*).[10] Since it is positive impurity, ignorance is called dirt (*mala*).[11] *Mala* is a term of the physical world, literally meaning "dirt" or "filth." Applied to consciousness, it means spiritual or mental impurity. It is the impurity with which consciousness, in its present state (the state of the bound individual) is tainted.

Since the impurity obscures Consciousness (the Self) from sight, it is called "darkness" (*timira* or *tamas*).[12] Since the impurity covers or veils Consciousness, it is called "covering" or "veil" (*āvaraṇa* or *ācchādana*);[13] it is like a curtain or cloak (*kañcuka*) that veils the real nature of the Self.[14] Since the impurity prevents the light of the Self from coming to the fore, it is called "obstruction" (*avarodha*). Since it binds consciousness, it is called "bondage" (*bandha*)[15] or "fetters" (*argalā*).

At this point it would be relevant to consider the question How is impurity (*mala*), which is bondage, related to Śiva?[16] From the point of view of Śiva, bondage is the free sportive activity (*krīḍā* or *līlā*) of Śiva — the sport of limiting oneself. Śiva's very desire to freely limit or cover Himself is itself the impurity.[17]

In the Tantric tradition, impurity is of three types: (a) *āṇava mala*, (b) *māyīya mala*, and (c) *kārma mala*. All three types of impurity are the products of *māyā*,[18] the limiting or covering principle. All three should thus be called *māyīya malas*. But the name *māyīya* is given to the one particular *mala* that consists of seeing difference or otherness from oneself. Abhinavagupta is aware of this linguistic discrepancy, and he writes "the name *māyīya* given to the impurity of seeing difference is just a name; all three *malas* are also *māyīya* by virtue of being the products of *māyā*."[19]

Āṇava mala means the identification of Consciousness with a limited individuality. Limited individuality is technically called "ego." *Āṇava* is thus the sense of ego. The word *āṇava* is the adjective of *aṇu*, which means the limited soul. *Aṇu* also means "the small." Here *aṇu* is taken not in the sense of being small in size, but in the sense of being limited or finite.

Since finitude or limitation means imperfection, *āṇava* means the sense of being imperfect (*apūrṇaṁ-manyatā*).[20] It should be noted here that Absolute Consciousness (Śiva) has not *really* become limited, what has happened is that the individual soul (*aṇu* or *paśu*), mistakes itself for a limited or imperfect being. This is like what happens in a dream. A king, when he becomes a beggar in a dream, does not *really* become the beggar; he mistakenly *thinks* he has become a beggar, as his mind is under an illusion. But this misapprehension of his real nature is such that it brings about a virtual change in his existence, and he is a beggar for all practical purposes, as long as the dream persists. Similarly, the individual (*aṇu*), which is really the perfect Śiva, mistakes itself for a limited person,[21] and this misapprehension turns it into a limited person for all practical purposes. This is the power of ignorance (*ajñāna*). The same is true of the other impurities (*malas*) also.

Furthermore, the individual (*aṇu*) takes itself to be imperfect because, although its real nature is the ubiquitous Self, it feels identified with an individuality that has its natural limitations. The individual becomes finite and therefore imperfect. As a result it feels lack or want in itself, which in turn creates hankering (*lolikā*)[22] in it for the desired but unacquired things.

In the *Īśvara-pratyabhijñā-kārikā*, Utpaladeva says that the *āṇava* can be understood in two ways: (a) "There is no freedom of Consciousness," and (b) "There is no consciousness of freedom." Both of these predicaments are due to the loss of one's real nature, which is Absolute Consciousness or Śiva.[23] Freedom (*svātantrya*), which means the absence of all limitation and therefore also means perfection, is the very nature of Pure Consciousness. This freedom of Consciousness is lost in the state of *āṇava* — Consciousness becomes bound or limited. *Āṇava* can thus be understood as the loss of the freedom of Consciousness. Second, in *āṇava*, one is not aware of this freedom (perfection) that is one's real nature. The freedom (perfection) already exists, but one does not recognize it. These two predicaments of the soul — namely the loss of the freedom of Consciousness and the non-cognition of this freedom — occur simultaneously and function in vicious reciprocity. It is like the case of the rope-snake illusion when one sees the snake because one does not see the rope, and one does not see the rope because one sees the snake in its place. In *āṇava*, one is not aware of one's real nature because one's real nature is not at the fore, and one's real nature is not at the fore because one is not aware of it. Reality and the awareness of reality are reciprocal.

Āṇava is the principal *mala*, as it holds all the other *malas* within it. It is the primordial *mala* that gives rise to the other two *malas*. The first thing that *māyā* does is make the all-ubiquitous Consciousness a limited person (*aṇu*), which offers the necessary ground or cause for the creation of the ego sense. This ego sense is the main obstruction to the realization of the Self. To use an analogy, the wave is separated from the ocean because it has taken an individuality, otherwise it is nothing but water or the ocean. The wave cannot become the ocean as long as it maintains its individuality. It is only when the wave loses its individuality that it becomes completely one with the ocean. The water has taken a particular form (*rūpa*) and the name (*nāma*) "wave" is given to it. The nameless and formless water has taken a particular name and form (*nāma-rūpa*). But what is the status of this *nāma-rūpa*? It is not a reality, for the reality is water. The moment the wave subsides, it becomes what it really is — pure water. Similarly, the ego is a *nāma-rūpa* that the Self (Consciousness) has taken on, and the moment this condition subsides, the individual consciousness merges into the ocean of the universal Consciousness. Whether the renunciation of the ego should be considered a case of suicide or one of self-fulfillment will be determined later.

Even in practical life we find that ego is the root cause of all evil. Ego and selfishness are two sides of the same coin. Ego is like a post upon which all the evil qualities hang. When this post of ego falls, all the evil falls too. We also find in practical life that the more the ego of a person is thinned or dissolved, the more the peace, power, beauty, illumination, and joy of the Inner Self flows in him or her and the more self-fulfillment the person feels.

The treatment of the ego that I have presented may suggest that since ego is the cause of evil and since it is Śiva who has created the ego, it is Śiva, and not the individual, who is responsible for the evil. But it would be a naive understanding of Absolutism to think that everything that we find on earth is a creation of God (Śiva). Humanity can also create many things of its own accord, as humans are not robots but beings possessed of free will. The vanity or egoism that goes with selfishness is entirely the creation of the individual (*paśu*), and therefore egoism is the responsibility of humanity. The egoism that is the actual cause of evil is different from the natural ego that attends the limited individuality created by Śiva through His power of ignorance. The natural ego is simply the knowledge of oneself as an individual different from others. This metaphysical or natural ego differs from the egoism (*abhimāna*) that is responsible for evil, which is the creation of the *paśu*, not of Śiva. When, for example, one asks a person, "Who are you?" the person replies, "I am so and so." What is at work here is the natural ego, which is really harmless and without which our behavior (*vyavahāra*) in the world is not possible. But when the person takes the credit for something, or imposes his or her will on others, this is the actual ego that causes evil. This natural ego, or the sense of limited individuality, may indirectly serve as a cause of the egoism in question. It may even be a necessary cause of it, for there can be no egoism without the sense of limited individuality, but it is not the sufficient cause, for it cannot itself create egoity. Egoism is the creation of our own free will. Śiva has created individuality, through the agency of ignorance, for the joyful pursuits of life. It is a sportive activity not only on the part of Śiva; it is meant for sport even on the part of the *paśu*, as is evident in the example of a child. Individuality becomes a cause for evil only when we add egoism to it. Egoism is perhaps the only thing that is entirely the creation of humanity — it further creates all the evil of the world.

Ego functions in two ways — the cognitive and the conative. When we take credit for the powers that are really not ours, as all powers belong to God or Nature, then this is a case of wrong understanding. This may be called the cognitive ego. When we try to impose ourselves on others or insist that our will be done, this too is ego. Since this ego involves willing or activity, this can be called the conative ego.

Māyīya mala means the sense of duality or difference — the false sense that one is different or separate from the rest of the world or that one's fellow beings are "other" than oneself.[24] The word *māyīya* is the adjective form of *māyā*; it means the impurity pertaining to *māyā*. The chief characteristic of *māyā* is that it creates the sense of difference, or duality, and *māyīya* knowledge would thus be the knowledge of duality.[25] Since *māyā* mainly consists of the sense of duality, the impurity (*mala*) of seeing difference is termed *māyīya*.

Māyīya mala presupposes *āṇava mala*, for there can be no apprehension of difference (*bheda*) unless one is limited to a particular individuality. When one becomes limited to one individuality, that means one becomes separated or cut off from the rest of the world. Spinoza has said that determination means negation (*determinatio est negatio*). To determine a thing means to limit that thing to a particular characteristic — the characteristic determined — and therefore to isolate or separate it from others. For example, when we determine the word "this" by saying "this is a table," we are actually limiting the word "this" to the table. This means that now "this" is the table alone; it is not the chair, not the stool, and so on. By determining or limiting "this" to the table, we are actually negating it from referring to the rest of the world. Similarly, when one is limited to one individuality, one is cut off from the totality; one cannot be all. The sense of difference is the result of the limitation to one individuality. *Māyīya mala* is a result of *āṇava mala*.

It is not difficult to understand why the sense of difference is an impurity (*mala*). Whatever obstructs our real nature, or takes us away from our real nature, is impurity. Our real nature is pure and perfect, and whatever defiles it, or makes it impure, is *mala* ("impurity"). In our real nature we are one with all, which is a state of supreme bliss. But the sense each of us has that he or she is just a limited personality, and not all, obscures our nature and causes our purity and bliss to disappear.

The word *kārma* is the adjective of *karma*, and thus *kārma mala* means the impurity pertaining to *karma* ("action"). *Karma* is voluntary action that we perform by exerting our will and that arises out of the sense of want or lack in us. This is in contrast to *kriyā*, which is the spontaneous, natural, or automatic flow of activity that naturally arises out of the fullness of bliss, not out of some want or lack. Since *karma* is voluntary action that we perform by exerting our will, it falls in the ethical realm of good and bad, or virtue and vice (*puṇya* and *pāpa*), involving the reaping of moral fruit generated by *karma*.

Karma thus has two important characteristics — (a) it arises out of the sense of lack or want, and (b) it is voluntary action performed by exerting the will. It is obvious that *karma* is possible only when one is in the state of imperfection, which in turn is possible only when one is ignorant (*ajñāna*) of one's real nature, which is the perfect Self. Thus *karma* is action done in the state of ignorance. In his *Īśvarapratyabhijñā-kārikā*, Utpaladeva describes *kārma mala* as the action done when the doer is ignorant of his real nature (*kartari abodhe*).[26] Commenting on this in his *Vimarśinī*, Abhinavagupta says, "*Kārma mala* comes when the doer is in the state of ignorance and imperfection, has the sense of duality, and performs action in the form of virtue and vice (*dharmādharma*), which leads to birth and reaping the fruit of actions."[27] Since one has to reap the fruits of one's actions, according to the Law of Karma, one has to take a new birth, and thus *karma* is the cause of the changing world of birth and death (*saṁsāra*).[28] The variety of existence is said to be due to *karma*.[29]

It is obvious that, like *māyīya mala*, *kārma mala* arises out of the principal *mala āṇava*. *Āṇava* is the sense of imperfection.[30] When due to *āṇava*, one becomes limited and imperfect, one naturally feels want or lack in oneself, and in order to fulfill that lack or want, one performs action. If one is already full — that is, all one's desires are fulfilled and one needs nothing — then what is the sense of performing action? One can perform action (*karma*) only in order to fulfill some lack; but if there is no lack or want, why should one perform action at all? *Kārma mala*, which pertains to the performance of action (*karma*), originates from *āṇava mala*;[31] in this sense *āṇava* is again the principal *mala*.[32]

In the state of perfection, although *karma*, or voluntary effortful action, is not possible, *kriyā*, or spontaneous activity arising out of fullness as the free and natural overflow of bliss, is very much possible. Moreover *kriyā*, unlike *karma*, does not create bondage, as *kriyā* is a natural and spontaneous flow of activity that is beyond the ethical categories of "good" and "bad."

Why should *karma* be bondage? All the systems of Indian philosophy consider *karma* to be bondage for the soul and detrimental to the attainment of *mokṣa*. If we understand the nature of *karma* and the nature of *mokṣa*, and also understand the distinction of *karma* from *kriyā*, we will see that *karma* and *mokṣa* are opposites, whereas *kriyā* and *mokṣa* go together. *Karma* becomes bondage for two reasons. First, *karma* takes us away from the inner Self. To express it allegorically, when one performs *karma*, one moves forward and does not relax in oneself. However, the Self is not forward, but backward as the inner ground of oneself; therefore, Self-realization is a matter of going back or withdrawing, not of moving forward. To use an analogy, suppose one is climbing up a rope hanging from the ceiling — this is action (*karma*), and this action will lead one toward the ceiling. But further suppose that one's aim is not to go to the ceiling but to the ground, then what should one do? One should not make the effort of climbing, for it will take one further away from the ground; rather one should undo what one is already doing — one should loosen one's grip on the rope so that one falls down to the ground automatically. *Mokṣa*, or Self-realization, is a matter of "falling down to the ground"; it is a question of withdrawing or receding, not moving forward or climbing up.

Action is primarily mental; it arises in the mind in the form of will and physical activity follows. When we perform action, the mind is not resting within ourselves but is moving outside of ourselves. In the language of yoga, action is tension, for the mind, while performing action, is not at rest but is exerting itself. But *mokṣa* is a state of relaxation, as opposed to action, which is a state of tension. *Mokṣa* is the state of being seated in or taking rest in Oneself (*ātma-viśrānti*). All the yogic forms of meditation consist of withdrawing into oneself by non-doing or non-thinking. When the mind is thinking or doing, it is switching outside; meditation is withdrawing inside — coming back to oneself.

Of course, when we withdraw or relax, automatic creative activity flows through us of its own accord, for spontaneous activity is the very nature of Consciousness (the Self). According to the Tantric tradition, this type of activity is called *kriyā*, not *karma*. This state of activity can be paradoxically described as the state of "actionless activity," or "relaxed activity," where one is a doer and yet not a doer. The activity is not performed by exerting the will; it flows automatically. The *karma* yoga of the *Gītā* is the same. It is not *karma* but *kriyā*. *Karma* is seen as bondage in the *Gītā*, too.[33] *Karma* yoga lies in surrendering the will to the Lord (the Higher Self) and allowing the spontaneous activity of the Self to flow through oneself. This is the state of "actionless activity" or "activity in relaxation," where one is a doer and yet not a doer.[34]

Kriyā, although a form of activity, is a state of relaxation, because one does not *do* the action by exerting one's will; one remains seated in the Self, and the action is automatically done. Or the action spontaneously flows while one is sitting silent, doing nothing. Thus *karma*, which takes us away from the Self, is bondage, while *kriyā*, which is action in a state of rest or relaxation, is not bondage.

The other reason why *karma* is bondage, is that we are bound to reap the moral fruit of our actions, good or bad.[35] *Karma* is what we perform voluntarily, so we are responsible for it. It falls in the moral (ethical) category — it may be "good" or "bad."[36] This binds us, as we are obliged to reap its fruit, both good and bad. If it is morally right action (*dharma*), it will result in pleasure or happiness; if it is sin (*adharma*), it will result in pain or suffering. And in order to be able to reap the fruits, we are forced by the Law of Karma into rebirth;[37] this is how we become bound in the world of birth and death (*saṁsāra*).[38]

It is worth noting that both bad and good actions are binding to the soul. Even the good action, by virtue of being *karma* which takes us away from the Self, binds. That is why it is said that both good and bad actions are fetters that bind — bad action is an iron fetter, whereas good action is a fetter made of gold. Good action leads to heaven and bad action to hell, but both destinations are within our bound state. This is like living in a universal prison as a prisoner and being rewarded or punished for good or bad actions done within the prison life. *Mokṣa* however, is the attainment of our natural state of absolute freedom, which is also the state of freedom from the prison of birth and death. After attaining *mokṣa* one can still remain in the prison if one likes, not as a prisoner but as a free visitor or as an administrative officer of the prison. The prisoner, in order to be able to attain his or her freedom, must rise above both good and bad actions. That is why the Indian tradition maintains that one has to rise above both virtue and vice, truth and falsehood.[39]

Needless to say, the state of *kriyā* is the state of freedom — freedom from prison. *Kriyā* does not bind one to the prison, as it does not fall within the ethical category of right and wrong (*dharma* and *adharma*). Although naturally good, it is itself beyond good and bad. It can be termed "spiritual" activity as opposed to the activity that binds, which falls in the ethical category of good and bad. Spirituality preserves in itself the merits of morality and is free from the demerits, as we shall see later.

Thus we see that *āṇava mala*, *māyīya mala*, and *kārma mala* are the three forms of impurity (*mala*) that bind the Self (Consciousness). All three are impurity because all obscure the Self, our real nature, and keep us away from the Self. Freedom from impurity is equal to going back to our real nature, the freedom of the Self.

If we look at the thirty-six categories of Creation accepted in Kashmir Śaivism, we will find that the *malas* are not enumerated among them. The reason they are not placed within the categories is that they themselves are not the actual things (*tattvas*) that evolve from Reality; they are the results or consequences of the function of certain *tattvas*. *Māyā*, together with the five sheaths (*pañca-kañcuka*) which evolve from her, is the *tattva* that evolves from Reality (Śiva). *Māyā*, the matrix of the *kañcukas*, is also called *kañcuka*, and when added to the five *kañcukas*, it makes six sheaths (*ṣaḍ-kañcuka*). It is the *ṣaḍ-kañcuka* that causes the *malas*. When the sheath functions, the result is *mala*. *Mala* is a functional consequence of the *kañcuka*. This is the reason the *malas* are not enumerated in the *tattvas*.

THE MEANING OF MOKṢA

Mokṣa, or *mukti*, has two meanings — a negative meaning and a positive one. The negative meaning of *mokṣa* is the freedom from impurity (*ajñāna* or *māyā*). This is suggested by the literal meaning of the word *mukti*. The word *mukti*, or *mokṣa*, literally means "release," "freeing," or "unbinding." As we have already seen, the soul is in bondage — the bondage of ignorance, or *māyā* — that obstructs the real nature of the soul. *Mokṣa* is the release or freedom from the bondage of ignorance. The soul is bound by limitations and *mokṣa* is freedom from limitations. It is not that one becomes free from *some* limitations for some time under some conditions; one becomes free from *all* limitations for all time under all conditions.[40] *Mokṣa* is not relative freedom but absolute freedom.

Since *mokṣa* is understood as release from something — ignorance or impurity — it follows that *mokṣa* is a negative attainment. We lose something in *mokṣa*, but what do we *gain*? We gain our own real nature that was hitherto obstructed.[41] When we clean a piece of cloth, cleaning is certainly a negative process — we separate the dirt from the cloth and we do not add anything to the cloth. But the negative process of cleaning leads to the positive attainment of the real nature of the cloth, which is clean in and of itself. We do not add cleanliness to the cloth. The cloth is clean by its very nature; that clean nature was only obstructed. Now that the dirt is removed, the cleanliness of the cloth comes to the fore. Or, to use another analogy, when a lion is released from captivity, it is not true that when it was in the bound state it was a goat and only when it is freed does it become a lion. The lion was already a lion, but its "lionness" was not in evidence as it was caged. Once it is freed from the cage, it becomes what it already really was.

Similarly, in *mokṣa* we become what we really are. Our real nature was obscured and now that the obstruction is cleared away, we attain our real nature. *Mokṣa* is thus also a positive attainment — the attainment of our real nature. Of course, this is not the attainment of a new thing; it is the "getting of the gotten" (*prāptasya prāptiḥ*).[42] This paradoxical statement is not a tautology; it means that the Self that we attain in *mokṣa* is already there; it is not a new thing. In this sense *mokṣa* is the "getting of the gotten." But the Self was previously obscured, and we have come to realize it only now; in this sense it is a new event. The Self, or Consciousness, was very much present, but its powers were blunted, just as in the case of a lion in a cage. So it is only when Consciousness is released from captivity that its powers are revealed, just as the powers of the lion come to the fore only when it comes out of the cage. The thing that is attained is thus already there, but the attainment itself is a new thing.

All the systems of Indian philosophy that accept *mokṣa* accept both the negative and positive meanings of *mokṣa*, namely (a) *mokṣa* is freedom from bondage and (b) *mokṣa* is the attainment of one's own real nature. All the systems are thus in agreement with regard to the meaning of *mokṣa* as the attainment of the real nature of the soul or self. But what is the real nature of the self or soul? It is here that the differences among the systems of philosophy start. The conception of *mokṣa* in a particular system depends upon the conception of the real nature of the soul accepted in that system. We find in the systems of Indian philosophy a hierarchical understanding of the real nature of the soul.

In Vaiśeṣika, the nature of the soul is only existence (*sat*); the soul exists but it has no knowledge, no activity, no pleasure, no pain. These are the accidental qualities of the soul. They naturally disappear in the state of *mokṣa*, as they are not part and parcel of the soul. In the state of *mokṣa*, as conceived by Vaiśeṣika, one virtually becomes like a stone, as one is devoid even of knowledge. The *mokṣa* of Vaiśeṣika is viewed by the other systems as a disvalue, and is also ridiculed by some of them. A Vaiṣṇava *bhakta*, for example, says, "I would rather forego *mokṣa*, and accept being born as a jackal in the forest of Vrindāvana (hallowed by the presense of Kṛṣṇa) than pray for the *mukti* of Vaiśeṣika."[43]

In Sāṁkhya, however, we find an improvement upon the Vaiśeṣika position with regard to *mokṣa*. According to Sāṁkhya, the nature of the soul (*puruṣa*) is both *sat* (being) and *cit* (knowledge), and thus the state of *mokṣa* is a state of knowledge. But here, too, the soul is devoid of joy (*sukha* or *ānanda*) and activity, as these are the qualities of matter (*prakṛti*). In *mokṣa* (or *kaivalya*, as it is called in Sāṁkhya) the soul (*puruṣa*) remains a seer or knower and not a doer; it is also devoid of bliss, as bliss goes with *prakṛti*, from which the *puruṣa* is completely dissociated in *mokṣa*.

Vedānta moves a step further and declares that the real nature of the self (soul or *puruṣa*) is not only *sat* ("existence") and *cit* ("knowledge" or "illumination"), but also *ānanda* ("joy" or "bliss"). Brahman, which is the real nature of the self, is *sat-cit-ānanda*. This idea is fully developed in Advaita Vedānta. According to Advaita Vedānta, one becomes *sat-cit-ānanda* in the state of *mukti*. But there, too, as in Sāṁkhya, the liberated soul remains inactive (*niṣkriyā*). There is no activity in the real nature of the Self, activity being relegated to *māyā*, which is transcended in *mokṣa*.

Kashmir Śaivism, as we have seen, accepts as the nature of the Self not only *sat-cit-ānanda* but also activity (*kriyā*, *vimarśa*, *spanda*, *śakti*, or *svātantrya*). This is spontaneous activity freely arising out of the fullness of the Self. Since freedom or activity (*svātantrya*) is the very nature of the Self, the liberated person is vibrant with joyful activity.

Bondage is a state of the forgetfulness of our real nature. This forgetfulness did not begin at a particular point in time; it is beginninglessly present with the existence of the individual soul, as if the soul were born blind. Since bondage is the forgetfulness of our real nature, *mokṣa*, naturally, is the state of remembrance of the same. Abhinavagupta says, "The enlightenment (*prakāśa*) that dawns in the state of *mokṣa* is like the remembering of a forgotten wealth, and the forgotten wealth is the state of one's unity with all."[44]

In the same vein it can be said that the joy (*ānanda*) that we obtain in *mokṣa* is the natural joy of the Self, which we realize by easing ourselves from the crushing load of ignorance we are carrying. Abhinavagupta further says, "The joy of *mokṣa* is not like the acquired pleasure of material wealth, women, and wine;[45] the joy of *mokṣa* is the joy of the freedom from the colossal sense of duality, like the joy of the unloading of a heavy weight."[46]

From the above treatment of *mokṣa*, two things become clear: (a) *mokṣa* is not a physical acquisition but a realization, a remembrance, or a re-apprehension of the Self; and (b) *mokṣa* is not a new acquisition; what we attain in *mokṣa* is already there — it is only a question of uncovering or discovering it.[47]

Since *mokṣa* is a process of going back to our original nature, not acquiring new things and undertaking new adventures, it sounds like retiring from life. It may appear that Kashmir Śaivism advocates a philosophy of life that leads to passivity and regression, undermining the activistic and progressive ideal of life. One may argue that it is not joy but social and scientific progress that is the ideal of life, and a progressive civilization should be the aim of our endeavors. In answer to this we may point out that work or scientific progress in itself cannot become the aim of life; life is ultimately meant for the welfare and happiness of mankind. The idea of work for the sake of work or progress for the sake of progress is absurd. The goal of life is finally happiness, or *ānanda*.

This understanding is not meant to denigrate the value of work and progress; it simply points out that progress is the means, not the end. Happiness, or *ānanda* is the end of all work and progress. Moreover, happiness is not only the *end* of all activity, but it is also the *ground* of activity and progress. Beautiful activity naturally emanates or flows from joy. If we are seated in happiness, the activity will flow not only in greater volume, but also in the proper direction so that the activity becomes both useful and enjoyable. In that state of mind, technological achievement becomes a thing of joy and beauty. What the present day scientific and technological atmosphere lacks is the spiritual sense, which alone can make scientific progress good and beautiful.

The value of activity, however, is by no means inferior. It is through activity that the joy of the individual self reaches its fullness or perfection. The *Gītā* advocates this idea in a systematic and detailed way. Just as a seed attains perfection through the process of the actualization of its potentialities in the form of a tree, the Self realizes its perfection through the process of activity, which is really a process of actualization of its potentialities. But in the process of the blossoming of a bud into flower, what is significant is not the process itself but the beauty that the flower exhibits through the process of blossoming. Similarly, what is important in the process of activity or growth is not the process of activity itself but the joy that is expressed through it.

SPECIAL FEATURES OF THE MUKTI OF KASHMIR ŚAIVISM

Since according to Kashmir Śaivism, Creation is a manifestation of the Self — a blissful dance of Śiva — and since free and spontaneous activity is the very nature of the Self, *mokṣa* need not be a rejection of the world but may be a free acceptance of the world and worldly activity. The *mokṣa* of Kashmir Śaivism is full, not only from the point of view of Śiva, but also from the point of view of the world. *Mokṣa* is aglow with both celestial and terrestrial beauty. *Mokṣa* is not opposed to *bhoga* ("enjoyment"). Even in enjoyment, what the Self-realized person enjoys is the bliss of the Self, not the joy of the object. A Self-realized person is far above the selfish and exploitative enjoyment of the ordinary person. Such a person is not bound by enjoyment. The Tantra says, "The sun sucks up everything of the world; the fire consumes everything (and yet the sun and the fire ever remain pure); so also the yogi, although accepting all enjoyments, is never defiled by sin."[48]

It is not the world and the enjoyable objects of the world that create bondage; it is attachment (*rāga*) that is the real bondage. Attachment can be overcome not by an attitude of negation, but by a positive attitude — a positive negation, as it were. It is possible to have enjoyment of worldly objects without attachment. Real enjoyment of the world and a happy material life is possible only when one is, even to a small extent, unattached. The poor person who is too tied up with the world cannot derive real joy from the world. One who treads the path of liberation (*mukti*) fully enjoys the world unattached. The liberated person (*jīvanmukta*) does this out of freedom and joy. With his or her senses under perfect control, he or she has no compulsion to indulge in the world. The bound person indulges in the world out of compulsion, from the instinctive urge; the freed person does not. The *Gītā* says, "One who enjoys the objects with senses that are free from attachment (*rāga*) and aversion (*dveṣa*) and are under one's full control, does the desirable thing and attains peace and happiness."[49] Kṛṣṇa is the perfect example of this. For Him everything is His own play (*līlā-vilāsa*). In this attitude one is in enjoyment yet at the same time transcends the enjoyment.[50]

Karma ("action"), which is generally taken to be bondage, becomes a means of liberation when it is performed in the same religious spirit. The *Gītā* is the champion of this idea. If the world, which consists of activity and enjoyment, were a hindrance to liberation, it would be a hindrance and bondage to the Creator also, which it is not. For the Creator the world is spontaneous activity (*kriyā*) and so it is for one who seeks to become one with the Creator.

One of the significant points in the Tantric philosophy and religion is that there is perfect compatibility and harmony between liberation (*jīvanmukti*) and socio-cultural activity. This becomes especially significant when compared with scholastic Advaitism, where socio-cultural activity is logically meaningless in the context of the attainment of liberation. In Advaitism, one who aspires to liberation tries to disassociate him- or herself from social activity, for all such activity detracts from one's effort for *mokṣa*. Indulgence in the world and worldly activities is not only useless for such a person but is also an obstruction to Self-realization. The world is unreal and valueless (*tuccha*); it is a superimposition on the Real, created by ignorance, and it must therefore be discarded and renounced in order to reach the Real. The ideal of liberation (*jīvanmukti*) can occur only with renunciation (*sannyāsa*) of the world. Renunciation of worldly activity (*nivṛtti*), not involvement therein (*pravṛtti*), is the Advaitic ideal.

Moreover, in scholastic Advaitism the person who attains liberation lives just to work out his or her leftover karma. He or she can do no positive work with regard to society; he or she must be inactive (*niṣkriyā*), for activity, according to the Advaitin, is due to ignorance (*avidyā*). Such a person is like one who has taken preparatory leave prior to retiring from one's career, counting the days until final retirement. Such a person loses all interest in the affairs he or she was previously involved in. Society cannot be benefitted by such a person for he or she has no incentive for doing good for society. All actions cease on his or her part and the world becomes a non-entity. He or she is lost to the world, as it were, and the world, in turn, is lost to him or her. In the Advaitic pattern each historical case of the attainment of liberation is a virtual loss to society.[51]

In the Āgamic tradition we find a different picture of the ideal of liberation. Socio-cultural activity goes hand in hand with Self-realization both before and after the attainment of liberation. Before the attainment of liberation activity serves as a means to Self-realization; after attainment, activity naturally flows in a spontaneous way, since spontaneous activity (*spanda* or *kriyā*) is the very nature of the Self. Activity arises not out of ignorance, as the Advaitin thinks, but out of the freedom to act (*svātantrya*).[52] We have already seen that indulgence in the world and performance of social and worldly activity is not a hindrance to Self-realization. Rather, activity (*pravṛtti*) is, in the Tantric tradition, taken to be a potent means of Self-realization. The aspirant for Self-realization therefore does not renounce the world. He or she, on the contrary, participates in the worldly affairs and takes part in socio-cultural activity.

In the Tantric tradition, unlike classical Advaitism, the Real (Śiva or Self) is not conceived of as inactive (*niṣkriyā*); spontaneous activity (*kriyā*) is seen as the very nature of the Self. The world is taken not as a superimposition on Śiva but as His free and active creation. As *kriyā* is the very nature of the Self or Śiva, the person who has attained Śivahood, like a Kṛṣṇa, a Christ, or a Buddha, becomes the ideal of free activity. Universal love is his or her very nature. He or she feels one with all and does good to all. Abhinavagupta says that doing good to others out of grace (*parānugraha*) is clearly manifest in the person who is in the state of Self-realization.[53] He or she spontaneously works for the cultural progress and betterment of society. The Self-realized person does not act to work out his or her leftover *karma*, this being already liquidated; he or she acts because spontaneous activity is his or her very nature. Such a person responds to every call; he or she takes an active interest in the affairs of the world. While the ordinary person (*paśu*) does this out of selfish interest and by straining his or her will, the liberated person does this out of universal love, in a free and relaxed way. While overflowing in external activity (*unmeṣa*), he or she always remains in the Self.

The liberated person, freed from the personal ego, actually identifies him- or herself with all. The Advaitin may say that as long as one sees others — as long as one sees the world in terms of duality — there can be no liberation, for to see "others" is ignorance (*avidyā*). The Tantrist would point out that it is not the physical presence of "others" and the objective world that is ignorance, but the act of seeing them *as others* — knowing them as different from oneself — is ignorance. The physical presence of duality is not bondage, for the physical duality is just a free manifestation or extension (*prasāra*) of the Self Itself; it is only the "sense" of duality — the wrong understanding that something is different from oneself — that is the bondage, and it is this that is called *māyīya mala* ("the ignorance consisting of the sense of duality"). When one freely creates an imaginary world in one's mind, one knows that the world is one's own creation and that one is one with it; though one sees it objectively, yet one's non-duality remains intact. But when the same imagination becomes a dream, one forgets the truth and takes the objective dream world to be different from oneself; it is then that one is bound. For the liberated person who has awakened from the dream of duality, the world does not cease to exist, but it is seen as the free expansion of his or her own Self. The presence of the world of duality does not hamper the liberated person's non-dual Self-realization. Utpaladeva says, "One who is identified with the Universal Self and knows 'all this is my own glory,' remains in Śivahood even in the face of prevailing determinations (or duality)."[54]

Thus we see that the world and secular activities are perfectly compatible with the attainment of Self-realization. Activity flows much more when the Self is attained. Energy, or activity, is natural to the Self; the ego is an obstruction to its flow; therefore the bound soul (*paśu*) is not *that* active. But when the ego is silenced or removed and the Self attained, the constrained energy is released — hence the greater flow of energy. The more one is seated in the Self — that is, the more the ego is relaxed or silenced — the more the Self expresses Itself in the form of creative activity. And since

Self-realization is the state of universal love, the creative activity is generally directed towards the welfare of society.

In the case of partial Self-realization this energy may, in spiritually untrained persons, take a destructive turn, but that is because the Self is now ignored and the ego takes charge of the released energy. The Indian mythology of demons (*asuras*) suggests this. Many of the famous *asuras* first performed *tapasyā* ("self-mortification" which is symbolic of the mortification of the ego) and did intense devotion to Lord Śiva. As a result the Lord, being pleased, granted them unusual power that they subsequently misused; they were then punished on that account. All energy, constructive or destructive, is from the Higher Self anyway. When one displays tremendous creativity and work in any field — secular or religious — one is, to a small degree at least, in unity with the Self.

Aesthetic creativity also ensues from the Self. The joy of the Self expresses itself in creativity in art. The Upaniṣads also maintain that the Self is of the nature of aesthetic joy.[55] That is why all the esoteric and mystical language that flows from that state becomes poetic. The Vedas and the Upaniṣads themselves are examples of this.

The sublime creative activity is not a result of the straining of the will, but is a spontaneous expression of the Self. A real poet does not compose by forcing his or her will; poetry in the true sense of the term flows — and it flows from the Self. The poet is, to some extent, in communion with the Self, which is the fountainhead of all beauty and creativity. The rich artistic creativity that we find in the history of Indian culture can be explained on the basis of this Tantric theory. According to classical Advaitism, however, all such creative activity is due to ignorance and not due to the Self — a theory that leads to the absurdity of thinking that all the great and inspired works of art are the creation of ignorant minds, not of enlightened ones.

As for the origin of almost all the arts, it is traditionally believed and also expressly stated in the Hindu scriptures, that they have come from Lord Śiva. All the arts — poetry, music, dance, architecture, and so on, are Āgamic. The origin of all the arts and aesthetic disciplines from Śiva may be sheer mythology but it suggests a truism, namely, that the artistic creativity originates from the Self or Śiva.

So the path of Self-realization, or *Śiva-prāpti*, is not devoid of earthly beauty; it is rich with creativity, fulfillment, and love for one's fellow beings. The celestial and the terrestrial, the spiritual and the secular, the transcendent and the immanent go hand in hand. The two poles are not exclusive of each other; in fact, the immanent, or the secular, is the free expression of the transcendent, or the spiritual; in this sense the two are one.

It also follows that the *nirvikalpa samādhi* advocated by Sāṃkhya and Pātañjala Yoga and also accepted by Advaita Vedānta, is not the highest realization. The highest or the ultimate is what is called *sahaja samādhi*. In the *nirvikalpa* stage all the modifications of the mind (*vikalpas*) are silenced, and therefore, all activity ceases. This is, according to Tantrism, a stage prior to the attainment of the final one. The *vikalpa* aroused from motives and desires must cease before the attainment of the ultimate stage; but this does not mean that the natural *vikalpas*, or the *vikalpas* aroused out of the freedom of the Self, should also cease. The "natural" (*sahaja*) state of Consciousness is desireless and egoless, and therefore, there are no *vikalpas* (or activity) caused by desire or motive; but natural and free *vikalpas* flow automatically. Hence spontaneous activity occurs in the state of *sahaja samādhi*. Mystic saints have always mentioned the *sahajāvasthā* as the highest form of *samādhi*.[56]

MOKṢA AS THE HIGHEST VALUE

In the Indian tradition we find a well developed theory of values called the theory of *puruṣārtha*. The word *puruṣārtha* means the "object (*artha*) to be achieved by man (*puruṣa*)." Hence *puruṣārtha* means the object or value desirable for man. There are four values accepted in the Indian scheme of *puruṣārtha*. These are wealth (*artha*), satisfaction of desires (*kāma*), morality (*dharma*), and liberation (*mokṣa*). In the history of Indian culture, some people have accepted the theory of *trivarga* — just three *puruṣārthas* consisting of *artha, kāma*, and *dharma*, but the majority accepted the theory of *caturvarga* — four *puruṣārthas*, including *mokṣa*.[57]

I am attempting in the following pages to show that while accepting *kāma* and *dharma* as ultimate values, the acceptance of *mokṣa* or at least the search for a principle like *mokṣa*, is warranted conceptually or at least semi-conceptually. I should also make it clear here that in making this attempt I have in mind a particular conception of *mokṣa* — the Tantric one — that may be quite different from some of the traditional conceptions.

It is obvious that there are two basic, ultimate, and absolute values — one is morality (*dharma*), which may also be called goodness, virtue, and so on; and the other is happiness, pleasure, or satisfaction of desires (*kāma* –– *artha* being a means to *kāma*). In technical terms, the former is called *śreya* — "the good," and the latter is called *preya* — "the pleasant." In actual life we often find a conflict between "the good" (*dharma*) and "the pleasant" (*kāma*); at many times *kāma* appears to be anti-*dharma*, and if one chooses to follow the path of *dharma*, one has to subdue the *kāma*. Not only is there an empirical conflict between the two, but there is also, as may be argued, a conceptually inherent dichotomy between morality (*dharma*) and the attainment of pleasure (*kāma*). Following the strict line in the analysis of morality, it may be argued that the more we suffer in discharging our moral duties, the more credit for morality we achieve; that is, the more we sacrifice *kāma* for the sake of *dharma*, the greater merit we acquire. This is conveyed in the *Mahābhārata* by the story of King Yudhiṣṭhira and the jackal, which shows that Yudhiṣṭhira, even while giving a sumptuous feast to thousands of Brahmins, could not acquire the merit equal to that acquired by a poor Brahmin family who, having suffered pangs of hunger for a week, fed a hungry person with their own modest food, choosing to suffer greater pangs of hunger.

This dichotomy between the good (*dharma*) and the pleasant (*kāma*) warrants thinking of a possible situation where the two are synthesized and the dichotomy ceases to exist. The question naturally arises, is there a situation or a state of being that is both naturally good and pleasant and from which the activities that flow are naturally both good and pleasant? It is a question of finding a principle that synthesizes the good and the pleasant, truth and beauty, or one's own good and the good of others. The ancient Indian thinkers faced this problem and saw a possible solution in what is called Self-realization or *mokṣa*.

If we analyze the nature of *mokṣa* as given in the Upaniṣads, the Tantras, and the *Gītā*, we will find that *mokṣa* (Self-realization) is said to fulfill the demands of both pleasure (*kāma*) and morality (*dharma*). In the beginning it appears that *mokṣa* is a means for the attainment of *kāma* and *dharma*, but a deeper analysis reveals that *mokṣa* is taken to be the underlying reality of *kāma* as well as of *dharma*. *Mokṣa* is envisaged as the ground of all the values, and therefore *mokṣa*, in this sense, can be said to be *the* value.

Not only do the Tantras, which advocate a highly positive approach to life, present *mokṣa* as the fulfillment of *kāma* and *dharma*, but the Upaniṣads and the *Gītā* do also. The *Chāndogya Upaniṣad* says, "He who finds the Self (*ātman*) and knows it, attains all the worlds and all desires."[58] This statement resonates with the theory that all talent and all power to work efficiently and beautifully in every walk of life comes from the Self. All creativity, artistic or otherwise, springs forth from the Self. It is from the Self that the illumined understanding of anything comes to the mind as a spontaneous flash — a phenomenon technically called *pratibhā*. Therefore, the more we are in line with the Self, the more power flows. Thus a person of Self-realization makes a better teacher, philosopher, scientist, leader, businessperson, manager, and so on. *Mokṣa* is not an otherworldly or after-death value but is the ground of overall success in our life.

All the beauties of worldly life, including the pleasures of *kāma*, emanate from our inner Self Itself. This idea is clearly and explicitly presented in detail in the tenth chapter of the *Gītā*, and the concluding verse says that whatever beauty, prosperity, and power we find in the world comes from the light of the Self.[59] This position is perfectly in line with the Upaniṣadic contention that everything of the world is illumined with the light of the Self.[60] The Upaniṣads and the *Gītā*, not to mention the Tantras, declare in unequivocal terms that even the pleasure of sex is nothing but the manifestation of the joy of Brahman (the Self) Itself. The *Taittirīya Upaniṣad* says, "Brahman is present in the sex organ as reproduction, immortality, and joy."[61] In the *Gītā*, Lord Kṛṣṇa, who symbolizes the higher Self, declares "I am the libido which causes reproduction"[62] and "I am, in living beings, the feeling of sex unopposed to morality."[63] The *Bhāgavata Purāna* also refers to the theory that sex is the manifestation of God.[64]

All the worldly pleasures, including the pleasure of sex, at all levels — physical, mental, and spiritual, are taken as manifestations of the Self. The theory is that the pleasure of the object does not come from the object itself but from the Self, just as the moon shines not by its own light but by the light of the sun. All the pleasure of the world comes from the Self, only indirectly. Thus if we are not seated in the Self, we are *not* able to enjoy the world; the pleasure we take from the world is proportionate to the degree of Self-realization we have achieved. The poet Coleridge, addressing Nature says, "O Lady, we receive but what we give," meaning that we receive from Nature or the world the joy that we unconsciously project on it.[65] If we observe life carefully we will find that even the enjoyment of worldly objects depends upon the subjective condition of the enjoyer. The situation and the object of enjoyment being constant, the degree and intensity, and also the quality of enjoyment varies with the variation in the subjective state of the enjoyer. This suggests that the above theory that Self-realization is the very ground of all enjoyment (*kāma*) is true.

I do not mean to argue in favor of the above-mentioned idealistic or spiritualistic theory of pleasure; I am simply suggesting that there is a strong possibility that this theory is true; and if the theory is true, then we are obliged to maintain conceptually that Self-realization or *mokṣa* is the very ground of enjoyment (*kāma*) or that *mokṣa* synthesizes *kāma* within itself. We can put forward the theory, as is maintained in the Indian tradition, that joy, or ānanda, is the very nature of the Self, just as illumination is the very nature of the sun, and each and every form of joy or pleasure in the world is a manifestation of the joy of the Self in varying degrees.

Self-realization (*mokṣa*) incorporates within itself not only pleasure (*kāma*) but also morality (*dharma*). Morality is said to be naturally present in *mokṣa* for two reasons. First, the Self that is attained in *mokṣa* is conceived of as naturally good. That is why it is called Śiva ("the benign"). It is illogical to think that bad actions could spring forth from a naturally benign Self. As Ramakṛṣṇa Paramahaṅsa used to say, just as only honey can drop from a honeycomb, only good actions can spring from the Śiva-state.

Second, in the state of *mokṣa* or self-realization, one feels one's unity with all,[66] and it is quite natural for such a person to do good to all.[67] What obstructs the Self is called *māyā* or *ajñāna* (ignorance), and ignorance is defined as the sense of duality (*dvaita-prathā* or *bhedabuddhi*),[68] that is, the sense that there are "others." When this sense of duality is dispelled and one's unity with all (*advaita-bhāvanā* or *abheda buddhi*) is realized — that is, universal love is attained — then one of the most essential characteristics of *mokṣa*, or Self-realization, is achieved.

It is obvious that selfishness or the sense of duality is the root of all immorality. One can exploit a person only when one considers him or her to be other than onself. But if one considers him or her to be one's own self, how can one exploit him or her? A Self-realized person will not exploit or harm anyone, as Self-realization is a state of perfect universal love. On the contrary, he or she will help all. Thus, Self-realization is a state of natural or spontaneous morality.

Thus morality is logically connected with Self-realization. If one considers so-called "other" people to be one's own, it logically follows that one will try to help them rather than harm them.

Moreover it is quite possible, as the advocate of the theory of Self-realization believes, that moral consciousness, or moral reason, is also a manifestation of the ultimate Consciousness or the Self. It may be argued that whatever is known, through any means of knowledge, is known by Consciousness. When we say that it is clear to us that morality is an ultimate value, a value in itself, this clarity comes from Consciousness. There is nothing illogical or irrational in maintaining, as a hypothesis, that this moral consciousness or reason is also a manifestation of the same higher Consciousness, the Self. It is not unreasonable to believe that we are conscious of morality because the natural reason of the Self is manifest in us. Animals have far less Self-realization than human beings, and that is why they do not seem to have moral consciousness. According to the theory of Self-realization, the more we advance towards Self-realization, the clearer the moral consciousness becomes. In the end morality just becomes natural. So Self-realization is the underlying principle in morality (*dharma*) and also the underlying principle in pleasure (*kāma*), as we have already seen.

Thus we see that Self-realization synthesizes within itself both pleasure (*kāma*) and morality (*dharma*) or the pleasant (*preya*) and the good (*śreya*). In Self-realization the good of oneself and the good of others become one; it is a state that is at once good and pleasant. In our empirical experience, too, we can find at least one phenomenon that is the example of this synthesis — the phenomenon of love. In love the good of the lover and the good of the beloved person become one. The mother, for example, feels her oneness with her child, and the mother herself feels happy in the happiness of the child. Love naturally prompts good action of the lover towards the beloved. Moreover, besides prompting beneficial activity towards the beloved person, love gives immense satisfaction and joy (*ānanda*) to the lover him- or herself. The rapture of love is so deep that only a true lover can fully understand it. So love benefits both the lover and the beloved. To use a phrase from Shakespeare, "it blesseth him that gives and him that takes."

Needless to say, love is the very nature of the Self, and a person of Self-realization will be a true lover. Love is the chief characteristic of the saints and sages who have achieved some amount of Self-realization. The more we realize the Self, the greater is the natural flow of love in us.

According to the theory of Self-realization, joy and goodness are naturally present in the Self. In empirical life the joy of the Self manifests in the form of pleasure and the goodness of the Self manifests in the form of morality. In love the two — joy and goodness of the Self — are manifest in one. This is quite a plausible theory, and in this way pleasure (*kāma*) and morality (*dharma*) logically fit together in Self-realization (*mokṣa*).

The question may be asked here, if pleasure and morality are synthesized in Self-realization as is claimed, how can Self-realization (*mokṣa*) be called a deeper or higher value or even a value independent from pleasure and morality? Presented in the above manner, Self-realization seems to be just a combination of pleasure and morality. The answer is that a synthesis is not just a combination. The principle that synthesizes and incorporates others within itself is not one of them; it transcends them and stands at a higher or deeper level, like the thread that penetrates the flowers and weaves them into one garland. Similarly, *mokṣa* should be regarded as belonging to an order different from that of the other human values and yet incorporating them all within itself.

A further question may be asked, if Self-realization is not one of the values or at par with them, how can it be called a value in the strict sense of the term? The answer is that it is true that Self-realization is not at par with the other values, but why should it not be called a value on that account? Rather, Self-realization can be called the highest value as it is the value underlying all values, as we have seen. Self-realization will lose its eligibility for being called a value only when it ceases to be a desirable thing. If it is a desirable thing, whether at par with pleasure and morality or different from them, it remains a value; and Self-realization is perhaps the most desirable thing, as it is the very ground of all the other values.

The contention that Self-realization is a value higher than even morality (*dharma*) raises an important question, namely, whether there can be a value higher than morality, for morality is absolutely binding on everyone. In this sense, morality is the highest value, which cannot be subsumed into any other value. But, if there is a value that incorporates within itself all the merits of morality and at the same time is free from its demerits, then that value can certainly be called higher than the moral value. Western thought in general takes morality to be the highest value, but the Indian thinkers have found some gaps in this concept, and therefore they seek a still higher value in which morality finds its perfection.

There are two difficulties in the moral consciousness. First, in moral consciousness there is a dichotomy between the good (*śreya* or *dharma*) and the pleasant (*preya* or *kāma*), and one has to undermine or even totally suppress the pleasant in favor of the good. Psychoanalytically speaking, this dichotomy may be a hindrance to the process of the integration of the personality. Second, moral consciousness may generate an ego sense that is not only morally undesirable but is also detrimental to mental and spiritual health. A person who egotistically sees him- or herself as moral or righteous may harm him- or herself and society as well.

Considering these difficulties of moral consciousness, there arises the need of a state of consciousness that, on the one hand, preserves the merits of moral consciousness, and on the other hand, is free from the demerits of same. Spiritual consciousness is the answer to this need. Here it should be made clear that spirituality is a very vague and ambiguous term. I use the term spirituality here in a technical sense that I believe is the true sense of the word. Spirituality is different from religiosity; one can be spiritual without accepting external forms of religious worship. Of course spirituality can be said to be the essence of religion; but just as morality, although an essential part of religion, is different from religion, spirituality, although being the essence of religion, is not religion itself. Spirituality is also different from theology, as one can be spiritual even without having any kind of theistic belief.

As a working definition of spirituality, we can understand spirituality as a state of egoless consciousness that is also a state of natural goodness and in which one's own good and the good of others become one. In other words, awareness of one's unity with "others," that is, universal love, is the core of spirituality. Thus love in itself is a spiritual value, different from both the moral and religious values, for spirituality in itself is different from morality and religion. But in a secondary sense, love can also be considered to be both a moral and a religious value, as love, or spirituality, is the very essence of morality as well as of religion.

There should be no difficulty in understanding that spirituality preserves the merits of morality, as spirituality is a state of natural or spontaneous morality — a state of egoless morality. Spirituality not only preserves the merits of morality but also improves the quality of morality, for spiritual morality, that is, natural or egoless morality, is more satisfying to oneself and others than ethical morality. Moreover, spiritual morality appeals to our natural reason to be more sublime. Second, the difficulties of moral consciousness, namely (a) the dichotomy between the good and the pleasant and (b) the egotistic pride in being moral or of doing the moral act, are absent in spirituality. The moral ego is absent in spirituality because in spirituality we do not perform an act deliberately or effortfully as we do in morality; the activity flows in a natural and spontaneous way.

Moreover, in the state of spirituality the good done to others is felt to be done to oneself, just as happens in love. The mother, for example, does good to the child not out of thinking that it is moral to do so, as we do in the case of charity, but out of love in a natural and spontaneous way. Moreover, she feels that the good that she is doing to the child is her own good, as there is self-identification with the child. Love, which is a spiritual value, is the best example of the rectification of both the defects of morality. There is nothing as good and pure as love. Where there is love, there can be no immorality; on the contrary, love is the natural ground of all morality. Moreover, there is nothing more satisfying than the experience of love. Love is the most sublime thing in the world.

It can also be noticed that the degree as well as the quality of morality is raised in the naturally moral activity that is the characteristic of spirituality. We are inclined to do good to others more out of love, which is a spiritual phenomenon, than out of moral consideration. A Buddha, Christ, or any other spiritual person for that matter, is led to do good for society not out of the thought that it is moral to do so, but out of love or compassion for the masses. Activities of social service flow in great volumes from love, and not from the moral sense alone. A moral person may restrict him- or herself to doing good for society in a negative way, that is, he or she may refrain from causing anybody harm but he may not feel the strong incentive or inclination to do positive good for society. This incentive is present in the spiritual consciousness in abundance. As I have already mentioned, the good that one does to others in love is more satisfying to oneself as well as to others and is also much more desirable. Just as natural beauty is more precious than artificial beauty, so also the natural activity of goodness to others is more valuable. We would, for example, consider it to be more valuable, and therefore we would like it more, if someone helps us out of love than if someone helps us out of charity.

Thus we see that spirituality is a state of consciousness that has four relative advantages over morality, namely, (a) spirituality preserves the merits of morality, as it is the state of natural morality, (b) spirituality enhances the degree and quality of morality by making it natural and spontaneous, (c) there remains no egotistic pride in being moral, and (d) there is no dichotomy between the good and the pleasant, or between one's own good and the good of others.

Therefore, spirituality can definitely be called a higher value than morality. Needless to say Self-realization, which is the state of complete spirituality, is therefore a value higher than morality.

There is a lot of wisdom in the fact that the incarnation of Rāma is taken to be inferior to Kṛṣṇa. Rāma is seen as a not-so-perfect incarnation having only twelve "degrees" (*kalās*), and Kṛṣṇa is the "complete incarnation" (*pūrṇāvatāra*) having the full sixteen degrees. The reason for this is obvious. Rāma stands for the moral ideal that is absolutely necessary for the individual and social life; but in Rāma's life there is a conflict between the good and the pleasant, and Rāma has to undergo mental suffering from glorifying the good by rejecting the pleasant. In Kṛṣṇa, on the contrary, we find a perfect synthesis of the good and the pleasant; his life is a play of joy (*līlā*), which at the same time is naturally beneficial for others. The goodness that the life of Kṛṣṇa exhibits is natural and spontaneous; Kṛṣṇa is an egoless personality, a perfect example of egoless goodness. The goodness that is seen in the divine is really spiritual goodness that incorporates within itself, in a natural way, the moral goodness also.

Some scholars hold that Self-realization (*mokṣa*), unlike the values of pleasure (*kāma*), wealth (*artha*), and morality (*dharma*) of the *trivarga* scheme, is a personal value, as in *mokṣa* one is concerned with one's own salvation or one's own bliss, however deep or exalted that bliss may be, and this has nothing to do with others. Morality consists in one's attitude towards others; in morality others are involved, that is, society is involved, thus morality is not a personal value; but there is no such thing in Self-realization.

If by saying that Self-realization is a personal pursuit what is meant is that Self-realization is attained and experienced by the individual, then Self-realization of course *is* personal, as it is a subjective experience of the individual. All experience is subjective and therefore all experience is personal in that sense. But this does not mean that Self-realization is restricted to the individual and others are not involved. The concept of Self-realization that I have put forth here necessarily involves consideration for others, for Self-realization, as we have already discussed, is by definition the state of universal love. If one does not love or feel one's unity with "others," one is not liberated or Self-realized. The Self of the Self-realized person is enlarged so much that it incorporates all within itself. Loving "others" and doing good to "others" is, as we have already seen, part of *mokṣa*-consciousness. In fact, in Self-realization, personal and impersonal, within and without, oneself and others, subjective and objective, become one.

Some people also maintain that Self-realization is not a functional value. Perhaps they think that, unlike morality (*dharma*), which performs the function of regulating wealth (*artha*) and pleasure (*kāma*), Self-realization is merely a state or structure; it does not perform any function. However the type of Self-realization that we are discussing is a functional one. As we have already seen, Self-realization performs the function of synthesizing the good and the pleasant and providing the ground for all around success in every field of life and in every aspect of life — material, moral, and spiritual. Of course in the Indian tradition there are some schools — like Sāṁkhya, scholastic Advaita Vedānta, or some schools of Buddhism — that define liberation (*mokṣa*, *kaivalya*, or *nirvāṇa*) in a non-functional way; but the *Śaiva* and *Vaiṣṇava* conceptions of liberation or Self-realization are quite different.

The Tantric concept of Self-realization in particular, which I consider to be perfectly in line with the original Upaniṣadic position but not the post-Sāṁkarite scholastic Advaitism, is both structural and functional. It combines both freedom-from and freedom-to. The nature of the Self, or Consciousness, that is realized in the state of liberation is, according to Tantrism, dynamic; this dynamism — technically called *spanda*, *kriyā*, *śakti*, or *vimarśa* enables the state of Self-realization to perform the functions logically assigned to it. The Self-realized person, for example, pays positive attention to the redemption of the suffering of the masses or to the betterment of society and aptly responds to any demand of the situation. The dynamism or *spanda* of the Self leads the liberated person to naturally and spontaneously take part in socio-political activities, to engage in artistic creativity, to successfully and pleasantly discharge his or her duties, and so on. Creative activity is the natural effulgence, or spontaneous emanation of the Self. Self-realization performs the function of providing all these things. It also provides, as we have already seen, the very ground of morality in the form of love and natural goodness. All the above-mentioned things are necessary for a healthy life, both individual and social. Thus, Self-realization is a highly functional value.

The question may be asked, if Self-realization is such an important value, why do people not desire it or why are they not inclined towards it? In answer to this I will say three things. First, the eligibility of something as a value does not depend upon its actually being desired by people: a value means something that *should* be desired not necessrily what *is* desired. Second, if people knew that Self-realization is the fulfillment of all values, material and moral, they would certainly be inclined to pursue it. Third, people may not desire Self-realization in the technical and traditional sense, but they do desire it in a very general way, and what is more, everyone desires Self-realization in this way. It is obvious that everybody desires happiness and tries to avoid sorrow. We want complete happiness and complete freedom from undesirable things. But this does not happen; we find ourselves encountering limitations on all sides, and therefore we are not able to attain complete happiness. We see ourselves as a finite or imperfect being, bound by countless limitations. Consciously or unconsciously we desire that all our chains be broken and we become completely free from limitations, for we know that to be completely happy means to be completely free from limitations. It means to become infinite. We may not be able to find the way out of our finitude, but we do wish to become perfect or to enjoy happiness. This is what is technically called *mokṣa* ("liberation"), which lies in Self-realization. Thus we can very well say that everyone is seeking *mokṣa* without knowing it by this technical name. Whether such a state of perfection, or liberation exists or not is a different question, and we will take it up later on.

The *Chāndogya Upaniṣad*, while positing the existence of Self-realization, does not start with Brahman; it starts with an inquiry into the human predicament of limitation or finitude. The Upaniṣadic seer clearly envisages the logical truth that to be happy means to be free from limitation. That is why the Upaniṣad says, "In that which is infinite (*bhūmā*), there lies happiness (*sukha*); there is no happiness in the finite (*alpa*)."[69] Liberation is thus not an unknown or undesired value but the highest value; it is both desired and desirable.

Finally, there is the question of the validity of the spiritual experience called Self-realization or liberation (*mokṣa*). It is obvious that the concept of Self-realization is based on the acceptance of an ontological reality called the Self or Consciousness. Now the question arises, what is the logical proof for this alleged ontological reality? How can we be sure that such a thing does exist? Normally, we do not find such a thing in our experience; it is not known by the empirical mode that is normally the only mode of knowing available to us. So, can we not say that the concept of Self-realization is just the speculation of an imaginative mind and is based on faith, not on actual experience? It is obvious that along with our bodies there is a knowing or thinking principle that we call the "I" (the self) or "consciousness." This "I" is postulated by the *cogito ergo sum* of Descartes, the *ya eva hi nirākartā tasyaivātmatvāt* ("One who denies the self, that denier itself is the self")[70] of Advaita Vedānta, and the *kartari jñātari svātmanyādisiddhe maheśvare* ("The self is present as the doer and the knower in the very beginning of all behavior")[71] of Kashmir Śaivism. But it is also clear that these arguments do not succeed in proving the ontological self; all they prove is that there is an epistemological principle of knowing or thinking. It is beyond our ability to know whether this epistemological principle is just Kant's "synthetic unity of pure apperception," which is just a formal unity, or is also a metaphysical reality or entity. It is from this point that metaphysical speculations as well as scientific hypotheses about the Self or Consciousness start.

It is reasonable to believe, as the spiritualist maintains, that the phenomenon of consciousness which we call the self or the "I" that appears at the surface level, is just the tip of a bigger reality lying deeper in us, like the iceberg, only a tiny portion of which is visible above the surface, or like an artesian spring that is invisibly connected with a deeper and vaster underground water reserve. If we accept this it follows that we can reach the deeper levels of our reality step by step. Self-realization can be achieved in degrees. Even at present we have some degree of Self-realization, as the power of Consciousness, which is called *kuṇḍalini* in the symbolic language of Tantric yoga, is already working in us in the form of the mental phenomena. Obviously it is possible that in different people this Consciousness becomes manifest in varying degrees, either naturally or by the deliberate process of unfolding the beauties of Consciousness. We can logically stretch this process to the extent of achieving the fullest manifestation of Consciousness — Self-realization or spiritual attainment in the highest degree.

The theory of Self-realization is not speculation nor is it based on faith; it is actually based on experience. In the Tantric tradition, Self-realization is accepted on the basis of inductive experience (*āgama*), as opposed to the authority of scripture, which is deductive (*nigama*). Of course this inductive experience is higher than ordinary sensory (empirical) induction. There is nothing illogical in maintaining that there could be modes of experience other than the strictly empirical one. To stick to the position that the empirical is the only mode of knowing is nothing short of irrational, rigid dogmatism.[72]

To conclude, I have in the foregoing pages tried to show that acceptance of the possibility of Self-realization is warranted in the consideration of the three-fold life values system and that it is the highest value, as it forms the very ground, or is the underlying reality, of all the values.

It is also clear from this treatment of Self-realization that it cannot be included in pleasure (*kāma*), as some people suggest. Some propose that if Self-realization is to be incorporated in the scheme of human values at all, it should be included in pleasure (*kāma*). But this proposal is not acceptable, as Self-realization is something basically different from pleasure. One may retort that the desire for perfection or freedom from limitations, that is, the desire for Self-realization, can by virtue of being a desire, be included within the realm of pleasure (*kāma*). In answer we might point out that the desire for perfection or complete freedom from limitations belongs to a different level, as it is the desire for the very ground or the underlying reality of all the values, including pleasure (*kāma*). The term *kāma* is used to denote a particular order of desires, namely, material or psycho-physical desires. *All* desires cannot be included in this realm. For example, in spiritually advanced people there is a natural desire for morality (*dharma*). Should the desire for morality be included in the category of pleasure (*kāma*) simply because it is a desire? Desires are not only of different types of the same order, but they are also of different orders or levels. The desire for Self-realization is certainly of a different order, and to include it within the realm of pleasure is an over-simplification.

To sum up the theory of human values (*puruṣārtha*), we can understand the values in a hierarchical order. Wealth (*artha*) is meant to represent the fulfillment of the gross physical or bodily needs like food, shelter, and so on. Gross physical or biological needs are certainly different from desires, which are more mental or psychological, and therefore, subtler and more refined. In this sense, pleasure (*kāma*) may be regarded as higher than wealth (*artha*) in the hierarchy of value. Morality (*dharma*) is still higher, for wealth and pleasure can be sacrificed in favor of morality.

If liberation is understood not in the negative sense of the absence of worldly life but in the positive sense of Self-realization — realizing and completely expressing the Consciousness that is present in every enjoyment and every activity of life, liberation will certainly be regarded as the highest value in life. Self-realization is the highest value, as it transcends all the other values and synthesizes them within itself. Since the synthesizing principle transcends the synthesized terms and stands at a deeper level, Self-realization should be regarded as belonging to an order different from that of the other life values and yet incorporating them all within itself.

STAGES OF THE SPIRITUAL EVOLUTION OF THE SOUL

Self-realization is not attained in one flash; it involves the gradual evolution of the soul. Self-realization is a question of self-purification; the more the consciousness is freed from impurity (*mala*), the more the light of the Self is revealed and the more the Self is realized. The removal of impurity is a negative process, and the positive side of the removal of impurity is Self-realization. Although there is really no difference in the nature of consciousness, a difference is seen because of the hierarchical state of freedom from impurity.[73] We can understand this position with the help of the analogy of light. When a brilliant light passes through a curtain, it becomes dim; when the obstruction is removed, the light is restored to its original brilliance. The more the curtain is thinned or made more transparent, the brighter the light becomes.

Similarly, the more the impurity (*mala*) is removed from a person, the more the light of the Self comes to the fore, which means the greater is the Self-realization. Even in our present state of impurity we have some amount of Self-realization, for the light of the Self, or Consciousness, is already working in and through us. The amount and degree of the expression of the light of Consciousness varies from person to person.

Moreover, in the analogy of the light we can see that it is the thinning or purification of the curtain, or obstruction, and not of the light itself; the light is ever pure. We call the light impure because of the impurity of the curtain. Similarly, Consciousness, or the Self, is ever pure. It is called impure because when it passes through the impurities, its nature is dimmed or obstructed.

Thus we can see that the removal of impurity and the realization of the Self go together in equal proportion.[74] Since there can be grades of self-purification, there can be grades of Self-realization also. This means, further, that there can be hierarchical variation among the different aspirants for Self-realization and also among those who have attained it.

The attainment of Self-realization is a gradual process — a development or growth of consciousness. It is not that one is in bondage and then all of a sudden one becomes liberated; there is no leap or jump from the stage of bondage to the stage of liberation. It is a gradual trek from one stage to the other.

This is not to suggest that there are degrees of Consciousness or degrees of Reality. There are actually no degrees in Consciousness or the Self. But we can still meaningfully use the term "degree" to suggest that there is a hierarchical variation in the removal of impurities from the heart, and subsequently, a hierarchical variation in the attainment of Self-realization.

Advaita Vedānta seems to suggest that there is no gradual attainment of Self-realization. According to Advaita, one is either bound or one is liberated, there is no such thing as half-bound or half-free. In the analogy of the rope-snake, either one sees the snake in ignorance, or one sees the rope in knowledge. In the dream analogy, either one is dreaming or one has awakened. There is a gap between the dream state and the waking state; the transition from the dream to the waking state is a single jump, not a gradual process.

What the Advaitin seems to forget is that this does not happen in the case of Self-realization. Self-realization is not a sudden jump from the state of bondage to the state of liberation. If someone seems to become liberated suddenly it is because he or she has been following the path of purification for a long time, maybe from previous births, and the veil, already thinned after a long process of purification, is finally removed.[75] Of course if purification is sudden,

Self-realization will also be sudden. But in actual life we find that purification is not sudden; it is not as easy and simple as the Advaitin thinks.

The reason why Advaita overlooks this fact of life is that it approaches the problem of Self-realization purely from the epistemic point of view; it sets aside the axiological consideration that is supreme in the Upaniṣads. The Advaitin would use the analogy of darkness and say that complete darkness can be set aside in a moment by just igniting a match and lighting a lamp; it does not take a long, arduous effort to demolish the darkness. Similarly he or she would argue bondage, which is ignorance, can be dispelled by a flash of knowledge; ignorance is not like a physical mountain that takes long years of effort to demolish. But again the Advaitin forgets that this ignorance is not mere intellectual ignorance (*bauddha-ajñāna*) but is *pauruṣa-ajñāna*, which captures the entire person in the form of spiritual impurity (*mala*). This cannot be removed simply by learning scriptures or hearing the teacher. Had it been so, all the great pandits of philosophy would have attained Self-realization. This type of ignorance can be removed only by doing the spiritual practice (*sādhanā*) of self-purification. The intellectual knowledge of Reality can help only when *pauruṣa-jñāna* is attained side by side with it.

Had the Advaitin also considered the issue from the axiological point of view, that is from the point of view of the actual attainment of Self-realization, he or she would have easily realized the limitation of the rope-snake analogy. But the Advaitin becomes complacent with the epistemic consistency of the theory and forgets that when this philosophy is applied to actual life situations it becomes logically absurd.

Since there is a gradual evolution of the state of consciousness moving towards Self-realization, the Tantric tradition accepts hierarchical grades of souls. Seven grades of souls are noted. They are called the seven "knowers" or seven "subjects" (*sapta-pramātā*). The soul is called the "knower" or "subject" (*pramātā*) because it is different from the insentient matter that is the "known" or the "object" (*prameya*). The essential nature of soul (consciousness) that distinguishes it from matter is that it is the knowing subject.[76] So, knower or *pramātā* may be taken as the synonym of soul or consciousness. The distinction among the seven knowers is based on considering in each how far limited individuality is undermined and Śivahood or divinity is manifest.[77] This depends upon how far the soul is purified or freed from *mala*.

The seven knowers are (a) *pralayākala* or *layākala*, (b) *sakala*, (c) *vijñānākala* or *jñānākala*, (d) *mantra*, (e) *mantreśvara*, (f) *mantra-maheśvara*, and (g) Śiva (*Śiva-pramātā*). The first three, *pralayākala*, *sakala*, and *vijñānākala*, belong to the impure stage of bondage or *mala* (impurity), and the remaining four, *mantra*, *mantreśvara*, *mantra-maheśvara*, and *Śiva-pramātā*, belong to the pure state. The term *sakala* is also used to denote the bound soul in general in distinction with the freed soul, which is called *niṣkala* or *akala*.[78] *Kalā*, with which the word for the bound soul is suffixed, denotes "impure *kalā*" or impure functioning of the soul (consciousness).

The *pralayākala*, or *layākala*, as the very name suggests, is the soul that is in the state of *laya* or *pralaya*("dissolution"). In the state of the dissolution of the world, the souls lie in a stupor. This is a state of deep, unconscious rest, as in deep sleep. *Pralayākala* is the primordial state of individual consciousness where consciousness is not functioning — this is the state of sleeping consciousness. The impurities exist, but since the soul is sleeping the impurities are also lying in a potential state,[79] they have not arisen or awakened. *Pralayākala* is the initial state of the bound soul — its primordial state.

Pralayākala is not there only when the world is dissolved. Actually *pralayākala* denotes the initial stage of consciousness where the consciousness is sleeping in an embryonic state, as it were;[80] the world, even if it is there, for all practical purposes has not yet arisen for the soul. Thus *pralayākala* stands for the initial stage from which the development of the soul starts. In this stage the soul does not do or know anything, but the potential capacity for the same is very much there.[81]

The second stage is that of *sakala.* This is the state of the soul awakened from the dissolution (*pralaya*). In this state the soul is fully conscious, although tainted with all three impurities (*malas*). In the *pralayākala* stage the impurities are not active, for the soul is sleeping, but in the *sakala* stage, since the soul is fully awake all the impurities become manifest and are at work. *Sakala* is the stage in which the people of the world normally are.

The *saṁskāras,* which were dormant during the state of *pralayākala,* are aroused in the state of *sakala* and bound souls (*sakalas*) move in the cycle of birth and death taking bodies merited by their *karma.*[82] In the process of the evolution of the soul it is necessary that the potential dispositions (*saṁskāras*), or seed desires, be actualized in order that they can be eliminated finally. Although the *pralayākala* state is free from the tumult of the world, as the soul is sleeping in ignorance, it is inferior to *sakala* in the hierarchy, for the *saṁskāras* are yet to be actualized. The sleeping soul, in order to achieve its freedom in the Śiva-stage, must pass though the *sakala* stage so that the soul works out its *karma* and exhausts its potentialities.

The third stage of the bound soul is *vijñānākala.* The special feature of *vijñānākala* is that it is free of *kārma-mala* and *māyīya-mala* and only *āṇava-mala,* which is responsible for limited individuality, exists there.[83] *Āṇava* is the last to go, for it was first to come. *Āṇava* generates the *māyīya* and *kārma malas.* In the *sakala* state all the *malas* are present, but when the soul moves upward, the last two *malas* (*māyīya* and *kārma*) take leave. This is a highly purified state, but since *āṇava,* sense of individuality, is still there, the soul at the *vijñānākala* stage is still bound. That soul stands at the threshhold of liberation; it has crossed the main stages of māyic bondage and is looking forward to entering into the state of pure knowledge, *śuddhavidyā.* That is why the *vijñānākala* soul is said to be above *māyā* and below *śuddhavidyā*;[84] the soul has reached the final exit gate of *māyā,* but has yet to enter into the realm of the pure categories (*śuddhādhvā*). In this state, impurity (*mala*) is in the final process of being destroyed,[85] but is yet to have all traces completely removed. That is why the soul in *vijñānākala* does not fully realize its unity with Śiva.[86]

Vijñānākala is so called because it is a fairly high stage of knowledge (*vijñāna* or *jñāna*), but it is knowledge alone, the divine dynamism (*kriyā*, or *śakti*) has not yet become manifest.[87] A soul at the level of *vijñānākala* is at the door of divinity; it has not yet attained divinity and is still awaiting the divine powers to manifest within it. The saints, devotees, good and pure hearted people, and so on, can be classified under the category of *vijñānākala*. Such persons have a fair degree of spiritual advancement by virtue of freedom from impurity but are yet to be liberated.

If we view the categories of *pralayākala*, *sakala*, and *vijñānākala* from the angle of the three qualities or *gunas* (*tamas*, *rajas*, and *sattva*), we find that *pralayākala* is pure *tamas*, for one in that state is sleeping. *Sakala* is the state of *rajas*, as one in that state is active. In *vijñānākala* one reaches the stage of pure *sattva*, as one is highly purified and consequently knowledge manifests in one. *Sattva* is the state of purity. It is also non-obstructive to knowledge or illumination of the Self. A person of *sattva* will have inner illumination, knowledge, or awareness, as *sattva* allows the illumination of Consciousness (Self) to shine forth, just as a thin white curtain does not impede the light but allows it to pass. The quality of *tamas* is like a heavy black curtain that fully obstructs the light; *rajas* is like a red curtain that allows some light to pass through. The color of *tamoguṇa* is seen as black, that of *rajoguṇa* as red, and that of *sattvaguṇa* as white. This is very significant and relates to the degree to which they obstruct light.

The model of the three *guṇas* (*sattva*, *rajas*, and *tamas*) set forth by the Sāṁkhya system and accepted by almost all the systems of Indian philosophy, is a very good model for understanding the personality differences and the different stages of the evolution of people. This model can easily be applied to the *pralayākala*, *sakala*, and *vijñānākala* stages. If we look to the characteristics of the three knowers (*pramātās*) and compare them to the *guṇas*, it will appear that the distinction between the three knowers is based on the consideration of the distinction of the three *guṇas*, although this is not explicitly mentioned. The chief characteristic of the *pralayākala* is his or her long stupor or sleep, which is nothing but the product of *tamoguṇa*. In *rajoguṇa* the person is awake and active, for activity *karma* is the characteristic of *rajoguṇa*. The *sakala* state is exactly this; the *sakala* is awake, performing action, and moving in different bodies. The chief characteristic of *sattvaguṇa* is *jñāna* ("knowledge"), which is also the chief characteristic of the *vijñānākala*. It is also comparable that *sattva*, although a high state of purification, is not the state of freedom or liberation; the *sāttvika* is still within bondage, although knocking at the door of freedom. This is also the case with *vijñānākala*. The point is that the model of the three *guṇas* can be applied to the three *pramātās* so perfectly that it leaves little doubt about the distinction of the *pramātās* being based on the consideration of the three *guṇas*. However, it is a puzzle why this is not explicitly mentioned.

The next four knowers (*pramātās*) — *mantra*, *mantreśvara*, *mantra-maheśvara*, and Śiva (Śiva-*pramātā*) — belong to the realm of pure categories (*śuddhādhvā*). The first three are the correlates, respectively, of *sadviḍyā*, *īśvara*, and *sadāśiva*, which are the stages of pure Creation (*śuddhādhvā*). The reason why they are called by the name *mantra* is that they ideate the Creation within themselves. The word *mantra* is formed from *manana* (*mananānmantraḥ*), which means "thinking" or "ideating." Creation is nothing but the thinking or ideating of Śiva, who is Consciousness or the Self. According to Kashmir Śaivism and Tantrism in general, Consciousness is the only Reality and Creation is within Consciousness; it is a projection of Consciousness and not a material creation, for there is no matter at all. So Creation is an ideation (*manana* or *mantraṇa*) of Śiva-Consciousness. Hence, while doing the activity of Creation, Śiva becomes the *mantra* ("one who ideates"). *Mantra-maheśvara*, *mantreśvara*, and *mantra* are the different hierarchical stages of Śiva's ideating activity of Creation.

Thus the three *mantra*-categories, which are the stages of pure Creation, are the free manifestations of Śiva himself.[88] When Śiva "wishes to create the world and enjoy Creation, He becomes *mantra-maheśvara*, who creates the world by mobilizing His *māyā-śakti*."[89]

Here a question may be asked, why does Śiva descend three stages to create the world, why does one stage not suffice? The answer is that there are naturally three stages in every creation. The first is the will to create (*icchā*, the Sadāśiva stage); in the second stage the world becomes an idea in the mind (*jñāna*, the Īśvara stage); finally, in the third stage, the world is projected externally (*kriyā*, the *sadvidyā* stage). All three stages are necessary in every creation. The division of Śiva into the three creational forms is based upon the prominence of the different aspects or *śaktis* needed for Creation.[90]

When the *vijñānākala* soul by shaking off its only remaining impurity, *āṇava-mala*, becomes free and enters into the realm of pure categories (*śuddhādhvā*), it first becomes or identifies itself with *sadvidyā*. At this stage it ideates the world as "I am and this is" (*ahaṁ ca idaṁ ca*). This is the *mantra* stage. Then it moves upward and identifies itself with Īśvara (*jñāna-śakti*) and ideates the world as "this I am" (*idamaham*). This is the *mantreśvara* stage. Then it reaches the initial stage of Creation and identifies with Sadāśiva (*icchā-śakti*), and ideates the world as "I am this" (*ahamidam*). This is the *mantra-maheśvara* stage. Thus the knower (*pramātā*), "realizing his unity with Śiva, gradually rises through *mantra* and *mantreśvara* to *mantramaheśvara* and finally reaches the Śiva-state by the grace of Śiva."[91]

The reason the *mantra* categories — *mantra*, *mantreśvara*, and *mantra-maheśvara* — are called "pure" (*śuddha*) even when there is the duality of the object at their stage, is that although the knower sees the object, it does not take the object to be different from or other than itself but takes the object to be its own projection and therefore one with it. In Kashmir Śaivism, the presence of the duality of the object is not itself impurity; what is impurity is the taking of the object to be different from oneself or other than oneself. This is the sense of duality (*dvaita-prathā*).

Mantra-maheśvara, or Sadāśiva, who is the sixth knower (*pramātā*), is the highest or the first stage of Creation, and *mantra*, or Sadvidyā, is the last stage of (pure) Creation. The seventh and highest knower is Śiva (Śiva-*pramātā*), which is not itself a category of Creation. Śiva, or the Śiva-*pramātā*, is beyond Creation, it is the matrix of all Creation.

There is no separate knower category for Śakti (no Śakti-*pramātā*), because although at the highest stage of the pure categories there are two principles — Śiva and Śakti — yet the two form one and the same state of Consciousness, called *parā* ("the transcendent"). Śiva is also Śakti or Śiva-Śakti. The Śiva-*pramātā* may also be called the Śakti-*pramātā* or the Śiva-Śakti-*pramātā*. This is because Śiva and Śakti, which form the transcendent state, are not *two* but one.

9

The Means of Mokṣa

We have already seen that liberation (*mokṣa*), which is a state of Self-realization, is attainable through the removal of ignorance (*ajñāna*), which is impurity (*mala*). The impurity can be removed because impurity is not part and parcel of the Self. If impurity was the nature of the Self (Śiva), it could not be removed, or it could not be removed without the removal of the Self Itself. There are efficacious means of removing the impurity and thereby attaining the Self. The way of attaining or realizing the Self by removing the impurity is called *upāya*. The word *upāya* is translated as "the means" or "the way." What is to be achieved is called the *upeya* or *sādhya* ("the end"), and the way to achieve it is called the *upāya* or *sādhana* ("the means").

The above position is very beautifully expressed in the Four Noble Truths (*ārya-satyas*) discovered by the Buddha. Suffering is a fact in the world that cannot be denied; suffering (*duḥkha*) is thus the first truth (*duḥkha-satya*). But the suffering is not an independent reality; it is caused or dependent (*pratītyasamutpanna*), and the cause is ignorance (*avidyā*). Thus the second truth is that suffering is dependent or caused (*samudaya-satya*). If suffering is dependent and not self-existent, this implies that if the cause of the suffering is destroyed, then the effect (suffering) will also be destroyed. And the nature of the cause is such that ignorance (*avidyā* or *ajñāna*), which is the cause of suffering, can be removed (*nirodha-satya*). If the cause of suffering can be removed, then there must also be a way (*mārga*) for removing it. The fourth truth is that there is such a path (*mārga-satya*).

The final question then is that of the path or means. There are a variety of paths. There are also different systems of philosophy and religion advocating the different paths.

EFFORT AND GRACE

Before we deal with the path or means (*upāya*) of liberation (*mokṣa*), it is relevant to consider the question of whether *mokṣa* is attained through self-effort or by the grace of God (Śiva). This is a profound question and philosophers have frequently addressed themselves to it. Buddhism and Jainism believe that liberation is attained through self-purification; purifying oneself is one's own business — it is something that one alone can do.[1] If one decides not to follow the path of self-purification leading to Self-realization, no guru or God can help one. The guru can at the most show one the path, but following it is completely up to the individual. According to Buddhism and Jainism then, one can attain liberation or Self-realization through one's own effort. Since Buddhism and Jainism lay emphasis on self-effort, they are called the *śramaṇa* tradition. The word *śramaṇa* comes from *śrama*, which means "labor" or "effort." *Śramaṇa* thus means one who believes in the effectiveness of effort or self-effort in the attainment of liberation.

The Vedic traditions, including the Vaiṣṇava and the Śaiva, believe in the power of grace (*anugraha*, *puṣṭi*, *kripā*, or *śaktipāta*) combined with self-effort. They accept the role of grace in the attainment of both worldly enjoyment (*bhukti*) and liberation (*mukti*).

Material things such as money and success, as well as Self-realization, can be attained by the grace of God.

It is not very difficult to understand that the powers with which the ego is endowed are not the powers of the ego itself; they are the powers of the higher Self (*paramātman*), or God. All power comes from a source beyond the ego. In order to realize this truth, it is not necessary to believe in God; even an atheist can see that the ego itself is not the source of power. A scientist, for example, can see that the power is Nature's, and the ego succeeds only when Nature is cooperating with it.

From this it follows that whatever the ego achieves, it achieves with the help of the power of God or Nature. If God or Nature withdraws the power, the ego can do nothing. The ego may falsely take the credit for itself and may be vain enough to think that it is the real doer, but the truth is otherwise. An athlete for example, may think that the power in his or her muscles comes from him- or herself, and he or she may take pride in that power, but it is really endowed by Nature. The moment Nature withdraws Her cooperation — say for example, when the athlete incurs a paralytic attack — the power of the muscles deserts him or her. The power of intelligence also exists because Nature has bestowed it; it is not the ego's creation. The same is true with any talent or any form of power. The ego in itself is a cipher; it works with the power that comes from a source other than itself.

This situation is explained by Kashmir Śaivism in terms of grace (*anugraha*) — the showering or automatic emerging of power (*śaktipāta*). Śiva (the Self) is the source of all power; nothing can work without being connected to this powerhouse.[2] The electricity that works at various levels flows from the powerhouse automatically. Likewise when we open the window blinds the light automatically comes in and dispels the darkness. We do not fetch or bring it; it comes of its own accord. Similarly when the impurity is removed, the illumination from the inner Self comes automatically, bringing with it self-fulfillment. This is what is called *grace* or *śaktipāta.*[3] It is called *grace* because the light of Consciousness comes automatically of its own accord; we do not cause it to come. If it chooses not to manifest, we cannot force it to; whenever it comes, it comes freely. We also cannot determine the sequence (krama) in which *śaktipāta* occurs, for Consciousness is free.[4]

Although grace (*śaktipāta*) is the free manifestation of Śiva-Consciousness, this does not mean that Śiva showers His grace arbitrarily. He showers it on deserving people only. If the undeserving also received the grace, it would go against reason and the moral governance of the world. It would also mean that arbitrariness exists in Śiva. Freedom is not arbitrariness. Śiva's freedom in the dispensing of grace means that there is no compulsion on the part of Śiva in showering grace. Of course, He *can* become arbitrary if He so chooses. But why should He? Why should He act in an illogical way by showering grace on the undeserving? He is not like a wanton child misusing its freedom, or like a whimsical king distributing gifts blindly. This is similar to the question, can God be bad? While God has the capacity to be bad, He prefers to be good and chooses goodness freely.

The grace (*kripā*) of God is called *ahetukī* ("without cause or motive"), and sometimes *ahetukī* is misinterpreted as "without the consideration of the worthiness of the candidate." Some thus believe that God can give His grace even to the undeserving. It is argued that if God gives grace only to the deserving, then God is not free, He becomes bound by this rule. But what the arguer forgets here is that this is, in essence, making the act of God arbitrary and acting arbitrarily is a demerit.

Actually, *ahetukī kripā* does not mean grace "without the consideration of worthiness;" it means grace "without any motive." If there is some selfish motive in the act of helping others, then it is not grace. God has no selfish motive in showering grace on the souls; He does it purely for their benefit. He has nothing to gain by it. This is the meaning of "grace without motive." Śiva, in order to shower grace on a person, requires only that person's surrender (*bhakti*), and does not consider his or her caste, profession, position, and so on.[5]

To summarize, grace (*śaktipāta*) has two characteristics: (a) it is completely motiveless; God does it purely for the benefit of the souls, not for any benefit to Himself; (b) it is a completely free act; there is no compulsion. Nothing can force God to bestow grace; He gives it freely.

The grace of God is not arbitrary. We receive grace only when we deserve it, and only to the extent that we deserve it. According to Kashmir Śaivism, the grace of God is showered equally on all, but we receive it and benefit from it only to the extent that we have opened up to it. Like the rainfall from heaven, it can only fill the jar if the jar is uncovered. Like the light of the sun waiting outside our house, it can enter inside only when we keep the shades open. Opening the window blinds is *our* part of the task. God, the Light, resides in us as our own higher Self with all its brilliance, but it only becomes manifest to the extent our heart is purified; the Light cannot reveal itself through a state of impurity.[6] It requires the effort of self-purification. In this sense grace *is* proportionate to self-effort.

The question may be raised here that if grace depends on self-effort, then it becomes a matter of right; it is earned by self-effort, and it no longer remains grace. In answer Kashmir Śaivism would point out that even then it is grace, for even if we are highly deserving, we cannot force God to bestow His grace if He chooses to withhold it. Suppose a rich person donates a scholarship to a school, laying down certain conditions for getting the scholarship. A student fulfills the conditions and gets the scholarship. The student may argue that he or she has earned the scholarship by fulfilling the conditions, so his or her good fortune is not due to grace. But is it not grace? However deserving the student may be, he or she could not get the scholarship if the donor had not established it in the first place. And donating the scholarship is the free choice of the donor.

Similarly, however deserving we may become, we cannot force God to shower His grace if He chooses to withhold it. God, like the benevolent donor, donates His grace and lays down the conditions for receiving it. It remains grace even when we deserve it.

Thus we see that grace and self-effort go together. *Mukti* or Self-realization, the highest value of life, is achieved by the grace merited by self-effort. It is natural for Śiva (the "Benign Lord") to shower His grace, but it is up to us to avail ourselves of that grace by opening up to Him. Showering grace is the *Lord's* part of the work, and making an effort in order to get its benefit is *our* part of the work. Grace is *God's* free activity and self-effort is *ours*— even the Lord does not interfere in our efforts. In the *Gītā*, Lord Kṛṣṇa, after delivering his message to Arjuna, says to him, "Now you can do as you like."[7] The Lord's duty is fulfilled once the divine message has reached humanity; then it is up to humanity to follow it. The attainment of Self-realization is entirely in the hands of the individual; in this sense the freedom of God and the freedom of humanity go together. There is thus no contradiction in the two statements "everything is obtained by grace" and "everything is obtained through self-effort."

THE UNITY OF THE MEANS AND THE END

In the path (*sādhanā*) leading to Self-realization (*mokṣa*), the end (the *upeya* or *sādhya*) and the means (the *upāya* or *sādhanā*) coincide. The reason for this is simple. One has to become what one already is. One is already Śiva, one's Śivahood is just veiled or obstructed for the time being. In order for the veil to be removed and for one to become Śiva, one has to recultivate the qualities that Śiva has. Śiva is goodness, love, truth, egolessness, and so on, and one has to have all these characteristics in order to become Śiva.

The Self is completely good; that is why it is called *śiva*, which means "good," "benign," or "noble." This goodness is spiritual goodness, which is also a state of natural morality. Spiritual goodness includes all conceivable goodness. When we say, "Śiva is good," this means that Śiva is good from all angles. In order to become one with Śiva, one has to become good. There are indirect ways of becoming good, and there is the way (*sādhanā*) of becoming good directly. Charity, service, love, kindness, compassion, devotion to God, meditation (or relaxation in the Self) — all these indirectly make one good. One who practices these becomes good. But we can also practice to become good directly. Becoming good is a deliberate act, and so the practice (*sādhanā*) of becoming good is a deliberate one that we can undertake every day. When a teacher tells us "be good," we do not ask him or her how to be good, for we know that we can become good directly if we so choose. Becoming good involves creating an attitude of goodness, which can be done deliberately also.

We may not be quite clear as to what goodness exactly consists of, but we do understand something by the term *goodness* when someone tells us to be good. Whatever concept of goodness we have or however we understand the meaning of "to be good," we can practice to become that ideal.

"To be good" also means "to be pure at heart." Purity of heart is the ultimate object of all disciplines. There may be other, indirect means of self-purification, but purity of heart can be directly practiced also. Again we may not be quite clear about the exact content of purity, but we do understand something by "purity of heart," and we have to practice that.

It is not enough that we decide to become good or pure. We have to make it a daily practice. The inner tendencies (*saṁskāras*) toward impurity and non-goodness exist in us and drive us again and again to impurity. We have to daily undertake the task of purifying our hearts or making ourselves good, and then a time will come when we are no longer in the state of "doing" good but have reached the state of "being" good, where purity and goodness automatically exist. But while we have not reached the state of "being" (*ātma-sthiti* in Kashmir Śaivism) and are still in the state of "doing," we have to practice regular self-purification, otherwise the undesirable inclinations (*saṁskāras*) will come up again.

Śiva is also Truth. This means not only the ontological truth of existence, but also the moral truth of righteous living. This is the spiritual truth that naturally includes the moral truth also, as we have already seen. For a man like Gandhi, God means nothing but Truth. The Buddha did not mention God but he did mention Truth, which he called *dharma*, and it is the life of *dharma* that he asked people to live. In order to reach Śiva, who is Truth, one has to live a life of truthfulness. Truthfulness does not necessarily and exclusively mean truth in speaking — that is, not telling lies; it means truthfulness of behavior, which further means an honest and straightforward life free from hypocrisy.

The most significant characteristic of the state of Śivahood is love. Śiva is aware of His unity with the entire universe of sentient beings and insentient objects. In the dualistic system of Śaiva Siddhānta (southern Śaivism), and also in Christianity, the essential nature of God is seen as love. God (Śiva) is perfect love for all creatures, and He acts for their good in a completely selfless way. Śiva has no selfishness at all; He has nothing to gain from anyone or anything. Śiva is the state of pure love. In order to attain Śivahood, we are required to adopt the practice (*sādhanā*) of universal love. Of all the ways to Self-realization, love is the most efficacious. It is also the most satisfying, as love is the experience of joy. Love is the surest means of Self-realization. Of all the systems of spiritual philosophy, Kashmir Śaivism is the one that lays the most emphasis on the practice of *advaita-bhāvanā* — universal love, the feeling of one's unity with all.

Again, like the practice of becoming good and pure, the practice of love also has to be cultivated. Love may be present in the human consciousness as an inherent disposition (*sthāyī-bhāva*) but it has to be made to flow. That is why the Buddha gave the practice of *maitrībhāvanā* in which one has to wish others well, as they are one's own self. The state of Śiva is a state of egolessness. Love and egolessness are logically connected. Ego limits the consciousness to one particular individuality and thereby differentiates it from others. Unless we come out of our ego shell, we cannot feel our unity with others and love them. When we love others, our ego is automatically dissolved; feeling one's unity with others is the way to come out of one's ego shell. Since Śiva is a state of complete egolessness, we have to be egoless in order to have Śiva-realization.

There is one more characteristic of Śiva that we have to achieve in order to become one with Śiva. That is joy (*ānanda*). This joy, or bliss, is not the diabolical pleasure that one derives from exploiting others; this joy is beauty (*sundaram*), which is one with goodness (*śivam*). This joy is expressed in what is called *spanda*, which is a spontaneous flow of activity in bliss. We catch a glimpse of it in aesthetic activity. Since Śiva, or the Self, is joy expressed in *spanda* or creative activity, all activity done in joy leads to the Self. The child who spontaneously plays in joy is near to the Self. Similarly the joyful *spanda* that exists in aesthetic activity like poetry, music, or any joyful creativity, is near to the Self. Following the path of spontaneous activity (*spanda*) that is an expression of joy also leads us to the Self.

Goodness, purity, truth, love, egolessness, joy, and so on, are ends as well as means. They are ends because they are in the nature of Śiva, which is our goal. They are means because they can be practiced, and the practice leads to the goal. All the spiritual practices that fall in the three classes of *āṇavopāya*, *śāktopāya*, and *śāmbhavopāya* tend to strengthen these characteristics or help reveal them. These characteristics are to be practiced, for they are our real nature and the practice of them leads to our real nature. In order to achieve the end, the end itself is to be practiced as means. In this sense the end and the means become one. This is characteristic of spiritual *sādhanā*.

That we can attain the Self by practicing the natural characteristics of the Self is analogous to the fact that we can succeed in life situations not by going against Nature but by following Nature. If we try to row a boat upstream, it will be an extremely difficult task, and moreover it will take us farther from the ocean that is our goal. But if we sail our boat downstream, it will require little effort on our part and the stream will easily take us to the goal. Similarly in the realm of spirit, the course of Nature has to be followed. If we practice to become what we really are not or what is against our nature, we will not succeed. But if we practice to become what is in line with our nature, we will easily succeed. Goodness, purity, truth, egolessness, love, joy, and so on, are our real nature; practicing these will easily bring success. It is our great fortune that goodness, love, and joy are in line with the law of Nature, and to follow the way of goodness is to follow the law of Nature. Therein lies the hope of humanity. We, out of egoism, try to go against the law of Nature, and we suffer in consequence.

One may suggest here that the demonic qualities like greed, selfishness, egoity, animal desire, and so on, are very much a part of our nature and to follow the way of Nature would thus be to follow the way of the devil. In answer we would point out that the devilish qualities, described in the *Gītā* as *āsurī* qualities, are not our real nature; they are unnatural accretions that we have accumulated out of egoism, like dirt on a cloth. They can be easily washed away in the divine current of our inner nature. The allegorical story in Hindu mythology of the fight between the gods and demons that culminates in the victory of the gods over the demons suggests that the real nature is ultimately victorious over the false nature.

Thus a means (*upāya*) becomes a means because it leads to our real nature. In the Tantric tradition, three categories of *upāyas* — *śāmbhavopāya*, *śāktopāya*, and *āṇavopāya* — are given. In addition, two more *upāyas* — *pratyabhijñopāya* and *anupāya* — are sometimes mentioned, although these are not real *upāyas*. *Pratyabhijñā* is not *one* of the means, but is *the* means underlying all the *upāyas*.

This is because *pratyabhijñā* is really the end, and the end is implicitly present in the means.

ANUPĀYA

Anupāya is also not really an *upāya*. The literal meaning of *anupāya* is "no-means," which sounds like a negation of all means. What does it really mean? *Anupāya* is used in the Tantric tradition and interpreted by Abhinavagupta in two ways. First, the Self, which is the ultimate goal of life, is already achieved for it already exists. It does not have to be created afresh. It is also not really covered, for it always shines in pristine purity, just as the sun is really not covered even when the clouds seem to cover it. There is thus really no question of acquiring the Self or doing any practice to attain it.

The realm of *anupāya* is the realm of what is called *anuttara* (the "Transcendent"), which is beyond everything and in which doing or achieving anything is irrelevant. It is already complete in itself. Ahbhinavagupta, in a beautiful piece of poetry, the *Anuttarāṣṭikā*, writes,

> In the Transcendent, where is the talk of the difference between the worship, the worshipper, and the worshipped? Who transits (into the Real), who makes one transit, and what is the process of transition? All this (difference) is false; there is nothing separate from the unity of Consciousness. Everything is the experience of the Self and is pure by its very nature; so worry ye not.[8]

He further writes,

> Here there is no going anywhere, no applying of any technique, no contemplating, no meditating, no reciting (of mantra), no practicing anything, no making effort, nothing. Then what is the real thing to do? The real thing to do is this — do not leave anything, do not take anything, take everything as it is.[9]

One does not have to *do* anything or *not* do anything, but just *be* as one is. One does not have to either do anything out of the ordinary or to resist doing anything that comes naturally; one just has to be perfectly relaxed and let everything go as it will. This means behaving in a completely natural way. This is *anupāya.*

In his *Tantrāloka*, Abhinavagupta further says, "There is no attainment of the Self, for it is eternally present."[10] "There is no question of making it known, for it is self-illumined."[11] "There is no question of uncovering or discovering it, for it cannot be covered by anything whatsoever."[12] "There is no entering into it, for there is nobody separate from it who would enter into it."[13]

The awareness or the realization that the Self is already attained and admits of no means will itself lead to Self-realization,[14] for this awareness will totally relax the mind and total relaxation will lead to the Self. But such an awareness can only come to a person who is highly evolved and in whose case the impurities are almost completely removed.[15]

The suggested meaning of *anupāya*, which follows from the first point, is that when one has attained a high degree of purification and is ready for Śiva-realization, then a "little" means (*upāya*) will do. *Anupāya* can also be translated as "a little means" (*isat upaya* — the negative in Sanskrit is sometimes used for "the little" or *alpa*).[16] For example, just by hearing from the guru or scripture that one is really the all-pervasive Self, one attains Self-realization and needs no other practice (*sādhanā*).[17] Once one knows what gold is, one does not need to be apprised of it again and again.

Anupāya stands at the highest point in the hierarchy of means (*upāyas*) and it is sometimes taken as the culmination of *śāmbhavopāya*, which is the highest in the triad of means *śāmbhavopāya, śāktopāya,* and *āṇavopāya.*[18] *Anupāya* is thus not merely the negation of means.[19]

ŚĀMBHAVOPĀYA

Pratyabhijñopāya and *anupāya* are not really *upāyas* in the technical sense of the term for they are mostly automatic, coming as the end or the result of spiritual practice, whereas an *upāya* involves spiritual practice or some activity on the part of the aspirant. In this sense the trio of *śāmbhavopāya*, *śāktopāya*, and *āṇavopāya* are the real *upāyas*. *Śāmbhavopāya* is the highest of the three.

Śāmbhavopāya, as described in the third chapter of the *Tantrāloka*, in the *Tantrasāra*, and elsewhere, is the practice (*sādhanā*) of unity — the practice of visualizing the entire world within oneself as the reflection or projection of one's own Consciousness or Self. It is actually the practice of identifying oneself with Śiva.[20] "He is the lord of the universe (Viśveśvara or Śiva), in whose consciousness this entire world of difference appears as reflection."[21] This unitary awareness presupposes an absolutist metaphysics that maintains that the entire universe is the expansion of one's own higher Self in the form of the appearance or reflection of Consciousness. That is why Abhinavagupta presents the theory of appearance or reflection (Ābhāsavāda or Pratibimbavāda), under the heading *śāmbhavopāya*.[22] When one lives this philosophy — that is, when one visualizes the whole world within oneself as the appearance of one's own Consciousness — then one becomes liberated (*jīvanmukta*).[23]

In *śāmbhavopāya* we can think of our unity with the universe in three ways: (a) "All this has sprung forth from me" (*matta evoditamidam*), (b) "All this is reflected in me" (*mayyeva pratibimbitam*), and (c) "It is not-different from me" (*madabhinnamidam*).[24] This is really the state of universal love where one feels one's unity with all.

The knowledge (*parāmarśa*) that the whole world is one's own projection and therefore one with oneself is not a case of deliberate thinking done in the form of mentally repeating the idea — it comes automatically or spontaneously. It is not an artificially created feeling; it comes as an automatic (*nirvikalpa*) realization. The thinking that we *do* is *vikalpa*; what comes to the mind automatically is *nirvikalpa*. Deliberate thinking (*vikalpa*) about unity belongs to *śāktopāya*, which is a lower path. In the case of *śāmbhavopāya*, such thought is automatic or spontaneous (*nirvikalpa*).[25]

Considered from the point of view of the Śaktis — *icchā, jñāna,* and *kriyā* — *śāmbhavopāya* belongs to the *icchā* stage, which is Sadāśiva where the universe is contained in Consciousness in the state of unity. That is why *śāmbhavopāya* is also called *icchopāya.*[26] *Icchā,* in the context of *upāya,* also implies that in the *śāmbhava* stage one enters the state of complete attunement with Śiva (Śiva-*samāveśa* or Śiva-*samādhi*) merely by willing. One has already crossed the levels of deliberate thinking (*bhāvanā*) and has reached a stage where one can enter into the state of Śivahood (*śivāvasthā*) at will.

Considered from the point of view of the hierarchy of physical, mental, and spiritual yoga, *śāmbhavopāya* belongs to the level of spiritual yoga. Spiritual yoga consists of becoming egoless and feeling one's unity with all; it is the yoga of universal love.

The *upāyas* can also be viewed from the angle of the level of the unfolding of *kuṇḍalinī* as conceived of in *kuṇḍalinī* yoga. *Śāmbhavopāya* is the level of *bodha-kuṇḍalinī,* the awakening of *kuṇḍalinī* at the spiritual level. At this stage the *kuṇḍalinī* is called *bodha* or *jñāna* because here one feels one's unity with the entire universe and overflows in universal love, a characteristic of liberated souls.

Since the *śāmbhava* state of thinking or visualizing (*parāmarśa*) is automatic (*nirvikalpa*) and not created or acquired, it is possible only when one has reached the highest stage of purification after crossing the stages of *āṇavopāya* and *śāktopāya.* The *śāmbhava* stage may thus be said to be the result of *āṇavopāya* and *śāktopāya.*

ŚĀKTOPĀYA

Śāmbhavopāya is spiritual yoga that consists of directly dissolving the ego and feeling one's unity with all (universal love); *śāktopāya* is mental yoga that involves deliberate mental activity, such as contemplation and so on. In *śāktopāya* one has to contemplate some idea or assimilate some truth by thinking it over again and again.[27] There is no need to articulate the idea (*uccāra*); the idea or mantra is repeated in the mind.[28]

The word *śākta* is from *śakti*, which is "thinking" (*vimarśa*). Since this means (*upāya*) involves thinking, it is called *śākta*. But the thinking here is not spontaneous as in *śāmbhavopāya*; this thinking is deliberate (*vikalpātmaka*). One has to exert one's will (*saṅkalpa*) and make an effort (*adhyavasāya*).[29] It is effortfully done, but in the end it becomes effortless (*nirvikalpātmaka*).[30]

Considered from the point of view of the śaktis — *icchā*, *jñāna*, and *kriyā* — *śāktopāya* belongs to the level of *jñāna śakti*. Therefore it is also called *jñānopāya*.[31] *Jñāna śakti* consists of ideation or thinking. What is thought of in the mind as an idea is held by the unity of the mind, or consciousness. We see the world, in the mind, as difference, but at the same time it is held in unity by the mind or consciousness. So, *śāktopāya* (*jñānopāya*) is a stage of unity-in-difference (*bhedābheda*), whereas *śāmbhavopāya* is the state of complete unity (*abheda*).

Since *śāktopāya* is the realm of created thinking or voluntary thinking (*vikalpa*), there is the sense of doing[32] or ego (*abhimāna*).[33] In the *śāmbhava* state there is no ego sense in doing, as all activity is natural or spontaneous.

Considered from the point of view of *kuṇḍalinī*, *śāktopāya* is the stage of *nāda kuṇḍalinī*. *Nāda kuṇḍalinī* works at the mental level in the form of thinking.

Bondage is a form of wrong thinking, and *śāktopāya* consists of thinking in the right direction. It consists of bringing certainty (*niścaya*) to the mind that one is really not bound. Abhinavagupta, in a poetic verse, writes,

> The *paśu* thinks, "I am ignorant," "I am bound by *karma*," "I am impure," "I am determined by others (I am not free)," and so on; and the reversal of this thinking leads to Śiva-realization.[34]

Śāktopāya is perhaps the most useful and the most necessary *upāya*. Normally what happens is that when we take an idea to be true, fix it in the mind, and decide to follow it, the idea slips away from the mind after some time. Thus it is necessary to repeat the idea in the mind again and again so that it is fixed in the mind and becomes part of one's existence. *Śāktopāya* is exactly this. All types of mental recitation or repetition of an idea (*japa*), meditation (*dhyāna*), contemplation (*bhāvanā*), concentration (*ekāgratā* or *ekāgracittatā*), and so on, fall into the category of *śāktopāya*. *Śāktopāya* is mental yoga. It thus differs from *āṇavopāya*, which is physical yoga and *śāmbhavopāya*, which is spiritual yoga.

ĀṆAVOPĀYA

Āṇavopāya consists of external physical means. The word *āṇava* is from *aṇu*, which means the individual person. Since the individual (*aṇu*) operates in the external world of difference, *āṇavopāya* consists of external means related to the physical world of difference and duality.[35] All forms of external worship and external yoga come under *āṇavopāya*. Rituals are forms of external worship, so all rituals fall under *āṇavopāya*.[36] In the Śaiva tradition we find external worship of the Śiva *liṅga*, the symbol of Śiva, and there are elaborate rituals that are used in its worship.

Since the word *nara* ("man") is a synonym for *aṇu* ("the individual soul"), *āṇavopāya* is also called *naropāya*.[37] *Nara* implies the individual person with a body; through the body one performs external activity, both secular and religious. *Āṇavopāya* is also called *kriyopāya*.[38] *Kriyā* is external activity. At the *āṇava* stage, the *upāya* consists of external physical activity (*kriyā*);[39] it also admits of external objects in the worship and rituals.[40] Since the external *upāyas* consist of different objects, there may be innumerable divisions and subdivisions of *kriyopāya*.[41] That is why we find innumerable forms of external worship. Since at the stage of *āṇavopāya*, the *aṇu* uses the external means that involve difference (*bheda*), *āṇavopāya* is also called *bhedopāya*, the *upāya* involving difference.

From the point of view of yoga, *āṇavopāya* is physical yoga. The physical aspect of yoga is called *haṭha yoga*, which consists of posture (*āsana*), breathing (*prāṇāyāma*), and so on. Considered from the point of view of *kuṇḍalinī*, *āṇavopāya* is the realm of *prāṇa-kuṇḍalinī*, which operates as the life force (*prāṇa*) in our body. Through the practice of *prāṇāyāma*, coupled with meditation (*dhyāna*), *prāṇa-kuṇḍalinī* is aroused in the body.

In *āṇavopāya* we also use external symbols. The greatest symbol used for external worship is the Śiva *liṅga*. The word *liṅga* means "sign" or "symbol." The Śiva *liṅga* is the symbol for Śiva. The oval-shaped *liṅga* has no form, so it serves as a good symbol of the formless Reality that is the Self or Consciousness and is called Śiva.

Abhinavagupta points out a very significant thing regarding external worship. He makes it clear that the external worship in itself has no power. It derives its power from the inner spiritual feeling that we attach to it. "Just as without virility a man is impotent, and without life the body is dead, so is the external worship (without the inner spiritual feeling)."[42] It is quite understandable that mechanically performed worship and rituals are meaningless. The recitation of *mantra* becomes efficacious only when the *mantra* is connected with consciousness. It is said, "Without consciousness (*caitanya*), the *mantras* are mere letters; they do not fructify even after being recited a million times."[43] The power or life of the external forms of worship comes from the inner spirit or consciousness. The *Mālinīvijaya Tantra* says, "One should worship the spiritual *liṅga* within which the entire world is contained; the power of the external *liṅga* is based on this."[44] But this does not mean that external worship and ritualistic practice (*sādhanā*) are useless. All it means is that the external derives its power from the internal, and that the external without the internal is meaningless. The observance of rituals and the worship of symbols, such as idols, have great meaning. If they are coupled with spiritual feeling, they not only become powerful, but they in turn make the spiritual feeling much more powerful. It is like the digits in the number 10. The 0 is valueless without the digit 1 before it. If the 1 is absent, the 0 is just a cipher. But when the 1 is placed in front of it, the 0 derives its value from the 1 and in turn makes the 1 ten times bigger. If the inner spiritual feeling is coupled with rituals and external worship, it is greatly intensified. This is the special significance of the rituals and external worship.

It is obvious that the external objects by themselves cannot purify the heart, but they can do so when they are combined with inner devotion or spiritual consciousness. For example, when one bathes in the Ganges river taking it to be just water, the physical river will not cleanse one's heart. But if one considers the Ganges to be holy water — "fluid Brahman" — and bathes with this feeling of reverence, then the Ganges will surely cleanse one's heart. What will really cleanse one's heart is not the water but the feeling of reverence that one projects on the water. The same thing happens when one bows down in reverence to some external object — a deity, guru, parent, or anything at all. What helps one is not the external object but one's own feeling of reverence and homage, which weakens the ego. But we should also not forget that the external object serves as a powerful medium for the projection of one's feeling. In this sense the external object has a very significant role to play.

When one accepts a particular form of the deity, it is not that the particular deity itself is God; God is inside as one's own higher Self, and while worshipping the deity, one unconsciously projects on it the God within oneself. Thus the worship of every external deity is an indirect worship of God as Self. Conceiving and installing the deity outside is therefore quite useful and sometimes even necessary, as it is difficult for people to worship the God inside them directly. For the very same reason we conceive of God as transcendent or the "holy other." Since we are ordinarily not able to see the immanent God as our own Self, we have to see God outside as the "holy other." Thus Tantrism comprehends within itself any kind of theism and any form of external divinization. But while worshipping

God externally in a particular form, one must at the same time be philosophically aware that what one is worshipping is not itself God, but a projection or a symbol of the real God, which is one's own higher Self. The Tantric attitude saves us from falling into bigotry, idolatry, and superstition. In this sense Tantrism is the most rational religion.

When one goes to see the holy (in the form of an idol) and bows down before the holy, one makes oneself holy. It is not the "holy" itself that matters, what matters is one's surrender to the holy. One's surrender tends to undermine one's ego and thereby allow the holiness of one's own self to come to the fore. The same rule operates in the worship of a guru. The guru may be an ordinary creature of the earth, but one's own attitude of respect and reverence helps one. Here we may add that one may be well aware of the weaknesses of one's guru, but this may not hinder one's attitude of reverence towards the guru. It is quite possible, on the one hand, to rationally understand the shortcomings of the guru and, on the other hand, to consciously and deliberately direct one's feeling of reverence to him or her. One may worship one's own little daughter as the Goddess, as in *kumārī-pūjā*, or worship one's son as Kṛṣṇa, and at the same time be aware of the mistakes they make as children and admonish them. What matters is one's deliberate attempt to create the feeling of reverence and holiness in oneself and direct it to any person or thing one likes. The person or thing to which one directs the feeling does not matter. The reason why this attitude helps is that it tends to dissolve one's ego, and the dissolution of the ego facilitates the flow of the holiness of one's own higher Self.

GENERAL EVALUATION OF THE UPĀYAS

We have seen that *āṇavopāya*, *śāktopāya*, and *śāmbhavopāya* are the three major means of spiritual realization. They are not three particular *upāyas*; they are really three types or classes of *upāyas*. The most significant point regarding the three *upāyas* is that they are not only particular means or *sādhanās*, but they also serve as a general model for understanding and classifying *all* the means of spiritual realization. All the physical means or *sādhanās* involving external activity and objects come under *āṇavopāya*; all the mental ways, involving thinking, ideation, meditation, and so on, come under *śāktopāya*, and all the spiritual *upāyas* of directly dissolving or surrendering the ego and thereby directly entering into the Self, are classified under *śāmbhavopāya*. All the practices of the world can be classified under one or the other of these three *upāyas*. Tantrism presents, in the three *upāyas*, a comprehensive model for understanding and classifying *all* conceivable paths or means of spiritual realization.

The three *upāyas* are not at par; they are placed in a hierarchical order. The hierarchy is based on what is called *adhikārī-bheda*, the different levels of fitness of various aspirants. People stand at different levels of spiritual evolution, and they need or deserve different levels of *sādhanā*. The *adhikārīs* themselves can be broadly classified into three levels. The lowest of them stand at the level of the physical external world of difference. They need the *upāya* involving physical objects and external activity. *Āṇavopāya* is suited to them. But there are many who have risen higher than the level of external worship; they will not remain satisfied with it. They need the mental *sādhanā* of thinking, ideation, meditation, and so on. These people deserve *śāktopāya*. The *adhikārīs* of the highest level, who have achieved a high degree of self-purification, are fit for directly entering into the kingdom of Consciousness. They deserve *śāmbhavopāya*.

Since there is a hierarchical order among these three *upāyas*, the lower can be called a means to the higher. *Āṇavopāya* can be taken as a means to *śāktopāya*, and *śāktopāya* as a means to *śāmbhavopāya*.[45] What is called *anupāya* can actually be seen as the culmination of *śāmbhavopāya*.[46]

We have already seen that *āṇavopāya* is the yoga of physical means; *śāktopāya*, the mental; and *śāmbhavopāya*, the spiritual.

Āṇavopāya is the level of difference (*bheda*); *śāktopāya* of unity-in-difference (*bhedābheda*); and *śāmbhavopāya* of unity (*abheda*).[47]

Considered from the point of view of "doing" and "being," *āṇavopāya* and *śāktopāya* are the *upāyas* of the state of "doing" — *āṇavopāya* the physical, and *śāktopāya* the mental. *Śāmbhavopāya* is the state of being. Here one does not "do" in the sense of voluntary and effortful action (*karma*), but one remains seated in the Self and spontaneous activity (*kriya* or *spanda*) flows automatically. At the *āṇava* and the *śakta* stages one has to "do"; at the *śāmbhava* level one has to "be."

Abhinavagupta has determined the position of mind, or the internal organ of thinking (*citta*) in the three *upāyas*. According to him, in *āṇavopāya* the mind attains rest or becomes peaceful,[48] in *śāktopāya* the mind becomes illumined or enlightened, [49] and in *śāmbhavopāya* the mind is dissolved.[50] The mind is the seat or matrix of the effortful voluntary thoughts and actions (*karma*). The mind makes us restless and takes us away from the Self. As such, the mind is an obstruction to the natural flow of both the knowledge (*jñāna*) and spontaneous activity (*kriyā*) of the Self. Yoga aims at the elimination, dissolution, or at least the pacification, of the mind (*citta*). The mind is not dissolved immediately; it takes a long time to be finally eliminated. The mind usually moves outside and thinks of the affairs of the external world and gets agitated. Through external worship, the agitated mind gets pacified, although it remains very much intact. In *śāktopāya*, since the mind does the *sādhanā* of thinking in the right direction, it becomes illumined or enlightened. Because of the predominance of good qualities in the person, the mind is thinned enough to allow the illumination of the Self. The "thinned" mind becomes ready to be dissolved in Consciousness (the Self). In *śāmbhavopāya* the mind is fully surrendered, and therefore dissolved. This destruction or dissolution of the mind does not mean the destruction of Consciousness; it means the removal of an obstruction, resulting in the free flow of Consciousness.

Śāmbhavopāya (Śivopāya, Paropāya)	Icchopāya (Icchā — willing)	Spiritual yoga	Bodha-Kuṇḍalinī	Abheda (unity)	The state of "being"
Śaktopāya	Jñānopāya (Jñāna — ideation)	Mental yoga	Nāda-Kuṇḍalinī	Bhedābheda (unity-in-difference)	The state of "doing" (mental action)
Āṇavopāya (Naropāya)	Kriyopāya (Kriyā — external activity)	Physical yoga	Prāṇa-Kuṇḍalinī	Bheda (difference)	The state of "doing" (physical action)

The Upāyas

THE PLACE OF NEGATION IN TANTRIC SĀDHANĀ

It would be a naive understanding of Tantrism to think that since Tantrism is a philosophy of positive acceptance and assimilation of the world, it has no place for negation. It is true that Tantrism is a philosophy of integration, but integration itself presupposes some negation. If the world is to be integrated with Śiva, it cannot be integrated as it is. For the world, as it is, purports to be independent and made of matter. This will be an impediment to the integration of the world with Śiva. For the purpose of integration, the world will have to be deprived of its independence and also of its materiality. We will have to accept that the world is not an independent reality, but is a manifestation of Śiva. Moreover, Śiva is Consciousness; matter, being a different reality, cannot be integrated with Consciousness. So we will have to further accept that the world is not a material reality, but is the projection or appearance (*ābhāsa*) of Consciousness (Śiva). The world will have to lose its independence and materiality in order to be integrated with Śiva.

Kashmir Śaivism, which is the central philosophy of Tantrism, is an absolutism. There can be no absolutism without negation in some respect. Every absolutism has to integrate or assimilate the world within the Absolute, and the world has to be changed in order to fit in the Absolute. Absolutism is a philosophy of unity, and at the least the multiplicity of the world will have to be denied in order to be consistent with this unity.

Moreover in Kashmir Śaivism philosophy, or metaphysics, is a way of life, a spiritual practice (*sādhanā*). What is negated on the plain of metaphysics is also negated in the realm of (*sādhanā*). We have already seen in the context of *śāmbhavopāya* that the world is to be taken not as the independent material reality that it claims to be, but as the reflection or projection of one's own (higher) Consciousness. Even in *śāktopāya* and *āṇavopāya*, the world is to be viewed not as the world but as Śiva, just as the waves of the ocean are to be viewed as the ocean itself. This is what is called

Śiva-*bhāvanā*, the *sādhanā* of feeling that everything is Śiva. When one sees the world as Śiva, one does not see the world, but one sees Śiva; that is, one negates the world *as world* and accepts it as *Śiva* — the manifestation of Śiva.

It follows that one has to negate the factor that has caused the misapprehension of Reality and separated one from one's real nature. This is, as we have already seen, the factor of impurity (*mala*) and the greatest impurity is the ego sense (*āṇava*) which generates the sense of duality (*dvaita-prathā*). This is another name for selfishness. Selfishness also generates attachment (*rāga*). Egoism and selfishness are the main causes of our plight as limited individuals (*paśu*). These are to be negated. When selfishness is gone, attachment (*rāga*) goes automatically.

It further follows that the world, or worldly activity, is not to be negated, for the world is not the cause of bondage. What is bondage is egoism and selfishness, not the world or worldly attainment. So renunciation, according to Tantrism, is the renunciation of the ego, not of the world. This is directly opposed to those who follow the path of renunciation of the world. Such people have turned their back on the world that could be used as a means of Self-realization. They follow the ascetic life — a life of self-mortification and repression of desires. This is called the life of renunciation (*nivṛtti*), or knowledge (*vidyā*), as opposed to the life of worldly involvement (*pravṛtti*), or ignorance (*avidyā*). It is a psychological truth that such a life of self-abnegation, unless the renunciate also practices universal love, leads to the disintegration of the personality. Such a person labors under self-deception and is therefore doubly ignorant.

In light of the above statement we can very well understand the Upaniṣadic condemnation of the life of renunciation (*nivṛtti/vidyā*) devoid of worldly involvement (*pravṛtti/avidyā*). The *Īśa Upaniṣad* criticizes the life devoted exclusively to renunciation when it says, "Those who worship *avidyā* (ignorance, in the sense of worldly involvement) enter into darkness, but those who are engrossed in *vidyā* (knowledge or renunciation) enter into still more darkness."[51]

The best way, therefore, is to reconcile the two. In that vein, the Upaniṣad continues, "One who comprehends both *vidyā* and *avidyā* crosses mortality with the help of *avidyā* and attains immortality with the help of *vidyā*."[52] Both *vidyā* and *avidyā*, or renunciation and involvement, become the means of spiritual realization; there is no opposition between the two. The Upaniṣadic philosophy that takes the world as a manifestation of the Self (Brahman) and accepts the world of *avidyā* as a means of "crossing mortality" was misinterpreted by the Advaitic scholiasts to mean that the world is a superimposition on Brahman, like the rope-snake, and that the world is utterly valueless (*tuccha*), meant to be ultimately rejected and eliminated. This is a gross misinterpretation of the Upaniṣadic position. The *Gītā* even more clearly rejects the life of asceticism and renunciation of the world and secular activities.

Of course, as we have seen earlier, the process of integration or assimilation presupposes some kind of negation. If one wants to assimilate within oneself the entire world, of which at present one is just a part, one will have to rise above it by first negating oneself from it. It is only when one rises higher that one can view the whole panorama; one cannot do so from inside the panorama. The synthesizing principle stands at a higher level than the things that are synthesized. One negates oneself from the world in order to rise higher, so that one can assimilate or integrate the world within oneself. Negation of the world is only half the truth, the full truth is the assimilation or integration of the world within oneself as one's own manifestation or projection. The Advaitic scholiast confines him- or herself to half the truth (negation) and seems to forget the full truth (assimilation). He or she clings to the Upaniṣadic statement that Brahman is beyond the world (*neti, neti*)[53] or (*neha nānāsti kiñcana*)[54] and overlooks the equally important Upaniṣadic statement that "all this is Brahman" (*sarvaṁ khalvidaṁ brahma*).[55] The Advaitin confines Brahman to the "freedom-from" and deprives Brahman of the "freedom-to."

THE RELAXED WAY OF LIFE

Abhinavagupta prescribes what in yoga is called a perfectly relaxed way of life. He says, "Do not reject and do not accept; enjoy everything as it is."[56] He also says, "Do not leave anything, do not take anything; be in yourself (the Self) and enjoy everything as it is."[57] This is the state of "being," not "doing," from which activities naturally and spontaneously arise. This is a state of complete relaxation, a state of relaxing in the Self (*ātma-viśrānti*). Now the question arises, is this not a state of passivity? Is this possible even when one is doing one's secular work? Will this way of life be a hindrance or a help in one's professional work? The answer is that it will be quite helpful.

Many people think that the path leading to liberation, or Self-realization, (*mokṣa*) is the path that leads us away from the world and the professional activities of the world. Moreover they seem to think that the *sādhanā* of liberation is the *sādhanā* of "not doing," as action (*karma*) is bondage; therefore the seeker of liberation will retire from the activity of the world. But this is a very erroneous view of the path of liberation. The *Gītā* corrects this view and declares that the yoga of action leads to liberation. The *Gītā* points out that the state of the yoga of action is the state of "actionless activity" where one is a doer and yet not a doer. Tantra provides the metaphysical basis for the concept of "actionless activity" by pointing out that spontaneous activity (*kriyā* or *spanda*), which is different from voluntary, effortful action (*karma*), is the very nature of Consciousness (the Self). The seeker of liberation (*mokṣa*) follows the path of activity (*kriyā*), which is called Karma yoga in the *Gītā*. Karma yoga, however, does not involve *karma* but *kriyā* — the spontaneous activity that automatically and naturally flows from the Self, in which one is a doer and yet not a doer. This *kriyā* not only fits in with professional work but also enhances the quality and quantity of that work.

Tantrism accepts liberation (*mokṣa*), the realization of one's real Self, as the ultimate goal of life towards which all our endeavors, both physical and spiritual, are ultimately aimed. It must be emphasized that liberation is not an otherworldly, after-death value; it is related to our present-day existence, no matter what our walk of life. It is evident that it is the human psyche, or consciousness, that is at work in all human striving, the only difficulty is that it is obstructed by many factors and therefore does not operate at its full potential. There is an undefiled form of this psyche that, according to the Indian tradition, is its real nature and is present in every individual in the form of the higher, or deeper Self from which the lower self, or the ego, derives all its power, beauty, joy, and illumination or knowledge. Self-realization is nothing but the attuning of oneself to this deeper Self that is one's own real nature.

To use an analogy, consciousness is like the electric current that is working in the lighted bulb or in the machine. The ultimate source of the electric current is the powerhouse to which all the machines are connected. When we turn on the switch for the operation of the electric current, it is not the switch that generates the power; the switch, together with the net of wires and connections, is simply a medium through which electricity passes; the electricity itself emerges from the powerhouse. And the less obstruction in the medium, the more the flow of the current. Similarly the ego which operates the various workings of life is like the switch, the power of consciousness that makes the various workings possible is like the electric current; and the higher Self, which is the source of the power of consciousness, is like the powerhouse. Thus it is the power of the Self that makes all our activities possible. The more the ego is attuned with the Self through purification, the greater is the flow of power and the better the quality of one's work life. The more we are in tune with the Self, the more success we attain in life. The Upaniṣads declare that everything of the world is illumined with the light of the Self.[58] The *Gītā* makes it clear that whatever beauty, power, and prosperity we find in the world comes from the light of the Self.[59]

In order to attain Self-realization it is necessary to work or perform action. Performing action is the process of actualizing the potentiality contained within ourselves. The seed, which is a potential tree, cannot actualize itself unless it sprouts and grows from the stage of a sapling to that of a fully grown tree. The process of actualization of the potentialities of the seed is the process of the self-realization of the seed, and this entire process is a colossal activity. Similarly the lower self, or the ordinary human psyche, is the potential Higher Self (*ātman*), and through activity it unfolds or actualizes itself.

The above position can also be stated in the language of tension and relaxation. Action, or work, is necessary for the release of inner tension, too. To use the analogy of the seed again, the seed which is the potential tree, can be said to be in a state of tension, as if the seed is under pressure to actualize its potentiality. When the seed begins to unfold itself in the form of a sapling, the inner tension of the seed begins to ease. When the potentialities of the seed are fully exhausted in the form of the fully grown tree, the tension is fully relaxed. Similarly the individual psyche, which is the potential *ātman* together with its seed-desires, is in a state of tension. This tension is eased through the process of Self-actualization, which is possible only through work or activity. It is commonly believed that relaxation is the opposite of action; few people know that action is equally necessary for the easing of tension. That is why the yoga of the *Gītā* provides an important insight — the working out of inner tension cannot be achieved without action. This is an insight that many modern yoga teachers lack.

The same position can be expressed in a still different language — the language of self-purification. The process of Self-actualization is also a process of self-purification, as the psyche, through activity, gets purged of its obstructions and thereby facilitates the flow of the energy of the higher Self through it. The *Gītā*, again, says, "The yogins perform unattached action for the sake of self-purification."[60]

The *Gītā* gives the same idea in a still different version, namely that one can perform one's activities, of whatever kind, as worship to the Lord — a method of doing each and every act as an offering to the Lord for His pleasure. The *Gītā* abolished the distinction between secular act and religious act; every act, however secular it may be, becomes a religious act if it is performed in the spirit of being an instrument for the Lord's work. In fact, all work is *His* work; in the *Gītā* the Lord says that it is He who has initiated the cycle of worldly activity, and one who does not follow it lives in vain.[61] This is another way of saying that the Lord has created the world as an eternal drama and has assigned different roles to the different individual actors. We have to play our roles fully.

The beauty of the above attitude on our part is that when we work in this spirit, every work becomes a thing of joy in itself. The work becomes play or sport (*līlā*). The difference between work and play is that in work we become happy only after the work brings the desired result, whereas in play the action itself gives joy, irrespective of the result it brings. In the play of football, for example, the striking of the ball itself gives joy. A futher distinction between the two is that in work we are in a state of tension, whereas in play we are in a state of relaxation. Of course, this play does not include so-called sports where the mode is competitive, the object being to defeat the opponent and win a prize. This is no sport at all.

The question may be asked here, if we try to discharge our duty in the spirit of play, will we not become irresponsible and spoil the work? In order for our duty to be discharged properly, we have to take it seriously. The answer to this question is that taking our duty as a sport does not spoil it, but on the contrary, it enhances the quality of our work. When we do the work in a state of tension — which is quite likely when we take the work very seriously — we are more likely to spoil it, whereas in the sporting attitude, we are relaxed and, therefore the ensuing work is naturally done in a better way.

Moreover, taking duty as sport does not mean taking it lightly; it only means that we do the work for the sake of the work itself and enjoy the work *in* itself. This has the merits of joy and absence of tension on the part of the worker and improvement of the quality of the work life. In other words, engaging in work as a sportive self-expression naturally brings better physical results, too. A tree does not grow with the deliberate purpose of giving fruit, shadow, or timber. The growth of the tree is a natural act of self-expression, and in that process the tree automatically gives fruit, shadow, timber, and so on. Similarly, playful work is a spontaneous act of self-expression, and as such it automatically brings the results of physical fulfillment, too. Tantric philosophy by no means underrates result-oriented work. The goal, in fact, is to synthesize work with joy (*ānanda*). The Tantric philosopher discovers that such work can not only be linked with a joy-giving principle on the part of the worker, but can also be made much more fruitful that way. Fulfillment of the earthly needs — what is called *yoga-kṣema* — is automatically accomplished, just as when the tree grows, it bears fruit naturally. One waters not the twigs but the roots of the tree.

There may be a question regarding work as worship of the Lord: If one believes in God, one can take all work as the worship of God; but if one does not believe in God, then how can one follow this prescription? The answer is that in that case one would be advised by the *Gītā* to renounce oneself, which means relaxing or silencing the ego and the individual will, and allowing the Self to express its spontaneous activity through the individual. In the *Gītā* this is called *śannyāsa* yoga or *jñāna* yoga. The way of regarding work as worship of God is called *karma* yoga, (and includes *bhakti* yoga), and the other two yogas (*jñāna* and *karma*, or simply Sāṁkhya and yoga) are declared to be one by the *Gītā*. Yoga — whether *jñāna* yoga or *karma* yoga — is a state of consciousness in which the ego, being silenced, gives way to the sublime flow of activity of the higher Self. All activity, including office and business work, becomes part of this greater and more sublime flow of activity. This process tones up the quality of the work life by pouring beauty, harmony, self-satisfaction, and self-expression into the hitherto lifeless work life.

One may again ask a question, if one resigns one's personal will, then won't one become totally passive? There can be no activity without willing, and resigning one's will would virtually amount to one's committing suicide. This is exactly the question in the mind of Arjuna when he hears from Kṛṣṇa that he should resign his will and fight as well. Vyāsa, the author of the *Gītā*, makes Arjuna question Kṛṣṇa for clarification, and then Kṛṣṇa says that resignation of will does not lead to absence of action, for it is not the individual will or the ego that generates activity. It is the Self from which all activity ensues. Spontaneous activity is the very nature of the Self, and the individual will, or the ego, is in fact, an obstruction to the free flow of this activity. When the will, or the ego, is silenced, the spontaneous activity of the Self, thus freed, begins to flow through the individual all the more fully. This is not an academic speculation on the part of the Indian seer; it can be seen in our experience too. In the case of neurasthenia, the patient feels as fatigued as if he or she were doing tremendous work, whereas visibly he or she is doing nothing. It is not that such a patient is deceiving him- or herself or others, as his or her subconscious mind is vigorously exerting itself, yet the net result in the form of fruitful activity is zero. And on the contrary, we can find persons who feel that they are really doing nothing as they are not exerting their will, and yet a lot of useful activity manifests through them. People of spiritual attainment — the yogins and the saints — are like this. The secret of fruitful activity lies not in the will or the ego but in the Self whose very nature is the emanation of effortless spontaneous activity.

One could still press the question that successful work demands initiative on the part of the doer, and if the person involved resigns his or her will there will be no initiative. In answer one could say that this objection begs the same question discussed earlier, namely that no action is possible when the will is resigned. I will add here that initiative seems to be a matter of the will, but it is not. If we analyze the psychology of initiative, we find that initiative does not come as a result of vigorous willing — it comes to the mind as a flash, as a spontaneous movement of the will. Indian spiritual psychology would add here that the source of this is the same Self. The phenomenon of spontaneous initiative is called *pratibhā* in the Tantric tradition. It is a sudden flash of inspiration.

I do not mean to underrate the value of initiative in work life; on the contrary, I am suggesting the method for enhancing the power of initiative. The power of initiative comes spontaneously in the form of *pratibhā*, and the way to develop *pratibhā* is to follow the spiritual path. History bears witness to the fact that spiritually enlightened persons had a tremendous power of initiative. Buddha, Socrates, and Christ did marvellous work inspired by this initiative. Śaṅkarācarya enacted so many measures for the establishment of the tradition of Advaita Vedānta and for the upliftment and unity of Indian culture. Swami Vidyāraṇya, a saint of the Advaita Vedāntic tradition, founded one of the most illustrious kingdoms of India — Vijayanagaram in the south. We all know of the tremendous power of initiative possessed by Vivekananda and Gandhi. It is said of Washington that during the time of the American Revolution, whenever he felt himself cornered and in difficulty, he knelt down and prayed to the Lord for help and guidance and help always came in the form of the right initiative. In all countries and at all times people of spiritual attainment — saints and sages — have always done something useful and beneficial for the society. Initiative is the result of one's attunement with the Self, and the resignation of the personal will, or ego, is the prerequisite for this attunement.

In the above-mentioned state of consciousness, one is a doer and not a doer at the same time. One is not a doer in the sense that one does not exert one's will; all activity flows automatically or spontaneously through one. This can be called a state of relaxed activity or "actionless activity."

There is a long tradition of "actionless activity" in Indian thought. The *Gītā* says that in this state one does not do anything, although one is participating in all sorts of activity.[62] In the *Yoga-vāśiṣṭha* the teacher Vaśiṣṭha advises Rāma to follow the same path. He says, "Have artificial willing without, and be devoid of willing within; move in the world, O Rāghava (Rāma), being a doer outwardly and a non-doer inwardly."[63] He further exhorts Rāma to "be heated in activity without, and be cool and calm within."[64] In the language of yoga, the state of "actionless activity" is called *sahaja samādhi*, to which the mystic saint Kabir referred when he said, "All actions are done by me, yet I am beyond all activity."

The metaphysics behind this philosophy of "actionless activity" is that the nature of the Self, or Consciousness, is not merely knowledge (*jñāna*) but also spontaneous activity (*kriyā, spanda, vimarśa,* or *śakti*). Consciousness (*citi*) is not a static entity but a dynamic force, and that is why it is called *citi-śakti* ("Consciousness-force"). Consciousness, therefore, is not merely Śiva but Śiva-Śakti (*jñāna-kriyā*, or *prakāśa-vimarśa*). The spontaneous activity (*spanda*) of Consciousness is symbolized by the cosmic dance of Śiva Naṭarāja. The Self (*ātman*) or Consciousness as a dynamic force, or energy, which is at once the true (*satyam*), the good(*śivam*), and the beautifual (*sundaram*), is the precious discovery of Tantric metaphysics.

In the context of "actionless activity" there can be a question from the point of view of the ideal of morality. The moral demand is that since one is paid for one's work, one should pay back in the form of honest work. In other words, one should do the work with the idea that one is obliged to do it as one's duty, even if there is nobody to press one to work or even if there is no punishment for not working. Now this is possible only when one has morality as the incentive, but the way of work suggested in the context of "actionless activity" does not seem to have morality as an ideal. In answer to the above question one could point out that the spiritual philosophy of work suggested in the foregoing pages does not exclude morality; rather it has a natural or spontaneous morality. The essence of morality is to do good to others and not exploit them. In an action motivated by love we do good to the beloved not because we think it is moral to do so. Love has natural morality. In fact, love is the ground of all morality. Noble and saintly persons do good to others just out of love or compassion, not out of a conscious consideration of the moral ideal. It is all the better if morality comes naturally and effortlessly.

Thus we see that the relaxed way of life or the life of surrender in the Self (*ātma-viśrānti*) is a state of "being" that naturally emanates spontaneous "doing." In this state we "do" nothing, and yet everything is done through us automatically or spontaneously. The spontaneous doing that naturally emanates from this state meets the demands of the life situations in which one is placed. What each situation demands is met in the best way, for it is within the power of the Self, but not of the ego, to meet the demand in the most appropriate way. When we are in the state of voluntary and effortful action (*karma*), then it is the ego that works, and it is not within the power of the ego to perform activity in the most proper and the most beautiful way. But when we are in the state of relaxed activity, which is a state of *kriyā* or *spanda*, then it is not the ego but the Self (*ātman*, or *paramātman*) that works, and what the Self spontaneously does is both good (*śivam*) and beautiful (*sundaram*).

10

The Left-Handed Doctrine (Kaula Sādhanā) and Sex Sublimation

THE RATIONALE BEHIND THE KAULA SĀDHANĀ

The Kaula *sādhanā*, or the left-hand ritual practice of the Kaula school, is the most significant but most misunderstood *sādhanā* of the Tantric tradition. This misunderstanding perhaps arose because this practice has always been a secret one, handed down from guru to disciple through the ages, never disclosed to the general public. It was deliberately kept secret to prevent it from falling into the hands of unqualified people. Unfortunately the practice was taken up by people who, either out of ignorance or by deliberate design, used it purely for their own physical pleasure. Pretending to be Tantrists, these people ate and drank forbidden substances and indulged in illicit sex. These pseudo-Tantrists brought a bad name to this otherwise powerfully effective spiritual practice. Tantrism's critics, seeing the behavior of these pseudo-Kaulas, declared that Kaulism was perverted hedonism.[1]

The rationale behind the Kaula *sādhanā* is little known; therefore the practice is not appreciated by people in general. Once the rationale behind it is understood and the true spirit of the practice grasped, people naturally become Kaulas. The purpose of this chapter is to *explain* this rationale.

In the twenty-ninth chapter of his *Tantrāloka*, Abhinavagupta sets out the Kaula *sādhanā* under the heading: "The secret technique (*rahasya-vidhi*) meant for qualified people."[2] The ritual part of this *sādhanā* is called *kula-yāga* ("the ritual of kula"). *Kula* is Śiva's power (*śakti*), which manifests as the entire world.[3] *Kula* literally means "family" or "extension." The world is an extension of Śiva. The power of Śiva that pervades the universe is also called *kuṇḍalinī* (literally: "female coiled serpent") or *kula-kuṇḍalinī*. *Kuṇḍalinī* is the force or power of Consciousness vibrating in the form of the whole universe. *Kuṇḍalinī* is also the vitality or life force (*prāṇa*) of individual bodies. At the bodily level this energy is known as *prāṇa-kuṇḍalinī*.

Since the entire world is an extension of Śiva and directly connected with Him, the world can be used as a means for ascending to Śiva. The Kaula *sādhanā* consists in seeing everything in the world as Śiva. The practice is also called Śiva-*bhāvanā*, which means feeling Śiva everywhere. The *sādhaka*, observing the objects of the world, sees not the things but Śiva. Rather than "looking at" the objects, the *sādhaka* is "looking through" them to their fundamental ground, Śiva. To use an analogy, when one sees the waves as ocean, one is not seeing the waves but seeing the ocean. One is looking *through* the wave *to* the ocean, or seeing the ocean in the waves. Similarly, when one sees the world as Śiva, one sees not the world but Śiva. The world simply becomes a medium to look through. One can see Śiva directly reflected in anything and everything of the world.

In the language of *bhakti* this would be seeing the beloved Lord in every form. Any and every form can become a medium *through* which one can look at the beloved Divine, for the forms are nothing but the Beloved appearing in different poses.

The things of the world are thus simply a medium through which the Tantric establishes contact with Śiva (or Śakti). The Kaula ritual (*kula-yāga*) is a means of "contacting" Śiva, or seeing Śiva in so-called mundane objects. Abhinavagupta writes that this contact can be established through six means: (a) the external world (*bahiḥ*), (b) the woman (*śakti*), (c) the male/female couple (*yāmala*), (d) the body (*deha*), (e) the process of breathing (*prāṇa-patha*), and (f) the workings of the mind (*mati*).[4] Through these media we can realize Śiva more easily and effectively. An example of the use of the second of these media is the Kaulic ritual of "virgin worship" (*kumārī pūjā*). The woman is seen not as a human being, but as the Goddess incarnate; in this way the *sādhaka* establishes contact with the Goddess. This is a deliberate process for raising worldly objects to the level of Śiva or bringing Śiva to the level of the physical world.

Actually, Śiva is already present in the world, but people ignorant of this fact do not see Śiva when they look at the world. Kaula *sādhanā* is a way to see Śiva in the world and the world as Śiva. Kaulism "transforms" the world into Śiva. It is a divine alchemy that turns everything into gold. When someone worships an object or person as if it is God, that object or person becomes God for the worshipper.

As a medium through which God can be recognized, the sex act is accorded special attention in Kaulism. The power of the entire universe (*kuṇḍalinī śakti*) is alive in the body in the form of sexual energy,[5] therefore in Kaulism, sex is the most important channel for reaching Śiva. As a result of this emphasis, Kaulism has been identified as a *sādhanā* based exclusively on sex, which it is not. Kaulism is the practice of using everything in the world as a means of realization, specifically including sex. Sexual energy (*kāma śakti*) is not confined to sexual expression alone. It is the general energy of pleasure (*ānanda śakti*) that expresses itself in every form of joyful activity.

Kaula *sādhanā*, which is at the heart of Tantrism, is known in the Indian tradition as *vāma-mārga*, the "left-hand way." The Vedic tradition is by implication the "right-hand path" (*dakṣiṇa-mārga*).

The Vedic followers called the Tantric practice the left-hand way because of its ritual use of five substances that they considered impure: wine, meat, fish, parched grain,[6] and sexual intercourse. The Vedic followers thus looked down on the Kaulas and called their practice the left-hand way to suggest that they were on the wrong track.

The Kaulas did not object to their practice being called the left-hand way. They accepted the label, but interpreted it differently. They took *vāmā* to mean "left half" as in the left half, or female side, of Śiva in his manifestation as the half man/half woman Ardhanārīśvara. *Vāmā* is thus one of the many names given to Śakti. Therefore the *vāma-mārga* or left-hand path is the way of worship of the left half, or Śakṭi.

Not all Tantrists use the ritual of the five "impure" substances; therefore not all Tantrists are Kaulas. While Kaulism in its general sense is synonymous with Tantrism, Kaulism in its special sense of the practice of using the five "illicit" substances is only a part of Tantrism. Even within Kaulism itself there are Tantrists who do not physically use the five substances. They instead work to change their attitude toward the "forbidden" pursuits without physically enacting the Kaula ritual. It is quite possible to bring about such a change in attitude without the accompanying physical acts, and such a practice is advisable in the face of prevailing social morality. Therefore even in Kaulism, the actual physical use of the five "impure" acts is not necessary. In fact, the physical use of these is prohibited in the case of ignorant people who do not aim at changing their attitude. The Tantra says, "The ignorant person (*paśu*) should not smell or see or touch or drink wine and meat; the use of these is efficacious (only) in the case of the Kaula *sādhakas*."[7]

The so-called left-hand way grew out of the Tantric insight that the act of finding divinity in avowedly profane objects and activities was a powerful tool for discovering the Divine in everything. The practice is taken to the extreme by some groups such as the Aghoris, who smear themselves with filth and excrement. What is generally taken as the most ignoble and profane is, in the Tantric *sādhanā*, to be taken as something sanctified and divine; it is to be taken as Śiva. Abhinavagupta says that in the ritual of Kaulic worship only those things that are prohibited in the scriptural tradition[8] are to be used. In the Aghorī *sādhanā*, even filth, urine, and excrement are employed. Urine, for example, is called the Holy Water (*śivambu*).[9] It is egoism and ignorance, the Tantrist would say, to regard things of the world as other than Śiva. The *vāmā-sādhanā* is an efficacious technique for curing one's egoism and ignorance.

The Tantra, of course, does not prescribe smearing filth on the body, nor does it denigrate cleanliness as a hygienic value. It aims instead at eradicating the feeling that the filth is something unholy. There is a difference between a thing's being unclean and its being unholy or religiously impure. Cleanliness is a secular value, while holiness or unholiness is a religious attitude. What the Tantrist seeks to remove is not the uncleanliness, but the feeling of unholiness regarding the dirt. For example, a *śudra* or *cāṇḍāla*, even if he or she has washed his or her body clean and is wearing clean clothes, is, in the orthodox tradition, considered unholy and the very touch of the *cāṇḍāla* would "impurify" anything. The Tantrist would call this a wrong and egotistical attitude of the orthodox tradition. In order to neutralize this wrong idea, Tantrism would prescribe the worship of the *cāṇḍāla* as Śiva.[10] In another example, meat is taken in the orthodox tradition to be unholy in itself, apart from the question of its involving killing or being heavy for the body. The same is the case with fish and wine. An orthodox religionist, for example, would not like to dine at a table on which meat and wine are also served. He or she would think that the very touch of meat and wine would defile his or her own food. Tantrism does not favor violence nor does it favor drinking, but it seeks to neutralize the feeling that the meat, fish, wine, or anything of that kind is unholy and that the very touch of it is sacrilegious.

Some people interpret the Kaula ritual use of wine, meat, fish, parched grain, and sexual intercourse as merely a symbolic practice, but in my view the description of the practice should be taken literally. The Tantras vividly and graphically describe the process of worship and the details of the ritual. Moreover, the actual Kaula ritual has been a living tradition in several parts of India, especially Kashmir, Assam, Bengal, and Orissa.

The goal of the left-hand practice of the Kaulas is the sublimination of desires. Underlying the practice is the psychological truth that as long as we have an *antagonistic* attitude toward our desires, particularly the sexual urge, we are unable to overcome them. Instead, we unconsciously repress them, resulting in self-deception and a dissociation of personality. On the other hand, if we develop a religious attitude towards sex and other activities normally undertaken in the fulfillment of our desires, and feel these activities to be no less sanctified than any others, then we are easily able to transcend those desires. Desires are a form of energy. This energy cannot be destroyed; it can only be sublimated or transformed into higher and subtler levels of expression such as love, aesthetic creativity, and so on.

THE NECESSITY OF SEX SUBLIMATION

Why sublimate sex? Why not continue to use it for physical pleasure? The Tantrist presupposes that sexual energy is identical with the energy of the universe that is responsible for all joy and all creativity in different areas of life. The same energy expresses itself in different forms — in the gross form of the physical sex act and in the subtle sublimated form of love and aesthetic enjoyment on the mental level. True joy and creativity are not possible unless the sex energy (*kuṇḍalinī*) is to some extent awakened. The Tantric practitioners made the following discoveries: (a) the same energy, that of the libido, is at work in every form of enjoyment, be it gross or refined; (b) this same energy is also at work in every form of creativity; (c) the more this libidinal energy is caused to express itself through higher channels, the more joy and creativity it brings; (d) the more the sex energy is elevated to higher levels, the more one's sexual problems automatically dissolve. The sublimation of the sexual energy thus brings desirable results on all levels, the sublimated energy being a synthesis of what is good (*śreya*) and what is pleasant (*preya*).

In the Tantric tradition the sexual energy is symbolized by a coiled serpent (*kuṇḍalinī*). In ordinary people the serpent is asleep, coiled face-downwards in the nerve plexus or *cakra* at the base of the sex-organ in the body (the *mūlādhāra cakra*). This indicates that the sex energy normally lies dormant within us. The little bit of awakening that it does have is on the lowest level, in the animal enjoyment of sex. The *kuṇḍalinī* is thus directed downwards. Tantric practice is aimed at awakening this *kuṇḍalinī*, causing it to raise its face upwards and ascend through the chain of *cakras* in the body, finally reaching union with Śiva in the *cakra* at the top of the head (the *sahasrāra cakra*). The ascension of the *kuṇḍalinī* is a metaphor for the process of the *transmutation* of the sex energy from the level of gross enjoyment to the level of divinity.

For the Tantrist, restricting sex to the gross level means draining one's energy, bringing less joy and less creativity. The energy that could be used to bring tremendous power is simply wasted. The Kaula *sādhanā* of sex was devised to address the problem of how to sublimate and elevate the sex energy so that it could be utilized in the best possible way.

THE ATTITUDE OF HOLINESS

The essence of the Kaula ritual regarding sex, and the rationale behind the practice, rests on the assumption that the participants cultivate two attitudes: (a) a feeling of reverence towards the sex act, and (b) a feeling of love towards the sex partner. The external, ritual paraphernalia exist merely to help cultivate these feelings.

Tantrism advocates cultivating a feeling that sex is to be sanctified, in contrast to the contemptuous attitude towards sex preached in negativistic, puritanic, and cynically ascetic traditions. One should practice feeling that sex is something holy and divine. The same attitude is to be cultivated towards the sexual partner. A man should look upon a woman as the incarnation of the divine Śakti; the woman should regard the man as Śiva.

This Tantric concept of the sanctity of sex does not lead to sexual license, but rather the contrary. When the attitude of holiness is successfully cultivated, sex no longer presents a problem for the Tantrist; he or she no longer feels the compulsion or inordinate desire to indulge in sex. Those who suppress the sexual urge, on the contrary, are always in a bitter confrontation with their desires and they never succeed in their quest to uproot these feelings. Tantrism is an antidote to the poisonous attitude that sex is somehow sinful. On the other hand, Tantrism does not condone hedonism. Self-indulgence in sex is neither the goal of Tantra nor the means of reaching the goal. The aim of the Tantric *sādhanā* is the sublimation of sex, and changing one's attitude towards sex from shame to holiness is the first step. Kaulism is against both hating sex as sinful and base, on the one hand, and using it for self-gratification, on the other.

In the Kaula *sādhanā* the actual sex act is done not for enjoyment (*bhoga*), but as an offering to the deity.[11] It is done not for sensual gratification, which is repeatedly said in the Tantra to be sinful,[12] but as a religious act. The *Kulārṇava Tantra*, which prescribes the Kaula *sādhanā*, clarifies, "If by merely having sexual intercourse with a woman one could become liberated, then all the creatures in the world would be liberated (*mukta*) through the sex act."[13]

We can now understand the significance of the phallic worship prescribed in the Tantras. The woman (*śakti* or *dutī*) participant in the ritualized sexual intercourse (*maithuna*) of the Kaula *sādhanā* is worshipped as the Goddess (*devī*). All the parts of her body, especially her sex organ, are worshipped by the male aspirant. She in turn worships him in the same fashion. Worship of the phallic symbol is well known. The male sex organ (*liṅga*) is taken to be Śiva; and the female one (*yoni*), on which the *liṅga* is placed, is regarded as Śakti.

The Śiva-*liṅga* can also be independently interpreted as the ultimate principle, Śiva-Śakti, without connecting it with the phallus; but in the Kaula tradition it is necessarily connected with the phallus. Perhaps the very symbol originated from the phallus and Śiva-Śakti worship is primarily Kaula worship.

Ancient Indians, it seems, had translated this Tantric wisdom into practice. They religiously worshipped the sex god as any other god. We find in ancient Sanskrit literature references to the worship of Madana or Kāma-deva (Lord Cupid) on a particular day of the year, Vasantapañcamī, the beginning of spring season.[14] Many of the temples in India, such as Khajuraho, Konarka, and so on, are amply carved with sex images. This may not be religious perversion or the expression of repressed sex — it seems to be a deliberate attempt, quite in line with the Tantric tradition, to give sex religious status so that people may understand that sex is as religious and holy as anything.

The snake, which is the symbol of sex,[15] is also an object of worship in the Hindu tradition. This is in contrast with the Christian tradition in which the serpent is taken to be a symbol of evil. The festival of snake worship on the day of Nāgapañcamī is a living tradition in India. Moreover according to Hindu mythology, Lord Viṣṇu rests on the Divine Serpent, Śeṣa, and the snake is the ornament of Lord Śiva's neck. This means that Viṣṇu and Śiva, the ideal integral personalities, have not killed or suppressed — but befriended or sublimated — the snake, or sex. There is also another myth that the earth rests upon the hood of Śeṣa, the Divine Serpent. This may mean that all the activities of the world are based on sex — an idea akin to that of Freud.

The attitude that sex is holy and divine, not profane, is an acknowledged characteristic of Tantrism, or the "left-hand" tradition of India. But this attitude can also be found in "right-hand" scriptures such as the *Bhāgavād Gītā* and the Upaniṣads. In the *Taittirīya Upaniṣad* the spiritual aspirant is advised as part of his or her *sādhanā* to feel that the working of the hands and the locomotion in the feet are Brahman.[16] It also states, "Brahman is present in the sex organ in the form of reproduction, nectar, and joy."[17] In the *Bhāgavād Gītā* the Lord says, "I am the libido that reproduces,"[18] and "I am the feeling of sex unopposed to morality in living beings."[19] In the *Śrīmadbhāgavāta* it is said, "Some others say, 'God is libido.'"[20] The *Bṛhadaraṇyaka Upaniṣad*, referring to sex sacrifice (*yajña*) says, "O Gautama, the woman is the fire, her sex organ is the firewood, the hairs on the sex organ are smoke, the vagina is the flame, the penetration is the *aṅgāra*, the sexual joy is the spark; in that the gods offer semen; and out of that oblation the *puruṣa* is born."[21] The almost identical passage occurs in the *Chāndogya Upaniṣad* also.[22]

An existentialist phenomenologist may ask why Tantra advocates taking sex as something divine instead of just accepting it as a natural physical function. From the Tantric point of view the sex energy is to be sublimated in the service of the goal of spiritual liberation. The Kaula *sādhanā*, or cultivation of a feeling of reverence towards sex, is a kind of yoga. If sex is used merely as it occurs in nature, it is not yoga but sensual enjoyment.

CULTIVATING LOVE TOWARDS THE SEX PARTNER

The second prescription of Kaulism regarding sex is that one should feel love for one's sex partner. The texts enjoin the aspirants to feel the sex partner to be completely their own. The man should see the woman as his own Śakti; the woman should see the man as her own Śiva. They should cultivate a sense of identity with each other, a sense of non-duality — that is, each partner should intensely love the other.

This type of love is essentially a spiritual quality. Loving a person has two mutually complementary aspects: (a) wishing the person well — that is, that he or she is well and happy, and (b) feeling oneness with the person, feeling that he or she is one's own self. There is yet a third aspect of love that cannot be cultivated; it flows automatically as a result of the first two aspects. This is the aesthetic aspect — the object of love appears beautiful and gives immense joy and satisfaction to the lover. The intensity with which the first two aspects are cultivated effects the intensity of feeling of the third aspect.

Love causes sex to be automatically sublimated. The entire sex act is transformed into love. Just as water when heated becomes vapor, so sex is transformed by the fire of love into the deep aesthetic satisfaction that is the third aspect of love. And just as vapor when cooled, returns to the grosser form of water, so love, when it cools, may again be transformed into the grosser form of sex. Love is the transforming factor. The second Tantric prescription, then, is that sex be engaged in not for mere sensual pleasure but as an expression of love. The feeling of love for the sex partner, combined with the sense of adoration outlined earlier, is the surest means for sublimating the sexual impulse.

The feeling of love sublimates the crude animal sex on the one hand, and it cures the mechanical and lifeless sex act of its insipidity and barrenness. It so happens in some cases that people, although indulging in sex in order to derive gratification and joy therefrom, do not get sufficient pleasure or satisfaction — sex becomes mechanical and lifeless. Sexual frigidity and impotence may also result. The insipidity and lifelessness of sex occurs not in isolated cases; this is the general predicament of the ultramodern free sex society. All free sex cultures suffer from this malady. This happens also in the case of married couples when over the course of time the warmth of love cools down and mechanical sex union takes its place. The dilemma of sex is that if sex is ignored and repressed, it creates psychological abnormality, but if sex is made an end in itself and enjoyed freely for its own sake, it becomes, after some time, devoid of relish and flavor. Therefore taking sex purely for enjoyment (*bhoga*) defeats its own purpose.

Kaulism is the way out of this dilemma; the cultivation of love is the remedy for the barrenness of the sex life. Sex becomes mechanical and lifeless only when it is devoid of love — that is, when the sex partner no longer remains an object of love and becomes just an object of enjoyment. It is love that cures sex of its insipidity and makes it pleasant and satisfying. Just as the light by which the moon shines does not belong to the moon itself, but comes from the sun, so also the joy of sex comes from love. Love is something independent; like the light of the sun it has independent joy, and it can give joy even without sex. But sex is dependent on love for its joy; sex without love has no life. If one is selfish and devoid of the capacity of loving, one is denied the real pleasure in sex. If sex, and not love, becomes the sole object of the male-female relationship, then it defeats its own purpose. This is the paradox of sex. Thus the malady of insipid sex from which the free sex culture suffers can be cured only by the cultivation of love.

Thus we see that love has a dual function in relation to sex: (a) it supplies joy and satisfaction to sex, and (b) in that very process it also sublimates sex by absorbing sex within itself. The feeling of sanctity towards sex mentioned earlier is incorporated in love, for there is a natural feeling of piety in love. There is nothing as holy and good as love. Thus, when sex is done as an act or expression of love and the minds of the persons involved are fixed not on sex enjoyment but on love, then the first injunction of the Kaula-*mārga*, namely the feeling of sanctity towards sex, is already fulfilled; love naturally sanctifies sex. The second injunction, namely the feeling of love towards the sex partner, therefore, is the complete way.

The Tantric or Kaulic way of life solves the Freudian dilemma. The dilemma that confronted Freud is that if sex is condemned and suppressed then it creates abnormality and disintegration of the personality; but if sex is given free rein then man becomes no better than an animal, and there is no social or cultural life worth the name. Sigmund Freud, although recognizing the sublimation of sex brought about by Nature itself, did not have the idea of conscious and deliberate methods of transforming or sublimating sex. Tantrism presents a deliberate method, a yoga, by which we can sublimate sex at will.

When sex is so sublimated, the problem of the dissociation of personality, as well as the problem of social and cultural life, automatically dissolves. The state of sex sublimation is a happy synthesis of the two — of what is called *preya* ("the pleasant") and *śreya* ("the good" or "the beneficial"). Love amazingly synthesizes within itself the pleasure of sex, also. The perfect lover finds his sex desire automatically gratified, even more intensely. When the sex feeling is transformed or sublimated to higher and subtler levels, it neither creates disintegration in the individual nor does it pose problems in social and cultural life. On the contrary, it integrates the individual personality on the one hand, and it adds to the richness and beautification of social and cultural life on the other.

The problem of sex crimes is also solved thereby. Sex crimes are indicative of the want of love in the offender. If the inordinate animal sex impulse is caressed by the soothing feeling of love, no sex crime is possible. I do not mean that sex crimes should not be punished — of course they must. What I suggest is that the internal education of sex through love and the feeling of sanctity should also be taken into account. Love naturally makes a person good and holy. It reconciles one's own good with the good of the person who is the object of one's sexual desire. If sex is perfectly in tune with love, nothing remains immoral or sinful in sex. In fact it is loveless sex that is the real sin; and it is this that activates sex crimes. What is sometimes termed love and is sometimes responsible even for the murder of the beloved by the lover is really not love; it is simply a violent flare of the sexual and emotional selfishness of the so-called lover.

The Tantric insight is to take the raw material, namely the sex life, and transform it. This is winning over Nature with the help of Nature's own laws. Sublimation or transformation is the law of Nature, just as the given material — sexual desire — is part of Nature. Human beings already engage in sex, so why not do it in such a way as to derive the best possible results? The Tantric treatment of sex can be likened to the agriculturalist's treatment of so-called waste material. The agriculturalist uses the waste matter to make fertilizer for the benefit of his crops. Nature has provided the plants with the power of transforming manure into nutrition. The foul odor of the excreta is turned into the fragrant smell of the flower. The nightsoil is changed into the edible fruit yielded by the plant. Likewise, the Tantrist recognizes the valuable material of sex and exploits it to serve a healthy and worthy purpose. Sublimated, sex blossoms into love, aesthetic enjoyment, and creativity in all walks of life. Sex sublimation is the key to the attainment of higher values of life, both secular and religious.

KAULA SĀDHANĀ AS THE MEANS OF SELF-REALIZATION

It has been established that the Kaula *sādhanā* is a means of sex sublimation, but it remains to be seen how it can bring realization (*mokṣa*), the highest value of life. It does this in two ways. First, it causes the aforementioned sex sublimation, which is essential for *mokṣa.* Second, it releases the flow of love, which is perhaps the most effective means of *mokṣa.* All texts of the Indian tradition, whether left-hand or not, aver that it is the feeling of oneness with all — universal love — that brings Self-realization. One cannot be realized unless one loves the entire universe.

One might object that while the Kaula practice may help in developing the feeling of love towards the sex partner, it does not necessarily serve to cultivate the *universal* love that is the means of realization. In response the Kaula would say that love for the opposite sex is the beginning of universal love. Tantrism exploits the inborn impulse towards love and sex to prompt a melting into universal love.

The cultivation of universal love can be easily and efficaciously begun from the point where one is already naturally loving — in a one-to-one relationship. When one reaches a sufficient degree of sexual sublimation, one can experience true love toward one's sex partner with the fullest intensity. In loving one's sex partner one can have the first glimpse of spiritual love. Sexual love, if mastered, naturally paves the way for universal love. The love experienced with one's sex partner can be redirected and focussed on the world as a whole.

Moreover, it does not really matter if the beloved object is a single person or the entire world; it is the quality of love that matters. If one has in one's heart a flow of true and pure love for even one person, one acquires the capacity to love the whole world. If the flow of love exists within the *sādhaka* it will saturate whatever object comes before him or her — be it an individual or a whole world. Thus it is that the exalted love stories found in the literature of so many cultures invariably depict the lovers as saintly and pure-hearted. This is not merely poetic imagination; it is a representation of a fact of life. The true lover cannot but become saintly.

There is yet another reason the *sādhanā* of sex sublimation may be said to be a means to Self-realization. We can reach the Self (Śiva) by catching the thread of spontaneity (*spanda*) in our experience and developing it more and more. Sex is perhaps the greatest spontaneous act in our physical experience. Of course, in ordinary life sex is tainted with impurity and therefore does not reflect perfect freedom, but it gives one a sense of that ultimate spontaneity or freedom. If we catch hold of that sense and cultivate it properly, we can reach the ultimate state of freedom.

STAGES OF KAULA SĀDHANĀ

The Tantra mentions three stages of the Kaula *sadhana* — animal (*paśu*), hero (*vīra*), and divine (*divya*) — which are meant for three different levels of people (*adhikārīs*). The animal stage, which is the lowest, is meant for ordinary people who have not sufficiently risen above selfishness and in whose case sex lies mostly on the crude physical level. At this stage the initiation of the married couple (*yāmala-dīkṣa*) alone is given. Sex is allowed only between husband and wife. In the hero stage extra-marital relations are allowed. But the conditions for qualifying as a hero are quite high. Although below the state of complete realization, the hero stands at a high level of sex sublimation. He or she has risen above selfishness and is capable of loving anyone as his or her own self. Only such highly-qualified people are allowed to perform the hero *sādhanā*. The third and highest stage is the divine or godly (*divya*). There are two characteristics of those qualified by this stage. First, the ego of the *sādhaka* has vanished; he or she has attained the state of universal love. Second, such people have no need of physical sex; they can feel the same intensity of love, or even more, without bodily union. This is the highest level of sex sublimation. Only saints and those who are *jīvanmukta* stand at this level.

This classification system and hierarchy in the Kaula *sādhanā* implies that all people do not stand at the same level spiritually. Tantra shares this understanding with Indian philosophical systems in general. Hence there are different levels of spiritual practice appropriate to different levels of competence (*adhikārī bheda*). If these barriers to participation by unqualified people are ignored, havoc may be the result. If, for example, a person at the animal level is allowed to perform the extra-marital sex acts that should be restricted to those of the hero and divine levels, definite harm to the individual and society will follow. That is why the Tantra enjoins its adherents to practice the Kaula *sādhanā* secretly and keep it away from the general public. It is said, "Just as one guards one's wealth from thieves, so should one guard the Kaulic practice from the laymen (*paśus*)."[23] The layman is warned that "treading the Kaulic path is more difficult than moving on the edge of a sword or riding a tiger or wearing a serpent."[24] Those who ignore the warning and use the Kaulic material for sensual enjoyment (*bhoga*) are vehemently criticized by the Tantra.[25]

THE KAULA SĀDHANĀ: AN APPRAISAL

That the Tantra could claim the Kaula *sādhanā* to be the best of all paths is quite understandable. This is more than just a self-eulogy. The sublimation of desires and the cultivation of universal love are the most essential ingredients for liberation. These two aims can be achieved easily and perfectly through the Tantric *sādhanā*. Tantrism, or Kaulism, is not merely a particular ritualistic sex worship; it is a general attitude towards life, an attitude of acceptance and integration of all aspects of life. It is a positive philosophy of life that assimilates life and makes it sublime. No one can be really liberated without this attitude. If Kaulism is understood in this wider sense it can be safely said that no one can be liberated without having the Kaula attitude. Thus, latter-day holy men such as Ramakrishna Paramahansa or Rama Maharishi, while they may not have actually followed the particular ritualistic Kaula practice, were certainly Kaula in their attitude towards life.

Finally, it should be made clear that in Kaulism the state of enjoyment (*bhoga*) does not preclude the state of transcendence. While participating in sense experiences the Kaula is seated in the transcendent Self enjoying the bliss of the Self, not the pleasure of the object of sense. The Kaula enjoys the pleasure of the Self *through* the object. While engaging in pleasurable activities, the Kaula places his or her attention on the Self, or on love, which is natural to the Self. The moment the attention is turned from the Self to the object of enjoyment, it is a fall. Of course it is very difficult to keep the attention fixed on the Self or love and not allow it to drift to the enjoyment; it is for this reason that the Kaula *sādhanā* is said to be as difficult as moving on the edge of a sword. But it is only difficult for the ego-bound individual who has not realized the purifying bliss of Love and is still confined to the level of selfish enjoyment; it is not difficult for the enlightened one, who easily identifies the enjoyed object with his or her own self.

The hedonist may suggest that if the attention is on the Self and not on the enjoyment then the action would not afford any pleasure and would be like not eating a tasty morsel but rather offering it into the sacrificial fire. In answer the Kaula would say that the pleasure can be felt even more so — both in quantity and in quality — than when the attention is on the enjoyment itself. The reason for this is simple: the pleasure derived from an object does not come from the object itself but from the Self, or from the love natural to the Self, just as the moon shines not by its own light but by the light of the sun. The Upaniṣads say, "When *that* shines, all this shines; all this shines by the light of *that* ".[26] All the pleasure of the world comes from the Self, only indirectly. If we are not seated in the Self, we are *not* able to enjoy the world. The pleasure we take from the world is proportionate to the degree of Self-realization we have achieved. The poet Coleridge, addressing Nature, says, "O Lady, we receive but what we give," meaning that we receive from Nature or the world the joy that we already unconsciously project on it.[27]

The Kaula would further retort that if the attention is only on the enjoyment and not on the Self, it is self-defeating. This is what happens in the case of those who enjoy sex for the pleasure of the sex itself; after some time sex becomes mechanical, insipid, and tasteless. The pleasure of the sex life is not independent; it depends on the Self, or love, which is *spiritual.*

A final question arises, if the pleasure comes from the Self itself and not from the object of enjoyment, then why does the Self, independent in bliss, accept the outside object of enjoyment? What need is there of indulging in sense pleasure? In answer the Tantrist would say that the Self, perfect and satisfied in itself, need not indulge in sense pleasures and yet it does so out of its free will (*svātantrya*) or what is called *spanda* (or *kriyā)* — a phenomenon we have already discussed and identified in our actual experience. This indulgence does not diminish or defile the Self, but on the contrary enriches it all the more. This is like a beautiful woman putting on ornaments: the ornaments are not beautiful in themselves, they derive their beautifying power from the beauty of the woman and, in turn, beautify her all the more. Of course in the case of the woman, the ornaments are different from her, so in that sense at least she is dependent on the ornaments. In the case of the Self, the ornaments (the enjoyable objects) are self-manifestations, so the Self is perfectly independent in its enjoyment of them. This is really an indirect way of self-enjoyment. It is part of the *līlā* or sport of the Self. Thus the enjoyment of the world (*jagadānanda* or *lokānanda*) is the free activity of the Self.[28]

Love is a concrete example of the above position. When we love a person in the true sense of the term, the love is independent — that is the love is self-satisfied even without physical contact with the beloved person. This is exactly what happens in the *divya* stage of the Kaula *sādhanā*, although we do not ordinarily find one hundred percent true love and therefore dependence on the physical contact is present to some degree. Yet the physical contact gives no joy, for the joy comes from love not from the physical contact. Yet when the love is present, the physical contact enhances it. Acceptance of physical contact is the free expression of true love.

Moreover in this case enjoyment (*bhoga*) is done not as *bhoga* but as the sportive expression of the benign joy (*ānanda*). That is, in this case *bhoga* rises from the crude animal level of selfish gratification to the level of the free and spontaneous expression of the joy (*ānanda*) of the Self. As such it does not remain *bhoga* at all but becomes *spanda*—joyful activity, free and spontaneous.

11

Conclusion

From the discussion in the foregoing pages it follows that the Tantric tradition, apart from being highly significant in its own right, is complementary to the Vedic, or Upaniṣadic, tradition. The Āgamic *kriyā* complements the Vedic *jñāna*, the positive complements the negative, the immanent complements the transcendent, yoga complements *sannyāsa*, the left complements the right. The *kriyā* concept, though not explicitly explained, is implicitly present in the Vedas and Upaniṣads. The implicit is made explicit in the Āgamas or Tantras. The Upaniṣadic utterances regarding Creation clearly suggest the *kriyā* principle in Brahman. It is said that the world comes out of or emanates from Brahman,[1] or that, "He willed, 'Let me become many and reproduce.'"[2] These statements tend to suggest *kriyā* or *spanda*. The statement "All these things come out of the bliss itself"[3] refers in unequivocal terms to *spanda*. These statements cannot be explained away by labeling them fables (*ākhyāyikās*) as the Advaitin does.

The seeds of the left-handed way (Kaula- or *vāmā-mārga*) can also be successfully traced to the Vedas and the Upaniṣads. The *Bṛhadāraṇyaka* and the *Chāndogya* Upaniṣads mention the sex act as a form of holy sacrifice (*yajña*).[4] Of course the aim there is to describe the proper process of reproduction and to enforce the proper attitude towards sexual union; the aim is not to promote sex sublimation as in the Kaula path. But certainly there is a reverential attitude towards sex there. We find the same reverential attitude towards sex in the *Gītā* also.[5] The Tantra maintains that the Kaula *sādhanā* that it advocates is not non-Vedic. The *Kulārṇava Tantra* quotes Vedic passages to show that the seed of the Kaula *sādhanā* is very much present in the Vedas.[6]

The Āgamic position does not differ from the original Upaniṣadic position but from the classical scholastic Advaita of Śaṁkara and later Vedāntins. The crux of the difference between the two positions rests on whether Brahman actively creates the world out of Itself as its *līlā*, or Brahman remains neutral and the world is a superimposition on Brahman like the rope-snake.

The Tantrist holds that the world is a self-projection of Śiva, whereas according to the Advaitin, Brahman, like the rope, ever remains neutral and inactive. The Upaniṣads themselves do not seem to subscribe to this non-active view; the Upaniṣadic Brahman actively or spontaneously manifests the world out of Itself. The Advaitin interprets the simple and direct sentences of the Upaniṣads concerning the process of Creation as fables invented by the Upaniṣadic seers in order to silence the unanswerable question of Creation. We also do not find a distinction between Brahman and Īśvara in the Upaniṣads nor is there any theory of superimposition. These are not found in the *Brahma Sūtras* either. All this is the formulation of the Advaitin.

Our criticism of scholastic Advaita is that if Brahman is not taken to be a creative power (*śakti*), the world cannot be unified with Brahman; it cannot be Brahman's manifestation. When the Advaitin advances the theory of world-as-appearance in order to unify the world with Brahman, he or she seems to forget the further logical necessity of accepting the world as the self-projection of

Brahman, in which case Brahman has to be accepted as creative. But the Advaitin starts with the presupposition that Brahman is inactive, which is a one-sided position. It takes a partial view of the Upaniṣadic philosophy. Advaita stretches the simple Upaniṣadic sayings to yield unusual meanings, and formulates novel doctrines in order to explain its position consistently — doctrines that the Upaniṣads themselves do not support. Moreover the Advaitin's position gives rise to many difficulties in understanding the Upaniṣads. The clear axiology of the Upaniṣads, for example, becomes difficult to understand in the Advaita exposition.

Moreover, in so far as Advaita takes the world to be a superimposition on Brahman created by ignorance (*avidyā*) and not as an active creation of Brahman, its position amounts to a duality between the neutral Brahman and the machinery of *avidyā* projecting the whole world on the unresponsive Absolute. The difficulty with this position is that Brahman and the world are separate. Advaita seems to overlook the fact that the non-duality of Brahman can be preserved only if the world is taken to be Brahman's self-projection, not merely a superimposition on a neutral and inactive Absolute. Advaita may have recourse to the concept of Brahman-with-qualities, or Īśvara, and say that there is no duality between Brahman and *avidyā* because *avidyā* is the *śakti* of Īśvara and the world is a self-projection of Īśvara through *avidyā śakti*. But since Advaita does not see Īśvara as ultimately real and maintains a difference between Brahman and Īśvara, the problem of duality remains — it only shifts from the duality of Brahman and *avidyā* to the duality of Brahman and Īśvara.

Advaita should eliminate the distinction between Brahman and Īśvara and admit that the self-projection of Īśvara is the self-projection of Brahman, otherwise it results in a duality between the *śakti-less* Brahman that has nothing to do with the world and the *śakti-full* Īśvara who is the creator and governor of the world. The problem cannot be solved simply by calling Īśvara and His world false, for the world is not pure nothing (*asat*). *As appearance* it has epistemic or ideal reality. As such it has to be given a place in the Real by making it a free expression *of* the Real and not merely a superimposition *on* the Real if the non-duality of the Real is to be preserved. This is exactly what Kashmir Śaivism does.

The Upaniṣadic position could be construed even more consistently and more comprehensively in a way other than that of the Advaitin. There could well be an Upaniṣadic Advaita different from the classical scholastic Advaita. The views of Vivekananda, Sri Aurobindo, Rabindranath Tagore, or even Ramana Maharsi are nearer to the Upaniṣads than classical Advaita is. The Upaniṣadic Advaita is not inactivistic, nor is it world-negating in the scholiast's sense. The transcendence of Brahman suggested by the Upaniṣadic phrase "Here there is no duality of any kind" (*nehanānāsti kiñcana*), does not mean that Brahman is inactive — it only suggests the freedom of Brahman. The Advaitin would construe this freedom of Brahman as "freedom from," not as "freedom to." But in the Upaniṣads "freedom to" is not only not denied but is also positively stated. As to the question of the compatibility of "freedom-to" with "freedom-from," we have already seen that the former, understood in the sense of *kriyā* (not *karma*) is quite compatible with the latter. The Upaniṣads do not take a negative, renunciatory view of life; the Upaniṣadic way of life is also a life of richness and fulfillment. As we have already pointed out, the Upaniṣads do not create a dichotomy between enjoyment (*bhukti*) and liberation (*mukti*); *bhukti* is compatible with *mukti.* They prescribe a synthesis of the two. One may wonder how the negativistic view of life held by Advaita is derived from the Upaniṣads. Upaniṣadic Advaita differs from classical scholastic Advaita, and the Āgamic position is *not* different from Upaniṣadic Advaita.

The philosophy of Kashmir Śaivism serves as a corrective to the wrong attitude created by the philosophy of illusion (Māyāvāda). Māyāvāda creates a damagingly negative attitude towards life and the world — an attitude that is logically absurd and axiologically foolish. In the foregoing analysis of Advaita Vedāntic scholasticism in different contexts, we have seen that the attitude of the scholiast is not only un-Upaniṣadic but also logically inconsistent and untenable. If the manifestation of the world is not accepted as a self-projection of Brahman and is seen merely as a superimposition (*adhyāsa*) on Brahman — Brahman being neutral and inactive — then there must be an independent machinery of superimposition different from Brahman that works against the non-duality of Brahman. From the real (*paramārtha*) point of view, the world can be appearance (*mithyā*) and not mere nothing (*asat*), for it is a fact that the world *appears*. We can deny the world as a material reality, but we cannot deny the world as an appearance or projection of Consciousness.

The Māyāvādic philosophy that the world is a superimposition on Reality and therefore an obstruction of it, naturally leads to the conclusion that in order to attain Reality, the world must be discarded. According to the Māyāvādin, the world, which is ultimately valueless (*tuccha*), not only has no place in the attainment of *mokṣa* but is also contradictory to *mokṣa*. Indulgence in worldly activities, even activities related to social and cultural upliftment, creates bondage and leads to the opposite of *mokṣa*.

If we throw a glance on the social and cultural history of India, especially the medieval period onwards, we find that the practical impact of the negativistic philosophy of Māyāvāda has been that the best brains of India, taking the path of *mokṣa*, turned their backs on social work, thinking that every type of worldly activity would ultimately lead to bondage. The result was that Indian society was led by mediocrities and ignoramuses. Indian society has been in perpetual need of social reformation and cleansing of the dirt accumulated in the name of the Vedic *varṇāśrama dharma*. Unfortunately the people who had the capacity to do this were uninterested in the endeavor, for they considered all such work to be inconducive to the pursuit of *mokṣa*. Indian society, in want of proper leadership, continued to degenerate. A weakened India could not resist the onslaught of foreign invaders and became a slave country, only to be liberated much later when the philosophy of *mokṣa* was reinterpreted in a positive way by leaders like Vivekananda, Tilak, Gandhi, Aurobindo, and others.

There is need of a reinterpreting and restructuring of the Advaitic-Māyāvādic philosophy that is mistaken for the representative philosophy of India. Kashmir Śaivism turns the negativistic philosophy of Māyāvāda into a positive idealism that accepts the world as a free manifestation of Brahman (Śiva). Kashmir Śaivism may be viewed as a reinterpretation and restructuring of Māyāvāda, setting Māyāvāda aright.

The correct interpretation of Māyāvāda is that the world is not a reality but a projection or manifestation of Consciousness. The true significance of Māyāvāda lies in the discovery that the world is an "ideal" reality — made of Consciousness, not matter — and as such it is an active creation of Consciousness, not a mere superimposition on it from outside. This implies the acceptance of activity, dynamism, or power (*śakti*) in Brahman. Unfortunately, Advaita is not ready to accept activity in Brahman, for it takes all activity to be *karma*, which is a sign of imperfection. The basic mistake of Advaita is that it does not recognize the truth of *spanda*, or *kriyā*, which is as important a truth as knowledge (*jñāna*). As we have already seen, *spanda* (*kriyā* or *vimarśa*) is free and spontaneous activity that naturally arises out of the fullness of bliss (*ānanda*) and is basically different from *karma*, the voluntary effortful action that arises out of some lack or want. Acceptance of Brahman as inactive (*niṣkriya*) is the root mistake of Advaita, which drives it to the logical absurdity of denying even the most obvious truths.

The thesis I have brought out while expounding the philosophy of Abhinavagupta has the following points:

1. The Tantra is complementary to the Veda, including the Upaniṣads, in the sense that what is implicit in the Veda is made explicit in the Tantra, and what is left out of the Veda is supplied by the Tantra. Further, the Tantra is more complete in itself, for it contains what the Veda *has* plus what the Veda lacks. The *spanda* or

kriyā principle, or the concept of dynamic consciousness (*śakti*), is implicitly present in the Upaniṣads; it is given explicit and elaborate treatment in the Tantra. Moreover the yogic *sādhanās* and the ways of life aimed at transforming worldly life into a means of liberation dwelt upon in the Tantric tradition are not very clearly given in the Vedic tradition.

2. Apart from being complementary to the Veda, the Tantra is highly significant in itself. It presents a complete philosophy of life that has the potential to answer all the problems of life. The Tantric philosophy is significant in all three aspects of philosophy — epistemology, ontology, and axiology.

3. Epistemologically, Tantra is *āgama* or *āgamana* ("induction"), a tradition of experience that is being tested and verified. In this sense, āgamic knowledge can be called "scientific." Veda is *nigama* or *nigamana* ("revelation"). For its confirmation, revelation requires experience; revelation without experience remains an object of faith and does not become knowledge. The Vedic revelation is confirmed in experience, and this experiential confirmation is the function of the Tantra.

A very significant Tantric insight regarding the nature of knowledge is that knowledge is not a passive state of consciousness but an activity of consciousness, though an effortless or automatic one. Knowledge is not really like the reflection of the moon in a pond, the classical analogy given by the passivity theorist; in knowledge there is an active "grasping" on the part of the knower. The pond does not become aware of, or "grasp," the reflection, but the mind does "grasp" the reflection of the object. If the mind does not actively "grasp," there can be no knowledge. This "grasping" of the object is an activity in consciousness, but since the activity is effortless and automatic, we take it to be non-existent.

4. The ontological significance of the Tantric philosophy lies in its conception of Consciousness, or Self, as a dynamic power (*śakti*)

and its conception of Reality as Śiva-Śakti (*jñāna-kriyā*, or *prakāśa-vimarśa*). The dynamism or spontaneous activity (*spanda*) of ultimate Consciousness (*parā-samvit*) is responsible for the manifestation of the world. In Tantra, Creation is conceived of as the sportive activity of Śiva, or the dance of Naṭarāja. The Tantric theory of creation is Līlāvāda to the Advaita and Mādhyamika Buddhist Māyāvāda.

5. The Tantric axiology, which logically follows from its ontology, aims at accepting the world and making it divine. Every object of natural Creation, except the evil that is willfully created by man, is to be viewed as divine and benign (*śiva*). In the Tantra there is a highly positive attitude towards the world and worldly values. The Tantra presents a way of life in which *bhoga* ("enjoyment") becomes yoga and the otherwise bondage-creating round of existence (*saṁsāra*) becomes a means to liberation. In the Tantric way, material life becomes spiritualized.

The Tantric *mokṣa*, or Self-realization, is not an otherworldly, after-death value but the ground of overall success in material life. Life in all its aspects — both individual and social — is fulfilled through Self-realization. Moreover, Self-realization is a state of joyful activity, a state of relaxed or actionless activity, which has both internal relaxation and external vigorous, dutiful activity in one.

6. The Tantric philosophy is also historically significant. In India we can find two divergent and contradictory traditions from the very beginning of known history. One is the way of renunciation (*nivṛtti*), and the other is the way of worldly involvement (*pravṛtti*). Tantra synthesizes the two. The Tantric way of life is a happy and perfectly successful amalgam or synthesis of these two opposite trends of Indian culture. This synthesis is an event that is of profound historical and cultural significance. Speaking from the point of view of cultural history, India presents, in the form of Tantra, a philosophy of life that is complete and perfect in all respects.

7. Not everything that goes in the name of Tantra is Tantric.

Many aberrations have arisen in the Tantric tradition. Practices like physical sacrifice (animal and human), black magic, use of sex for the sake of sensual enjoyment, and so on are highly un-Tantric, but they usually mascarade as Tantra. It is unreasonable to think that the Goddess is pleased with the killing of her own creatures in sacrifice. Moreover, no psychic or spiritual power can be attained by sacrifice. Similarly, black magic is an abuse of the psychic powers. Like scientific technology, psychic power is meant for helping others not harming them. In the same way, the *sādhanā* of sexual union is meant not for lust (*bhoga*) but for changing one's mental attitude. There are imposters and pseudo-Tantrists who need to be carefully separated from genuine Tantra when an analysis of Tantra is undertaken.

8. Of all the Tantric denominations, the Śaiva, or Śaiva-Śakta, tradition is the most comprehensive one. We find the full and complete picture of the Tantric world in Śiva-Śakti Tantrism. Within this tradition, the Trika system, or Kashmir Śaivism, is the most comprehensive; thus it is the truly representative system of the Tantric tradition. Having an integral and all-accommodative approach, Kashmir Śaivism synthesizes within itself all the other systems of the Tantric tradition. Other systems represent Tantrism partially, whereas Kashmir Śaivism does it fully. It not only contains all the elements of Tantrism but it also presents them in the most appropriate form, spelling them out fully. Thus Kashmir Śaivism can be called the central philosophy of Tantrism.

9. The contribution of Abhinavagupta to Tantric thought is especially significant. (a) Abhinavagupta presents the otherwise difficult philosophy of Tantra in a cogent and coherent way; he makes Tantra rationally understandable. (b) In Kashmir Śaivism, he provides the thread of unity among the different sub-trends of the school — namely, the Krama, Kaula, Spanda, and Pratyabhijñā branches. He picks up the concept of Pratyabhijñā and successfully uses it as a thread to weave into one single garland the different flowers of the

sub-trends of Kashmir Śaivism. For him, Prayabhijñā becomes *the* philosophy in which all the other forms are organically incorporated. (c) Even in the Pratyabhijñā philosophy, Abhinavagupta makes the special contributions of (1) correcting and modifying the positions of his predecessors, especially Somānanda's attitude towards the linguistic philosophy of Bhartṛhari, in order to make the system fully consistent, and (2) fully spelling out the potentialities of the Pratyabhijñā philosophy. (d) Abhinavagupta's contribution to the Indian aesthetic theory is highly significant. His *rasa* theory, propounded in the light of his Śaiva philosophy, has greatly influenced aesthetic thought since his time.

10. The key concept of Kashmir Śaivism is *kriyā*, or *spanda*, which means free and spontaneous activity. *Kriyā* is different from *karma*, which is effortful voluntary action that is suggestive of imperfection and bondage; *karma* produces *kārma mala*, which is one of the spiritual impurities. *Kriyā*, or *spanda*, is the freedom (*svātantrya*) of the Self or Consciousness. The Self exhibits its freedom even at the *paśu* level, although in a limited form. The self at the *paśu* level, which has only limited freedom, can attain its potential freedom in fullness through *sādhanā*. Emphasis on the freedom (*svātantrya*) of the Self is a unique feature of Kashmir Śaivism.

It is the *kriyā* principle, the natural dynamism in the Self, that makes self-consciousness possible even in the ultimate non-dual Consciousness, Śiva. According to Advaita Vedāntic logic, awareness of the not-Self is the occasion for becoming aware of oneself, and since Brahman is absolutely devoid of the "other," there is no self-consciousness in Brahman. Kashmir Śaivism provides an alternative factor — the natural dynamism of Consciousness — that makes the non-dual Śiva self-conscious. In Kashmir Śaivism, *kriyā* is the logic of self-consciousness. The Self, or Consciousness, devoid of self-consciousness is no better than insentient matter (*jaḍa*).

11. The central problem of Kashmir Śaivism is that of Self-recognition (*pratyabhijñā* or *ātma-pratyabhijñā*), around which the

entire philosophy and religion of the system move. *Kriyā* is the key concept, and *pratyabhijñā* is the key problem. The problem starts with the question, who am I and how am I related to the world? By breaking through the surface self with the help of *sādhanā*, one reaches one's deeper Self, which is Śiva; and then one realizes that Nature, or the world, is not "other." One realizes one's unity with all beings; Self-realization naturally carries the sense of unity (*advaita-bhāvanā*).

12. Ābhāsavāda, the theory of the world as appearance that forms the cosmology of Kashmir Śaivism, clearly recognizes the truth that appearance (*ābhāsa*) *as appearance*, or as the process of self-projection, is real. In the case of appearance, the real material object that is posed by the appearance is false and the *appearance itself* is not false, just as the reflection in a mirror cannot be rejected *as reflection*; it can be rejected only as a real object, just as a cinema-projection *as projection* is very real. The world as appearance is not a superimposition on Śiva like the rope-snake but is the self-projection of Śiva like that of a magician or a yogin. This means that Śiva is actively involved in Creation and does not lie neutral and inactive like the Brahman of Advaita Vedāntic scholasticism.

The world appearance (*jagadābhāsa*) is a free manifestation or free spontaneous activity (*kriyā* or *spanda*) of Śiva. Śiva is not obliged to create or project the world out of Himself. When He creates or projects, He does so out of freedom, or freely out of joy (*ānanda*). Thus Ābhāsavāda fits perfectly with Svātantryavāda. The ultimate Consciousness, Śiva, has not only "freedom-from" but also "freedom-to" — the freedom to act or appear as It likes.

13. It logically follows from the above point that Creation is a sportive activity (*līlā*) or dance of Śiva, as Creation is a free manifestation out of the bliss of Śiva. The presence of evil in the world is not due to Śiva Himself but to humankind; people deliberately exercise their free will in favor of the abuse or misuse of their powers. Man, although substantially one with Śiva, is functionally and exis-

tentially different. Śiva has introduced the cosmic game of Creation in which the individual souls take part as players. But the individual souls are not like robots; they have free will. They deliberately choose, out of their free will, to violate the rules of the game. They hit the heads of their co-players instead of hitting the ball. Śiva of course punishes them for such violations. He has also introduced into this grand game a law of punishment in the form of the Law of Karma.

It is theoretically possible, therefore, that the world play could become absolutely free of evil if the players — the souls or *paśus* — chose not to violate the rules of the game. Just because there is the violation of the rules of the game on the part of the individual players out of their own free will, and the subsequent punishment of this violation in the form of suffering, this does not mean that the world is not a sport, or that it does not arise out of the bliss of Śiva.

14. In Kashmir Śaivism the emphasis is on practical *sādhanā*; philosophy is meant for life. Abhinavagupta, in his *Tantrāloka*, has categorized and classified all the *sādhanās*. The remarkable thing in this context is that Kashmir Śaivism has given three hierarchical categories of *sādhanās*, or ways, technically called *upāyas*; all the possible means for spiritual realization can be classified under one or the other of the three *upāyas* — *āṇavopāya*, *śāktopāya*, and *śāmbhavopāya*. *Āṇavopāya*, or *kriyopāya*, includes all physical and external forms of worship and *sādhanā*. *Śāktopāya*, or *jñānopāya*, comprises all the mental forms of *sādhanā*, such as meditation. *Śāmbhavopāya*, or *icchopāya*, contains all the spiritual *sādhanās* such as surrender of the ego, realization of universal unity, and universal love. The *upāyas* are hierarchical and meant for different levels of aspirants.

15. A very significant *sādhanā* that is unique to Tantrism is that of the Kaula-*mārga* or *vāma-mārga* — the left-handed way of spiritual *sādhanā* in which the five M's (*pañcamakāra*) are used as objects of worship. Apart from the natural and real difference

between the good and the bad, we have artificially created many false disctinctions of good and bad, or religious and profane. By using the so-called impure objects in worship, Kaula-*sādhanā* aims at freeing the spiritual aspirant from false and vain distinctions.

Moreover, the *sādhanā* related to sex has the added significance of bringing about sex sublimation. The Tantric seers realized that sex is the most potent psychophysical energy and, if sublimated, can work wonders. The Tantric wisdom lies in winning over Nature with the help of the laws of Nature itself. In accordance with the natural law of transformation, or sublimation, the Tantric seers devised ways for transforming the base desires, especially sexual desire, into nobler and finer forms. Sex energy, if sublimated, can be made to flow through the highly beneficial channels of love, aesthetic creativity, devotion (*bhakti*), social service, and so on, on the one hand, and be used as the means of Self-realization on the other. The sexual attraction between man and woman may be transformed into true love between them, and then the conjugal love may be channeled into universal love, which is the sure means of Self-realization. This is the rationale of the Kaula-*sādhanā*. This much-misunderstood and much-abused *sādhana* is of colossal significance if practiced in its true spirit.

śivārpaṇamastu
"Dedicated to Śiva"

Notes

CHAPTER 1

1. Abhinavagupta authored a voluminous work entitled *Tantrāloka* (literally "the light of Tantra") in which he systematized the philosophy and religion of Tantra in a cogent and coherent way. The *Tantrāloka* is the most rational and logical presentation of the Tantric position in existence.
2. *yotovā imāni bhūtāni jāyante.* TAITTIRĪYA UPANIṢAD 3.1.
3. *tadaikṣata bahusyām prajāyeyeti.* CHĀNDOGYA UPANIṢAD 6.2.3.
4. *ānandāddhyeva khalvimāni bhūtāni jāyante.* TAITTIRĪYA UPANIṢAD 3.6.
5. Further, the golden Umā, or Pārvatī, (*umā haimavatī*) that appears in the famous story of the *Yakṣa* in the *Kena Upaniṣad* suggests that Brahman is Śiva, and Umā, Śakti. In the Tantric tradition, *Umā* is a synonym for *Śakti.*
6. *anubhava-sampradāyopadeśa-pariśīlanena* . . . . P.T.V., p. 161. For a complete discussion of *āgama* ("induction"), see Chapter 2.
7. *svātmā sarvabhāvasvabhāvaḥ svayaṁ prakāśamānaḥ svātmānameva svātmāvibhinnena praśnaprativacanāt praṣṭṛ-prativakṭṛ-svātmamayena ahaṁtayā camatkurvan vimṛśati* . . . . IBID., pp. 14-15.
8. *guru-śiṣya-pade sthitvā svayaṁ devo sadāśivaḥ/*
   pūrvottarapadairvākyaiḥ tantraṁ samavatārayat// IBID., p. 12.
9. The Tantric tradition existed in oral form from the time of the Vedas; it was only written down in the post-Vedic period.
10. *ṣaḍdarsanāni meṅgāni pādau kukṣiḥ karau śiraḥ/*
    teṣu bhedantu yaḥ kuryānmamāṅgaṁ chedayattu saḥ//
    etānyeva kulasyāpi ṣaḍaṅgāni bhavanti hi/
    tasmād vedātmakaṁ śāstraṁ viddhi kaulātmakaṁ priye//
    KULĀRṆAVA TANTRA 2.84–85.
11. This will be covered in detail in Chapter 2.
12. *sarvabhūtātmabhūtātmā.* BH.G. 5.7.

13. *sarvabhūtahite ratāh.* IBID. 5.25.
14. *dvaitaprathā tadajñānaṁ tucchatvād banda ucyate.* T.A. 1.30.
15. *karṇāt karṇopadeśena samprāptamavanītalam.* YOGINĪHṚDAYAM 1.3. Also, *ṣaivādīni rahasyāni pūrvamāsanmahātmanām, ṛṣīṇāṁ vaktrakuhare . . .* Ś.D. 7.107.
16. The theory of the Dravidian origin of Tantrism is probably based on a survey of the ethos of the tribal people in India, who have a very positive attitude towards life and a very liberal and Tantra-like view of sex. This is especially noticeable in the tribals of Bastar and Surguja. The sexual dormitories (*ghotuls*) of Bastar are famous. The tribals of India enjoy life fully even in financial and technological deprivation, and they seem to take life as sport, or play (*līlā*). But this in itself is not a sufficient reason for theorizing that the Indian tribals are the descendents of Dravidians and that the Tantric way of life is specifically Dravidian.
17. The philological research of Dr. S. S. Mishra, Professor of Linguistics at Banaras Hindu University, among others, tends to suggest that Aryans originally inhabited Indian plains, and went from India to middle Asia and other places, not that they originally came from middle Asia to India. Professor S. S. Mishra discusses the issue at length in his work, *Aryan Problem: A Linguistic Approach* (at press).
18. *mā śiśnadevā api gurṛtaṁ naḥ. Ṛgveda* 7.21.5. Also, *ghnañchiśnadevān api varpasā bhūt.* IBID. 10.99.3.
19. *bhogo yogāyate sākṣāt pātakaṁ sukṛtāyate/*
mokṣāyate ca saṁsāraḥ kuladharme kuleśvari// KULĀRṆAVA TANTRA 2.24.
20. *andhantamaḥ praviśanti ye-avidyāmupāsate/*
tato bhūya iva te tamo ya u vidyāyāṁ ratāḥ// ĪŚA UPANIṢAD, verse 9.
21. *vidyāṁ cāvidyāṁ ca yastadvedobhayaṁ saha/*
avidyayā mṛtyuṁ tīrtvā vidyayāmṛtamaśnute// IBID., verse 11.
22. Sometimes in the Buddhist Tantric tradition the case is just the reverse — man is taken as the symbol of activity and woman as that of knowledge. However, the difference in the symbol does not make any difference in the symbolized.
23. In Vaiṣṇava Tantrism, Kṛṣṇa and Rādhā are frequently used for Śiva and Śakti; Rāma and Sītā are not so frequently mentioned. However, many of the Vaiṣṇava Bhakta poets have explicitly accepted Rāma-Sītā as Śiva-Śakti. Tulasīdāsa, for example, clearly sees Rāma-Sītā as Śiva-Śakti when he says, "Sītā and Rāma are different only in name and really not different, like the word and its meaning or like the water and the wave." (*girā-aratha jala-bīci sama, kahiyata bhinna na bhinna; bandau sītā-rāma-pada . . .*) RĀMA-CARITA-MĀNASA 1.18.

24. *sa eva hi ahambhāvātmā devasya krīḍādimayasya śuddha pāramārthikyau jñāna-kriya, prakāśarūpatā jñānaṁ tatraiva svātantryātmā vimavśaḥ kriyā* I.P.V. 1.8.11, p. 338.
25. *anāghreyam anālokyam aspṛśyañcāpyapeyakam. madyaṁ māṁsaṁ paśūnāntu kaulikānāṁ mahāphalam.* KULĀRṆAVA TANTRA 2.124.
26. *adhikāriṇyaṇau jātikulavarṇādyanādarāt.* M.V.V. 2.277.
27. *parīkṣitāya dātavyaṁ vatsarārdhoṣitāya ca.* YOGINĪHṚDAYAM 1.5.
28. In this connection mention of the controversial Rajneeshis is unavoidable. Bhagwan Rajneesh, as he is called by his devotees, was superb in his theoretical presentation of the *sādhanā* of sex-sublimation. He might also have personally practiced the *sādhanā* in its true spirit. But what occurs with some, or most, of the Rajneeshis is quite dubious. In the Tantras, hierarchical forms of the sex *sādhanā* are prescribed in accordance with the different levels of competence (*adhikārī-bheda*) of the practitioners. The *paśu-sādhaka*, who is at the lowest stage and has the attitude that sex is for sensual enjoyment (*bhoga-dṛṣṭi*), is not allowed extramarital sex; he or she is given the initiation of the married couple (*yāmala-dīkṣā*). Extramarital sex is reserved for the *vīra-sādhaka*, who has risen above *bhoga-dṛṣṭi* and has attained a high degree of love. And even in this case the sexual *sādhanā* is not allowed to be practiced publicly, lest it give the wrong impression to others. The left-handed path is meant to be kept secret (Kulārṇava Tantra 11.82). It seems that Rajneesh committed the mistake of allowing the ordinary *paśu-sādhakas* to perform *vīra-sādhanā*, and that, too, in public! Allowing *vīra-sādhanā* to be practiced by the ordinary person of the animal (*paśu*) level is hazardous for both the individual and society. It will confuse the *paśu-sādhaka* and will create sexual chaos in society.
29. T.A.V. (commentary by Jayaratha) 1.18.
30. *ataśca bheda-bhedābheda-abheda pratipādakaṁ śivarudra-bhairavākhyaṁ tridhaivedaṁ śāstramudbhūtam.* T.A.V. 1.18, p. 45.
31. Actually this has happened. Śaiva-Siddhānta originated from the *bheda* Āgamas, Vīra Śaivism from the *bhedābheda* ones, and Kashmir Śaivism from the *abheda* ones.
32. *sarvametat pravṛttyarthaṁ śrōtṝṇāṁ tu vibhedataḥ/ arthabhedāttu bhedo' yamupacārāt prakalpyate//* MĀLINĪVIJAYA-VĀRTIKA 2.275.
33. IBID., 2.277.
34. The Mādhyamika Buddhist, while explaining the difference in philosophical beliefs, holds that everyone is by temperament of a particular philosophical type or clan (*gotra*). We accept a particular philosophy not because it is

true, but because we unconsciously like it or are attuned to it by temperament. It is said about the Buddha that he preached apparently contradictory ideas to different persons. He is said to have been a physician who prescribed different medicines (*sādhanās*) according to the needs of the patients suffering in *saṁsāra*.

35. T.A.V. 1.18, p. 45.
36. *puṣpe gandhastile tailaṁ dehe jīvo jale' ṛtam, yathā tathaiva śāstrāṇāṁ kulamantaḥ pratiṣṭhitam.* T.A. 35.34. Also quoted by Jayaratha in his commentary, 1.18, p. 45, with a variation of *ale rasaḥ*'.
37. . . .*paramādvayāmṛtapariplāvitaṁ vidadhyāt, anyathā hyasya parapadaprāptinimittatvaṁ na syāt.* IBID. 1.18, p. 45.
38. *pūrvapakṣatayā yena viśvamābhāsya bhedataḥ/*
abhedottarapakṣāntarnīyate taṁ stumaḥ śivam//
I.V.P. 1.2, p. 51 —*maṅgalācaraṇa.*
39. Leo Tolstoy in his interesting philosophical story "The Coffee-house of Surat" presents the different positions regarding the concept of God with the ingenuity of an artist and concludes by showing that the more comprehensive the concept of God is, the nearer it is to the truth.
40. *sāmudro hi taraṅgaḥ kvacana samudro na tāraṅgaḥ.* Part of a verse ascribed to Śaṅkarācārya.
41. The Lord (who is the unity of all beings) affirms in the *Gītā*, "All beings (i.e., difference) are held by me, but I am not held by them." (*matsthāni sarvabhūtāni na cāhaṁ teṣvavasthitaḥ*). BH.G. 9.4.
42. *svasiddhāntavyavasthāsu dvaitino niśritā dṛḍham/*
parasparaṁ virudhyante tairayaṁ na virudhyate//
MĀṆḌŪKYA-KĀRIKĀ 3.17.
43. *daśāṣṭādaśavasvaṣṭabhinnaṁ yacchāśanaṁ vibhoḥ/*
tatsāraṁ trikaśāstraṁ hi . . . // T.A. 1.18, 37.17. This statement refers to the three traditional positions regarding the number of authentic Tantras (Āgamas). The first tradition accepts ten Tantras as authentic, the second accepts twenty-eight; and the third, sixty-four.
44. Ś.D. 7.107-122. T.A. 36.11-12.
45. Ś.D. 7.107-8.
46. IBID. 7.121.
47. *sāṁsiddhikaṁ yadvijñānaṁ taccintāratnamucyate.* T.A. 13.150.
48. Mahāmohopādhyaya Paṇḍita Gopīnātha Kavirāja has prepared an extensive bibliography of Tantric literature, entitled *Tāntrika Sāhitya* (in Hindi), published by Hindi Samiti, Lucknow, 1972.
49. T.A. 1.18, 37.17, and M.V.V. 2.276.
50. T.A. 37.24-25.
51. *na tadastīha yanna śrī-mālinī-vijayottare.* T.A. 1.17.

. . . . yacchāśanaṁ vibhoḥ/
tatsāraṁ trikaśāstraṁ hi tatsāraṁ mālinīmatam// IBID. 1.18.

52. A *Vārtika* is an independent treatise written in line with a particular text with a view to explaining and expounding on the subject matter of the original text.
53. T.A. 13.149-50.
54. Pandey, K. C., *Abhinavagupta: An Historical and Philosophical Study*, Chowkhamba Sanskrit Series, Varanasi, 1963, p. 45.
55. *śrīsomānandanāthasya vijñānapratibimbakaṁ*. I.P.V., AVATARAṆIKĀ (Introduction to verse 2).
56. See Pandey, K. C., *Op. Cit.* The first part of this book deals extensively with the history and works of Abhinavagupta.
57. There seems to be a controversy regarding the authorship of the *Tantra-vaṭa-dhānikā*. M. M. Mukunda Rama Shastri, the editor of the *Tantra-vaṭa-dhānikā*, believes that the work might have been authored by a different Abhinavagupta. The same position is maintained by Dr. Kamala Dvivedi in her *Paramārthasāra* (Hindi), Motilal Banarsidas, Varanasi, 1984, p. 32. Professor K. C. Pandey, in his *Abhinavagupta: An Historical and Philosophical Study*, p. 55, refutes the view of M. M. Mukunda Rama Sastri and maintains that the same Abhinavagupta is the author. I think Professor Pandey's position is more justified.
58. Professor K. C. Pandey has published these smaller works in Appendix C (pp. 943 to 956) of his book.
59. PŪRṆATĀ-PRATYABHIJÑĀ 1.15.
60. T.A. 1.7-16.
61. *dvaita-prathā tadajñānam . . .* T.A. 1.30.
sarvādvaitapadasya vismṛtanidheḥ prāptiḥ prakāśodayaḥ.
ANUTTARĀṢṬIKĀ, Verse 4.
62. Rastogi, N., THE KRAMA TANTRICISM OF KASHMIR, Vol. I, Motilal Banarsidas, 1979, p. 6.
63. *vaiyākaraṇasādhūnāṁ paśyantī sā parā sthitiḥ.* Ś.D. 2.1. *Parā, paśyantī, madhyanā,* and *vaikharī* describe levels of manifestation in the creative art, whether it is creation of the world by Śiva, or of a pot by a potter. The terms also relate to levels of speech. *Parā* (literally "the transcendent") is the highest level, the state before manifestation begins. *Paśyantī* is the level of will (*iccha*), wherein the will to create (or speak) first arises. *Madhyamā* (literally "middle") is the state wherein the creation exists, but only as an *idea*, not as an outside manifestation. *Vaikharī* ("external") is the final state wherein the creation exists as an actual object.

CHAPTER 2

1. Part of this chapter has already been published in my book, *Significance of the Tantric Tradition*, Arddhanārīśvara Publications, Varanasi, 1981.
2. *ya eva hi nirākartā tasyaivātmatvāt.* SĀRIRAKA-BHĀṢYA 1.1.4.
3. *kartari jñātari svātmanyādisiddhe maheśvare.* I.P.V. 1.1.2.
4. *tasmin hi nirasite sarvamidaṁ meghāvaraṇavigamaneva svaprakāśabhānu-kiraṇavṛndamatyantasvacchaṁ bhāsate nānyathā* . . . . Ś.D. 2.1., p. 36.
5. This idea became clear to me while discussing the issue with Professor S. Barlingey, Head of the Department of Philosophy, Poona University; I acknowledge my indebtedness to the learned professor for this.
6. The Nyāya system of Indian philosophy is a typically complete realism and objectivism. According to it, everything, including the knowing subject and its knowledge, can be known as object. (*sarvaṁ jñeyam* — "everything is knowable.") Other systems, however, do not subscribe to this view.
7. *na ca bodhasya vedyatvaṁ kadācidupapadyate.* M.V.V. 1.58.
8. In the literature of Advaita Vedānta, the idea of *svayamprakāśa* (or *svaprakāśa*) has been outlined with the utmost clarity. Citsukhācārya, for example, in his *Tattvapradīpikā* (popularly known as *Citsukhī*) has devoted an important section to the concept of *svaprakāśa*. In the Tantric tradition, however, the idea is just accepted and maintained throughout.
9. *tatra jñānaṁ svataḥsiddham* . . . I.P.K. 1.1.5.
10. *pramāṇāni pramāveśe svabalākramaṇakramāt,*
    yasya vaktrāvalokīni prameye taṁ stumaḥ śivam. I.P.V. 2.3.1 (Introduction), p. 60.
11. *pramāṇānyapi vastūnāṁ jīvitaṁ yāni tanvate, teṣāmapi paro jīvah sa eva parameśvarah.* IBID.
12. *āgamastu nāmāntaraḥ śabdanarūpo draḍhīyastamavimarśatmā citsvabhāvasya īśvarasya antaraṅga eva vyāpāraḥ pratyakṣaderapi jīvitakalpah.* I.P.V. 2.3.2., p. 80.
13. *jaḍameva hi mukhyo' tha puṁsprakāśo' sya bhāsanam/*
    bahiḥsthasyaiva tasyāstu buddheḥ kim kalpanā kritā// T.A. 9.197.
14. *upāyairna śivo bhāti bhānti te tatprasādataḥ/*
    sa evāhaṁ svaprakāśo bhāse viśvasvarūpakaḥ// T.A.V. 2.2, p. 3. Also, tradition gives us *upāyajālairna śivaḥ prakāśate ghaṭena kiṁ bhāti sahasradīdhitiḥ*. T.S. 2, p. 9. "Śiva (consciousness, or the self) is not illumined by other means. Can the sun be illumined by the pitcher? (The pitcher is illumined by the sun, not the sun by the pitcher.)"
15. *kartari jñātari svātmanyādisiddhe maheśvare/*
    ajaḍātmā niṣedhaṁ vā siddhiṁ vā vidadhīta kaḥ// I.P.K. 1.1.2.

16. *samvit-tattvaṁ svaprakāśam ityasmin kiṁ nu yuktibhiḥ/ tadabhāve bhaved viśvaṁ jaḍatvād aprakāsakam//* T.A. 2.10. Also, *tadaprakāśe hi viśvam andhatamasaṁ syāt*. . . . I.P.V. 1.1.5, p. 46.
17. *avaśyaṁ cidātmā aparokṣo bhyupetavyaḥ, tadaprathāyāṁ sarvasyāprathanene jagadānhyaprasaṅgāt.* BHĀMATĪ. S.S.S. SASTRI, T.P.H., Madras, 1933, ADHYĀSA-BHĀṢYA, p. 42.
18. SĀṄKHYA-KĀRIKĀ, 17.
19. *ya eva nirākartā tasyaivātmatvāt.* ŚĀRĪRAKA-BHĀṢYA 1.1.4.
20. I.P.V. 2.3.2, p. 80.
21. P.T.V. pp. 14-15.
22. *brahma veda, brahmaiva bhavati.* MUṆḌAKA UPANIṢAD, 3.2.9.
23. *parīkṣya bhikkhavo grāhyam madvacaḥ na tu gauravāt.*
24. *nāsato vidyate bhāvo nābhāvo vidyate satah/ Ubhayorapi dṛṣṭo' ntastvanayostattvadarśibhiḥ//* BH.G. 2.16.
25. P.T.V., p. 161.
26. *karṇāt karṇopadeśena samprāptamavanītalam.* YOGINĪHṚDAYAM 1.3
27. *pratyakṣañca pramāṇāya sarveṣām prāṇinām priye/ upalabdhibalāttasya hatāḥ sarve kutārkikāḥ// parokṣaṁ ko' nujānīte kasya kiṁ vā bhaviṣyati/ yadvā pratyakṣaphaladaṁ tadevottamadarśanam//* KULĀRṆAVA TANTRA 2.88-89.
28. *kulaṁ pramāṇatāṁ yāti pratyakṣaphaladaṁ yataḥ.* IBID. 2.87.
29. The Cārvākas, in their efforts to expose proponents of higher experience as frauds, have floated an interesting and humorous story. The story goes that there was once a notorious cheat. The king of the country had the cheat's nose cut in punishment. The cheat left the country and went to a far-off place where nobody knew him. There he sat in a public place pretending to enjoy supernatural bliss as if in *samādhī*. He told the people gathered around him out of curiosity that he was enjoying supernal bliss. Asked if they could also obtain that bliss, he readily replied, "Oh yes, provided you get your nose cut." Nobody in the beginning was prepared to take the risk, but at last someone ventured to make the experiment and had his nose cut. He did not receive any bliss and complained to the professed master. The cheat told him privately "Yes, I know that no bliss can be had by getting one's nose cut; but as your nose is already cut, please say that you are now enjoying bliss." There was no option before the embarrassed man, and he obeyed. In this way a whole race of the nose-cuts came about. The story is meant to illustrate the point that the alleged phenomenon of higher experience is the invention of crooks and the whole affair is a case of mass deception.
30. *bhrāntibodhasya svasaṁvedanāṁśe prakāśamāne na bhrāntitā, tatra vaiparītyābhāvāt;*

yastu tatra adhyavasīyate svākāraḥ sa viparītatayā asvākāreṇa arthatayā — iti tatra aṁse bhrāntitā. I.P.V. 1.3.5., p. 102.

31. *na hi draṣṭurdṛṣṭeḥ viparilopo vidyate.* BṚHADĀRAṆYAKA UPANIṢAD 4.3.23.
32. KENA UPANIṢAD 1.4-8.
33. *kapilo yadi sarvajñaḥ sugato neti kā pramā/*
    ubhāvapi sarvajñau matabhedastayoḥ katham//
34. *ekaṁ sad viprāḥ bahudhā vadanti.*
35. *kintu mohavaśādasmin dṛṣṭepyanupalakṣite....* I.P.K., 1.1.3.
36. *svayameva yato vetti bandhamokṣatayātmatām/*
    tat prātibhaṁ mahājñānaṁ śāstrācāryānapekṣi yat// T.A. 13.132.
37. *yathā yathā parāpekṣātānavaṁ prātibhe bhavet/*
    athā tathā gururasau śreṣtho vijñānapāragaḥ// T.A. 13.138.
38. *viveko' tīndriyastveṣa yadāyāti vivecanam/*
    paśupāśapatijñānaṁ svayaṁ nirbhāsate tadā// T.A. 13.177.
39. There is continuity between lower consciousness and higher consciousness. But this does not mean that the two are exactly the same. The higher one is pure, whereas the lower one is tainted with impurity (*mala*). The difference between the two is analogous to the difference between a bright (pure) light and the same light becoming dim (impure) after passing through a curtain. The thinner or lighter the curtain, the brighter or purer the light. Similarly the less the impurity, the greater the flow of higher consciousness.
40. KENA UPANIṢAD 1.4-8.
41. *tameva bhāntamanubhāti sarvam, tasya bhāsā sarvamidaṁ vibhāti.* MUṆḌAKA UPANIṢAD 2.2.10.
42. *itthaṁ prātibhavijñānaṁ kiṁ kiṁ kasya na sādhayet/*
    yatprātibhādvā sarvaṁ cet....// T.A. 13.146.
43. *pratibhā paramevaiṣā sarvakāmadughā yataḥ.* T.A. 13.156.
44. *arthakriyābhāso' pi ca ābhāsāntaram eva iti arthakriyākāritvamapi na bhāvānāṁ sattvam.* I.P.V. 1.8.6., p. 330. Here the word "appearance" (*ābhāsa*) is used just in the epistemological sense, meaning what appears as real.
45. *bādhābhāve prāmāṇyam ityetadartham avaśyasamarthyo yo bādha-vyavahāraḥ...* I.P.V. 1.7.6, p. 290.
46. *aprāmāṇyaṁ hi bādhabalāt bhavati...* I.P.V. 1.7.6 (introduction), p. 289.
47. *ayaṁ bādhyabādhakabhāvaḥ satyāsatya-pravibhājanāya viśveṣāṁ vyavahārāṇāṁ jīvitabhūtaḥ.* I.P.V. 1.7.6., p. 290.
48. Tantrism may be taken to be an idealism, as the non-dualistic Tantras are clearly idealistic; Kashmir Śaivism, which is the major system of the Tantric tradition, is an idealism.
49. *ityapūrṇakhyātirūpā akhyātireva bhrāntitattvam.* I.P.V. 2.3.13., vol. II, p. 113.

50. *ajñānam iti na jñānā bhāvaścātiprasaṅgataḥ* T.A. 1.25
51. *nanu ajñānaśabdasya apūrṇaṁ jñānamarthaḥ.* T.A.V. 1.25., (introduction), p. 57.
52. *ato jñeyasya tattvasya sāmastyenāprathātmakam, jñānameva tadajñānaṁ śivasūtreṣu bhāṣitam.* T.A. 1.26.
53. *māyāpadaṁ hi sarvaṁ bhrāntiḥ, tatrāpi tu svapne svapna iva gaṇḍe sphoṭa iva apareyaṁ bhrāntirucyate.* I.P.V., 2.3.13., p. 114.
54. (a) *dvaitaprathā tadajñānaṁ tucchatvād bandha ucyate.* T.A. 1.30, p. 59.
    (b) *tasmāt saṁvidadvaitātmanaḥ pūrṇasya rūpasya akhyānāt dvaitaprathā eva ajñānam.* T.A.V. 1.30, p. 61.
55. *viśvabhāvaikabhāvātma-svarūpaprathanaṁ hi yat/*
    aṇūnāṁ tatparaṁ jñānaṁ tadanyadaparaṁ bahu// T.A. 1.141, p. 181.
56. *yattu jñeyasatattvasya pūrṇapūrṇaprathātmakam/*
    taduttarottaraṁ jñānaṁ tattat saṁsāraśāntidam// T.A. 1.23, p. 63.

CHAPTER 3, PART I

1. *kartari jñātari svātmanyādisiddhe maheśvare/*
   ajaḍātmā niṣedhaṁ vā siddhiṁ vā vidadhīta kaḥ// I.P.K. 1.2.
2. *sa tu viśudhasvabhāvah śivātmā, māyāpade tu sañkucitasvabhāvaḥ paśuḥ.* I.P.V. 2.2.3, p. 39.
3. *pṛthagdīpaprakāśānāṁ srotasāṁ sāgare yathā/*
   avirudhāvabhāsānāmekakāryā tathaikyadhīḥ// I.P.K. 2.3.7, p. 96.
4. (a) *śiva eva gṛhītapaśubhāvaḥ.* P.S. 5.
   (b) *ahaṁ rūpā tu saṁvittirnityā svaprathanātmikā.* T.A. 1.127.
5. (a) *tasyadevātidevasya parāpekṣā na vidyate/*
   parasya tadapekṣatvātsvatantro' yamataḥ sthitaḥ// T.A. 1.59.
   (b) *anapekṣasya vaśino....* T.A. 1.60.
6. *paraṁ parasthaṁ gahanād anādim ekaṁ viśiṣṭaṁ bahudhā guhāsu sarvālayaṁ sarvacarācarasthaṁ tvāmeva śaṁbhuṁ śaraṇaṁ prapadye.* P.S. 1.
7. *mahāguhāntarnirmagnabhāvajātaprakāsakaḥ jñānaśaktipradīpenayaḥ sadā taṁ stumaḥ śivam.* I.P.K. 1.5, p. 151.
8. Spinoza defined substance, which is God, not only as self-existent, as Descartes did, but also as self-known. Since substance in Spinoza is Spirit or Consciousness, and not matter, it is natural for the Substance to be self-known.
9. (a) *tasya pratyavamarśo yaḥ paripūrṇo' hamātmakaḥ/*
   sa svātmani svatantratvādvibhāgamavabhāsayet// T.A. 3.235.

(b) *mayyeva bhāti viśvaṁ darpaṇa iva nirmale ghaṭādīni/*
mattaḥ prasarati sarvaṁ svapnavicitratvamiva suptāt// P.S. 48.

10. (a) *pṛthvī prakṛtirmāyā tṛtayamidaṁ vedyarūpatāpatitam/*
advaitabhāvanabalād bhavati hi sammātrapariśeṣam// P.S. 41.
(b) *vibhutvātsarvago nityabhāvādādyanta varjitaḥ/*
viśvākṛtitvāccidacittadvaicitryāvabhāsakaḥ// T.A. 1.60.

11. The same problem arises in Advaita Vedānta also. The Upaniṣads declare that Brahman is Consciousness (*cit*), and Brahman (*cit*) alone exists (*ekamevādvitīyaṁ Brahma, neha nānāsti kiñcana*, etc.). At the same time, the Upaniṣads also declare, "All this is Brahman" (*sarvaṁ khalvidaṁ Brahma*). Now, the problem arises: how can "all this," which appears to be material substance different from Consciousness, be Brahman, which is not matter but consciousness? In answer, Śaṇkarācārya presents Māyāvāda. The world, although apparently material, is an appearance, or a dream-like projection of Consciousness. Hence, what appears to be a material object is really consciousness. It can be argued on Śaṇkarācārya's part that in order to preserve the non-dualism of the Upaniṣads and to understand the sentences of *śruti* (the Upaniṣads) consistently, we have to accept Māyāvāda even if it is not clearly stated in *śruti.*

12. (a) *mahāprakāśarūpā hi yeyaṁ saṁvidvijṛmbhate/*
sa śivaḥ śivataivāsya vaiśvarūpyāvabhāsitā// T.A. 15.265-266.
(b) *saṁvidātmani viśvo' yaṁ bhāvavargaḥ prapañcavān/*
pratibimbatayā bhāti yasya viśveśvaro hi saḥ// T.A. 3.268.
(c) *tena saṁvittimakure viśvamātmānamarpayat/*
nāthasya vadate' muṣya vimalāṁ viśvarūpatām// T.A. 3.44.
(d) *so' yaṁ samasta evādhvā bhairavābhedavṛttimān/*
tatsvātantryātsvatantratvamaśnuvāno' vabhāsate// T.A. 11.54, p. 45.
(e) *sarvo mamāyaṁ vibhava ityevaṁ parijānataḥ/*
viśvātmano vikalpānāṁ prasare' pi maheśatā// I.P.V. 4.1.12, p. 266.

13. (a) *sadā sṛṣṭi vinodāya sadā sthitisukhāśine/*
sadā trbhuvanāhāratṛptāya svāmine namaḥ// Ś. St. 20.9.
(b) *nijaśakti vaibhavabharād aṇḍacatuṣṭayamidaṁ vibhāgena/*
śaktirmāyā prakṛtiḥ pṛthvī ceti prabhāvitaṁ prabhuṇā// P.S. 4.
(c) *tasya pratyavamarśo yaḥ paripūrno' hamātmakaḥ/*
sa svātmani svataṁtratvādvibhāgamavabhāsayet// T.A. 3.235.
(d) *tasmādeko mahādevaḥ svātantryopahitasthitiḥ/*
dvitvenabhātyasau bimbapratibimbodayātmanā// T.A. 3.11, p. 13.

14. (a) *cinmayatve' vabhāsānāmantareva sthitiḥ sadā,*
māyayā bhāsamānānāṁ bāhyatvādbahirapyasau. I.P.K. 1.8.7., p. 331.
(b) *mayyeva bhāti viśvaṁ darpaṇa iva nirmale ghaṭādīni/*
mattaḥ prasarati sarvaṁ svapnavicitratvamiva suptāt// P.S. 48.

(c) *ata evāntaraṁ kiṁciddhīsaṁjñaṁ bhavatu sphuṭam/*
yatrāsya vicchidābhānaṁ saṁkalpasvapnadarśane// T.A. 3.64, p. 71.

15. *svātantryamātrasadbhāvā yā tvicchā śaktiraiśvarī/*
śivasya saiva karaṇaṁ tayā vetti karoti ca// T.A. 10.17, p.11

16. *yathā nyagrodhabījasthaḥ śaktirūpo mahādrumaḥ/*
tathā hṛdayabījasthaḥ viśvametaccarācaram// Kṣemarāja quoted this verse in his Parāpraveśikā.

17. (a) *bījamaṇkurapatrāditayāpariṇametacet/*
a tatsvabhāvavapuṣaḥ sa svabhāvo na yujyate// T.A. 9.14, p. 25.
(b) *niyamaśca tathārūpabhāsanāmātrasārakaḥ/*
bījādaṅkura ityevaṁ bhāsanaṁ nahi sarvadā// T.A. 9.25, p. 32.

18. See the next chapter for a discussion of *spanda.*

19. (a) *ātmaiva sarvabhāveṣu sphurannirvṛtacidvibhuḥ/*
aniruddhecchāprasaraḥ prasaraddṛkkṛyaḥ śivaḥ// Ś.D., 1.2.
(b) *cidātmaiva hi devo' ntaḥ sthitamicchāvaśādbahiḥ/*
yogīva nirupādānamarthajātaṁ prakāśayet// I.P.K., 1.5.7, p. 182.

20. (a) *na śivaḥ śaktirahito na śaktiḥ śivavarjitā.* Quoted in T.A., 3.67, p. 80.
(b) *śaktiśca nāma bhāvasya svaṁ rūpaṁ mātṛkalpitam/*
tenādvayaḥ sa evāpi śaktimatparikalpane// T.A. 1.69.

21. (a) *tasya pratyavamarśo yaḥ paripūrno' hamātmakaḥ/*
sa svātmani svatantratvādvibhāgamavabhāsayet// T.A., 3.235.
(b) *tena bodhamahāsindhorullāsinyaḥ svaśaktayaḥ.* T.A. 3.102.

22. Dr. L. N. Sharma, in line with his teacher Professor T. R. V. Murti, has termed the Absolute of Kashmir Śaivism the Will-Absolute. Sharma, L. N., KASHMIR ŚAIVISM, Bharatiya Vidya Prakashan, Varanasi, 1972, p. 139.

23. *tasmādanuttaro devaḥ svācchandyānuttaratvataḥ/*
visargaśaktiyuktatvātsaṁpanno viśvarūpakaḥ// T.A. 3.195-96.

24. *na sanna cāsatsadasanna ca tannobhayojjhitam/*
durvijneyāhi sāvasthā kimapyetadanuttaram// T.A. 2.28.

25. A classical illustration of this point is the story of a beggar boy. The boy, after hearing about a king for the first time, asked his father what the king was like. The reply of the father was that the king was a very happy man. Upon hearing this the boy commented, "Now I understand: the king has a lot of sugar to eat." The point is that the beggar boy cannot understand the happiness of a king, for the boy does not have the category for such understanding. He can grasp the royal happiness in terms of his own category, namely the eating of sugar, because this is the only category of pleasure he has.

26. *samastalakṣaṇāyoga eva yasyopalakṣaṇam* .... Ś. ST., 2.6.

27. (a) *no bhāvo nāpyabhāvo na dvayaṁ vācāmagocarāt/*
akathyapadavīrūḍhaṁ śaktisthaṁ śaktivarjitam// T.A. 2.33.
(b) T.A. 2.28.

28. (a) *yattu sarvāvibhāgātma svatantraṁ bodhasundaram/*
saptatṛṁśaṁ tu tatprāhustattvaṁ paraśivābhidham// T.A. 11.21-22.
(b) Abhinavagupta wrote his *Tantrāloka* in thirty-seven chapters. Tradition maintains that thirty-six of the chapters stand for the thirty-six *tattvas* that are accessible to thought; the thirty-seventh chapter stands for the all-elusive Parama-Śiva that is beyond our conception.
29. *tasyāpyuktanayādvedyabhāve' tra parikalpite/*
yadāste hyanavacchinnaṁ tadaṣṭātriṁśamucyate// T.A. 11.22-23, p. 15.
30. *yato vāco nivartante aprāpya manasā saha.* TAITTIRĪYA UPANIṢAD 2.4.1., also 2.9.1.
also, *yo buddheḥ paratastu saḥ.* BH.G. 4.42.
31. *yasyāmataṁ tasya mataṁ, mataṁ yasya na veda saḥ/*
avijñātaṁ vijānatām vijñātamvijānatām// KENA UPANIṢAD 2.3.
32. (a) T.S. 1, pp. 3-4.
(b) T.A. 1.47.
33. *viśvamayatve' pyasya svasvarūpānna pracyāvaḥ ityāśayaḥ.* T.A.V. 1.65.
34. (a) *nahi tasya svatantrasya kāpi kutrāpi khaṇḍanā.* T.A. 2.47.
(b) *svatantratā ca cinmātra vapuṣaḥ parameśituḥ/*
svatantraṁ ca jaḍaṁ ceti tadanyonyaṁ virudhyate// T.A. 9.9, p. 12-13.
35. *uktaṁ ca kāmike devaḥ sarvākṛtirnirākṛtiḥ/*
jaladarpaṇavattena sarvaṁ vyāptaṁ carācaram// T.A. 1.66.
36. *ittham nānāvidhaiḥ rūpaiḥ sthāvaraiḥ jaṅgamairapi/*
kṛḍayā prasṛto nityameka eva śivaḥ prabhuḥ// T.A.V. 1.159.
37. *asatye vartmani sthitvā tataḥ satyaṁ samīhate.* VĀKYAPADĪYAM. 2.238.
38. T.A. 3.195-96.
39. (a) *mādhyasthyavigame yāsau hṛdaye spandamānatā*
ānanda-śaktiḥ śaivoktā yataḥ sahṛdayo janaḥ. T.A. 3.210.
(b) *prakāśamātraṁ yatproktaṁ bhairavīyaṁ paraṁ mahaḥ/*
tatra svatantratāmātram adhikaṁ pravivicyate// T.A. 3.1.
40. T.A. 10.269, p. 182.
41. T.A. 1.127.
42. *saṁvidrūpe na bhedosti vāstavo yadyapi dhruve/*
tathāpyāvṛti nirhrāsatāratamyātsa lakṣyate// T.A. 1.138.
43. (a) *śiva eva gṛhītapaśubhāvah.* P.S. 5.
(b) *sa tu viśuddhasvabhāvaḥ śivātmā, māyāpade tu saṁkucita svabhāvaḥ paśuḥ.* I.P.V. 2.2.3, p. 39.
44. *tena bodhamahāsindhorullāsinyaḥ svaśaktayaḥ.* T.A. 3.102.
45. Quoted in T.A.V. 1.204.
46. *prakāśasyātmaviśrāntirahaṁbhāvo hi kīrtitaḥ.* Quoted in T.A.V. 1.55.
47. *ahaṁrūpā tu saṁvittirnityā svaprathanātmikā.* T.A. 1.127.

48. *ata eva sā svarasena cidrūpatayā svātmaviśrāntivapuṣā uditā satatam anas tamitā nityā ahamityeva.* I.P.V. 1.5.14, p. 206.
49. RADHAKRISHNAN: INDIAN PHILOSOPHY Vol. II, Allen & Unwin, 1958, p. 659.
50. IBID., p. 659. Here we may add that up to Śaṅkara the problem does not arise very much. His treatment of the Absolute is such that it could also be interpreted in a positive way. It is only the post-Śaṅkara scholiasts in whom the fully abstract and negative picture of Brahman comes out. The potentiality of such a position, however, is very much present in Śaṅkara.
51. Pointing out the benefit of this dialectical treatise, *Khaṇḍana-Khaṇḍakhādya*, Śrī Harṣa says that those who want to attain victory over their opponents in the polemic duel (*śāstrārtha*), can do so even by simply repeating like parrots what he has said: *dhīrā yathoktamapi kīravadetaduktvā, lokeṣu digvijayakautukamātanudhvam.* KHAṆḌANA-KHAṆḌAKHĀDYA 1.3.
52. There is an implicit claim among the Āgamic philosophers — sometimes it finds explicit expression — that their philosophy is akin to the Upaniṣadic position. The Āgamic tradition, they believe, completes and complements the Vedic and Upaniṣadic tradition by making explicit what is left implicit in the Vedas and Upaniṣads.
53. (a) *etadrūpaparāmarśamakṛtrmamanābilam/*
    ahamityāhureṣaiva prakāśasya prakāśatā// T.A. 4.132.
    (b) *tasya pratyavamarśo yaḥ paripūrṇo' hamātmakaḥ/*
    sa svātmani svatantratvādvibhāgamavabhāsayet// T.A. 3.235.
    (c) *ekameva paraṁ rūpaṁ bhairavasyāhamātmakam.* T.A. 3.208.
54. *uktañca kāmike devaḥ sarvākṛtirnirākṛtiḥ.* T.A. 1.66.
55. *tasya pratyavamarśo yaḥ paripūrṇo' hamātmakaḥ.* T.A. 3.235.
56. *prakāśasyātmaviśrāntirahambhāvo hi kīrtitaḥ.* T.A.V. 1.55.
57. *anuttaravisargātma śivaśaktyadvāyatmani/*
    parāmarśo nirbharatvādahamityucyate vibhoḥ// T.A. 3.203-204.
58. *ahaṁrūpā tu saṁvittirnityā svaprathanātmikā.* T.A. 1.127.
59. (a) *nirāśansāt pūrṇādahamiti purā bhāsayati yad....*
    I.P.V. (*maṅgalācarana*).
    (b) *bhārūpaṁ paripūrṇaṁ svātmani viśrāntito mahānandam/*
    icchāsaṁvitkaraṇairnirbharitam anataśaktiparipūrṇam// P.S. 10.
60. *yovai bhūmā tatsukhaṁ nālpe sukhamasti....*
    CHĀNDOGYA UPANIṢAD 7.23.1.
61. (a) *parasya tadapekṣatvāt svatantro' yamataḥ sthitaḥ/* T.A. 1.59.
    sva-svātantryāt svātmadarpaṇe... ābhāsayati// T.A.V. 2.246.
    (b) *tasya svatantrabhāvo hi kiṁ kiṁ yanna vicintayet.* T.A. 1.136.
    (c) *nahi tasya svatantrasya kāpi kutrāpi khaṇḍanā.* T.A. 2.47.
    (d) *sva-svātantrya-prabhāvodyat....* T.A. 3.117.

CHAPTER 3 — PART II

1. Part of this chapter is already published in my book SIGNIFICANCE OF THE TANTRIC TRADITION, Arddhanārīśvara Publications, Varansi, 1981.
2. (a) *prakāśamātraṁ yatproktaṁ bhairavīyaṁ paraṁ mahaḥ/ tatra svatantratāmātramadhikaṁ pravivicyate//* T.A. 3.1.
   (b) *prakāśavimarśātmakameva saṁvidrūpam.* I.P.V. 1.8.1., p. 317 (footnote).
3. The term *kriyā* in the Tantric tradition is sometimes used to denote the gross external activity as in the triad of *icchā-jñāna-kriyā.* But it is also used to denote the general dynamism of Consciousness, technically called *spanda* ("spontaneity"). The word *kriyā* ("activity") is juxtaposed with the word *jñāna*, or *dṛk* ("knowledge"), and Reality is said to be both together (*dṛk-kriyā* or *jñāna-kriyā*).
   sa eva hi ahaṁbhāvātmā vimarśo devasya krīdādimayasya, śuddhe pāramārthikyau jñāna-kriye, prakāśarūpatā jñānaṁ tatraiva svātantryātmā vimarśaḥ kriyā. I.P.V. 1.8.11, p. 338.
4. *prakāśamātraṁ yatproktaṁ bhairavīyaṁ paraṁ mahaḥ/ tatra svatantratāmātram adhikaṁ pravivicyate//* T.A. 3.1.
5. (a) *bhāvagrahādiparyantabhāvī sāmānyasaṁjñakaḥ/ spandaḥ sa kathyate śāstre svātmanyucchalanātmakaḥ//* T.A. 4.183, p.213.
   (b) *spandanaṁ ca kiñcit calanam, eṣaiva ca kiñcidrūpatā yat acalamapi calam ābhāsate iti, prakāśasvarūpaṁ hi manāgapi nātiricyate atiricyate iva iti acalameva ābhāsabhedayuktameva ca bhāti iti.* I.P.V. 1.5.14, p.208-209.
6. By using words like "partial" and "complete" perfection I do not mean to suggest that perfection admits of degrees. Perfection here means freedom from wants, which can certainly be partial or complete. Generally, the complete freedom from wants is called perfection.
7. When using the English substitute of these words, I will use "action" for *karma* and "activity" for *kriyā*, although "activity" is not really an adequate translation of *kriyā.*
8. *evasyaiṣa svabhāvo' yam āptakāmasya kā spṛhā.* MĀṆḌŪKYA-KĀRIKĀ 1.9.
9. It is true that in the examples of *kriyā* cited above and earlier we may find some amount of motivation and, therefore, of compulsion, as our ordinary activity is tainted with *mala* ("dirt"). But the point is that there is at least some amount of motivelessness and freedom that gives rise to *kriyā.* Certainly there is considerable difference between (a) a student working hard at his studies in order to pass the examination, and (b) the same student

playing joyfully after the examinations are over. In the former case the student has a motive and is compelled to work, whereas in the latter case he is comparatively motiveless and free from compulsion, and yet the activity of playing is there in full swing. Where does the activity of playing come from? What we want to point out is that there is an amount of freedom and desirelessness that gives rise to such activities.

10. *anandāddhyeva khalvimāni bhūtāni jāyante.* TAITTIRĪYA UPANIṢAD 3.6.
11. This is akin to what Swami Chetanananda calls "dynamic stillness" in his book, DYNAMIC STILLNESS. Cambridge: Rudra Press, 1990.
12. *karmaṇyabhipravṛtto' pi naiva kiñcit karoti saḥ.* BH.G. 4.20.
13. *tasya kartāramapimāṁ viddhyakartāramavyayam.* IBID., 4.13.
14. *naiva kiñcit karomīti yukto manyeta tattvavit.* Ibid. 5.8.
15. *bahiḥ kṛtrima saṁrambho hṛdi saṁrambhavarjitaḥ/*
    kartā bahirakartāntar loke vihara rāghava//
16. *bahistaprontarāśītaḥ loke vihara rāghava.*
17. *saba hī karma hamāre kīye, hama karmana te nyāre ho.*
18. Even the question of freedom in *karma*, on which the notion of *puruṣa-tantra* is based, is controversial. While doing action (in the sense of *karma* and not *kriyā*) we are not free, at least not completely free, as our action is determined by external and internal factors. Even the choice to do or not do or do in a different manner (*kartum akartum anyathā vā kartum*) is conditioned by the same factors. It is only in *kriyā*, on the contrary, that one is free, as there is no determination, external or internal, whatsoever.
19. *kriyā kāla kramānugā.* I.P.K. 2.4.18, 3.1.1.
    Also, *nanu ca kramikatvameva kriyāyāḥ svarūpam.* I.P.V. 2.1.2, p. 5 of volume II.
20. *krama eva ca kālo, na anyo' sau kaścit* and *bhinneti kāla eva kramaḥ, krama eva kālaḥ.* I.P.V. 2.1.3, p. 9.
21. *sakramatvaṁ ca laukikyāḥ kriyāyāḥ kālaśaktitaḥ/*
    ghaṭate na tu śāśvatyāḥ prābhavyāḥ syāt prabhorīva// I.P.K. 2.1.2.
22. *sā sphurattā mahāsattā deśakālāviśeṣiṇī/*
    saiṣā sāratayā proktā hṛdayaṁ parameṣṭhinaḥ// I.P.K. 1.5.14, p. 208.
23. *nanu ca kramikatvameva kriyāyāḥ svarūpaṁ, kramaśca kāla kalanāhīne cinmaye bhagavati nāsti, iti katham asya sā bhavet.*
    I.P.V. 2.1.2, AVATARAṆIKĀ (introduction).
24. *yathā prabhoḥ sakramatvamasambhāvyaṁ tathā tasyā api.* I.P.V. 2.1.2.
25. In the TANTRĀLOKA 3.128-29, Abhinavagupta gives the answer implicitly, and Jayaratha makes it somewhat explicit in his commentary.
26. ... *cinmaye bhagavati*.... I.P.V. 2.1.2., introduction.
27. *sakramatvaṁ ca laukikyāḥ.* I.P.V. 2.1.2., p. 6-7.
28. *pākādistu kriyā kālaparicchedātkramocitā.* T.A. 3.129.

29. *ataśca pākāderlaukikyā eva kriyāyāḥ sakramatvaṁ, na punaḥ śāśvatyāḥ saṁvillakṣaṇāyā iti.* T.A.V. 3.129.
30. *ucchalantyapi samvittiḥ kālakramavivarjanāt/*
    uditaiva satī pūrṇā mātṛmeyādirūpiṇī// T.A. 3.128-129.
31. (a) . . . *saṁvinmātrarūpatvāpracyāvāt niyamena anastamitarūpā ityarthaḥ, ata eva pūrnā—svātmamātra viśrāntirūpatvādananyāpekṣiṇi ityarthaḥ.* T.A.V. 3.128.
    (b) *ityantena parameśvare paramārthato' kramā kriyā, parimitasāṁsārikapramātṛgate kramāvabhāsanayogāt sakramāpi ca, iti.* I.P.V. 2.1, p. 2.
    (c) *kriyā naikasya sakramā.* I.P.V. 2.1.1, p. 2.
32. I acknowledge my indebtedness to Professor Dr. Richard Sorabji from the United Kingdom, who gave this example in his lecture on the concept of Time, in the Department of Philosophy, Banaras Hindu University, and also in his private discussion with me in the after-lecture session.
33. Bhartṛhari applied the adjective *abhinna* ("non-sequential" or "non-differential") to Time (*Kāla*) and points out that it is only in our ordinary activity that the *abhinna-kāla* assumes difference (*bheda*).

    tasyābhinnasya kālasya vyavahāre kriyākṛtāḥ/
    *bhedā iva trayaḥ siddhāḥ yānlloko nātivartate//*Vākyapadīyam. 3.9.48
34. (a) *na śivaḥ śaktirahito na śaktiḥ śivavarjitā/ yāmalaṁ prasaraṁ sarvam . . .* // Quoted in T.A.V. 3.67.
    (b) *tayoryadyāmalaṁ rūpaṁ sa saṁghaṭṭa iti smṛtaḥ.* T.A. 3.68.
    (c) *paraiva sūkṣmā kuṇḍalinī-śaktiḥ śivena saha paraspara-sāmarasya-rūpa-mathya-manthaka-bhāvātmakaṁ śaṅghaṭṭamāsādya utthitā satī . . .* T.A.V. 3.67.
35. (a) *śaktayo' sya jagatkṛtsnaṁ śaktimānstu maheśvaraḥ.* Quoted in T.A.V. 3.67.
    (b) *akulasyāsya devasya kulaprathanaśālini.*
    kaulikī sā parā śaktir aviyukto yayā prabhuḥ. T.A. 3.67.
36. . . .*na hi śaktiḥ śivāt bhedamāmarśayet.* P.T.V. 1, p.3.
37. *parameśvaraśāstre hi na ca kāṇādadṛṣṭivat/*
    śaktīnāṁ dharmarūpāṇām āśrayaḥ ko' pi kathyate// T.A. 1.158.
38. *nanu yadi kāṇādadarśanavad ihāpi dharmadharmibhāvasya nirūpaṇaṁ kriyate, tadā ko doṣaḥ syādityāśaṅkyāha —*
    tataśca dṛkkriyecchādyā bhinnāścecchaktayastathā.
    ekaḥ śiva itīyaṁ vāg vastuśūnyaiva jāyate. T.A. 1.159, together with introduction.
39. *phalabhedādāropitabhedaḥ padārthātmā śaktiḥ.* T.A.V. 1.69.

40. *ko bhedo vastuto vahnerdagdhṛpaktṛtvayoriva.* T.A. 1.70.
41. *evaṁ parameśvarasya parikalite' pi śaktīnāṁ ānantye na kaścidbhedaḥ iti na kadācidīśvarādvayavādakṣatiḥ.* T.A.V. 1.70.
42. (a) *iti śaktitrayaṁ nāthe svātantryāparanāmakam* . . . T.A. 1.94.
(b) *tena svātantraśaktyaiva yukta ityañjaso vidhiḥ/ bahuśaktitvamapyasya tacchaktyaivāviyuktatā//* T.A. 1.68.
43. *prakāśatrūpatā cicchaktih.* T.S. 1, p. 6.
44. The word *icchā* in Sanskrit is used for both "desire" and "will." Desire (for food, sex, etc.) arises in us naturally, it is not our willful doing. "Will" totally depends upon us, it is *our* doing, not Nature's. The correct Sanskrit substitute for "Will" is *saṅkalpa*, which is volitional and which may be effortful. But since in the case of Śiva the *saṅkalpa* is spontaneous and not a result of the exerting of the will, it is called *icchā*, perhaps in order to convey both spontaneity and willfullness.
45. *taccamatkāra icchāśaktiḥ.* T.S. 1, p. 6.
46. The word "mind" or "mental" is used here in the sense of "consciousness," it is not used in the technical sense of *manas*, which is an evolute of the material *prakṛti.*
47. *āmarśātmakatā jñānaśaktiḥ.* T.S. 1, p. 6.
48. *sarvākārayogitvaṁ kriyāśaktiḥ.* T.S. 1, p. 6.
49. Utpaladeva in his *Śivastotrāvalī* offers his salutations to Śiva as One who *always* does the acts of creation, preservation, and destruction out of his sportive nature.

sadā sṛṣṭivinodāya sadā sthitisukhāsine, sadā tribhuvanāhāratṛptāya svāmine namaḥ. Ś.ST. 20.9.
50. The Advaita Vedānta system has the proclaimed view that Creation is an accidental characteristic (*taṭasthalakṣaṇa*) of Brahman; and yet the father-Advaitin, Gauḍapāda, says, "This (Creation) is the nature of the Lord; what shall a perfect being desire?" (*devasyaiṣa svabhāvo' yam āptakāmasya kā spṛhā.* MĀṆḌŪKYA-KĀRIKĀ. 1.9) Naturally he means that in the Lord there is no motive for Creation; he cannot mean that creation is a necessary and eternal act of Brahman.
51. *iti śaktitrayaṁ nāthe svātantryāparanāmakam/ icchābhirabhikhyābhir gurubhiḥ prakaṭīkṛtam//* T.A. 1.94.
52. *yad iyaṁ svacamatkṛtimayī svātmanyeva prakāśanamaye viśramya sphurati tadevaṁ sphuṭitamavicchinnatāparamārtham aham iti.* P.T.V. 1, p. 6.
53. *jñānaṁ vimarśānuprāṇitaṁ, vimarśa eva ca kriyeti/ na ca jñāna-śakti vihīnasya kriyāyogaḥ//* I.P.V. 3.1.1, p. 190.
54. *prakāśyaṁ sarvavastūnāṁ visargarahitā tu sā/ śaktikuṇḍalikā caiva prāṇakuṇḍalikā tathā//*

visargaprāntadeśe tu parā kuṇḍalinīti ca/
śivavyometi paramaṁ brahmātmasthānamucyate// T.A. 3.139-40.

55. Please see the section entitled Creation as Vāk ("Speech") in Chapter 4.

CHAPTER 4

1. P.S. 11.
2. I.P.K. 2.4.1, p. 136.
3. *viśve hi bhāvāstasyaiva śaktirūpeṇa svarūpātmatvena sthitāḥ.* I.P.V. 2.4.1, p. 136.
4. STAVA-CINTĀMAṆI 9.
5. *ātmaiva sarvabhāvesu sphurannirvṛtacidvibhuḥ/ aniruddhecchāprasaraḥ prasaraddṛkkriyaḥ śivaḥ//* Ś.D. 1.2.
6. I.P.K. 1.8.7, p. 331, 1.5.1, p. 153.
7. *sārametatsamastasya yaccitsāraṁ jaḍaṁ jagat.* T.A. 4.185.
8. *cidātmaiva hi devo' ntaḥ sthitamicchāvaśādbahiḥ. yogīva nirupādānamarthajātaṁ prakāśayet.* I.P.K. 1.5.7, p. 182.
9. *carīkarti barībharti sañjarīharti līlayā.*
10. *svātantryācca maheśasya tirobhūto' pyasau svayam/ paradvāreṇa vābhyeti bhūyo' nugrahamapyalam//* T.A. 14.20.
11. *tirodhiḥ pūrṇarūpasyāpūrṇatvaṁ tacca pūraṇam.* T.A. 13.111.
12. (a) *namaḥ śivāya satataṁ pañcakṛtya-vidhāyine.* P.H. 1, *mangalācaraṇa.*
    (b) *itthaṁ sṛṣṭisthitidhvaṁsatirobhāvamanugrahaḥ/ iti pañcasu kartṛtvaṁ śivatvaṁ saṁvidātmanaḥ//* T.A. 14.24.
13. *rātriḥ svapnāya kalpitā.*
14. (a) *yasyonmeṣādudayo jagataḥ . . . viśvasya hi sphuṭatvaṁ bāhyatvam unmeṣaṇaṁ, nimeṣaṇaṁ tvasphuṭatvāpādanamantārūpatodrecanam — iti nimeṣaḥ.* I.P.V. 3.1.3, p. 194.
    (b) *svarūpādunmeṣaprasaraṇanimeṣasthitijuṣaḥ, tadadvaitaṁ vande paramaśivaśaktyātma nikhilam.* I.P.V. 1.1, *mangalācaraṇa.*
15. *nimeṣaṇaṁ tu . . . antārūpatodrecanam.* I.P.V. 3.1.3, p. 194.
16. *mahāprakāśarūpā hi yeyaṁ saṁvidvijṛmbhate.* T.A. 15.265.
17. *mayyeva bhāti viśvaṁ darpaṇa iva nirmale ghaṭādīni/ mattaḥ prasarati sarvaṁ svapnavicitratvamiva suptāt//* P.S. 48.
18. *yāvacchivaikavedyo' sau śiva evāvabhāsate. tāvadekaśarīro hi bodho bhātyeva yāvatā.* T.A. 10.166.
19. Ś.D. 1.36-38.
20. *ha hi viśvasya vācyavācakātmanā dvidhā avabhāsaḥ.* T.A. 3.67.

21. (a) *sā sphurattā mahāsattā deśakālāviśeṣiṇī/*
saiṣā sāratayā proktā hṛdayaṁ parameṣṭhinaḥ// I.P.K. 1.5.14.
(b) *vibhāgābhāsane cāsya tridhā vapurudāhṛtam/*
paśyantī madhyamā sthūlā vaikharītyabhiśabditam// T.A. 3.236.
22. The starting point of the philosophical position of the Grammarian is the discovery that thinking is linguistic. Bhartṛhari says, "There is no conception or thought that is devoid of language; all knowledge is illumined as if penetrated by speech (or language)."

na so' sti pratyayo loke yaḥ śabdānugamādṛte/
anuviddhamiva jñānaṁ sarvaṁ śabdena bhāsitam//
VĀKYAPADĪYAM 1.123.
23. *vimarśaśca śabdajīvitaḥ.* I.P.V. 2.3.2, p. 70.
24. In the Bible the world is said to have come from the "Word." "Before the world was created, the Word already existed; he was with God. From the very beginning the Word was with God. Through him God made all things; not one thing in all creation was made without him. The Word was the source of life, and this life brought light to mankind." GOOD NEWS BIBLE; John 1.1-5, p. 118.
25. Kālidāsa in his Mālavikāgnimitram, 2nd act, uses the word (*antarvacana*) "inner speech" for the inner feeling or thought: *angairantarnihitavacanaih* . . . .
26. *svasaṁvitsiddhāyāṁ yaiva parā-vāgbhūmiḥ saiva . . . paśyantyādidaśāsvapi vastuto vyavasthitā, tayā vinā paśyantyādiṣu aprakāśatāpattyā jaḍatāprasaṅgāt.* P.T.V. 1, p. 5.
27. I pointed out in the very beginning that Śiva and Śakti are *two* in connotation only; in denotation the two are one and the same, and therefore, the reality is one and the same.
28. *citiḥ pratyavamarśātmā parā vāk svarasoditā.* I.P.K. 1.5.13.
29. *ekameva paraṁ rūpaṁ bhairavasyāhamātmakam.* T.A. 3.207.
30. *tadaikṣata bahusyāṁ prajāyeyeti.* CHĀNDOGYA UPANIṢAD 6.2.3.
31. (a) *icchāśaktiraghorāṇāṁ śaktīnāṁ sā pārā prabhuḥ.* T.A. 3.72.
(b) *yo' nuttaraḥ paraḥ spando yaścānandaḥ samucchalan/*
tāvicchonmeṣasaṁghaṭṭādgacchato' tivicitratām// IBID.,3.93-94.
(c) *anuttarānanda citī icchāśaktau niyojite/*
trikoṇamiti tatprāhurvisargāmodasundaram// IBID.3.94-95.
32. *tatastu paśyantī yadyad abhīpsitaṁ tattadeva samucitakāraṇaniyamaprabodhitaṁ bodhasūtramātreṇa vimṛśati.* P.T.V. 1, p. 4.
33. *nahi prathamajñānakāle bhedo' tra asphurat, yatra vācyavācakaviśeṣayoḥ abhedaḥ.* P.T.V. 1, p. 4-5.

34. (a) *madhyamā punaḥ tayoreva vācyavācakayoḥ bhedamādarśya sāmānādhikaraṇyena vimarśavyāpārā.* P.T.V. 1, p. 5.
(b) *jñātavyaviśvonmeṣātmā jñānaśaktitayā sthitaḥ.* T.A. 3.73-74.
35. *paśyantyāṁ yatra bhedāṁśasyāsūtraṇaṁ,*
yatra ca madhyamāyāṁ bhedāvabhāsaḥ .... P.T.V. 1, p. 6.
36. *vaikharī tu tadubhayabhedasphuṭatāmayyeva.* P.T.V. 1, p. 5.
37. *Artha* primarily means the thing (*vastu*). The word stands for thing; and it is, therefore, the thing (*artha*) that gives meaning to the word — the thing (*artha*) is the meaning of the word. Hence, *artha* secondarily means "meaning."
38. *yā tu sphutānāṁ varṇānāmutpattau kāraṇaṁ bhavet/*
sā sthūlā vaikharī yasyāḥ kāryaṁ vākyādi bhūyasā// T.A. 3.244-45.
39. *ahameva sā parāvāgdevīrūpaiva sarvavācyavācakāvibhaktatayā evamuvāca.* P.T.V. 1, p. 9.
40. Although Śiva and Śakti are numbered as two in the hierarchy of the thirty-six categories, they are one and the same. As I have already explained, they are two only connotatively; denotatively they are one single reality. Therefore the *two* are classified under one and the same level of Reality, namely, the *parā*.
41. *svātmapratyavamarśo yaḥ prāgabhūdekavīrakaḥ/*
jñātavyaviśvonmeṣātmā jñānaśaktitayā sthitaḥ// T.A. 3.73-74.
42. *dvaita-prathā tadajñānaṁ tucchatvād bandha ucyate.* T.A. 1.30.
43. *tadevaṁpañcakamidaṁ śuddho' dhvā paribhāṣyate/*
*tatra sākṣācchivecchaiva kartryābhāsitabhedikā//*T.A. 9.60.
44. *sarvo mamāyaṁ vibhava ityevaṁ parijānataḥ/*
*viśvātmano vikalpānāṁ prasare' pi maheśatā//*I.P.K. 4.1.12.
45. ... *śiva eva gṛhīta paśu-bhāvaḥ.* P.S. 5.
46. *ātmapracchādanakrīḍāṁ kurvato vā kathañcana/*
māyārūpamitityādi śaṭtriṁśattattvarūpatāṁ// Ś.D. 1.32.
Also, *svātmapracchādanakrīḍāpaṇḍitaḥ parameśvaraḥ.* T.A. 4.10.
47. *iti bandhamokṣacitrāṁ krīḍāṁ pratanoti paramaśivaḥ.* P.S. 33.
48. *paramaṁ yat svātantryaṁ durghaṭasaṁpādanaṁ maheśasya/*
devī māyāśaktiḥ svātmāvaraṇaṁ śivasyaitat// P.S. 15.
49. *māyā kalā rāgavidye kālo niyatireva ca/*
*kañcukāni ṣaḍuktāni saṁvidastatsthitau paśuḥ//*T.A. 9.204.
50. *sarvo mamayaṁ vibhavaḥ* .... I.P.K. 4.1.12.
51. T.A. 9.208, 9.172, 9.176, 9.213, 9.215.
52. *sarvaviṣayamabhilāṣamātraṁ hi rāgatattvam* .... T.A.V. 4.17.
53. ... *tayā niyatisaṅgataṁ rāgatattvamuktaṁ sāmānyena* ... T.A.V. 4.17.
54. *dvaita-prathā tadajñānam* ... T.A. 1.30.
55. T.A. 9.202; T.S. 8, p. 82.

56. *kārya-kāraṇa-bhāvo yaḥ śivecchāparikalpitaḥ.* T.A. 9.7.
57. The mythical story about the sage Mārkaṇḍeya goes that he was fated (according to his *karma*) to die at the age of sixteen. Knowing this, the boy Mārkaṇḍeya developed intense devotion for Lord Śaṁkara (Śiva). When at the appointed hour Yamarāja, the Lord of Death, approached Mārkaṇḍeya to take his life, he (Mārkaṇḍeya) totally surrendered himself to Lord Śaṁkara. Lord Śaṁkara appeared and drew His trident (*triśūla*) to attack Yamarāja. Yamarāja bowed and submitted, "I am simply doing my duty in fulfilling the Law of Karma which is Your own law." The Lord retorted, "Don't you know that one who totally surrenders to me, becomes free from the Law of Karma?" The point is that the *paśu* is bound by the Law of Karma, the Law of Karma is the law of God, and one who comes totally in line with God, or the Self, transcends the Law of Karma.
58. *niyatiryojanāṁ dhatte viśiṣṭe kāryamaṇḍale.* T.A. 9.202.
59. *krama eva ca kālo, na anyo' sau kaścit*. . . . I.P.V. 2.1.3, p. 9.
60. T.A. 13.206 (p. 129).
61. I.P.V. 2.2.4, p. 43.
62. *māyāparigrahavaśād bodho malinaḥ pumān paśurbhavati/*
*kāla-kalā-niyativaśād rāgavidyāyaśena sambaddhah//*P.S. 16.
63. The Upaniṣad describes Brahman as "smaller than the smallest and bigger than the biggest" (*aṇoraṇīyān mahato mahīyān*). Here the word *aṇu* is used for "small."
64. *tadevaṁ puṁstvamāpanne pūrṇe' pi parameśvare/*
tatsvarūpāparijñānaṁ citraṁ hi puruṣāstataḥ// T.A. 8.293.
65. *atrāpi vedyatā nāma tādātmyaṁ vedakaiḥ saha.* T.A. 10.165.
66. T.A. 9.227, p. 182.
67. T.A. 9.235.
68. P.S. 21.
69. IBID. 22.
70. T.A. 9.280-296.
71. Berkeley, the Idealist, maintains that the existence of the object depends upon our perceiving the same (*esse est percipi*).
72. In his *Krama-stotram*, Abhinavagupta brings out this idea beautifully. He says that "the Lord's power, although adopting a variety of changes in *krama*, does not really undergo any change."

ataścitrācitrakramataditarādisthitijuṣo vibhoḥ śaktiḥ śaśvad vrajati na vibhedaṁ kathamapi. [KRAMA-STOTRAM]11.
And, "Because of the absence of *krama*, the thinking of time is totally gone."
kramābhāvādeva prasabha vigalatkālakalanam. IBID.,13.

73. *namaḥ saṁsārarūpāya niḥsaṁsārāya śambhave.* Ś.ST. 2.8.
74. T.A. 11.21-22.
75. IBID. 11. 22-23.
76. KENA UPANIṢAD 1.4-8.
77. *saṁsāraikanimittāya saṁsāraikavirodhine/*
*namaḥ saṁsārarūpāya niḥsaṁsārāya sambhave//*Ś.ST. 2.8.

CHAPTER 5

1. *anubhava-sampradāyopadeśapariśīlanena....* P.T.V. 9, p. 161.
2. *sārametatsamastasya yaccitsāraṁ jaḍaṁ jagat.* T.A. 4.185.
3. *tadevamubhayākāram avabhāsaṁ prakāśayan/*
vibhāti varado bimba-pratibimbadṛśākhile// T.A. 3.11.
4. *nirmale makure yadvad bhānti bhūmijalādayaḥ/*
amiśrāḥ tadvadekasmin cinnāthe viśvavṛttayaḥ// T.A. 3.4
5. *tena saṁvittimakure viśvamātmānamarpayat/*
nāthasya vadate' muṣya vimalāṁ viśvarūpatām// IBID.3.44
6. *saṁvidātmani viśvo' yaṁ bhāvavargaḥ prapañcavān/*
pratibimbatayā bhāti yasya viśveśvaro hi saḥ// IBID.3.268.
7. *antarvibhāti sakalaṁ jagadātmanīha yadvad vicitraracanā mukurāntarāle/*
bodhaḥ paraṁ nijavimarśarasānuvṛttyā viśvaṁ parāmṛśati no
mukurastathā tu// T.A. 1, p. 19, also quoted in T.A.V. 3.65, p. 73.
8. (a)... *tatra hi bimbapratibimbayordvayorapi sāmarthyamiti bhāvah.*
T.A. 3.51 (Comm., p. 61).
(b)... *tasmādeko mahādevaḥ svātantryopahitasthitiḥ.*
dvitvena bhātyasau bimbapratibimbodayātmanā.
Quoted in T.A. 3.11, p. 13.
9. *mayyeva bhāti viśvaṁ darpaṇa iva nirmale ghaṭādīni/*
mattaḥ prasarati sarvaṁ svapnavicitratvamiva suptāt// P.S. 48.
10. (a) *arthakriyābhāso' pi ca ābhāsāntaram eva iti arthakriyākāritvamapi na*
bhāvānāṁ sattvam. I.P.V. 1.8.6, p. 330.
(b) *arthakriyāpi sahajā nārthānāmīśvarecchayā/*
niyatā sā hi tenāsyā nākriyāto' nyatā bhavet// I.P.K. 2.3.12, p. 111.
11. *tattadrūpatayā jñānaṁ bahirantaḥ prakāśate/*
jñānādṛte nārthasattā jñānarūpaṁ tato jagat//
nahi jñānādṛte bhāvāḥ kenacidviṣayīkṛtāḥ/
jñānaṁ tadātmatāṁ prāptametasmādavasīyate//
Quoted in T.A. 3.57, p. 66.

12. *yugapadvedanād jñāna-jñeyayorekarūpatā.* Quoted in T.A. 3.57, p. 66.
13. *nanu bimbasya virahe pratibimbaṁ bhavet katham.* T.A. 3.52.
14. *kiṁ kurmo dṛśyate taddhi* . . . . T.A. 3.52.
15. . . . *yathā bimbābhāve' pi nimittāntareṇa pratibimbaṁ bhavettathā ihāpi* . . . . T.A.V. 3.64, p. 72.
16. *evam bahiḥ smṛtyādau yathā bimbābhāve' pi nimittāntareṇa pratibimbaṁ bhavetathā ihāpi ityāha, ato nimittaṁ devasyaśaktayaḥ santu tādṛśe.* T.A. 3.64-65, p. 72.
17. . . . *svātantryaśaktimātraparamārtha eva iti nijaiśvaryamātrādeva asya svātmani viśvākāradhāritvam* . . . . T.A.V. 3.64-65, p. 72.
18. *itthaṁ viśvamidaṁ nāthe bhairavīyacidambare/*
    pratibimbamalaṁ svacche na khalvanyaprasādataḥ// T.A. 3.65.
19. (a) *yogināmapi mṛdbīje vinaivecchāvaśena tat/*
    ghaṭādi jāyate tattatsthirasvārthakriyākaram// I.P.K. 2.4.10, p. 151.
    (b) *nirupādānasaṁbhāramabhittāveva tanvate/*
    jagaccitraṁ namastasmai kalāślāghyāya śūline//
    STAVACINTĀMAṆI 9.
20. *viśve hi bhāvāstasyaiva śaktirūpeṇa svarūpātmatvena sthitāḥ.* I.P.V. 2.4.1, p. 136.
21. . . . *cetano hi svātmadarpaṇe bhāvān pratibimbavadābhāsayati, iti siddhāntaḥ.* IBID. 2.4.11, p. 153.
22. (a) T.A. 3.4, 3.44, 3.268.
    (b) PARAMĀRTHA-CARCĀ 5.
    (c) *darpanabimbe yadvan nagaragrāmādi citramavibhāgi/*
    bhāti vibhāgenaiva ca parasparaṁ darpaṇādi ca// P.S. 12.
23. . . . *ciddarpaṇe rājate.* *Anuttarāṣṭikā* 8.
24. *māyeyaṁ na cidadvayāt paratayā bhinnāpyaho vartate.* ANUTTARĀṢṬIKĀ 3.
25. *yadyad bhāti na bhānataḥ pṛthagidam* . . . . PARAMĀRTHA-DVĀDAŚIKĀ 3.
26. *vartamānāvabhāsānāṁ bhāvānāmavabhāsanam/*
    antaḥsthitavatāmeva ghaṭate bahirātmanā// I.P.K. 1.5.1, p. 153.
27. (a) *mayyeva bhāti viśvaṁ darpaṇa iva nirmale ghaṭādīni/*
    mattaḥ prasarati sarvaṁ svapnavicitratvamiva suptāt// P.S. 48.
    (b) *svapne ghaṭapaṭādīnāṁ hetutadvatsvabhāvatā/*
    *bhāsate niyamenaiva bādhāśūnyena tāvati//*T.A. 9.27.
28. I.P.V. 1.1.3, p. 35-37.
29. *tatra svatantratā mātram adhikaṁ pravivicyate.* T.A. 3.1.
30. *tatsvātantrayarasāt punaḥ śivapadād bhede vibhāte param* . . . . T.A. 9.2.

31. *tena svātmarūpameva viśvaṁ satyarūpaṁ prakāśātmatāparamārthamatruṭitaprakāśābhedameva sat prakāśaparamārthenaiva bhedena prakāśayati maheśvaraḥ.* I.P.V. 2.4.20, p. 181.
32. *niḥsatye capale prapañcanicaye svapna-bhrame peśale....* ANUTTARĀṢṬIKĀ 6.
33. (a) ... *rajjubhujaga-cchāyāpiśāca bhramo....* ANUTTARĀṢṬIKĀ 2.
    (b) *rajjvāṁ nāsti bhujaṅgaḥ trāsaṁ kurute ca mṛtyuparyantam/ bhrāntermahatī śaktir na vivektum śakyate nāma//* P.S. 28.
34. ANUTTARĀṢṬIKĀ 2,6; P.S. 28.
35. *niḥsatye capale....* ANUTTARĀṢṬIKĀ 6.
36. *mithyāmohakṛdeṣa....* IBID. 2.
37. *saṁsāro' sti na tattvatas tanubhṛtāṁ bandhasya vārtaiva kā.../ mithyāmohakṛdeṣa rajjubhujaga cchāyāpiśācabhramo...//* ANUTTARĀṢṬIKĀ 2.
38. *nahi draṣṭurdṛṣterviparilopo vidyate.* BṚHADĀRAṆYAKA UPANIṢAD 4.3.23.
39. *svatantratā ca cinmātra vapuṣaḥ parameśituḥ/ svatantraṁ ca jaḍaṁ ceti tadanyonyaṁ virudhyate//* T.A. 9.9, p. 12-13.
40. *prakāśamātraṁ yat proktaṁ bhairavīyaṁ paraṁ mahaḥ/ tatra svatantratāmātram adhikaṁ pravivicyate//* T.A. 3.1.
41. *citisaṅkocātmā cetano' pi saṅkucitaviśvamayaḥ.* P.H. 4.
42. *tathāpi tadvat pañcakṛtyāni karoti.* P.H. 10.
43. *tasmāt vāstavaṁ cidekatvamabhyupagamyāpi tasya kartṛtvalakṣaṇābhinnarūpasamāveśātmikā kriyā nopapadyate; parāmarśalakṣaṇaṁ tu svātanryaṁ yadi bhavati tadopapadyate sarvam.* I.P.V. 2.4.20.
44. *parāmarśalakṣaṇaṁ tu svātantryam...* IBID.
45. *na me pārthāsti kartavyaṁ triṣu lokeṣu kiñcana. nānavāptamavāptavyaṁ varta eva ca karmaṇi.* BH.G. 3.22.
46. *ānandāddhyeva khalvimāni bhūtāni jāyante....* TAITTIRĪYA UPANIṢAD 3.6.
47. *tatsvātantryarasāt punaḥ śivapadād bhede vibhāte param.* T.A. 9.2.
48. *citrākāraprakāśo' yaṁ svatantraḥ parameśvaraḥ.* T.A. 13.264.
49. *pūrvapakṣatayā yena viśvamābhāsya bhedataḥ/ abhedottarapakṣāntar nīyate taṁ stumaḥ śivam//* I.P.V. 1.2.1, *maṅgalācaraṇa*, p. 51.
50. (a) *tadevāsyātidurghaṭakāritvalakṣaṇaṁ svātantryam aiśvaryam ucyate.* I.P.V. 2.4.20.
    (b) *paramaṁ yatsvātantryaṁ durghaṭasampādanaṁ maheśasya.* P.S. 15.
51. *svecchayā svabhittau viśvamunmīlayati.* P.H. 2.

52. *dve satye samupāśritya buddhānāṁ dharmadeśanā/*
lokasamvṛtisatyañca satyañca paramārthataḥ//
MADHYAMAKA ŚĀSTRA 24.8.
53. *māyāpadaṁ hi sarvaṁ bhrāntiḥ, tatrāpi tu svapne svapna iva gaṇḍe sphoṭa iva apareyaṁ bhrāntirucyate.* I.P.V. 2.3.13, p. 114.
54. *ityapūrṇakhyātirūpā akhyātireva bhrāntitattvam.* I.P.V. 2.3.13, Vol. II, p. 113.
55. *viśvabhāvaikabhāvātma-svarūpaprathanaṁ hi yat/*
aṇūnāṁ tatparaṁ jñānaṁ tadanyadaparaṁ bahu// T.A. 1.141.
56. Referring to the distinction in *paramārtha* and *vyavahāra* and the abuse of this theory by many of the Advaitic pandits, Dr. Ram Manohar Lohia, the socialist leader, used to say that hypocrisy exists in every country, but India is the only country where there is also a philosophy (the philosophy of *paramārtha* and *vyavahāra*) to justify hypocrisy! Dr. Lohia may not be completely correct, but the main thrust of what he says is true.

CHAPTER 6

1. Referring to the mythological story of Bhṛgu Muni who in anger gave a severe kick to Lord Viṣṇu (the manifest form of God) on His chest, the Bengali poet Kazi Nazrul Islam angrily admonishes God in one of his Verses. He says:
   āmi vidrohī bhṛgu
   āmi bhagavān bu ke ik dibo padaciñha,
   eyi śok-tāp-dātāya khayāle vidher
   vakkha kari' vacūrna.
   "I am the rebel Bhṛgu; I will give the Lord a kick; I will break into pieces the chest of this whimsical God who gives sorrow and suffering."
2. Pained at the sight of indiscriminate killings by the Moghul soldiers at the time of Babar's invasion of India, Guru Nānak makes a severe complaint to God:
   khurāsāna khasamānā kīyā hindustānu ḍarāyiyā.
   āpai dosa na deī karatā jamu kari mugal caḍhāyiyā.
   etī māra payī karalāne tain kī daradu na āyiyā.
   "O Lord, You sent the Moghul as Yamarāja (the Lord of Death) who terrorized India. You do not take the responsibility on Yourself; but were You not moved to see the pangs of suffering of the people at the striking hands of the cruel Moghuls?"
   GURU GRANTH SĀHIB, p. 360. (Also see p. 417.)

3. *śiva eva gṛhīta paśubhāvah.* P.S. 5.
4. *iti bandhamokṣacitrām krīḍām pratanoti paramaśivaḥ.* IBID. 33.
5. The author of the *Pratyabhijñāhṛdayam* catches hold of this truism and points out that the *paśu,* as a replica of Śiva, performs the five-fold activities of creation, and so on (*pañcakṛtya*) of Śiva, although in a limited way. *tathāpi tadvat pañcakṛtyāni karoti.* P.H. 10.
6. The Existentialists are quite aware of the freedom of man, although, as they say, it is "anguished freedom." Kashmir Śaivism fully respects the existence of man, and in that respect it can be said to be a form of existentialism; the only difference would be that it supplements the philosophy of existence with a philosophy of essence, or a philosophy of higher existence, based on the actual experience of the sages and the seers. "Anguished freedom" is the existential reflection of man whose real nature is perfect freedom that can be achieved in this very life.
7. "Everyone is tied by the thread of his own karma" (*svakarmasūtragrathito hi lokaḥ*), is the famous dictum accepted by Indian seers. TRADITIONAL.
8. Swami Rāmakṛṣṇa Paramahansa, using an analogy, says that just as the water, falling from the different rooftops through different channels, comes from one and the same source — the cloud — similarly the teachings coming out of the mouths of different sages really come from one and the same source — God.
9. The proverb goes, "animate beings live by eating other animate beings." (*jīvo jīvasya jīvanam*). TRADITIONAL.
10. *jñāninām api cetāṁsi devī bhagavatī hi sā/*
balādākṛṣya mohāya mahāmāyā prayacchati// DURGĀ-SAPTAŚATĪ 1.55.
11. *prakṛteḥ kriyamāṇāni guṇaiḥ karmāṇi sarvaśaḥ/*
ahaṇkāra-vimūḍhātmā kartāhamiti manyate// BH.G. 3.27.
12. *īśvaraḥ sarvabhūtānāṁ hṛddeśe' rjuna tiṣṭhati/*
bhrāmayan sarvabhūtāni yantrārūḍhāni māyayā// BH.G. 18.61.
13. One is reminded here of Spinoza, an advocate of Divine determinism, who maintains that all human action is determined by the Divine will, yet a person falsely thinks that he or she is a free agent, as if a falling stone thinks that it is falling of its own accord.
14. The *Gītā* says, "The Lord does not give vice (*pāpa*) or virtue (*puṇya* or *sukṛta*) to anybody," that is, it is not the Lord who causes anybody to enact vice or virtue. "Knowledge is covered by ignorance, and that is what prompts the creatures to act."
nādatte kasyacitpāpaṁ na caiva sukṛtaṁ vibhuḥ/
ajñānenāvṛtaṁ jñānaṁ tena muhyanti jantavaḥ// BH.G. 5.15.
15. In the same *Gītā* that declares God to be the real doer, the Lord says to Arjuna, "I have related to you the wisdom that is the secret of all secrets;

think over it from all points, and then *do what you like.*"
iti te jñānamākhyātaṁ guhyādguhyataraṁ mayā/
vimṛśvaitadarśeṣeṇa vathecchasi tathā kuru// BH.G. 18.63.

16. A popular Hindi verse using this analogy says that God is like the digit (*aṇka*) of "1" (one), and all the worldly means are like the zero; the efficacy of the means is derived from God, just as the zero becomes ten times more valuable when the digit "1" is placed by its side, but it becomes nothing when the digit "1" is removed.
rāma nāma ika aṇka hai, saba sādhana hai sūna/
aṇka gaye kachu hātha nahi, aṇka rahe dasagūna// TRADITIONAL.
17. The famous story of the *yakṣa* (*Yakṣopākhyāna*) in the *Kena Upaniṣad* relates the incident of Brahman's withdrawing His powers from the gods (Agni, Vāyu, and so on). They became absolutely helpless and then realized the nothingness of their egos. This story depicts the truth that the powers of the ego really belong to the Higher Self; when these powers are withdrawn, the ego becomes nothing.
At one place the *Taittirīya Upaniṣad* says, "The power of action in the hands and the power of locomotion in the feet come from Brahman."
karmeti hastayoḥ, gatiriti pādayoḥ. TAITTIRĪYA UPANIṢAD 10.2.
18. In the "Questions of King Milinda" (MILINDAPANHO), Nāgasena, using the analogy of the chariot, makes this point clear to King Milinda. No constituent of the so-called chariot — not the axle, wheels, frame, reins, yoke, spokes, or goad — can be called "chariot." What exists in reality is the axle, wheels, and so on, not the thing called a chariot. "Chariot" is a mere name, just a practical designation given to the aggregate of the parts. So the "chariot," which is a mere name and is nothing in itself, has taken possession of everything — the axle, wheels, and so on. That which is really nothing (the chariot) has become the principal thing; and that which really is the thing (the axle, wheels, and so on) is lost. Similarly, it is the five components of the individual (*pañcaskandha*) — body, mind, sense-organs, and so on, that are the real things, and what is called the ego, or the ātman as the Buddhist would call it, is a mere name like the chariot. But this ego that is a mere nothing has taken possession of all the body components and has become the master reality.
19. DURGĀ-SAPTAŚATĪ 1.55.
20. When the ego or the individual will is surrendered, what ensues is not voluntary, effortful action (technically called *karma*) but the spontaneous, joyful activity of the Self, which is called *spanda* or *kriyā*. Unlike *karma*, which results from imperfection, *spanda* is at once both good and joyful; it is the state of the natural synthesis of *śreya* ("the good") and *preya* ("the pleasant or beautiful"). A God-surrendered or Self-realized person is not in the state

of *karma*, but the state of *spanda* or *kriyā*, naturally and spontaneously emanating activity that is at the same time benign and blissful.

21. *krīḍayā duḥkhavedyāni karmakāriṇi tatphalaiḥ/*
sambhatsyamānāni tathā narakārṇavagahvare//
nivāsīni śarīrāṇi gṛhṇāti parameśvaraḥ/
yathā nṛpaḥ sārvabhaumaḥ prabhāvāmodabhāvitaḥ//
krīḍankaroti pādātadharmānstaddharmadharmataḥ/
tathā prabhuḥ pramodātmā krīḍatyevaṁ tathā tathā// Ś.D. 1.36-38.
22. *ajñānenāvṛtaṁ jñānaṁ tena muhyanti jantavaḥ.* BH.G. 5.15.
23. *iha tāvatsamasteṣu śāstreṣu parigīyate/*
ajñānaṁ saṁsṛterheturjñānaṁ mokṣaika-kāraṇam// T.A. 1.22.
24. *avaśyameva bhoktavyaṁ kṛtaṁ karma śubhāśubham.* TRADITIONAL.
25. The poet Tulasīdāsa uses this very analogy and says that just as a mother overlooks the impatient cries of the child in order that the child be free from disease, so also the Lord relieves His devotee of his ego.
jadapi prathama dukha pāvayī rovayi bāla adhīra/
vyādhināsa hita jananī ganati na so sisupīra//
timi raghupati nija dāsa kara harahi māna hita lāgi/
tulasidāsa aise prabhuhi kasa na bhajahu bhrama tyāgi//
RĀMACARITAMĀNASA, UTTARAKĀṆḌA, 74(a) & 74(b).
26. The mystic poet Kabir, referring to the distinction between "to do" and "to be" says, "One who does or acts is my son (i.e., is inferior to me), and one who merely talks is my grandson (is much more inferior to me); but one who is or lives the life of ideal consciousness is my guru; I prefer to be with him."
karanī kare so pūta hamārā, kathanī kare so nātī/
rahanī rahe so guru hamārā, hama rahanī ke sāthī//
27. The eminent psychoanalyst, Sigmund Freud, says, ". . . it is by no means the rule that virtue is rewarded and wickedness punished, but it happens often enough that the violent, the crafty, and the unprincipled seize the desirable goods of the earth for themselves, while the pious go empty away." NEW INTRODUCTORY LECTURES ON PSYCHOANALYSIS, 1933, p. 228, quoted in "Problems of Suffering in Religions of the World" by John Bowker, Cambridge, 1970, pp. 1-2.
28. There is a story about Guru Nānak that illustrates that the rich are not necessarily happy. A rich man privately narrated his plight to Nānak. It seems his beautiful wife once fell seriously ill and she expressed her fears that after her death he would marry another woman. In order to assure her of his fidelity, he ripped his sexual organ. His wife then recovered, but as the husband was now sexually impotent, she began flirting with other men. This caused unbearable agony to the helpless husband.

The rich are sometimes the most miserable people on earth. Some of them are unfit for spiritual pursuits. As Christ said, "It is easier for a camel to go through the eye of a needle than for a rich man to enter into the Kingdom of God."

29. *kṣīyante cāsya karmāṇi tasmin dṛṣṭe parāvare.*
MUṆḌAKA UPANIṢAD 2.2.8.
30. *yathaidhānsi samiddho' gnir bhasmasāt kurute' rjuna/*
jñānāgniḥ sarvakarmāṇi bhasmasāt kurute tathā// BH.G. 4.37.
31. *kaha kabīra santa koyi sūramā, karma kī rekha pai mekha mārai.*
32. *sanmukha hoyi jīva mohiṁ jabahīṁ/*
janma koṭi agha nāsahiṁ tabahīṁ//
RĀMACARITA-MĀNASA, SUNDARAKĀṆḌA 43.2.
33. *iti te jñānamākhyātaṁ guhyādguhyataraṁ mayā/*
vimṛśyaitadaśeṣeṇa yathecchasi tathā kuru// BH.G. 18.63.

CHAPTER 7

1. According to the Reminiscence theory of Plato, the soul has come from the perfect world of Ideas, the memory of which it unconsciously preserves; it thus tries to reapprehend its real home.
2. *prakāśātmatayā satatam avabhāsamāne' pi ātmani bhāgena aprakāśanavaśād anupalakṣite . . . pūrṇatāvabhāsanasādhyām arthakriyām akurvati, tatpūrṇatāvabhāsanātmakābhimāna viśeṣasiddhaye pratyabhijñā . . . pradarśyate.* I.P.K. 1.1.3.
3. (a) . . . *śiva evāham* . . . T.A. 3.286.
(b) IBID. 3.283-86.
(c) *sa tu viśuddhasvabhāvah śivātmā, māyāpade tu saṁkucitasvabhāvaḥ paśuḥ* . . . . I.P.V. 2.2.3, p. 39.
(d) *tadayaṁ pramātā jñānakriyāśaktiyogād īśvara iti vyavahartavyaḥ prāṇāgamādiprasiddheśvaravat.* I.P.V. 1.1.4, p. 43-48.
4. *antato' pi sāmānyātmanā vā jñātasya punarabhimukhībhāvāvasare pratisandhitaprāṇitameva jñānaṁ pratyabhijñā* . . . I.P.V. 1.1.1, p. 20.
5. *nṛpatiṁ prati pratyabhijñāpito' yam ityādan* . . . I.P.V. 1.1.1, p. 20
6. I.P.K. 4.2.2.
7. . . . *dṛṣṭe' pyanupalakṣite.* I.P.K. 1.1.3.
8. . . . *pūrṇaśaktisvabhāve īśvare sati svātmanyabhimukhībhūte tatpratisandhānena jñānam udeti, nūnaṁ sa eva īśvaro' ham — iti* . . . . I.P.V. 1.1.1, p. 21.
9. *śaktyāviṣkaraṇeneyaṁ pratyabhijñopadarśyate* I.P.K. 1.1.3.
10. There is no perfect substitute in English for *pauruṣa ajñāna. Pauruṣa* means

pertaining to *puruṣa* ("person"). Hence *pauruṣa ajñāna* means the ignorance that pertains to the entire person (and not merely the intellect). For lack of a better word, I call *pauruṣa jñāna* existential knowledge.

11. *malamajñānamichhanti saṁsārāṅkurakāraṇam.* T.A. 1.23.
12. *na hi bauddhājñānamātranivṛttau mokṣo bhavet.* T.A.V. 1.24.
13. *pauruṣe punarajñāne dīkṣādinā nivṛtte sati . . . jīvanmuktiṁ pratyapi kāraṇaṁ bhavet.* IBID. 1.24.
14. *ajñānasya pauruṣabauddhātmakatvena dvaividhye' pi iha pauruṣameva vivakṣitaṁ syānnānyat . . . .* IBID. (introduction).
15. . . . *kevalena punastena na kiñcit setsyati ityuktaprāyaṁ.* IBID. 1.24.
16. *pauruṣaṁ punarjñānamuditaṁ sat anyanirapekṣameva mokṣakāraṇam.* IBID.
17. . . . *na kārakavyāpāro bhagavati nāpi jñāpakavyāpāro' yam, api tu mohā pasāraṇamātrametat* . . . I.P.V. 1.1.3, p. 38.
18. MUṆḌAKA UPANIṢAD 3.2.9.
19. *dvaitaprathā tadajñānam* . . . . T.A. 1.30.
20. *yastu sarvāṇi bhūtāni ātmanyevānupaśyati/*
    sarvabhūteṣu cātmānam . . . // IŚA UPANIṢAD 6.
    Also, *sarvabhūtātmabhūtātmā* . . . BH.G. 5.7.
21. This issue is thoroughly discussed in the Advaita Vedānta system; in the Tantric tradition, however, it is simply accepted.
22. I use the word *innate* not in the sense of being congenital but in the sense of coming automatically by itself. The word *innate* is not the best translation for the Sanskrit word *pratibhā* (mostly used in the Tantric tradition), for the word *innate* is generally used in the sense of meaning something congenital or present at birth. *Pratibhā* does not primarily mean what exists at birth; it means the illumination or knowledge that comes by itself or dawns automatically.
23. (a) *saiva bhagavato māyā vimohinī nāma śaktiḥ, tadvaśāt prakāśātmatayā satatam avabhāsamāne' pi ātmani bhāgena aprakāśanavaśād anupalak site* . . . . I.P.V. 1.1.3, p. 37.
    (b) The Upaniṣads say, "The face of Reality (Truth) is covered with a golden pot." (*hiraṇmayena pātreṇa satyasyāpihitaṁ mukham*). ĪŚA UPANIṢAD 15.
24. I.P.K. 1.1.3.
25. (a) *śaktyāviṣkaraṇeneyaṁ pratyabhijñopadarśyate.* I.P.K. 1.3.
26. The Upaniṣads say that one can see the Self by "turning one's eyes back" (*āvṛttacakṣuḥ*): *kaściddhīraḥ pratyagātmānamaikṣad āvṛttacaksur amṛtatvamicchan.* KATHA UPANIṢAD 2.1.1.
27. pratīpam ātmābhimukhyena jñānaṁ prakāśaḥ pratyabhijñā. I.P.V. 1.1.1, p. 19-20).

28. The story goes that there were ten idiots in a village. They were sitting idle, doing nothing, and the villagers were fed up with them. One day the villagers told them, "You people are ten, go to the city and try to earn your livelihood." Then all ten idiots started for the city. On the way they had to cross a riveret. When they reached the other side of the riveret, a doubt occurred in the mind of one of them as to whether someone was drowned in the riveret. So he asked the others to fall in line so that he could count them in order to ascertain if anyone had drowned. The others obeyed and he counted up to nine, as there were nine persons standing before him, omitting himself, for the idea to count himself did not occur to him (idiot as he was). Every one of them counted in the same way, and they all came to the conclusion that one of them was drowned in the riveret! They began to cry over the loss of the tenth idiot.
   A wiseman who was passing that way saw them crying and asked them the cause of their weeping. Hearing the entire story from them, he was amazed to see that all ten people were present. He tried to assure them that nobody was lost, but they did not agree. He then immediately understood that there was some fault in the counting. So he asked them to show him how they counted. Then one of them, following the previous procedure, counted up to nine and, being confident of his conclusion, said to the wiseman, "Tell me, where is the tenth?" Then the wiseman, pointing to him, said, "Thou art the tenth (*daśamastvamasi*)." Then the tenth man saw himself and realized the truth that he himself was already there although he had not counted himself. The point of the story is that our attention is normally directed towards the external world and we are not able to see our own selves. The moment we "turn our eyes back" (*āvṛttacakṣuḥ*), we realize our own reality.
29. *kiraṇāyāṁ tathoktaṁ ca gurutaḥ śāstrataḥ svataḥ.* T.A. 13.162.
30. *svayameva yato vetti bandhamokṣatayātmatam/*
    tatprātibhaṁ mahājñānaṁ śāstrācāryānapekṣi yat// T.A. 13.132.
31. *sa tāvatkasyacittarkaḥ svata eva pravartate/*
    sa ca sāṁsiddhikaḥ śāstre proktaḥ svapratyayātmakaḥ// IBID. 4.40-41.
32. *sāṁsiddhikaṁ yad vijñānam....* IBID. 13.150.
33. *... śiva eva gṛhītapaśubhāvaḥ.* P.S. 5.
34. *tathāpi tadvat pañcakṛtyāni karoti.* P.H. 10.
35. *satyapi bhedāpagame nātha tavāhaṁ na māmakīnastvam/*
    sāmudro hi taraṅgaḥ kvacanasamudro na tāraṅgaḥ// TRADITIONAL.
36. *brahma veda brahmaiva bhavati.* TRADITIONAL.
37. In the systems of Indian philosophy we can find basic differences in the nature of the Self and, subsequently, in the conception of *mokṣa*. The Nyāya-Vaiśeṣika system regards the Self as devoid of knowledge, activity,

pain and pleasure, and so on, as these are accidental qualities of the Self, and so in *Mokṣa* the self remains in itself devoid of all these things. In Sāṁkhya, knowledge is accepted as the nature of the self, but there too, activity, pain, and pleasure are alienated, as these belong to *prakṛti* and not to *puruṣa*. In the Advaita Vedānta system, knowledge or illumination (*cit*) and bliss (*ānanda*) are both regarded as the very nature of the Self (*saccidānanda*). We can say that in the Nyāya-Vaiśeṣika the Self is only *sat* ("existence"), in Sāṁkhya it is *sat* and *cit* ("knowledge" or "Consciousness"), and in Advaita Vedānta it is *sat-cit-ānanda*. In the Tantric system, however, *kriyā* or *spanda* ("spontaneity") is accepted in the nature of the Self in addition to *sat-cit-ānanda*.

CHAPTER 8

1. In the previous chapter, "The Concept of Pratyabhijñā," we examined what is called *pratyabhijñā* or *ātma-pratyabhijñā* ("Self-recognition or Self-realization"), which is technical language used by the Kashmir Śaiva philosopher to explain *mokṣa*. Thus we have already discussed aspects of *mokṣa*. Here we will examine only those points relating to *mokṣa* that are not covered in the chapter on *pratyabhijñā*.
2. The Cārvāka (materialist) does not accept the existence of the soul, therefore he or she also denies the existence of *mokṣa*. The Kṣaṇabhaṅgavāda Buddhist, who advocates the theory of momentariness, does accept *nirvāṇa* (*mokṣa*) but is generally believed not to accept the existence of the soul. This leads to questions of how the no-soul theory fits with *nirvāṇa*. But this is all a misunderstanding of the Kṣaṇabhaṅgavāda position. The Kṣaṇabhaṅgavādin does not believe in a permanent soul. He or she sees the soul as a flux or continuum, of momentary selves (*vijñānas*); this continuum is present in *nirvāṇa* also. If we do not accept even this then *nirvāṇa* has no meaning. Only sentient beings attain *mokṣa* or *nirvāṇa*, so it is logically necessary to maintain that there is a sentient being — a soul, or self.
3. *kartari jñātari svātmanyādisiddhe maheśvare.* I.P.K. 1.1.2.
4. (a) *kintu mohavaśādasmin . . . .* I.P.K. 1.1.3.
   (b) *cidvattacchaktisaṁkocāt malāvṛtaḥ saṁsārī.* P.H. 9.
5. This has been explained in Chapter 7, and we need not review it here.
6. (a) *nanu ajñānaśabdasya apūrṇaṁ jñānamarthaḥ.* T.A.V. 1.25.
   (b) *ato jñeyasya tattvasya sāmastyenāprathātmakam/*
   jñānameva tadajñānam . . . // T.A. 1.26
7. See the section entitled "The Theory of Error" in Chapter 2.

8. *dvaitaprathā tadajñānaṁ tucchatvād bandha ucyate.* T.A. 1.30.
9. (a) *viśvabhāvaikabhāvātma-svarūpaprathanaṁ hi yat/ anūnāṁ tatparaṁ jñānam//* T.A. 1.141.
   (b) *yastu sarvāṇi bhūtāni ātmanyevānupaśyati/ sarvabhūteṣu cātmānam . . . //* ĪŚA UPANIṢAD 6.
   (c) *sarvabhūtātmabhūtātmā* . . . . BH.G. 5.7.
10. *pumān aśuddho bhedamayatvāt.* T.A.V. 1.189, p. 217.
11. (a) *malamajñānamicchanti saṁsārāṇkurakāraṇam.* T.A. 1.23.
    (b) *māyāparigrahavaśād bodho malinaḥ pumān paśurbhavati.* P.S. 16.
12. (a) *ajñānaṁ timiram* . . . . T.A.V. 1.23, p. 55.
    (b) *andhantamaḥ praviśanti ye' vidyāmupāsate/ tato bhūya iva te tamo ya u vidyāyāṁ ratāḥ//* ĪŚA UPANIṢAD 1 (see also verse 12).
13. *svātmapracchādanecchaiva vastubhūtastathā malaḥ.* T.A. 9.66.
14. (a) *malaścāvaraṇam* . . . . T.A. 9.71.
    (b) *svarūpagopanāsatattvam apūrṇaṁ jñānaṁ, tadeva cāṇavaṁ malam* . . . . T.A.V. 1.23, p. 55.
    (c) . . . *svātmāvaraṇaṁ śivasyaitat.* P.S. 15.
    (d) *hiraṇmayena pātreṇa satyasyāpihitaṁ mukham.* ĪŚA UPANIṢAD 15.
    (e) *dhūmenāvṛyate vahniryathādarśo malena ca/ yatholbenāvṛto garbhastathā tenedamāvṛtam//* BH.G. 3.38.
    (f) *malenāvṛtarūpāṇām aṇūnām* . . . . T.A. 9.72.
15. (a) *jñānaṁ bandhaḥ.* Ś.S. 1.2.
    (b) *dvaitaprathā tadajñānaṁ tucchatvād bandha ucyate.* T.A. 1.30.
16. We have considered this issue in detail in Chapter 3, "Absolute Consciousness" and Chapter 4, "The Process of Creation," and we will not repeat it here.
17. *svatantrasya śivasyecchā ghatarūpo yathā ghaṭaḥ/ svātmapracchādanecchaiva vastubhūtastathā malaḥ//*T.A. 9.65-66, p. 59.
18. . . . *māyāśaktyaiva tattrayam.* I.P.K. 3.2.5.
19. *bhinnasya yat prathanaṁ tasya māyīyam iti saṁjñāmātram, māyā-kṛtatvena māyīyatā malatrayasyāpi.* I.P.V. 3.2.5, p. 221.
20. (a) *aṇūnāṁ lolikā nāma niṣkarmā yābhilāṣitā/ apūrṇaṁ-manyatā-jñānaṁ malaṁ sāvacchidojjhitā//* T.A. 9.62.
    (b) *apūrṇaṁ-manyatā ceyaṁ tathārūpāvabhāsanam.* IBID. 9.65.
21. . . . *ata eva apūrṇaṁ-manyatā, ata eva pūrṇajñānātmakasvarūpākhyāterajñānaṁ — saṅkucitajñānaṁ, ata eva svarūpāpahānyā malam.* T.A.V. 9.62, p. 57.
22. *aṇūnāṁ lolikā nāma* . . . . T.A. 9.62.
23. *svātantryahānirbodhasya svātantryasyāpyabodhatā/ dvidhāṇavaṁ malamidaṁ svasvarūpāpahānitaḥ//* I.P.K. 3.2.4.

24. (a) *bhinnavedyaprathātraiva māyākhyam* .... I.P.K. 3.2.5.
    (b) ... *svarūpasaṅkoce vṛtte bhinnasya yatprathanaṁ tasya māyīya iti saṁjñāmātraṁ.* I.P.V. 3.2.5, p. 229.
25. T.A. 1.30.
26. *kartaryabhodhe kārmaṁ tu* .... I.P.K. 3.2.5.
27. *tatra karturabodharūpasya dehāderbhinnavedya prathane sati dharmādharmarūpaṁ kārmaṁ malaṁ, yato janma bhogaśca.* I.P.V. 3.2.5, p. 221.
28. (a) *tatrāpi kārmamevaikaṁ mukhyaṁ saṁsārakāraṇam.* I.P.K. 3.2.10.
    (b) *saṁsārakāraṇaṁ karma saṁsārāṅkura ucyate.* T.A. 9.88.
29. *caturdaśavidhaṁ bhūtavaicitryaṁ karmajaṁ yataḥ.* T.A. 9.89, p. 75.
30. *apūrṇaṁ-manyatā-jñānaṁ malam* .... T.A. 9.62.
31. ... *kārma malaṁ, tasyāpi kāraṇam āṇavamiti.* T.A.V. 9.88-89, p.75.
32. *evaṁ kārmasyaiva malasya mukhyatayā saṁsārakāraṇatve' pi etadeva hi prādhānyenoktaṁ yattasyāpīdaṁ kāraṇamiti.* IBID. 9.62., p. 57.
33. *yajñārthātkarmaṇo' nyatra loko' yaṁ karmabandhanaḥ.* BH.G. 3.9.
34. (a) *karmaṇyabhipravṛtto' pi naiva kiñcit karoti saḥ.* BH.G. 4.20.
    (b) *tasya kartāramapi māṁ viddhyakartāramavyayam.* BH.G. 4.13.
    (c) Also see BH.G. 5.8-9, 18.17.
35. *avaśyameva bhoktavyaṁ kṛtaṁ karma śubhāśubham.*
36. (a) ... *dharmādharmarūpaṁ kārmaṁ malam* .... I.P.V. 3.2.5.
    (b) *dharmādharmātmakaṁ karma sukhaduḥkhādilakṣaṇam.* T.A. 9.121.
37. *yā tvasya karmaṇaścitraphaladatvena karmatā* .... T.A. 9.99.
38. (a) ... *kārmamevaikaṁ mukhyaṁ saṁsārakāraṇam.*
    Quoted in T.A.V. 9.62, p. 56.
    (b) *saṁsāra-kāraṇaṁ karma saṁsārāṅkura ucyate.* T.A. 9.88.
39. *taja dharmamadharmaṁ ca ubhe satyānṛte tyaja/*
    ubhe satyānṛte tyaktvā yena tyajasi tattyaja// TRADITIONAL.
40. *tasmānmukto' pyavacchedādavacchedāntarasthiteḥ/*
    amukta eva, muktastu sarvāvacchedavarjitaḥ// T.A. 1.34.
41. *mokṣo hi nāma naivānyaḥ svarūpaprathanaṁ hi saḥ.* T.A. 1.156.
42. *apravarititapūrvo' tra kevalaṁ mūḍhatāvaśāt,*
    śaktiprakāśaneśādivyavahāraḥ pravartyate. I.P.K. 2.3.17.
43. *varaṁ vṛndāvane ramye śṛgālatvaṁ vṛṇomyaham/*
    na ca vaiśeṣikīm muktiṁ prārthayāmi kadācana//
44. *sarvādvaitapadasya vismṛtanidheḥ prāptiḥ prakāśodayaḥ.*
    ANUTTARĀṢṬIKĀ 4.
45. *ānando na hi vittamadyamadavan naivāṅganāsaṅgavat.* IBID. 46.
    harṣaḥ saṁbhṛtabhedamuktisukhabhūr bhārāvatāropamaḥ. IBID. 47.
    tadapararaṇameva hi parameśvaratālābho muktiḥ I.P.V. 2.3.17, p. 130.

48. *sarvaśoṣī yathā sūryaḥ sarvabhogī yathā' nalaḥ/*
yogī bhuktvākhilān bhogān tathā pāpairna lipyate//
KULĀRNAVA TANTRA 9.76.
49. *rāgadveṣaviyuktaistu viṣayānindriyaiścaran/*
ātmavaśyairvidheyātmā prasādamadhigacchati// BH.G. 2.46.
50. It is said in the *Paramarthasāra* that just as the grain separated from the husk is not bound by the husk although living with it, the liberated person (*jīvan-mukta*), free from the traces of past actions, is not touched by them although living with them in the world.
tadvat kañcukapataliprthakkṛtā samvidatra saṁskārāt/
tiṣṭhantyapi muktātmā tatsparśavivarjitā bhavati// P.S. 106.
51. Dr. C. P. M. Namboodiry in his brilliant and somewhat controversial paper, "Advaita and Indian Tradition" published in *Vedānta and Buddhism* (CASP, Benares Hindu University, 1968), has carefully analyzed the Advaitic position to successfully show that the ideal of liberation in scholastic Advaitism is incompatible with the ideal of the betterment of society. He says, "Either he (the Advaitin) must find some explanation why a person who has realized Brahman still continues in the world of *avidyā*, and this would be tantamount to accepting that *avidyā* can in some sense survive Brahmajñāna . . . or he must totally deny the very possibility of *jīvanmukti*, which would go against the Upaniṣadic tradition . . . while the *mumukṣu* might at least take a passive interest in the affairs of the world or society, in so far as he still forms part of it, the *jīvanmukta* is totally and permanently dissociated from it." He further says, ". . . the real has never had, nor can ever have, any relation with the illusory. . . . In the progress from the illusory to the real, nothing that was in any way connected with the illusory is taken up; as far as the real is concerned, every accretion is illusory." He concludes, "Advaita has no concept of social progress and has no ideal of humanitarian service." By "Advaita" Dr. Namboodiry means the classical scholastic Advaita, not the original Advaita of the Upaniṣads.
52. *kriyā ca kartṛtārūpāt svātantryānna purnarmalāt.* T.A. 9.99.
53. *parānugrahakāritvam atrasthasya sphuṭaṁ sthitam.* T.A. 3.290.
The *Gītā* also says that such persons are engaged in doing good to all (*sarvabhūtahite ratāḥ*). BH.G. 5.25
This is quite consistent with their knowledge of oneness with all (*sarvabhūtātmabhūtātmā*). BH.G. 5.7.
54. *sarvo mamāyaṁ vibhava ityevaṁ parijānataḥ/*
viśvātmano vikalpānāṁ prasare' pi maheśatā// I.P.K. 4.1.12.

55. *raso vai saḥ rasaṁ hyevāyaṁ labdhvānandībhavati.* TAITTIRĪYA UPANIṢAD 2.7.1.
56. *santoṅ sahaja samādhi bhalī.* KABIR.
57. Professor Rajendra Prasad has presented a brilliant critique of the theory of *puruṣārtha* in his two papers entitled (a) "The Concept of Mokṣa" (Philosophy of Phenomenological Research, Vol. XXXI, No. 3, March 1971), and (b) "The Theory of Puruṣārthas: Revaluation and Reconstruction" (*Journal of Indian Philosophy* 9, 1981; D. Reidel Publishing Co., Dordrecht, Holland, and Boston, U.S.A.). In "The Theory of Puruṣārtha: Revaluation and Reconstruction," Professor Prasad has pointed out that *mokṣa* is a redundant value and the theory of *trivarga* is a better social-functional theory. I feel an obligation to answer Professor Prasad and show that *mokṣa* is a necessary value.
58. *sa sarvānśca lokānāpnoti sarvānśca kāmān yastamātmānamanuvidya vijānāti.* CHĀNDOGYA UPANIṢAD 3.7.1.
59. *yadyad vibhūtimatsattvaṁ śrīmadūrjitameva vā/*
    tattadevāva gaccha tvaṁ mama tejoṁsasambhavam// BH.G. 10.41.
60. *tasya bhāsā sarvamidaṁ vibhāti.* MUṆḌAKA UPANIṢAD 2.2.10.
61. *prajātiramṛtamānanda ityupasthe.* TAITTIRĪYA UPANIṢAD 10.2-3.
62. *prajanaścāsmi kandarpaḥ.* BH.G. 10.28.
63. *dharmāviruddho bhūteṣu kāmosmi bharatarṣabha.* BH.G. 7.11.
64. *puṁsaḥ kāmamutāpare.* ŚRĪMADBHĀGAVATA 4.11.22.
    Following the same line, Paṇḍitarāja Jagannātha, in his *Rasagaṅgādhara*, contends that aesthetic enjoyment (*rasa*) is nothing but the Self or Consciousness uncovered (*bhinnāvaraṇā cideva rasaḥ*). His point is that *rasa*, or aesthetic joy, is the very nature of the Self; it is only obstructed, and the experiencing of an aesthetic object or situation — say, drama, poetry, music, etc. — removes the obstruction from consciousness, and the joy or (ānanda) of the Self comes to the fore.
65. "O Lady! we receive but what we give,
    And in our life alone does Nature live; . . .
    Ah, from the soul itself must issue forth
    A light, a glory, a fair luminous cloud
    Enveloping the Earth." Samuel Taylor Coleridge, "Dejection: An Ode."
66. *sarvabhūtātmabhūtātmā.* BH.G. 5.7.
67. *sarvabhūtahite rataḥ.* BH.G. 5.25.
68. T.A. 1.30.
69. *yo vai bhūmā tatsukhaṁ, nālpe sukhamasti.* CHĀNDOGYA UPANIṢAD 7.23.1.
70. ŚĀRĪRAKA-BHĀṢYA 1.1.4.

71. ĪṢVARAPRATYABHIJÑĀ-KĀRIKĀ 1.1.2.
72. This question is discussed in detail in Chapter 2.
73. *samvidrūpe na bhedo-sti vāstavo yadyapi dhruve/ tathāpyāvṛtinirhrāsatāratamyāt sa lakṣyate//* T.A. 1.138.
74. *bandhaprakṣayo nāma mokṣah.* T.A.V. (introduction) 4.31, p. 35.
75. This reminds me of part of a poem that runs:
    The heights that great men reached and kept
    Were not of a sudden flight.
    But they while their companions slept
    Were toiling upward in the night.
76. *jñānamālāyāḥ antaḥsūtra-kalpaḥ svasamvedanātmā pramātā jīvitabhūtaḥ.* P.T.V. 2.2.3., p. 39.
77. *mātāramadharīkurvan svāṁ vibhūtiṁ pradarśayan/ āste hṛdayanairmalyātiśaye tāratamyatā//* T.A. 1.175.
78. *tadāsau sakalaḥ prokto niṣkalaḥ śivayogataḥ.* T.A. 3.218.
79. *layākale tu saṁskāramātrāt satyapyasau bhidā.* T.A. 10.129.
80. *etatkārmamalaṁ proktaṁ yena sākaṁ layākalāḥ/ syurguhāgahanāntasthāḥ suptā iva sariṣṛpāḥ//* T.A. 9.138.
81. *tadānīṁ pralayākalādyavasthāyāṁ yogyatayaiva vedyatā bhāvadharmaḥ* .... T.A.V. 10.143, p. 101.
82. *tataḥ prabuddhasaṁskārāste yathocitabhāginaḥ/ brahmādisthāvarānte' smin saṁsaranti punaḥ punaḥ//* T.A. 9.139.
83. *kevalaṁ pārimityena śivābhedamasaṁspṛśan/ vijñānakevalī proktaḥ śuddhacinmātrasaṁsthitaḥ//* T.A. 9.91-92.
84. *māyordhve śuddhavidyādhaḥ santi vijñānakevalāḥ.* T.A. V. 9.91, quoted p. 78.
85. *malaḥ karotu tenāyaṁ dhvaṁsamānatvamaśnute.* T.A. 9.118.
86. ... *śivābhedamasaṁspṛśan.* Ibid. 9.91.
87. (a) *vijñ ānakevalī proktaḥ śuddhacinmātrasaṁsthitaḥ.* T.A. 9.91-92.
    (b) *vijñānakevalī vijñānaṁ bodhātmakaṁ rūpaṁ kevalaṁ svātantryarahi tam asya iti.* T.A.V. 9.91-92, p. 78.
88. *tathāhi svasvatantratvaparipūrṇatayā vibhuḥ/ nihsaṁkhyairbahubhī rūpairbhātyavacchedavarjanāt//* T.A. 9.53-54.
89. *bhogecchorupakārārtham ādyo mantramaheśvaraḥ/ māyāṁ vikṣobhya saṁsāraṁ nirmimīte vicitrakam//* IBID. 9.148-49.
90. *ekaikatrāpi tattve' smin sarvasaktisunirbhare/ tattatprādhānyayogena sa sa bhedo nirūpyate//* T.A. 9.51-52.
91. *sa punaḥ śāmbhavecchātaḥ śivābhedaṁ parāmṛśan/ kramānmantreśa-tannetri-rūpo yāti śivātmatām//* T.A. 9.92-93.

CHAPTER 9

1. In the case of a patient suffering from some physical ailment, medicine can be forced into the patient's body even against his or her will and it will cure the patient. But in the case of the spiritual aspirant, *sādhanā*, which is the medicine, cannot be forced on him or her. Doing *sādhanā* is entirely up to the aspirant.
2. *viśuddhasvaprakāśātmaśivarūpatayā vinā/*
   na kiñcid yujyate tena heturatra maheśvaraḥ// T. A. 13.113.
3. T.A. 13.50-52.
4. *tasmānna manmahe ko' yam śaktipātavidheḥ kramaḥ.* T. A. 13.101.
5. *kulajātivapuṣkarmavayonuṣṭhānasampadaḥ/*
   anapekṣya śive bhaktiḥ śaktipāto' phalārthinām// T. A. 13.117-8.
6. *nānirmalacitaḥ puṁso' nugrahastvanupāyakaḥ.* T. A. 2.47.
7. *... yathecchasi tathā kuru.* BH.G. 18.63.
8. *pūja-pūjaka-pūjya-bhedasaraṇiḥ keyaṁ kathānuttare/*
   saṁkrāmaḥ kila kasya kena vidadhe ko vā praveśakramaḥ//
   māyeyaṁ na cidadvayātparatayā bhinnāpyaho vartate/
   sarvaṁ svānubhavasvabhāvavimalaṁ cintāṁ vṛthā mā krithāḥ//
   ANUTTARĀṢṬIKĀ 3.
9. *saṁkrāmotra na bhāvanā na ca kathā yuktirna carcā na ca/*
   dhyānaṁ vā na ca dhāraṇā na ca japābhyāsaprayāso na ca//
   tatkiṁ nāma suniścitaṁ vada paraṁ satyaṁ ca tacchrūyatām/
   na tyāgī na parigrahī bhaja sukhaṁ sarvaṁ yathāvasthitaḥ//
   ANUTTARĀṢṬIKĀ 1. See also T. A.V. 2.24-26, 2.37.
10. *na svarūpalābho nityatvāt.* T.S. 2, p. 8.
11. *na jñaptiḥ svayamprakāśamānatvāt.* IBID.
12. *na āvaraṇavigamaḥ āvaraṇasya kasyacidapi asambhavāt.* IBID.
13. *na tadanupraveśaḥ anupravaṣṭuḥ vyatiriktasya abhāvāt.* IBID.
14. *upāyajālairna śivaḥ prakāśate ghaṭena kiṁ bhāti sahasradīdhitiḥ/*
    vivecayannitthamudāradarśanaḥ svayamprakāśaṁ śivamāviśetkṣaṇāt//
    T. S. 2, p. 9
15. *tatra ye nirmalātmāno....* T. A. 2.7
16. *... ityanupāyatvam .... alpopāyatvamityarthaḥ.* T.A.V. 2.2, p. 30.
17. *sakṛjjñāte suvarṇe kiṁ bhāvanā karaṇaṁvrajet/*
    ekavāraṁ pramāṇena śāstrādvā guruvākyataḥ//
    jñāte śivatve sarvasthe pratipattyā dṛdhātmanā/
    karaṇena nāsti kṛtyaṁ kvāpi bhāvanayāpi vā//
    Ś.D. 7.5-6, also quoted in T. A. 2.48.
18. *sākṣādupāyena iti śāmbhavena ... sa eva parāṁ*
    kāṣṭhāṁ prāptaścānupāya ityucyate. T. A.V. 1.142

19. *ata eva anupāyaḥ iti nopāyaniṣedhamātram*... IBID.
20. *tenāvikalpā samvittirbhāvanādyanāpeksinī/ śivatādātmyamāpannā, samāveśo' tra śāmbhavaḥ//* T. A. 1.178
21. *samvidātmani viśvoyaṁ bhāvavargaḥ prapañcavān/ pratibimbatayā bhāti yasya viśveśvaro hi saḥ//* T. A. 3.268
22. Philosophy, or metaphysics, is taken by Abhinavagupta and by the entire Tantric tradition, as a way of life (*sādhanā*) meant to bring one to the realization of one's real nature. To the Western mind this may appear as a confusion of philosophy with religion. But the Indian philosopher considers it a plus, for he or she would ask, what is the use of philosophy if it is not meant for life?
23. *ityevaṁ sakalaparāmarśaviśrāntimātrarūpaṁ pratibimbitasamasta-tattv-abhūtabhuvanabhedam ātmānaṁ paśyato nirvikalpatayā śāmbhavena samāveśena jīvanmuktatā.* T. S. 3, p. 19.
24. *matta evoditamidam mayyeva pratibimbitam/ madabhinnamidaṁ ceti tridhopāyaḥ sa śāmbhavaḥ//* T. A. 3.280.
25. (a) *tenāvikalpā samvittirbhāvanādyanapekṣiṇī*... T. A. 1.178
    (b) *avikalpapathārūḍho*... IBID. 1.211
    (c) *nirvikalpe parāmarśe śāmbhavopāyanāmani.* IBID. 3.274.
26. *tatrādye svaparāmarśe nirvikalpaikadhāmani/ yatsphuret prakaṭam sākṣāt tadicchākhyaṁ prakīrtitam//* T. A. 1.141.
27. *bhūyobhūyo vikalpāṁśaniścayakramacarcanat/ yatparāmarśamabhyeti jñānopayaṁ tu tadviduḥ//* T. A. 1.148
28. *uccārarahitaṁ vastu cetasaiva vicintayan/ yaṁ samāveśamāpnoti śāktaḥ sotrābhidhīyate//* IBID. 1.169. This is a verse from the MĀLINĪVIJAYA TANTRA quoted by Abhinavagupta.
29. *abhimānena saṅkalpādhyavasāyakrameṇa yaḥ/ śāktaḥ sa māyopāyo' pi tadante nirvikalpakaḥ//* T. A. 1.215
30. *tadante nirvikalpakaḥ.* IBID.
31. ...*jñānopāyaṁ tu tadviduḥ.* T. A. 1.148.
32. *evaṁ vaikalpikī bhūmiḥ śākte kartṛtvavedane.* T.A. 1.217
33. *abhimānena saṅkalpādhyavasāyakrameṇa yaḥ.* IBID. 1.215.
34. *yo niścayaḥ paśujanasya jaḍo' smi karmasaṁpāśito' smi malino' smi parerito' smi/ ityetadanyadṛḍhaniścayalābhasiddhyā sadyaḥ patirbhavati viśvava-puścidātmā//* T. S. 4, p. 32.
35. *aṇurnāma sphuṭo bhedastadupāya ihāṇavaḥ.* T. A. 1.221
36. *uccārakaraṇadhyāna varṇasthānaprakalpanaiḥ/ yo bhavet sa samāveśaḥ samyagāṇava ucyate//*T. A. 1.70. This is a verse of the MĀLINĪVIJAYA TANTRA, quoted by Abhinavagupta.

37. *śāktopāyo naropāyaḥ kālopāyo' tha saptamaḥ.* T.A. 1.279.
38. *kriyopāyaṁ tadāmnātam . . .* IBID. 1.149
39. Here the word *kriyā* is used in the sense of external activity as in the triad of *icchā-jñāna-kriyā*, not in the sense of the ultimate *śakti* or *vimarśa.*
40. *yattu tatkalpanāklṛpta-bahirbhūtārthasādhanam/ kriyopāyaṁ tadāmnātam bhedo nātrāpavargagaḥ//* T.A. 1.149.
41. *kriyopāye' bhyupāyānāṁ grāhya-bāhya-vibhedināṁ/ bhedopabhedavaividhyānniḥsaṁkhyatvamavāntarāt//* IBID. 1.164.
42. *vīryaṁ vinā yathā ṣaṇṭhastasyāpyastyatha vā balam/ mṛtadeha iveyaṁ syād bāhyāntaḥ parikalpanā//* T. A. 5.158
43. *caitanyarahitāḥ mantrāḥ proktā varṇāstu kevalam/ phalaṁ naiva prayacchanti lakṣakoṭijapādapi//* KULĀRṆAVA TANTRA 15.61
44. *yajedādhyātmikaṁ liṅgaṁ yatra līnaṁ carācaram/ bahirliṅgasya liṅgatvamanenādhiṣṭhitaṁ yataḥ//* MĀLINĪVIJAYA TANTRA 18.42, quoted in T. A.V. 5.120.
45. *tasya śāmbhavasya upāyaḥ śāktaḥ . . . tasyāpi upāya āṇavaḥ.* T. A.V. 1.142
46. *sākṣādupāyena iti śāmbhavena . . . sa eva parāṁ kāṣṭhāṁ prāptaścānupāya ityucyate* Ibid.
47. *abhedopāyamatroktaṁ śāmbhavaṁ śāktamucyate bhedābhedāt makopāyaṁ bhedopāyaṁ tadāṇavam.* T. A. 1.230.
48. *āṇavaḥ citta viśrāntirūpaḥ.* T. S. 3, p. 17.
49. *śāktaḥ cittasambodhalakṣaṇaḥ.* IBID.
50. *śāmbhavah cittapralayarūpaḥ.* IBID.
51. *andhantamaḥ praviśanti ye' avidyāmupāsate tato bhūya iva te tamo ya u vidyāyāṁ ratāḥ.* ĪŚA UPANIṢAD verse 9
52. *vidyāṁ cāvidyāṁ ca yastadvedobhayaṁ saha/ avidyayā mṛtyuṁ tīrtvā vidyayāmṛtamaśnute//* IBID. verse 11.
53. BṚHADĀRAṆYAKA UPANIṢAD 2.3.6., 3.9.26
54. IBID. 4.4.19
55. CHĀNDOGYA UPANIṢAD 3.14.1.
56. *na tyāgi na parigrahī bhaja sukhaṁ sarvaṁ yathāvasthitaḥ.* ANUTTARĀṢṬIKĀ 1.
57. *mā kiñcittyaja mā gṛhāna vilasa svastho yathāvasthitaḥ.* IBID. 2.
58. *tasya bhāsā sarvamidaṁ vibhāti.* MUṆḌAKA UPANIṢAD 2.2.10
59. *yadyadvibhūtimatsattvaṁ śrīmadūrjitamevavā tattadevāva/ gacchatvaṁ mama tejoṁśasambhavam//* BH.G. 10.41.
60. *yoginaḥ karma kurvanti saṅgaṁ tyakvātmaśuddhaye.* BH.G. 5.11.
61. *evaṁ pravartitaṁ cakraṁ nānuvartayatīha yaḥ/ aghāyurindriyārāmo moghaṁ pārtha sa jīvati//* BH.G. 3.16.
62. *karmaṇyabhipṛavṛtto' pi naiva kiñcit karoti saḥ.* BH.G. 4.20

63. *bahiḥ kṛtrima-saṁrambho hṛdi saṁrambha-varjitaḥ/*
kartā bahirakartāntarloke vihara rāghava//
YOGAVĀŚIṢṬHA (*upaśama prakaraṇa*) 18.22
64. *bahistaptontarāśītaḥ loke vihara rāghava.* IBID.

CHAPTER 10

1. The poet Tulasīdāsa lists the Kaula as the first of the fourteen most wretched persons, no better than the dead:
kaula kāmabasa kṛpina vimūḍhā. . . .
RĀMACARITAMĀNASA, LAṄKĀKĀṆḌA 31.1.
2. *atha samucitādhikāriṇa uddiśya rahasya ucyate' tra vidhiḥ.* T.A. 29.1.
3. *kulaṁ ca parameśasya śaktiḥ sāmarthyamūrdhvatā/*
svātantryamojo vīryaṁ ca piṇḍaḥ samviccharīrakam. IBID. 29.4.
4. *bahiḥ śaktau yāmala ca dehe prāṇapathe matau*
iti ṣoḍhā kulejyā syāt pratibhedaṁ vibhedinī// T.A. 29.7.
5. *bījaṁ sā pīdeyate rasaśalkavibhāgato' tra kuṇḍalinī/*
adhyuṣṭapīthanetrī kandasthā visvato bhramati// T.A. 29.68.
6. The word for parched grain — *mudrā* — has many meanings in everyday speech, such as "seal," "metallic currency," "physical posture," and so on. However, in the context of the five M's it means parched grain — particularly parched gram — that is taken along with wine, and so forth.
7. *anāghreyam anālokyam aspṛśyañcāpyapeyakam/*
madyaṁ māṁsaṁ paśūnāntu kaulikānāṁ mahāphalam//
KULĀRṆAVA TANTRA 2.124.
8. *atra yāge ca yaddravyaṁ niṣiddhaṁ śāstrasantatau/*
tadeva yojayeddhīmān vāmāmṛtapariplutam T.A. 29.10
9. *Śivāmbu*, or the "holy water" (urine), has medicinal value also. In Āyurveda, the ancient Indian system of medicine, urine is characterized as a neutralizer of poison (*viṣahara*). Many people in India regularly take *Śivāmbu* in order to cure various bodily ailments.
10. There is a famous story that Lord Śiva appeared in the form of a *cāṇḍāla* (untouchable) before Śaṅkarācārya in Kāśī (Varanasi) in order to teach the erring non-dualist the lesson of equality. The story goes that Śaṅkarācārya wanted the *cāṇḍāla* to keep away, lest the *cāṇḍāla*' s touch make him impure. But the *cāṇḍāla* conversed in a cryptic language, and the repentant Śaṅkarācārya, recognizing him as Lord Śiva, fell on his feet. Many saints are reported to have used the Tantric methods in order to correct some of their rigid disciples.

11. *madyaṁ māṁsañca matsyañca mudrā maithunameva ca/ makārapañcakaṁ devi devatāprītikārakam//* KULĀRṆAVA TANTRA 10.5.
12. *mādi pañcakamīśāni devatā-prītaye sudhīh/ yathāvidhi niṣeveta tṛṣṇayā cet sa pātakī//* IBID. 10.6.
13. *śakti-sambhoga mātreṇa yadi mokṣo bhaveta vai/ sarvepi jantavo loke muktāḥ syuḥ strīniṣevanāt//* IBID. 2.119.
14. (a) *ahaṁ punarjānāmi na bhavato na kāmadevasya mamaivaikasya brāhmaṇasyāyaṁ madanamahotsavo yasya priyavayasyenaivaṁ mantryate.* ŚRĪHARṢAḤ, "Ratnāvalī," Motilal Banarsidass, p. 22.
    (b) *kāñcanamāle, pratiṣṭhāpayāśokamule bhagavantaṁ pradyumnam.* IBID., p. 40.
    (c) *kusumasukumāramūrtidadhatī niyamena tadanuttaraṁ madhyam/ ābhāti makaraketoḥ pārśvasthā cāpayaṣṭiriva//* IBID.
    (d) *vasantotsavopāyanalolupenāryagautamena kathitaṁ tvaratāṁ bhaṭṭinīti.* KĀLIDĀSAḤ, "Mālavikāgnimitram," Kālidāsa Granthāvalī, B. H. U., pp. 289-90.
15. Depth-psychologists, while studying snake dreams and snake phobia, have found that the snake symbol is somehow unconsciously related to sex. The attitude towards the snake is thus suggestive of the attitude towards sex.
16. *karmeti hastayoḥ gatiriti pādayoḥ.* TAITTIRĪYA UPANIṢAD 10.2-3.
17. *prajātiramṛtamānanda ityupasthe.* IBID.
18. *prajanaścāsmi kandarpaḥ.* BH.G. 10.28.
19. *dharmāviruddho bhūteṣu kāmo' smi bharatarṣabha.* IBID. 7.11.
20. *puṁsaḥ kāmamutāpare.* ŚRĪMADBHĀGAVATA 4.11.22.
21. *yoṣā vāgnirgautama, tasyā upastha eva samit, lomāni dhūmo, yonirarciḥ, yadantaḥ karoti te' ṅgārā, abhinandā visphuliṅgāḥ; tasminnetasminnagnau devā reto juhvati, tasyā āhutyai puruṣaḥ sambhavati.* BṚHADĀRAṆYAKA UPANIṢAD 6.2.13.
22. CHĀNDOGYA UPANIṢAD 5.8.1-2.
23. *yathā rakṣati caurebhyo dhanadhānyādikaṁ priye/ kuladharmaṁ tatha devi paśubhyaḥ pariraksayet//* KULĀRṆAVA TANTRA 11.82.
24. *kṛpāṇadhārāgamanāt vyāghrakaṇṭhāva lambanāt/ bhujaṅgadhāraṇānnūnamaśakyaṁ kulavartanam//* IBID. 2.122.
25. See the Kulārṇava Tantra, Chapter III, verses 113 to 123.
26. *tameva bhāntamanubhati sarvam tasya bhāsā sarvamidaṁ vibhāti* MUṆḌAKA UPANIṢAD 2.2.10; KAṬHA UPANIṢAD 2.2.15; SVETĀŚVATARA UPANIṢAD 6.6.14.
27. O lady! We receive but what we give,
    And in our life alone does Nature live . . . .
    . . . Ah; from the soul itself must issue forth

A light, a glory, a fair luminous cloud
Enveloping the Earth . . . .
SAMUEL TAYLOR COLERIDGE, "Dejection: an Ode"

28. *lokānandaḥ samādhisukham.* Ś.S. 1.18.

CHAPTER 11

1. *yatovā imāni bhūtāni jāyante.* TAITTIRĪYA UPANIṢAD 3.1.
2. *tadaikṣata bahusyāṁ prajāyeyeti.* CHĀNDOGYA UPANIṢAD 6.2.3.
3. *ānandāddhyeva khalvimāni bhūtāni jāyante.* TAITTIRĪYA UPANIṢAD 3.6.
4. (a) BṚHADĀRAṆYAKA UPANIṢAD 6.2.13.
   (b) IBID. 6.4.2-22.
   (c) CHĀNDOGYA UPANIṢAD 5.8.1-2.
   (d) TAITTIRĪYA UPANIṢAD 10.2-3.
5. BH.G. 7.11, 10.28.
6. KULĀRṆAVA TANTRA 2.140-41.

Selected Bibliography

The following bibliography consists mainly of the non-dualistic Śaiva Tantric literature pertaining to Kashmir Śaivism. A few works of dualistic Śaiva and Śākta Tantrism, however, are also included. A complete bibliography of works on Tantrism, covering the Śākta, Buddhist, and Vaiṣṇava strands, would take volumes. Since our present work is concerned with Kashmir Śaivism and Abhinavagupta in particular, a select bibliography is given here.

ORIGINAL SOURCES

Aitareya-Upaniṣad (*Śāṅkara-bhāsya*). Gorakhpur: Gita Press, Samvat 2009.

Aghorītantra. Hindi translation and commentary by Pandit Gaurīśankara Śarmā. Bombay: Gaṅgāviṣṇu Śrīkṛṣṇadāsa, 1951.

Ajadapramātṛsiddhi of Utpaladeva, included in his *Siddhitrayi,* M.S. Kaul, ed. Kashmir Series of Texts and Studies, (K.S.T.S.), no. XXXIV, 1921.

Akulavīra-tantra. P.C. Bagchi, ed. In the *Kaulajñāna-nirṇaya,* pp. 84-106, Calcutta, 1934.

Amaraugha-śāsanam of Gorakṣanātha. M.R. Shastri, ed. K.S.T.S., no. XX, 1918.

Ānandalaharī. In *Wave of Bliss,* A. Avalon, ed. and trans. 4th ed. Madras: Ganesh & Co., 1953.

Anubhava-nivedana-stotra of Abhinavagupta. In *Abhinavagupta: An Historical and Philosophical Study*, by K.C. Pandey, 2nd ed. Varanasi: Chowkhamba Sanskrit Series, 1963.

Anuttara-prakāśa-pañcāśikā of Ādyanātha. M.R. Shastri, ed. K.S.T.S., no. XIII, 1918.

Anuttarāṣṭikā of Abhinavagupta. K.S.T.S., no. XIII, 1918.

Ātmavilāsa of Amṛtavāgbhavācārya with his own commentary *Sundarī*. B.N. Pandit, ed. Shri Peeth Shodha Sansthana, Samvat 2039 (1981).

Bhagavadgītā with the *Sarvatobhadra* of Rāmakaṇṭhā. M.R. Shastri, ed. K.S.T.S., no. LXIV, 1943.

Bhagavadgītārtha-saṅgraha, a commentary by Abhinavagupta on the Bh.G. Laksman Raina, ed. Srinagar, 1933.

Bhairavānukaraṇa-stotra of Kṣemarāja. Raniero Gnoli, ed. *East & West*, New Series, 1958.

Bhairava-stotra of Abhinavagupta. In *Abhinavagupta: An Historical and Philosophical Study*, by K.C. Pandey. Varanasi: Chowkhamba Sanskrit Series, 1963.

Bhāskari. 3 vols. Sarasvati Bhavana Texts, nos. 70 (1938), 83 (1950), and 84 (1954). The first two volumes consist of the commentary of Bhāskarakaṇṭha on the I.P.V. of Abhinavagupta. The third volume is an English translation of the I.P.V., together with K.C. Pandey's "Outline of the History of Śaiva Philosophy."

Bhāvopahāra of Cakrapāṇi, with *vivaraṇa* by Ramyadeva Bhaṭṭa. M.R. Shastri, ed. K.S.T.S., no. XIV, 1918.

Bodhapañcadaśikā of Abhinavagupta with *vivaraṇa* by Hara Bhatta Shastri. J.D. Zadoo, ed. K.S.T.S., no, LXXVI, 1947.

Brahma-sūtra (*Śāñkara-Bhāsya*), with *Bhāmatī*, *Kalpataru*, and *Parimala*. A.K. Sastri, ed. 2d ed. re-edited by Bhargava Sastri. Nirnaya Sagar Press, 1938.

Bṛhadāraṇyakopaniṣad (*Śāñkara-bhāsya*). 3d ed. Gorakhpur: Gita Press, Samvat 2013.

Chāndogya-Upaniṣad, (*Śāñkarabhāsya*), 3d ed. Gorakhpur: Gita Press, Samvat 2013.

Cid-gagana-Candrikā. Trivikrama Tirtha, ed. Calcutta: Tantrik Texts, XX, 1936.

Dakṣināmūrti stotram of Śaṁkarācārya. Bombay: Nirnayasagar, 1902.

Dattātreya-Tantra. B.M. Pandey, ed. Varanasi, 1963.

Dehasthadevatācakrastotram of Abhinavagupta. In *Abhinavagupta: An Historical and Philosophical Study*, by K.C. Pandey, 2d ed. Varanasi: Chowkhamba Sanskrit Series, 1963.

Devī-bhāgavata. 2 vols. Mansukhrai Mor, ed. Calcutta: Gurumandal Series, no. XXI, vol. 1, 1960 and vol. II, 1961.

Devī-māhātmya. Vasudeva S. Agrawal, ed. and trans. Varanasi: Kashiraj Trust, 1963.

Devī-nāma-vilāsa by Sahib Kaul, ed. M.S. Kaul, ed. and trans. K.S.T.S., no. LXIII, 1942.

Devī-Upaniṣad. A. Mahadeva Sastri, ed. In *The Śākta Upaniṣads*. Madras: Adyar, 1950.

Dhvanyāloka of Ānandavardhana with *Locana* of Abhinavagupta. Mahādeva Śāstrī and Paṭṭābhirāma Śāstrī, eds. Varanasi: Chowkhamba Sanskrit Series, 1963.

Dhyānabindu-Upaniṣad. N.R. Ācārya, ed. In *Īśādiviṁśatyuttaraśatopaniṣadaḥ*. Bombay, 1948; translated by J. Varenne in *Upaniṣads du Yoga*. Paris, 1971.

Gauḍapāda-Kārikā. Ratna Gopal Bhatta, ed. Varanasi: Haridas Sanskrit Series, no. 1, 1910.

Gāyatrī-tantra. Tārakanātha Bhattācārya, ed. Kashi Sanskrit Series, no. 143, 1946.

Haṭhayogapradīpikā of Svātmārāma. Swami Digambarji, ed. Poona: Lonavla, 1970.

Īśādyaṣṭottaraśatopaniṣadaḥ. Vasudeva Laksmana Sastri, ed. Bombay: Nirnaya Sagar, 1932.

Īśāvāsyopaniṣad (*Śāñkara-bhāsya*). Gorakhpur: Gita Press, Samvat 2008.

Īśvara-pratyabhijñā-kārikā of Utpaladeva with *vṛitti.* M.S. Kaul, ed. K.S.T.S., no. XXXIV, 1921.

Īśvara-pratyabhijñā-vimarśinī, by Abhinavagupta. 2 vols. M.R. Shastri and M.S. Kaul, eds. K.S.T.S. nos., XXII (1918) and XXXIII (1921). A commentary on the I.P.K. of Utpaladeva.

Īśvara-pratyabhijñā-vivṛtivimarśini by Abhinavagupta. 3 vols. M.S. Kaul, ed. K.S.T.S. nos. LX (1938), LXII (1941), and LXV (1943). A detailed commentary on the *vivṛti* of the I.P.K. of Utpaladeva.

Īśvara-pratyabhijñā-vimarśinī. Hindi translation by Krishnanand Sagar. Shivoham Sagar Granthamala, 1979.

Īśvara-siddhi of Utpaladeva. In *Siddhitrayī.* M.S. Kaul, ed. K.S.T.S., no. XXXIV, 1921.

Janma-maraṇa-vicāra of Bhaṭṭa Vāmadeva. M.R. Shastri, ed. K.S.T.S., no. XIX, 1918. (With the *Amaraughaśāsanam* of Gorakṣanātha and the *Tantra-vaṭadhānikā* of Abhinavagupta.)

Jñānārnava-tantra. G.S. Gokhale, ed. Poona: 1952.

Kāma-Kalā-Vilāsa of Puṇyānandanātha with anonymous commentary. M.R. Shastri, ed. K.S.T.S., no. XII, 1918.

Kāma-Kalā-Vilāsa with commentary by Naṭanānandanātha. Arthur Avalon, ed. and trans. Madras: Ganesh & Co., 1961.

Karpurādistotra. Hymn to Kālī, Arthur Avalon, ed. and trans. Madras: Ganesh & Co., 1961.

Kaṭhopaniṣad (*Śāñkara-bhāsya*). Gorakhpur: Gita Press, Samvat 2008.

Kaulajñānanirṇaya. P.C. Bagchi, ed. Calcutta, 1934.

Kenopaniṣad (*Śāñkara-bhāsya*). Gorakhpur: Gita Press, Samvat 2008.

Khaṇḍanakhaṇḍakhādya of Śrī Harsa. Swami Yogindrananda, ed. and trans. (Hindi). Varanasi: Udāsina Sanskrit Vidyālaya, 1979.

Kramadīpikā of Keśava. D.P. Shukla, ed. Varanasi: Chowkhambha Sanskrit Series, 1917.

Krama-stotra of Abhinavagupta. In *Abhinavagupta: An Historical and Philosophical Study*, by K.C. Pandey. Varanasi: Chowkhamba Sanskrit Series, 1963.

Kulacūdāmani-tantra. G.C. Vedāntatīrtha, ed. Calcutta: Tantrik Texts, IV, 1915.

Kulacūdāmani-tantra. Arthur Avalon, ed. and trans. Madras: Ganesh & Co., 1956.

Kulārṇava-tantra. T. Vidyaratna, ed. Calcutta: Tantrik Texts, V, 1917.

Kumāra-tantra of Rāvana. J. Filliozat, ed. and trans. (French). Paris, 1937.

Lakṣmī-tantra. V. Krishnamacharya, ed. Adyar, 1959.

Lakṣmī-tantra. Sanjukta Gupta, trans. Leiden, 1972.

Lalitāsahasranāma with the commentary of Bhāskararāya. R.A. Sastry, trans. 3d ed. Madras, 1951.

Lalleśvarī-vākyāni. In *The Word of Lalla, the Prophetess*, Richard Temple, ed. Cambridge, 1924.

Lalleśvarī-vākyāni. In *The Wise Sayings of Lal Ded.* George A. Grierson and L.D. Barnett, eds. and trans. London: Asiatic Society Monograph, no. XVII, 1929.

Layayogasaṁhitā. Varansi: Mahāmaṇḍala Publishers, 1970.

Luptāgama-saṅgraha Pt. I. Gopinath Kaviraj, ed. Varanasi: Sanskrit University, Samvat 1892.

Mahānayaprakāśa of Śītikāṇṭha. M.R. Shastri, ed. K.S.T.S., no. XXI, 1918.

Mahānirvāṇa-tantra. In *The Great Liberation.* Arthur Avalon, ed. and trans. Madras: Ganesh & Co., 1953.

Mahārthamañjarī of Maheśvarānanda with his *Parimala.* M.R. Shastri, ed. K.S.T.S. no. XI, 1918.

Mahārthamañjarī. Ganapati Shastri, ed. Trivandrum Sanskrit Series, no. 66, 1919.

Mahārthamañjarī. Vrajavallabha Dviveda, ed. with introduction in Sanskrit. Varanasi: Yogatantra Granthamālā, vol. V, 1972.

Mahārthamañjarī. Lilian Silburn, trans. (French). Paris, 1968.

Mahimnastotra of Puṣpadanta with the commentary of Madhusūdana Sārasvatī. Varanasi: Chowkhamba Sanskrit Series, 1964.

Mahimnastotra of Puṣpadanta. Arthur Avalon, ed. 4th ed. Madras: Ganesh & Co., 1963.

Mahopadeśaviṁśatikam of Abhinavagupta. In K.C. Pandey's *Abhinavagupta: An Historical and Philosophical Study.* 2d ed. Varanasi: Chowkhamba Sanskrit Series, 1963.

Mālinīvijaya-vārtikam of Abhinavagupta. M.S. Kaul, ed. K.S.T.S., no. XXXI, 1921.

Mālinīvijayottara-tantra. M.S. Kaul, ed. K.S.T.S., no. XXXVII, 1922.

Māṇḍūkya-Upaniṣad (*Śāñkara-bhāṣya*), Gorakhpur: Gita Press.

Mātṛkābheda-tantra. C. Bhattacharya, ed. Calcutta, 1933.

Mātṛkābheda-tantra. Bhadraśīla Śarma, ed. Allahabad, Samvat 2017.

Mṛgendra-tantra with the commentary of Nārāyaṇakaṇṭha. M.S. Kaul, ed. K.S.T.S., no. L, 1930.

Muṇḍaka-Upaniṣad (*Śāñkara-bhāṣya*). Gorakhpur: Gita Press, Samvat 2009.

Nareśvaraparīkṣā of Sadyojyoti with *Prakāśa* by Rāmakaṇṭha. M.S. Kaul, ed. K.S.T.S., no. XLV, 1926.

Netra-tantra with the *Udyota* of Kṣemarāja. M.S. Kaul, ed. K.S.T.S., nos. XLVI (1926) and LXI (1936).

Nityāṣoḍaśikārṇava (A part of the *Vāmakeśvara-tantra*). With two commentaries: *Ṛjuvimarśinī* by Śivānanda and *Arthara-tnāvalī* by Vidyānanda. Vrajavallabha Dviveda, ed. Varanasi: Yogatantra Granthmālā, vol. I, 1968.

Nityāṣoḍaśikārṇava with *Setubandha* of Bhāskara Rāya. Poona: 1908.

Nityotsava by Umānandanātha. A.M. Sastri, ed. Baroda: Gaikhur Oriental Series 23, 1923, revised edition by Swami Trivikrama Tirtha, Baroda, 1948.

Pādukāpañcaka. T. Vidyāratna, ed. Tantrik Texts, II. Calcutta, 1913.

Pādukāpañcaka. Arthur Avalon, trans. In *The Serpent Power*, 8th ed. Madras: Ganesh & Co., 1972.

Paramārtha-carcā of Abhinavagupta with the *Vivarana* of Pandit Hara Bhatta Shastri. J.D. Zadoo, ed. K.S.T.S., no. LXXVII, 1947.

Paramārtha-carcā. In *Abhinavagupta: An Historical and Philosophical Study*, by K.C. Pandey, 2d ed. Varanasi: Chowkhamba Sanskrit Series, 1963.

Paramārtha-dvādaśikā of Abhinavagupta. In *Abhinavagupta: An Historical and Philosophical Study*, by K.C. Pandey, 2d ed. Varanasi: Chowkhamba Sanskrit Series, 1963.

Paramārthasāra of Abhinavagupta with *vivṛti* by Yogarāja. J.C. Chatterji, ed. K.S.T.S., no. VII, 1916.

Paramārthasāra of Abhinavagupta. L.D. Barnett, ed. and trans. Journal of The Royal Asiatic Society, London, 1910.

Paramārthasāra of Abhinavagupta. Prabha Devi, ed. and trans. Srinagar: Ishwar Ashram, 1977.

Paramārthasāra of Abhinavagupta. Lilian Silburn, ed. and trans. (French). Paris, 1957.

Paramārthasāra of Abhinavagupta. Kamala Dvivedi, trans. Delhi: Motilal Banarasidass, 1984.

Parā-prāveśikā of Kṣemarāja. M.R. Shastri, ed. K.S.T.S., no. XV, 1918.

Parā-prāveśikā. Purnanda Saraswati, trans. (Hindi). Varanasi: Dakshinamurti Math, 1986.

Paraśurāma-Kalpa-sūtra with the commentary of Rāmeśvara, 2d ed. S.Y. Sastri Dave, ed. Baroda: Gaikhur Oriental Society, no. XXII, 1950.

Parātriṁśikā with *vivarana* by Abhinavagupta. M.R. Shastri, ed. K.S.T.S., no. XVIII, 1918.

Parātriṁśikā. Published in an Italian magazine "RSO" in two parts—the first one in 1959 and the second one in 1965.

Parātrīśikā-Laghuvṛtti by Abhinavagupta. J.D. Zadoo, ed. K.S.T.S., nos. LXVIII & LXIX, 1947.

Parātrīśikā-Laghuvṛtti. R. Gnoli, trans. (Italian). *La trentino della Suprema.* Torino, 1965.

Parātrīśikā-tātparyadīpikā. J.D. Zadoo, ed. K.S.T.S., no. LXXIV, 1947.

Parātrīśikā-vivṛti of Lakṣmīrāma. J.D. Zadoo, ed. K.S.T.S., no. LXIX, 1947.

Paryantapañcāśikā of Abhinavagupta. V. Raghavan, ed. Madras, 1951.

Pātañjala-Yoga-Sūtra. In the *Ṣaḍdarśanam.* Banaras City: Chowkhamba Sanskrit Book Depot, 1912.

Prāṇatoṣiṇi, by Rāmatoṣaṇa Bhattacharya, J. Vidyasagar Bhattacharya, ed. Calcutta, 1898. A collection from the Tantras.

Prapañcasāra-tantra, ascribed to Śaṅkarācārya. T. Vidyaratna, ed. Calcutta: Tantrik Texts, III, 1914.

Praśnopaniṣad (*Śāñkara-bhāṣya*), Gorakhpur: Gita Press, Samvat 2009.

Pratyabhijñā-hṛdayam of Kṣemarāja. J.C. Chatterji, ed. K.S.T.S., no. III, 1911.

Pratyabhijñā-hṛdayam. Under the title *The Secret of Self-Recognition.* K.F. Leidecker, trans. Adyar: 1938.

Pratyabhijñā-hṛdayam. Under the title *The Secret of Self-realization.* J.K. Taimni, trans. Madras: Adyar, 1974.

Pratyabhijñā-hṛdayam. Jaideva Singh, ed. and trans. Delhi: Motilal Banarsidass, 1963.

Pratyabhijñā-hṛdayam. Jaideva Singh, trans. (Hindi). Delhi: Motilal Banarsidass, 1973.

Pratyabhijñā-hṛdayam. Pitāmbarapīṭhastha-Svāmī, trans. (Hindi). Datia (Madhya Pradesh).

Pratyabhijñā-hṛdayam. Vishal Prasad, ed. and trans. Delhi: Tripathi National Publishing House, 1969.

Pratyabhijñā-hṛdayam. S.A. Awasthi, comm. (Hindi). Varanasi: Chowkhamba, 1970.

Pratyabhijñā-hṛdayam. Kamala Devi Bawa, trans. and comm. (Hindi). Srinagar, 1973.

Pūrṇata-pratyabhijñā, by Ācarya Rāmeśvara Jhā. Kamalesh Jha, trans. (Hindi). Varanasi: Joshi Brothers, 1984.

Rahasyapañcadaśikā of Abhinavagupta. In *Abhinavagupta: An Historical and Philosophical Study*, by K.C. Pandey, 2d ed. Varanasi: Chowkhamba Sanskrit Series, 1963.

Rauravāgama. N.R. Bhatta, ed. 3 vols. Pondicherry, 1961-72.

Rudrayāmala-tantra (*Uttaratantra*). J. Vidyasagar, ed. Calcutta, 1937.

Śaiva Upaniṣads with the commentary of Upaniṣadbrahmayogin. A. Mahadeva Shastri, ed. Adyar Library, 1950.

Śaktisaṅgama-tantra. B. Bhattacharya, ed. 3 vols. Baroda: Gaikhur Oriental Series, nos. 61, 91, 104, 1932-47.

Śāktavijñānam of Somānanda. J.D. Zadoo, ed. K.S.T.S., no. 74, 1947.

Sambandha-siddhi of Utpaladeva. Included in *Siddhitrayī.* M.S. Kaul, ed. K.S.T.S., no. XXXIV, 1921.

Sāmbapañcāśikā. Swami Lakṣmaṇaji, ed. and comm. (Hindi). Srinagar: Ishwar Ashram, Samvat 2000.

Sāṁkhya-kārikā of Īśvarakṛṣṇa. Sitaram Sastri, ed. Varanasi, 1953.

Śāradātilaka of Lakṣmaṇa, with commentary *Padārthādarśa* of Rāghva Bhaṭṭa. M.J. Bakshi, ed. Varanasi: Kaśi Sanskrit Series 107, 1963.

Sarvadarśana-saṁgraha of Sāyaṇa-mādhava. V. Shastri Abhyankar, ed. Poona: Gaikhur Oriental Series, (class Z), no. 4, 1951.

Sarvadarśana-saṁgraha. V.S. Sharma, trans. (Hindi). Chowkhamba Sanskrit Series, 1964.

Sarvadarśana-saṁgraha. E.B. Cowell and A.E. Gough, trans. Chowkhamba Sanskrit Series, 1961.

Ṣaṭcakranirūpaṇa by Pūrṇānanda. T. Vidyaratna, ed. Calcutta: Tantrik Texts, II, 1913.

Ṣaṭcakranirūpaṇa. In *The Serpent Power*, 8th ed. Arthur Avalon, trans. Madras: Ganesh & Co., 1972.

Saṭtriṁśattattvasandoha with the *vivarana* of Rājānaka Ānanda. M.R. Shastri, ed. K.S.T.S., no. XIII, 1918.

Saundaryalaharī of Śaṅkarācārya. R. Anantakrishna Sastri and K. Rāmamūrthy Garu, ed. and trans. Madras, 1957.

Saundaryalaharī. W.N. Brown, trans. Harvard Oriental Series, 43.

Saundaryalaharī. V.K. Subramanian, trans. Motilal Banarsidass, 1977.

Siddha-siddhānta-paddhati of Gorakṣanātha. Kalyani Mallik, ed. Poona Oriental Book-house, 1954.

Siddhitrayī of Utpaladeva. M.S. Kaul, ed. K.S.T.S., no. XXXIV, 1921.

Śivadṛṣṭi of Somānanda with the *vṛtti* of Utpaladeva. M.S. Kaul, ed. K.S.T.S., no. LIV, 1934.

Śivadṛṣṭi. R. Gnoli, trans. and comm., 1st Chapter of *Śivadṛṣṭi*. In *East & West*, New Series, VIII, 1957.

Śivadṛṣṭi. An Italian translation of the 2nd chapter of the *Śivadṛṣṭi* was published in the Italian magazine "RSO," 1959.

Śivadṛṣṭi. Radheshyam Chaturvedi trans. (Hindi). Varanasi: Varanaseya Sanskrit Sansthan, 1986.

Śivaśaktyavinābhāva-stotra of Abhinavagupta, in the *Bhagavadgītārtha-saṅgraha*. LakṣmaṇaRaina, ed. Srinagar, 1933.

Śivastotrāvalī of Utpaladeva, with the *vivṛti* of Kṣemarāja. Rājānaka Lakṣmaṇa, ed. and trans. (Hindi). Varanasi: Chowkhamba, 1964.

Śivastotrāvalī. Krishnanand Sagar, trans. (Hindi). Shivoham Sagar Granthamala, 1985.

Śiva-sūtra of Vasugupta with the *vṛtti* of Bhāskara. In the *Śiva-sūtra-vārtika* of Bhāskara. J.C. Chatterji, ed. K.S.T.S., no. IV, 1916.

Śiva-sūtra with the *vārtika* of Bhāskara. J.C. Chatterji, ed. K.S.T.S., no IV, 1916.

Śiva-sūtra with the *vārtika* of Varadarāja. M.S. Kaul, ed. K.S.T.S., no. XLIII, 1925.

Śiva-sūtra with the *Vimarśinī* of Kṣemarāja. J.C. Chatterji, ed. K.S.T.S., no. I, 1911.

Śiva-sūtra P.T. Srinivasa, trans. Allahabad: Iyengar, 1912.

Śiva-sūtra with commentary *Ṛjvatthabodhinī* of Pītāmbarapīṭhastha Svāmī Datia (Madhya Pradesh). Samvat, 2017.

Śiva-sūtra. Under the title *The Ultimate Reality and Realization.* J.K. Taimni, trans. Madras, Adyar: 1976.

Śiva-sūtra. As *Siva-sutra: the Yoga of Supreme Identity.* Jaideva Singh, trans. Delhi: Motilal Banarsidass, 1979.

Śiva-sūtra. R. Gnoli and P. Boringhieri, trans. (Italian). In *Testi dello Sivaismo,* Torino, 1962.

Śiva-sūtra with four commentaries. Krishnanand Sagar, ed. and comm. Shivoham Granthamala, 1984.

Spanda-Kārikā. Vṛtti of Kallaṭa. J.C. Chatterji, ed. K.S.T.S., nos. IV & V, 1916.

Spanda-Kārikā. Vivṛti of Rāmakaṇṭha. J.C. Chatterji, ed. K.S.T.S., no. VI, 1913.

Spanda-Kārikā. Nirṇaya of Kṣemarāja. M.S. Kaul, ed. and trans. K.S.T.S., no XLII, 1925.

Spanda-Kārikā. Sandoha of Kṣemarāja. M.R. Shastri, ed. K.S.T.S., no. XVI, 1917. A commentary on the first verse of the *Spanda-kārikā.*

Spanda-Kārikā. Pradīpikā of Utpala Vaiṣṇava. Gopinath Kaviraj, ed. Varanasi: Yogatantra-Granthamala no. 3, 1970.

Spanda-Kārikā with the *Nirṇaya.* Under the title *Spanda-Kārikā: The Divine Creative Pulsation.* Jaideva Singh, trans. Delhi: Motilal Banarsidass, 1980.

Spanda-Kārikā with *vṛtti.* 2d ed. Neel Kantha Gurtu, trans. and comm. Motilal Banarsidass, 1984.

Spanda-Kārikā with four Sanskrit commentaries. Krishnananda Sagar, ed. Shivoham Granthamala, 1984.

Stavacintāmaṇi of Bhaṭṭa Nārāyaṇa with *vivṛti* of Kṣemarāja. M.R. Shastri, ed. K.S.T.S., no. X, 1918.

Stutikusumāñjali by Jagaddhara Bhaṭṭa. 2d ed. Kashi: Achyuta Granthamala, 1954.

Svacchanda-tantra with the *Udyota* of Kśemarāja. 6 vols. M.S. Kaul, ed. K.S.T.S., nos. XXXI, XXXVIII, XLIV, XLVIII, LI LIII, LVI, 1921-1935.

Svetāśvatara-Upaniṣad (*Śāñkara-bhāṣya*). Gorakhpur: Gita Press, Samvat 2009.

Taittirīya-Upaniṣad (*Śāñkara-bhāṣya*) Gorakhpur: Gita Press.

Tantrāloka of Abhinavagupta with the *Viveka* of Rājānaka Jayaratha. 12 vols. Vol. I edited by M.R. Shastri and vols. II-XII edited by M.S. Kaul. K.S.T.S., nos. XXIII (1918), XXVIII (1921), XXX (1921), XXVI (1922), XXXV (1922), XXIX (1921), XLI (1924), XLVII (1926), LIX (1938), LII (1933), LVII (1936), LVIII (1938).

Tantrāloka. 8 vols. Introduction by Navajivan Rastogi and R.C. Dvivedi. Motilal Banarsidass, 1987.

Tantrāloka. Chapters 1 to 14 with the *Viveka*, 2 vols. Krishnanand Sagar, Shivoham Granthamala, 1984. Chapters 15 to 37 are yet to come.

Tantrāloka. Ranīero Gnoli, trans. (Italian). Under the title *Luce Delle Sacre Scritture (Tantraloka) di Abhinavagupta.* Torino: Unione Tipographico Editrice Torinese, 1972.

Tantrasāra of Abhinavagupta. M.R. Shastri, ed. K.S.T.S., no. XVII, 1918.

Tantrasāra. Under the title *Essenza dei Tantra.* R. Gnoli and P. Boringhieri, trans. (Italian). Torino, 1960.

Tantrasāra of Kṛṣṇānanda. Rasikmohan Chatterji, ed. Basumati Press, Calcutta, 1929. Varanasi: Chowkhamba Sanskrit Series, no. 88. A text of the Śakti Tantrism of Bengal; not to be confused with the *Tantrasāra* of Abhinavagupta.

Tantra-Vaṭa-dhānikā of Abhinavagupta. M.R. Shastri, ed. K.S.T.S., no. XXIV, 1918.

Tantrarājatantra. Part I, Lakṣmaṇa Sastri, ed. Part II, Sadashiva Mishra, ed. Tantrik Texts, VIII and XII. London, 1918, and Calcutta/London, 1926.

Tantrasamuccaya of Nārāyaṇa. 2 vols. V.A.R. Sastri and K.S.M. Sastri, eds. Trivandrum Sanskrit Series, vols. 151 & 169.

Tantra-sāra-saṁgraha of Nārāyaṇa. Duraiswami Ayangar, ed. Madras, 1950.

Tantra-saṁgraha. Part I & II. Gopinatha Kaviraj, ed. Varanasi: Yoga-tantra-Grathamālā vols. III & IV, 1970.

Tattvapradīpikā of Citsukha with the *Nayana-prasādinī* of Pratyaksvarūpa. Swami Yogindranand, ed. and trans. (Hindi). Varanasi: Udasina Sanskrit Vidyalaya, 1956.

Tripurārahasya (*Jñānakhaṇḍa*) with *Tātparyadīpikā* of Śrīnivāsa. 2d ed. Gopinath Kaviraj, ed. Varanasi: Sarasvati Bhavana Granthamālā, vol. 15, A.V. Vasavada, trans. Chowkhamba, 1965.

Uḍḍānareśvara-tantra. J.D. Zadoo, ed. K.S.T.S., no. LXX, 1947.

Vākyapadīyam of Bhartṛharī. K.V. Abhyānkar and V.P. Limaye, eds. Sanskrit and Prākrit Series Vol. II, Poona University, 1965.

Vāmakeśvarīmatam with the *vivarana* of Jayaratha, M.S. Kaul, ed. K.S.T.S., no. LXVI, 1945.

Varivasyārahasya by Bhāskararāya Makhī with his own commentary *Prakāśa.* S. Subrahmanya Sastri, ed. and trans. Adyar Library, 1948.

Vātulanātha-sūtra with *Vṛtti* of Anantaśaktipāda. M.S. Kaul, ed. and trans. K.S.T.S., no. 39, 1923.

Vātulanātha-sūtra. Lilian Silburn, trans. (French). Publications de L'Institute de Civilisation Indienne, serie 8. Paris, 1959.

Vidyārṇavatantra, by Vidyāraṇya Yati. Bhadraśīla Śarmā, ed. Allahabad, Samvat 2023.

Vijñānabhairava-tantra with the commentary *Udyota* partly by Kṣemarāja and partly by Śivopādhyāya. M.R. Shastri, ed. K.S.T.S., no. VIII, 1918.

Vijñānabhairava-tantra with the *Kaumudi*, by Ānanda Bhaṭṭa. M.R. Shastri, ed. K.S.T.S., no. IX, 1918.

Vijñānabhairava-tantra. Vrajavallabha Dvivedi, comm. Delhi: Motilal Banarsidass, 1978.

Vijñānabhairava-tantra. Jaideva Singh, trans. Motilal Banarsidass, 1979.

Vijñānabhairava-tantra. Lilian Silburn, trans. (French). Publications de L'Institute de Civilisation Indienne, fasc. 15. Paris, 1961.

Virūpākṣa-pañcaśikā, with the commentary of Vidyācakravarti. Ganapati Sastri, ed. Trivandumit Sanskrit Series no. IX, 1910.

Virūpākṣa-pañcaśikā. In the *Tantrasaṁgraha*, Part I. Gopinath Raviraj, ed. Yogatantra-Granthamālā no. 3. Varanasi, 1970.

Yogadarśanam (the *Yoga-sūtras* of Patañjali), with the Hindi commentary by Prabhudayal. Kṣemarāja Śrīkṛṣṇadāsa, ed. Bombay, Samvat 2009.

Yogavāśiṣṭha, 5 vols. Srikrishna Pant Shastri, ed. and trans. (Hindi). Varanasi: Achyuta Granthamālā. Vols. 1-3, Samvat 2004, Vol. 4, 2005, and Vol. 5 2006.

Yoginīhṛdayam, with the commentaries *Dīpikā* of Amṛtānanda and *Setubandha* of Bhāskararāya. 2d ed. Gopinath Kaviraja, ed. Sarasvatī Bhavana Granthamālā, Vol. 7. Varanasi, 1963.

Yoginīhṛdayam with *Dīpikā*. Vrajavallabha Dviveda, ed. and trans. (Hindi). Motilal Banarsidass, 1988.

Yoginī-tantra. Pandit Kanhaiyalal Mishra, ed. 2d ed. Kalyan-Bombay, 1956.

SECONDARY SOURCES

Anand, M.R. *Kamakala: Some Notes on the Philosophical Basis of Hindu Erotic Sculpture.* New York: Nagel, 1958.

Anand, M.R. and Kramrisch, Stella. *Homage to Khajuraho.* Bombay, 1960.

Auboyer, J. *Khajuraho.* The Hague, 1960.

Aurobindo, Sri. *Bases of Yoga.* Calcutta: Arya Publishing House, 1948.

________. *Essays on the Gita.* New York: The Sri Aurobindo Library, 1950.

________. *Light on Yoga.* Howrah: Sri Aurobindo Library, 1935.

________. *Synthesis of Yoga.* New York: The Sri Aurobindo Library, 1950.

Avalon, Arthur. *The Garland of Letters (Varnamala)*, 3d ed. Madras: Ganesh & Co., 1955.

________. *The Great Liberation (Mahanirvana Tantra).* Madras: Ganesh & Co., 1963.

________. *Introduction to Tantra-Sastra*, 6th ed. Madras: Ganesh & Co., 1973.

________. *Principles of Tantra*, 3d ed. Madras: Ganesh & Co., 1960. English rendering of the Bengali *Tantratattva* of Sivacandra Vidyarnava Bhattacarya.

________. *The Serpent Power*, 8th ed. Madras: Ganesh & Co., 1972.

________. *Shakti and Shakta.* Madras: Ganesh & Co., 1956.

________. *Tantraraja Tantra: A Short Analysis.* Madras: Ganesh & Co., 1954.

________. *The World as Power*, 2d ed. Madras: Ganesh & Co., 1957.

Avasthi, S.S. *Mantra aur Matrkao(m) ka Rahasya.* Varanasi: Chowkhamba, 1966.

Bagchi, Prabodh Chandra. *Studies in the Tantras.* Calcutta: University Press, 1939.

Banerjee, J.N. *Pauranic and Tantric Religion.* Calcutta, 1966.

Basu, Arabindu. "Kashmir Saivism," in *Cultural History of India,* vol. IV, pp. 79-97.

Basu, M. *Tantra: A General Study.* Calcutta, 1976.

Beane, W.C. *Myth, Cult and Symbols in Sakta Hinduism: A Study of the Indian Mother Goddess.* Leiden, 1977.

Bernard, Theos. *Hindu Philosophy.* Bombay: Jaico Publishing House, 1958.

Bhandarkar, R.G. *Vaishnavism, Saivism and Minor Religious Systems.* Reprint. Varanasi, 1965.

Bharati, Agehananda. *The Tantric Tradition.* New Delhi: B.I. Publications, 1976.

Bhattacharya, B. *Saivism and the Phallic World,* vol. I. New Delhi: Oxford & IBH Publishing Co., 1975.

Bhattacharya, N.N. *History of Sakta Religion.* Delhi, 1974.

Bose, D.N. and Haldar, H. *Tantras, their Philosophy and Occult Secrets,* 3d ed. Calcutta: Oriental Publishing House, 1956.

Bose, M.M. *The Post-Caitanya Sahajiya Cult of Bengal.* Calcutta, 1930.

Briggs, G.W. *Gorakhanath and the Kanphata Yogis.* Calcutta, 1938.

Chakravarti, Chintaharan. *The Tantras: Studies on Their Religion and Literature.* Calcutta, 1963.

Chakravarti, P. *The Linguistic Speculations of the Hindus.* Calcutta, 1933.

Chatterji, J.C. *Kashmir Shaivaism.* Kashmir Series of Texts and Studies, no. II, 1914.

Coomaraswamy, A.K. *The Dance of Shiva.* New York: Noonday Publication, 1957.

________. "The Tantric Doctrine of Divine Bi-unity," in ABORI, vol. 19, pp. 173-183, 1938.

Coward, Harold G. *Sphota Theory of Language.* Delhi: Motilal Banarsidass, 1980.

Das Gupta, S.N. "General Introduction to Tantra Philosophy," in his *Philosophical Essays.* Calcutta: University Press, 1951.

________. *History of Indian Philosophy,.* 5 vols. Cambridge, 1922-1955.

________. *Indian Idealism.* Reprint. Cambridge, 1962.

David-Neel, Alexandra. *Magic and Mystery in Tibet.* London: Corgi Books, 1971.

De Riencourt, Amaury. *The Eye of Siva: Eastern Mysticism and Science.* Souvenir Press, Ltd., 1980.

Desai, Devangana. *Erotic Sculpture of India, A Sociological Study.* New Delhi, 1975.

Devasenapati, V.A. *Saiva Siddhanta.* University of Madras, 1958.

Dhavamony, M. *Love of God According to Saiva Siddhanta.* Oxford: Clarendon Press, 1971.

Dimock, Edward C. *The Place of the Hidden Moon: Erotic Mysticism in the Vaisnava Sahajiya Cult of Bengal.* Chicago, 1966.

Douglas, Nik. *Tantra Yoga.* Delhi: Munshiram Manoharlal, 1971.

Dvivedi, Hajari Prasad. *Natha Sampradaya.* Allahabad, 1960.

Dyczkowski, Mark. *The Canon of the Saivagamas and the Kubjika Tantra of the Western Kaula Tradition.* Albany: SUNY Press, 1988.

________. *The Doctrine of Vibration: An Analysis of the Doctrines and Practices of Kashmir Saivism.* Albany: SUNY Press, 1987.

Evans-Wentz, W., ed. *The Tibetan Book of the Dead.* London, 1949.

________. *Tibetan Yoga and Secret Doctrines.* Oxford, 1935.

Farquhar, J.N. *An Outline of the Religious Literature of India.* Reprint. London, 1968.

Foucher, Max-Pol. *Erotic Sculpture of India.* London: Allen & Unwin, 1959.

Ghose, A.B. "The Spirit and Culture of the Tantras," in CHI vol. IV, 2d ed., pp. 241-251, 1956.

Ghosh, A.B. *Siva and Sakti.* Rajshahi, 1935.

Gnoli, Raniero. *The Aesthetic Experience According to Abhinavagupta,* 2d ed. Varanasi: Chowkhamba, 1968.

Goudriaan, Teun and Gupta, Sanjukta. *Hindu Tantric and Sakta Literature.* Wiesbaden: Otto Harrassowitz, 1981.

Guenther, Herbert V. *Yuganaddha: The Tantric View of Life.* 2d ed. Chowkhamba Sanskrit Series, 1964.

Gupta, Sanjukta; Hoens, Dirk Jan; and Gupta, Sanjukta. *Hindu Tantrism.* Leiden: E.J. Brill, 1979.

Gurudatta, K. *Kashmir Saivism.* Bangalore, 1952. A pamphlet.

Jash, P. *History of Saivism.* Calcutta: Ray & Chaudhury, 1974.

Joshi, B.L. *Kashmir Saivadarsana aur Kamayani.* Chowkhamba Sanskrit Series, 1968.

Jung, Carl. "On Mandala Symbolism," in *Archetypes and the Collective Unconscious.* R.F.C. Hull, trans. London, 1955.

Kane, P.V. *History of Dharmasastra,* vol. V. Poona: Government Oriental Series (Class B) no. 6, BORI, 1962.

Kaviraj, Gopinath. *Bharatiya Sanskrti aur Sadhana*, 2 vols. Patna: Bihar Rashtrabhasha Parishad, vol. 1, 1923; vol. 2, 1964.

________. *Tantra O Agama-sastrer Digdarsana*. Calcutta Sanskrit College Research Series, no. XXV, studies no. 12, 1963.

________. *Tantrika Sahitya*. Lucknow: Hindi Samiti, 1972. A catalogue of the Tantric Literature.

________. *Tantrika Vanmaya mem Sakta Drsti*. Ratna, 1963.

Kaw, R.K. *The Doctrine of Recognition*. Hoshiarpur, 1967.

Kosambi, D.D. *Myth and Reality*. Bombay, 1962.

Kramrisch, Stella. *The Presence of Siva*. Delhi: Oxford University Press, 1981.

Kulasamghasekhara, Pandit Deviprasada. *Pancamakara tatha Bhavatattva*. Allahabad: Kalyan Mandir, 1954.

Kumaraswamiji. "Vira Saivism," in *Cultural History of India*, vol. IV, pp. 98-107.

Kundu, Nandu Lal. *Non-dualism in Saiva and Sakta Philosophy*. Calcutta.

Lorenzen, L.N. *The Kapalikas and Kalamukhas. Two Lost Saivite Sects*. Los Angeles: University of California Press, 1972.

Mahadevan, T.M.P. *Outlines of Hinduism*. Reprint. Bombay: Chetana Ltd., 1977.

________. *The Pancadasi of Bharatitirtha Vidyaranya: An Interpretative Exposition*. University of Madras, 1975.

Masson, J.L. and Patwardhan, M.V. *Santarasa and Abhinavagupta's Philosophy of Aesthetics*. Poona: BORI, 1969.

Mishra, Kailash Pati. *Kashmir Saiva Darshana: Mula Siddhanta*. Varanasi: Arddhanarisvara Publication, 1982.

________. *Saiva-Siddhanta Darsana.* Varanasi: Arddhanarisvara Publication, 1982.

Mishra, Kamalakar. *Significance of the Tantric Tradition.* Varanasi: Arddhanarisvara Publications, 1981.

Mookerjee, A. *Tantra Art: Its Philosophy and Physics.* New Delhi, 1968.

Mudaliar, N.M. *The Relevance of Saiva Siddhanta Philosophy.* Annamalai University, 1968.

Murti, T.R.V. *The Central Philosophy of Buddhism*, 2d ed. London: Allen and Unwin, 1960.

Nandimath, S.C. *Handbook of Vira Saivism.* Dharwar, 1942.

Narayan, C.V. *Origin and Early History of Saivism in South India.* Ayyar: University of Madras, 1974.

O'Flaherty, Wendy D. *Asceticism and Eroticism in the Mythology of Siva.* London, 1973.

Pandey, K.C. *Abhinavagupta: An Historical and Philosophical Study*, 2d ed. Varanasi: Chowkhamba Sanskrit Series Office, 1963.

Pandit, B.N. *Aspects of Kashmir Saivism.* Srinagar: Utpala Publications, 1977.

________. *Kashmir Saiva Darsana.* Jammu: Ranabir Sanskrit Vidyapitha, 1973.

Pandit, M.P. *Lights on the Tantra.* Madras, 1957.

________. *Studies in the Tantras and the Veda.* Madras: Ganesh & Co., 1964.

Paranjoti, V. *Saiva Siddhanta.* 2d ed. London: Luzac, 1954.

Pathak, V.S. *Saiva Cults in Northern India.* Varanasi, 1960.

Payne, E.A. *The Saktas.* Calcutta, 1939.

Poddar, H.P., ed. *Kalyana (Sivanka).* Gorakhpur: Gita Press, 1990.

________. *Kalyana (Saktyanka).* Gorakhpur: Gita Press, 1991.

Pratyagatmananda, Swami. "Philosophy of the Tantras," in *Cultural Heritage of India*, vol. III, pp. 437-448.

________. "Tantra as a Way of Realization," in CHI, vol. IV, 2d ed., pp. 227-240, 1956.

Probsthain, Arthur. *Mohenjo-daro and the Indus Civilization.* London, 1931.

Radhakrishnan. *The Hindu View of Life.* London: Allen & Unwin.

________. *Indian Philosophy.* New York: Macmillan, 1958.

Radhakrishnan, S., ed. *History of Philosophy: Eastern & Western.* London, 1952.

Rajneesh, Acarya. *The Book of the Secrets.* Poona: Rajneesh Foundation, 1974. Discourses on the *Vijnanabhairava Tantra.*

________. *Siva Sutra.* Swami Chaitanya Kirti, ed. Poona: Rajneesh Foundation, 1975.

Raju, P.T. *Idealistic Thought of India.* London, 1953.

Ramkrishna Mission Institute of Culture. *Cultural Heritage of India.* 5 vols. 1958-78.

Rao, Pandurang. *Srisahasrika.* Published by the author, 1985.

Rao, T.A. Gopinath. *Elements of Hindu Iconography*, vol. II. Varanasi: Indological Book House, 1971.

Rastogi, Navjivan. *The Krama Tantricism of Kashmir*, vol. I. Delhi: Motilal Banarsidass, 1979.

Rawson, Philip. *Tantra: The Indian Cult of Ecstasy.* London: Thames and Hudson, 1973.

Rudrappa, J. *Kashmir Saivism.* Mysore: Prasarang University, 1969.

Sastry, T.V. Kapali. *Sidelights on the Tantra.* Pondicherry, 1971.

Satprem. *Sri Aurobindo or The Adventure of Consciousness.* Tehmi, trans. Pondicherry: Sri Aurobindo Ashram, 1968.

Sharma, L.N. *Kashmir Saivism.* Varanasi: Bharatiya Vidya Prakashan, 1972.

Sharma, Pushpendra Kumar. *Sakti Cult in Ancient India With Special Reference to the Puranic Literature.* Varanasi, 1974.

Shastri, Gaurinath. *The Philosophy of Word and Meaning.* Calcutta Sanskrit College Series no. V, 1959.

Shastri, Govinda. *Tantra-Vijnana.* Sadhana Pocket Books, 1983.

Shastri, K.A. Nilakantha. "An Historical Sketch of Saivism," *Cultural Heritage of India,* vol. IV, pp. 63-78.

Shukla, Vanshidar. *Vamamarga.* Allahabad: Kalyan Mandir, 1951.

Siddhantashastree, R.K. *Saivism Through the Ages.* Delhi: Munishiram Manoharlal Publishers, 1975.

Singh, L.P. *Tantra: Its Mystic and Scientific Basis.* Delhi: Concept Publishing Co., 1976.

Sinha, Jadunath. *Schools of Saivism.* Calcutta: Sinha Publishing House, 1970.

Sircar, D.C. *The Sakta Pithas.* 2d ed. Calcutta, 1973.

________, ed. *The Sakti Cult and Tara.* University of Calcutta, 1967.

Sivaraman, K. *Saivism in Philosophical Perspective.* Varanasi: Motilal Banarsidass, 1973.

Sundaram, S. Sivapada. *The Saiva School of Hinduism.* London: Allen & Unwin, 1934.

Tantrika Sanskrti. Varanasi: Sanskrit University, 1965.

Thomas, P. *Kamakala: the Indian Ritual of Love.* Bombay, 1956.

Tirtha, Swami Omananda. *Patanjali-Yoga-pradipa*, 3d ed. Gorakhpur: Gita Press, 2016.

Tirtha, Swami Vishnu. *Devatma Shakti (Kundalini)*, 3d ed. Rishikesh, 1974.

Upadhyaya, V.N. *Madhyakalina Hindi Kavya ki Tantrika Prsthabhumi.* Allahabad, 1963.

Venkararamanayya, N. *Rudra Siva.* Madras University, 1941.

Zimmer, Heinrich. *Philosophies of India.* Joseph Campbell, ed. New York: Meridien Books, 1957.

Index of Sanskrit Terms

B